Tutor Group:　　　Date:

FOUNDATION
SCiENCE to

Stephen Pople

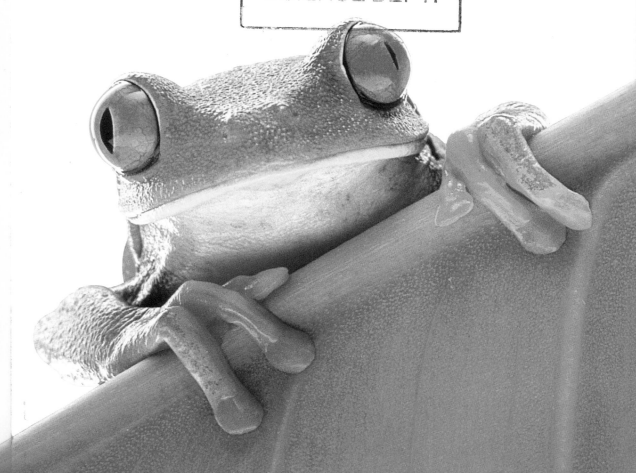

Oxford University Press, Great Clarendon Street, Oxford OX2 6DP

Oxford New York

Athens Auckland Bangkok Bogota Buenos Aires
Calcutta Cape Town Chennai Dar es Salaam
Delhi Florence Hong Kong Istanbul Karachi
Kuala Lumpur Madrid Melbourne Mexico City
Mumbai Nairobi Paris São Paulo Singapore
Taipei Tokyo Toronto Warsaw
and associated companies in
Berlin Ibadan

Oxford is a trade mark of Oxford University Press

First published 1997

Reprinted 1997, 1998

A CIP catalogue record for this book is available from the British Library.

Typeset in Folio light/medium

Printed in Spain by Gráficas Estella

ISBN 0 19 914683 7

Acknowledgements

The publisher would like to thank the following agencies for their kind permission to reproduce the following photographs:

Allsport /Didier Klein p 85, p 89, /David Cannon p 90, /Bob Martin p 92; J Allen Cash p 38 (bottom), p 56, p 96; Bruce Coleman Ltd / Dr Frieder Sauer p 11, / David Davies p 15, /Kim Taylor p 42, / Gerald Cubitt p 44 (bottom right), /Kim Taylor p 44 (bottom left), / Gordon Langsbury p 44 (top left), / Frank Greenaway p 45 (top right), /Kim Taylor p 45 (top left), p 46, /John Murray p 66 (bottom right), / Dieter & Mary Plage p 68, /George McCarthy p 71(centre left), / Mr Jens Rydell, p 74 (bottom right); G.S.F. Picture Library, p 74 (centre right and centre left), /Dr B Booth p 75 (top left), and top right; Oxford Scientific Films p 66 (bottom left), /Doug Allan p 74 (bottom left), /Edward Parker p 94 (top left); Science Photo Library / David Scharf p 28, / Petit Format/Nestle p 30 (top left), (top middle), (top right), / Katrina Thomas p 31, /Dr Tony Brain p 34, / Alex Bartel p 62 (bottom right), /European Space Agency p 70, /Gordon Garradd p 76, /Takeshi Takahara p 91, /Photo Library International p 94 (top right), /Johnny Autrey p 103, /David Nunuk p 109, /NASA p 116 (bottom left), /David Parker p 116 (bottom right), /National Snow and Ice Data Services p 116 (top right), /NASA p 117; Tony StoneWorldwide /Tom Tietz p 38 (top), p 64; Tony Waltham, p 74 (top right).

Additional photography by Peter Gould and Martin Sookias

Cover photograph Tony Stone Images

The illustrations are by: Chris Duggan, Jones Sewell, Pat Murray, Mike Ogden, Oxford Illustrators, Pat Thorne, Borin Van Loon, Pamela Venus and Mike Nicholson

Introduction

If you are working towards Key Stage 3 (levels 2 to 5) of the Science National Curriculum, then this book is for you. It explains the science ideas that you will meet, and helps you find what you need to know. The topics are covered in double-pages which we have called *spreads*.

Contents Here, you can see a list of all the spreads in the book.

Test and check Try answering these questions when you revise. Next to each group of questions, there is a number. This tells you which spread to look up if you need to find out more.

Spread 1.1 This should help you with your investigations.

Spreads 2.1 to 4.22 These are grouped into three sections, matching Attainment Targets 2, 3, and 4 of the National Curriculum.

Summaries These tell you the main points covered in each spread.

Answers to questions on spreads Here, there are brief answers to all the questions in spreads 2.1 to 4.22. But try the questions before you look at the answers!

Index Use this if there are scientific words which you need to look up.

To be a good scientist, you need to carry out investigations. This book should help you understand the scientific ideas behind your investigations. I hope that you will find it useful.

Stephen Pople

Contents

Test and check

Can you answer these questions? If not, the spread number tells you where to find out more.

1. Why do animals and plants need food?
2. In what ways are animals and plants the same?
3. What are cells?

2.1

4. Where is food made in a plant?
5. How does a plant get the energy to make its food?
6. What gas is made when an animal 'burns up' its food?

2.2

7. In a flower, where are the male cells and where are the female cells?
8. What does 'pollination' mean?
9. Why do some flowers have bright colours?

2.3

10. How is a flower fertilized?
11. How are seeds scattered?
12. What does 'germination' mean?
13. What does a seed need to germinate?

2.4

14. In your body, how do food, water, and oxygen get to your cells?
15. What job is done by the heart?
16. What job is done by the kidneys?

2.5

17. Why do you need a skeleton?
18. What job is done by the skull?
19. What is the main mineral in bone?
20. What moves your joints?

2.6

21. What are the main parts of the gut?
22. What happens to food in digestion?
23. What are enzymes?
24. What happens to food when it has been digested?

2.7

25. How does the heart work?
26. What do arteries do?
27. What do veins do?
28. Where does blood get rid of carbon dioxide?

2.8

29. What job is done by the lungs?
30. How does oxygen get into blood?
31. Which way does your diaphragm move when you breathe in?

2.9

32. In a woman, what do the ovaries do?
33. What happens to an egg during fertilization?
34. In a man, where are sperms stored?

2.10

35. In humans, how many months are there between fertilization and birth?
36. Before a baby is born, how does it get its food and oxygen?

2.11

37. Why do you need to eat proteins?
38. What foods are rich in vitamin C?
39. What substances give you most of your energy?

2.12

40. What are germs?
41. How can germs spread from one person to another?
42. What do antibiotics do?

2.13

43. What problems can you have if your diet is poor?
44. Why is smoking harmful?
45. Why is sniffing solvents dangerous?

2.14

46. Can you list *similar* and *different* features of an owl and a gull?
47. Can you use a key to work out the name of an animal or plant?

2.15

48. What are 'vertebrates'?
49. What are the five main groups of vertebrates?
50. What group do humans belong to?

2.16

51. What is a 'habitat'?
52. How do humans change the habitats of animals and plants?
53. How can pollution harm wildlife?

2.17

54. Can you describe how one animal is adapted to its way of life?
55. Why do many trees lose their leaves in the autumn?

2.18

56. Can you give an example of a food chain?
57. What is a 'predator'?
58. What is a 'prey'?

2.19

Test and check

Can you answer these questions? If not, the spread number tells you where to find out more.

1 How many grams are there in a kilogram?
2 What is a measuring cylinder used for?
3 Water has a 'density of 1000 kg/m^3'. Can you explain what this means?
4 How is a liquid different from a solid?
5 How is a gas different from a liquid?

3.1

6 What does a liquid become when it evaporates?
7 What is the temperature of boiling water?
8 Why are small gaps left at the ends of bridges?

3.2

9 Can you name a material which is a heat insulator?
10 Can you name a material which is an electrical conductor?
11 Can you list some of the properties of metals?

3.3

12 About how many elements are there?
13 What are the two main types of element?
14 What is the smallest bit of an element called?
15 What is a compound?

3.4

16 What is meant by a 'pure' substance?
17 What is an alloy? Can you give an example of an alloy?
18 What do 'solute', 'solvent', and 'solution' mean?

3.5

19 How would you separate sand from water?
20 How would you separate salt from water?
21 How would you separate inks in a mixture?

3.6

22 If an acid is 'dilute', what does this mean?
23 What effect does an alkali have on an acid?
24 How does an acid affect litmus paper?
25 How does an alkali affect litmus paper?

3.7

26 Can you give an example of a chemical change?
27 What are the signs of a chemical change?
28 Can you give an example of a physical change?

3.8

29 How could you show that about 1/5th of the air is oxygen?
30 Can you describe a simple test for oxygen?
31 What three things are needed for burning?

3.9

32 What two things are needed for iron to go rusty?
33 Gold is 'unreactive'. What does this mean?
34 Can you write down some of the useful properties of aluminium?

3.10

35 What are the two main gases in air? Which of these gases is there most of? Which of these gases do animals and plants need to stay alive?
36 Can you name one other gas in air? Can you describe any uses of this gas?

3.11

37 Can you explain how water in the sea can end up coming out of your tap?
38 What is the temperature of freezing water?
39 What damage can water cause when it freezes?

3.12

40 What happens to a rock during 'weathering'?
41 Can you give three causes of weathering?
42 What is 'erosion'?
43 Can you explain how bits from one rock can end up forming new rock?

3.13

44 How are igneous rocks formed?
45 How are sedimentary rocks formed?
46 How are metamorphic rocks formed?
47 Can you give examples of an igneous, a sedimentary, and a metamorphic rock?

3.14

Test and check

Can you answer these questions? If not, the spread number tells you where to find out more.

1 What materials conduct electricity?
2 What types of charge repel?
3 What types of charge attract?

4.1

4 Can you draw a circuit with a bulb, battery, and switch in it? Can you add meters to measure the voltage across the battery, and the current?

4.2

5 Can you draw a circuit with a battery and two bulbs in series?
6 Can you draw a circuit with a battery and two bulbs in parallel?

4.3

7 Can you draw the magnetic field round a bar magnet?
8 How is an electromagnet made?
9 Can you explain how a relay works?

4.4

10 What is a newtonmeter used for?
11 What is measured in newtons?
12 Can you give an example of balanced forces?

4.5

13 When you push in a drawing pin, is the pressure greatest under your thumb, or under the point? Can you explain why?

4.6

14 How can you get a stronger turning effect from a spanner?
15 What is a 'centre of gravity'?

4.7

16 Can you explain what a 'speed of 10 metres per second' means?
17 Can you give an example of friction being useful?

4.8

18 What is measured in joules?
19 Can you give some examples of different forms of energy?

4.9

20 Can you think of something which has a high temperature but not much heat?
21 Can you give an example of something that stores energy?

4.10

22 Can you describe how a fuel-burning power station works?
23 What is 'hydroelectric power'?

4.11

24 What are 'fossil fuels'?
25 What are 'renewable' energy supplies?
26 Where does the energy in your food come from?

4.12

27 Can you explain how most of the world's energy comes from the Sun?

4.13

28 What are 'sound waves'?
29 How are sounds made?
30 Why do you see lightning before you hear it?

4.14

31 Can you describe how the ear works?
32 If a guitar string vibrates faster, how does this affect the sound? How do bigger vibrations affect the sound?

4.15

33 How are shadows formed?
34 Can you draw a diagram showing how a ray of light reflects from a mirror?

4.16

35 What does 'refraction' mean?
36 What happens to a ray of light when it goes into a glass block?

4.17

37 What is the difference between a convex lens and a concave lens?
38 How is an image formed in a camera?
39 How is an image formed in the eye?

4.18

40 How would you produce a spectrum?
41 How could you make white using three beams of coloured light?
42 Why does a red book look red?

4.19

43 Why do we get day and night?
44 How long does the Earth take to go round the Sun?

4.20

45 How long does the Moon take to go round the Earth?
46 Can you describe some of the jobs that satellites are used for?

4.21

47 Can you describe how the planets move round the Sun?
48 Can you list the planets in order, starting with the one nearest the Sun?

4.22

Doing an investigation

Here is an investigation:

> Find out if sugar dissolves more quickly in
> hot water than in cold

I'm going to measure the time it takes sugar to dissolve in cold water – and then in hot.

You could do this like the girl on the right. But first, you need to know about the following:

▷ Key factors

In any investigation, you must decide what the **key factors** are. These are the things which affect what happens. In this investigation, the key factors are:

> type of sugar
> amount of sugar
> amount of water
> whether you stir or not
> temperature of water
> time for sugar to dissolve

▷ A fair test?

In the investigation, you must make sure that each test is fair.

For a fair test, you change just one factor (the temperature) and see how this affects one other factor (the time to dissolve):

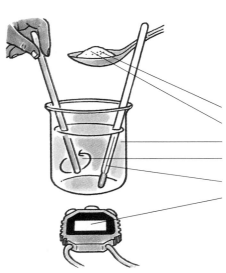
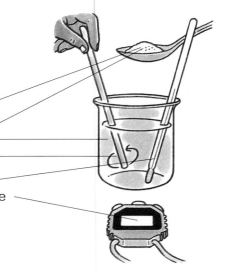

Fair test
Same type of sugar
Same amount of sugar
Same amount of water
Same stirring
Different temperature
Different time to dissolve

The test below is not a fair one. Lots of factors change as well as the temperature. So you cannot tell what effect the temperature is having:

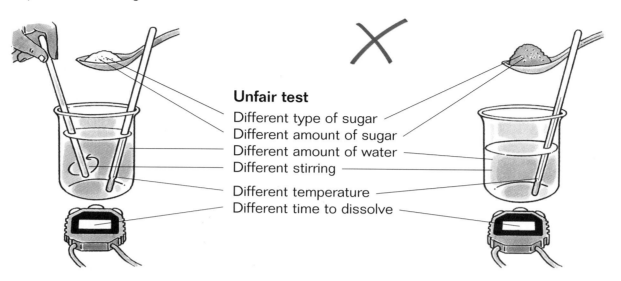

Unfair test
Different type of sugar
Different amount of sugar
Different amount of water
Different stirring
Different temperature
Different time to dissolve

Table.....

When you take readings, write them down in a table like this:

Temperature in °C	Time in seconds
20	75
30	52
40	36
50	

.....and graph

If you have several sets of readings, plot a graph. It will show you if the readings follow a pattern:

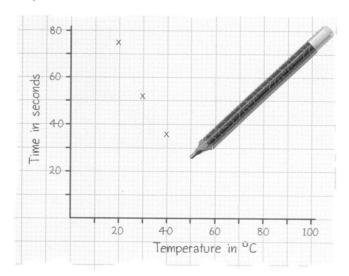

Conclusion

Your **conclusion** is what you found out. For example, from the points on the graph, your conclusion might be this:

The hotter the water, the less time it takes the sugar to dissolve

Looking at life

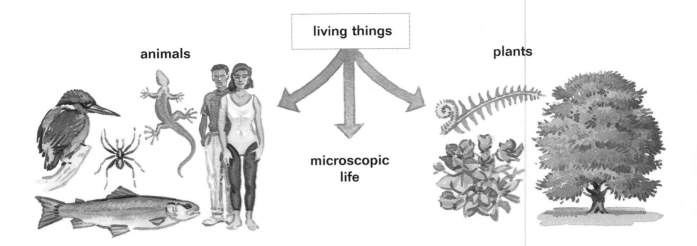

animals

living things

plants

microscopic
life

Animals and plants are living things. This is what living things are like:

They need food
It gives them energy.

They use air
They use it to 'burn
up' food in their
bodies. It is a special
type of burning with
no flames.

Their bodies make waste
You breathe out waste
gas and go to the toilet.
Plants get rid of waste
gas and water.

They reproduce
Animals have babies. New plants can grow
from seeds.

They grow
Babies grow into adults. Seedlings grow into
bigger plants.

They react
Animals react to light and noise. Plants grow
towards the light.

They move
Animals move most. But even plants move a
little.

▶ Made from cells

Living things are made from tiny bits called **cells**.
Your body is made from millions of cells.

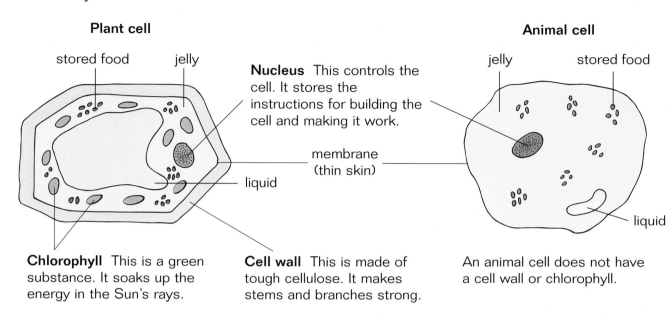

Plant cell

stored food   jelly

Nucleus This controls the
cell. It stores the
instructions for building the
cell and making it work.

liquid

membrane
(thin skin)

Chlorophyll This is a green
substance. It soaks up the
energy in the Sun's rays.

Cell wall This is made of
tough cellulose. It makes
stems and branches strong.

Animal cell

jelly   stored food

liquid

An animal cell does not have
a cell wall or chlorophyll.

1 *cells   animals   body   plants   nucleus*
   Copy the sentences below. Fill in the blanks,
   choosing words from those above:
       Animals and ____ are living things.
       Living things are made from ____.
       There are millions of cells in your ____.
       A cell is controlled by its ____.

2 Write down *one* example of each of these:
   a An animal getting energy.
   b A plant reproducing.
   c An animal reacting.
   d A plant reacting.

3 Copy the diagrams below. Write in these labels:
   animal   plant   nucleus   cell wall

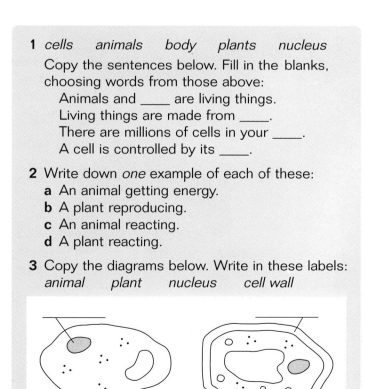

_____ cell   _____ cell

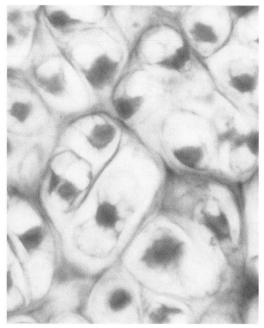

Human cheek cells, magnified 1500
times

Making and using food

Animals have to find their food. But plants make their own.

A plant takes carbon dioxide gas from the air, and water from the soil.....

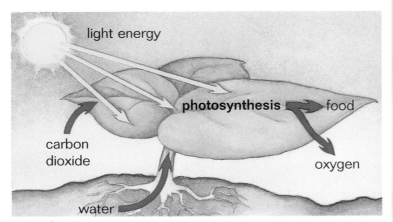

light energy

photosynthesis ➔ food

carbon dioxide

oxygen

water

.....Using the energy in sunlight, it turns these into food (sugar) and oxygen gas.

Food-making using light energy is called *photosynthesis*.

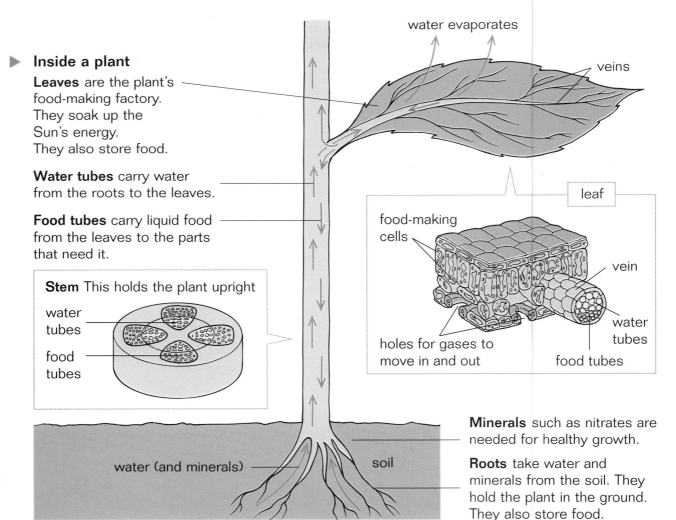

▶ **Inside a plant**

Leaves are the plant's food-making factory. They soak up the Sun's energy. They also store food.

Water tubes carry water from the roots to the leaves.

Food tubes carry liquid food from the leaves to the parts that need it.

water evaporates

veins

leaf

food-making cells

vein

water tubes

food tubes

holes for gases to move in and out

Stem This holds the plant upright

water tubes

food tubes

Minerals such as nitrates are needed for healthy growth.

water (and minerals)

soil

Roots take water and minerals from the soil. They hold the plant in the ground. They also store food.

▶ Burning up food

Plants make and store food. Animals can get this food by eating plants. That is why you eat fruit and vegetables.

To get energy, animals 'burn up' their food. For this, they need oxygen from the air. That is why you have to breathe in air.

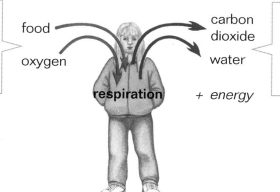

Burning up food makes carbon dioxide gas and water. So these things are in the air you breathe out.

Plants also need oxygen to burn up their food. But they make more oxygen than they can use.

Getting energy by burning up food is called *respiration*.

▶ Gas changes in the air

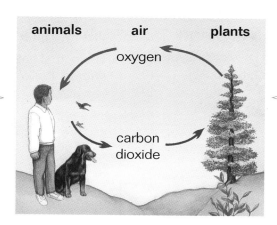

Animals use up oxygen and make carbon dioxide.

Plants use up carbon dioxide and make oxygen.

Plants replace the oxygen that animals use up.

---

1 Copy the diagram on the right.
   Shade in the parts where the plant makes its food.
   Label them 'Food is made here'.

2 *sunlight   oxygen   carbon dioxide   leaves*
   Copy the sentences below. Fill in the blanks, choosing words from those above. (You may use the same word more than once.)
   To make their food, plants use the energy in ____.
   Plants take in ____ gas and give out ____ gas.
   Animals take in ____ gas and give out ____ gas.
   To burn up their food, animals need ____.

3 Describe how water gets to the leaves of a plant.

4 Describe how a plant gets the minerals it needs.

5 Describe how gases get in and out of a leaf.

2.3 Flowers

New plants grow from seeds.
Seeds come from flowers.

Flowers have **sex cells** inside them. To make a
seed, a **male cell** must join with a **female cell**.

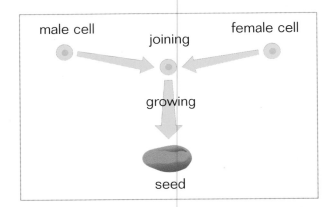

▶ Parts of a flower

Stamen This has a bulge at the end
called an **anther**. It holds thousands of
tiny grains of **pollen**. There is a male cell
in each grain.

When the **anther** splits open, the pollen
grains fall out.

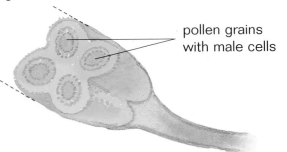

pollen grains
with male cells

Carpel This has an **ovary** inside, where
tiny eggs grow. The eggs are called
ovules. There is a female cell in each one.

The carpel has a sticky end called a
stigma. Pollen can stick to this.

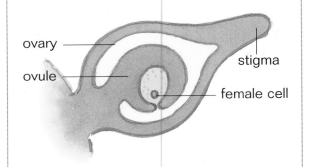

ovary

ovule

stigma

female cell

Petal This may be
brightly coloured to
attract insects.

Nectary This contains nectar,
a sugary food for insects.

▶ Pollinating flowers

Before a male cell can join with a female cell, pollen must get across to a stigma and stick to it. This is called *pollination*. Usually, the pollen is carried across to another flower.

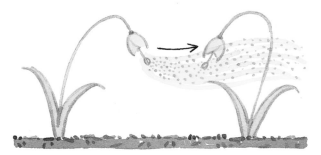

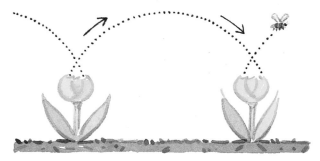

Some flowers are pollinated by wind Their flowers have stamens that hang out in the wind. When their pollen is blown away, some lands on other flowers.

Some flowers are pollinated by insects The insects are attracted by the scent or bright colours. As they search for nectar, they get covered in pollen and carry it to other flowers.

After pollination, the male and female sex cells can join. To find out how, see the next page.

1 *pollen   ovules   nectar   petal*

Copy the diagram below. Fill in the blanks, choosing words from those above:

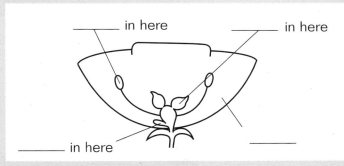

2 *pollination   male   female   flowering*

Copy the sentences below. Fill in the blanks, choosing words from those above:

In each ovule, there is a ____ cell.
In each pollen grain, there is a ____ cell.
When pollen sticks to a stigma, this is called ____.

3 Look at the photograph on the right.
 a Explain why the flower is brightly coloured.
 b Explain what the bee is doing.
 c Explain how a bee pollinates flowers.

Fruits and seeds

▶ **Fertilization**

After pollination, when pollen grains stick to a stigma, this is what happens:

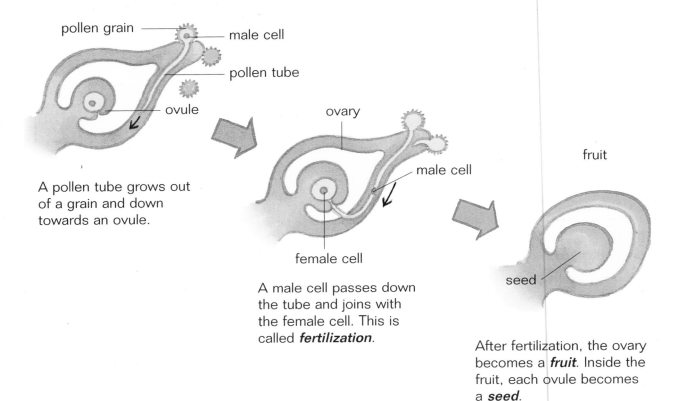

A pollen tube grows out of a grain and down towards an ovule.

A male cell passes down the tube and joins with the female cell. This is called **fertilization**.

After fertilization, the ovary becomes a **fruit**. Inside the fruit, each ovule becomes a **seed**.

▶ **Scattering seeds**

Flowers try to scatter their seeds over a wide area. This is so that more may survive and grow into new plants. A scattering of seeds is called **dispersal**.

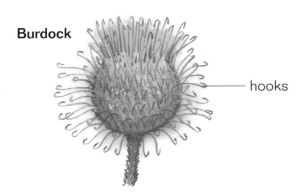

Some fruits and seeds have hooks so that they are carried by animals.

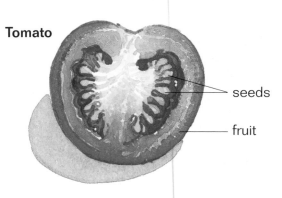

Some fruits are eaten by animals. The seeds come out with their droppings.

Sycamore

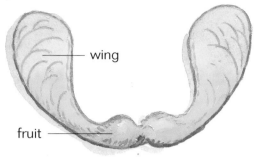

Some fruits and seeds are shaped so that they can be carried by the wind.

Pea

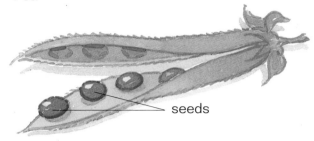

Some seeds are in pods. When dry, these pop open and flick out the seeds.

▶ **Germination**

A seed has a store of food inside it.

When a seed starts to grow, this is called *germination*.

To germinate, a seed needs.....

water	warmth	air

When a seed germinates:
A tiny **shoot** grows upwards towards the light.
A tiny **root** grows downwards into the soil.

Germination of a broad bean

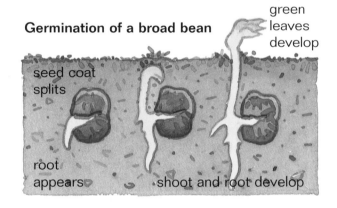

seed coat splits

green leaves develop

root appears

shoot and root develop

---

1 *germination   fertilization   scattering*
   Copy the sentences below. Fill in the blanks, choosing words from those above:
       A male cell joining with a female cell is called ____.
       A seed starting to grow is called ____.

2 Copy these sentences in the correct order:
       A male cell joins with a female cell.
       Pollen sticks to a stigma.
       A male cell passes down the pollen tube.
       The ovule becomes a seed.
       Pollen is carried from one flower to another.
       A pollen tube grows down towards an ovule.

3 Write down *three* things which seeds need to germinate.

4 Look at the diagram on the right.
   Describe how you think the seeds are scattered.

Dandelion

fruit

2.5 Organs of the body

An **organ** is any part of the body with a special job to do. The next page shows some of the main organs of the human body. The organs are all made of tiny cells.

▶ The body at work

Your body takes in food, water, and oxygen. The blood carries them to all your organs. There, the cells use them for growth and for getting energy.

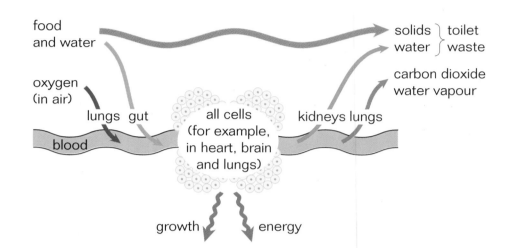

Your body gives out waste. Some is unused food that goes right through you. But cells also make waste, such as carbon dioxide and water. The blood carries these to the organs that get rid of them:

The **kidneys** get rid of water (through your bladder).

The **lungs** get rid of carbon dioxide and water (as damp air).

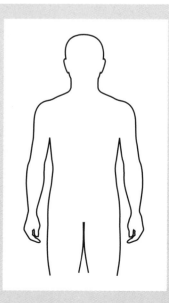

1 Here are some organs:

  stomach   lung   heart   kidney   bladder

  Write down the organ which does each of these:
  a Stores food when you eat it.
  b Puts oxygen into the blood.
  c Pumps blood through all the organs.
  d Cleans the blood by making urine.

2 Copy the diagram on the left.
  Draw in the organ which controls the whole body.
  Label it, using one of the words below.
  Draw in an organ which gets rid of carbon dioxide.
  Label it, using one of the words below.

  lung   kidney   heart   brain

3 Write down *three* things that the body must take in.

4 Write down *two* ways in which the body can get rid of water.

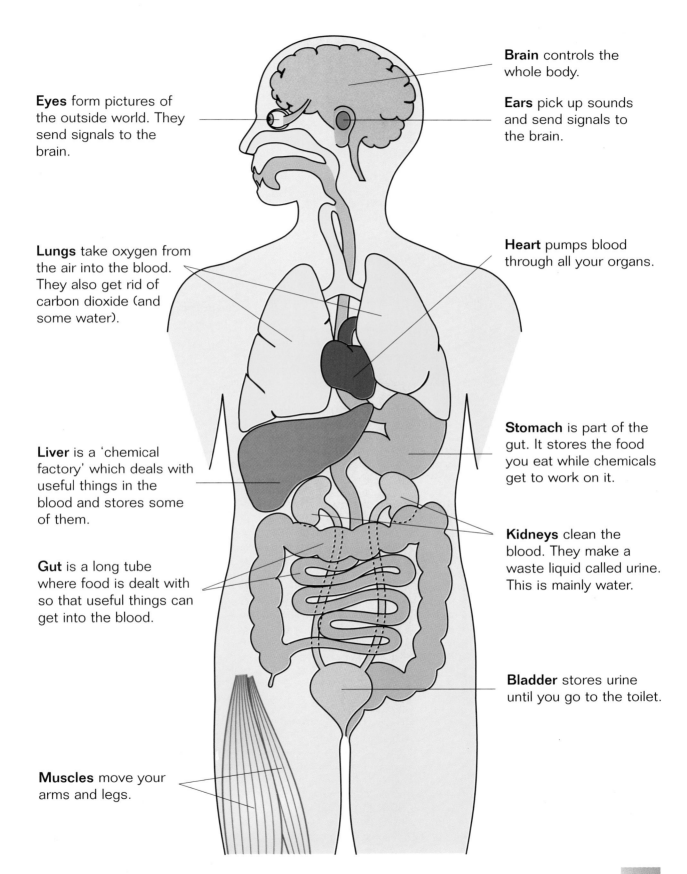

Brain controls the whole body.

Eyes form pictures of the outside world. They send signals to the brain.

Ears pick up sounds and send signals to the brain.

Lungs take oxygen from the air into the blood. They also get rid of carbon dioxide (and some water).

Heart pumps blood through all your organs.

Liver is a 'chemical factory' which deals with useful things in the blood and stores some of them.

Stomach is part of the gut. It stores the food you eat while chemicals get to work on it.

Gut is a long tube where food is dealt with so that useful things can get into the blood.

Kidneys clean the blood. They make a waste liquid called urine. This is mainly water.

Bladder stores urine until you go to the toilet.

Muscles move your arms and legs.

Bones, joints, and muscles

▶ The skeleton

Your body is held up by a *skeleton*. This has several jobs to do:

Support The skeleton lets you stand upright. It also supports organs inside you.

Protection The skeleton protects many organs.

Movement The skeleton has joints so that you can move bits of your body. The joints are moved by muscles.

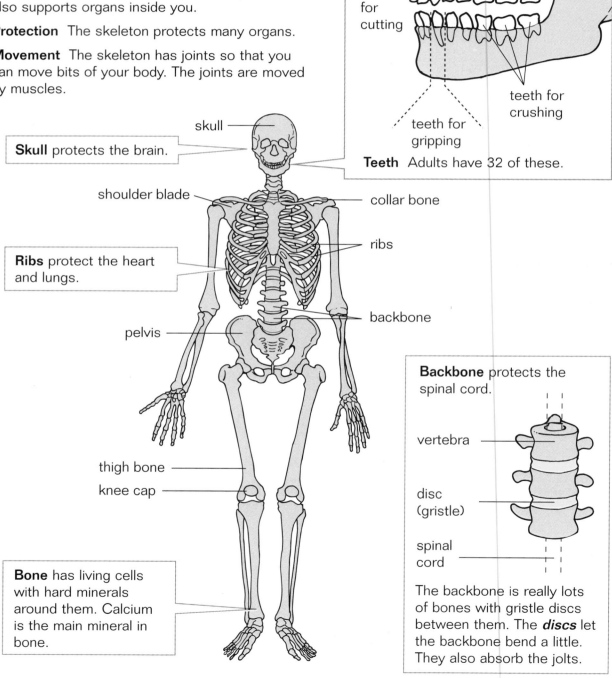

teeth for cutting

teeth for crushing

teeth for gripping

Teeth Adults have 32 of these.

skull

Skull protects the brain.

shoulder blade

collar bone

ribs

Ribs protect the heart and lungs.

backbone

pelvis

Backbone protects the spinal cord.

vertebra

disc (gristle)

spinal cord

The backbone is really lots of bones with gristle discs between them. The *discs* let the backbone bend a little. They also absorb the jolts.

thigh bone

knee cap

Bone has living cells with hard minerals around them. Calcium is the main mineral in bone.

► Joints and muscles

To bend a joint, a muscle contracts (gets shorter). But it cannot get longer again by itself. So muscles are arranged in pairs. One muscle pulls the joint one way, the other pulls it back again.

Raising arm

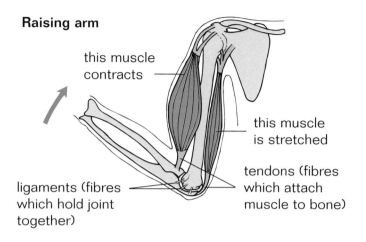

this muscle contracts

this muscle is stretched

tendons (fibres which attach muscle to bone)

ligaments (fibres which hold joint together)

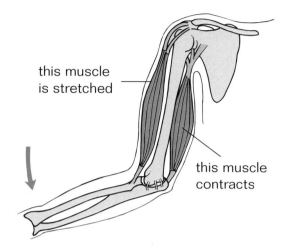

this muscle is stretched

this muscle contracts

► Nerves

To control your muscles, signals are sent along **nerves**.

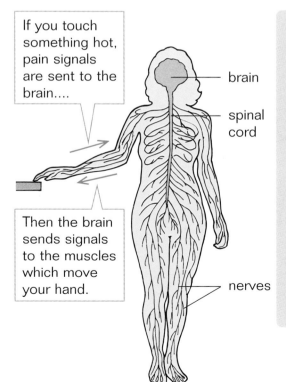

If you touch something hot, pain signals are sent to the brain....

Then the brain sends signals to the muscles which move your hand.

brain

spinal cord

nerves

1 *backbone   skull   ribs   pelvis*
Copy the sentences below. Fill in the blanks choosing words from those above:
    The ____ protects the brain.
    The ____ protect the heart and lungs.
    The ____ protects the spinal cord.

2 Here are some parts of the body:
    nerves   muscles   discs   teeth
    Write down which of these do the following:
    a Cut, grip, or crush food.
    b Move joints.
    c Carry signals to or from the brain.

3 Copy and complete these sentences:
    The main mineral in bone is....
    Fibres which hold joints together are called.....
    Fibres which attach muscle to bone are called.....

2.7 Dealing with food

▶ **The gut**

This is a long tube that runs from your mouth down through your body. This is where food is dealt with.

The main parts of the gut are:

mouth, gullet, stomach, small intestine, large intestine.

When you eat, the useful things in your food must get into your blood. But first, they must be changed into a liquid. This is called *digestion*.

In your gut, there are special chemicals for digesting food. These are called *enzymes*.

Your gut is over 6 metres long.

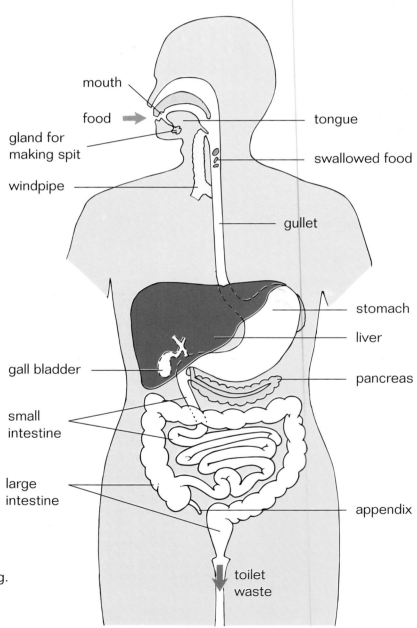

mouth

food

gland for making spit

windpipe

tongue

swallowed food

gullet

stomach

liver

gall bladder

pancreas

small intestine

large intestine

appendix

toilet waste

What happens to your food

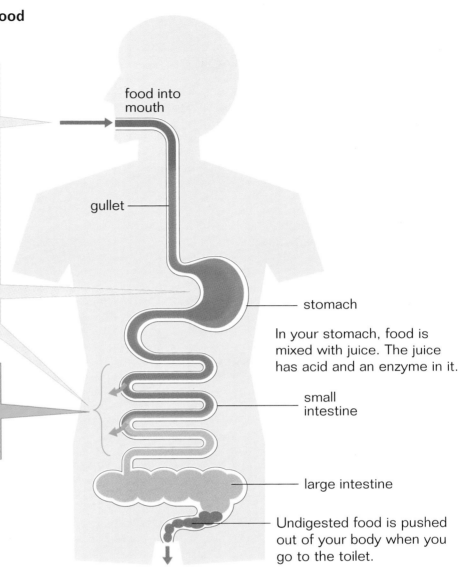

Digestion
Digestion starts in your mouth. When you chew, food gets mixed with spit. The spit has an enzyme in it. This changes solid bits of starch into liquid sugar.

Enzymes turn food into liquid. This mainly happens in the stomach and small intestine.

Absorption
Digested food (liquid) seeps into the blood. This mainly happens in the small intestine.

food into mouth

gullet

stomach

In your stomach, food is mixed with juice. The juice has acid and an enzyme in it.

small intestine

large intestine

Undigested food is pushed out of your body when you go to the toilet.

1 *absorption   digestion   enzymes   blood*
Copy the sentences below. Fill in the blanks, choosing words from those above.
   The useful things in your food must get into your ____.
   Changing solid food into liquid is called ____.
   Your food is digested by chemicals called ____.

2 Copy these sentences in the correct order:
   In the stomach, food is mixed with acid and an enzyme.
   Undigested food passes through the large intestine.
   Food is chewed and mixed with spit.
   Undigested food goes down the toilet.
   In the small intestine, digested food seeps into the blood.
   Food passes down the gullet.

2.8 Blood and the heart

▶ Jobs done by the blood

- Bringing oxygen, water, and food to cells all round the body.
- Taking away carbon dioxide and other waste from the cells.
- Carrying heat round the body.
- Carrying **hormones**. These are chemicals which control how different organs work.
- Carrying things which fight germs.

▶ Blood

Blood is a mixture of things. This is what it would look like through a powerful microscope.

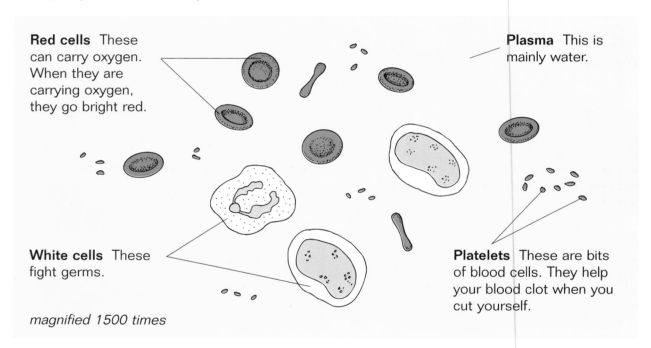

Red cells These can carry oxygen. When they are carrying oxygen, they go bright red.

Plasma This is mainly water.

White cells These fight germs.

Platelets These are bits of blood cells. They help your blood clot when you cut yourself.

magnified 1500 times

▶ Circulating blood

The heart pumps blood round the body through tubes called arteries, capillaries, and veins:

Arteries These carry blood away from the heart.

Capillaries These are thousands of narrow tubes running from arteries to veins. Every cell in the body is close to a capillary so that blood can bring the cell the things it needs.

Veins These carry blood back to the heart.

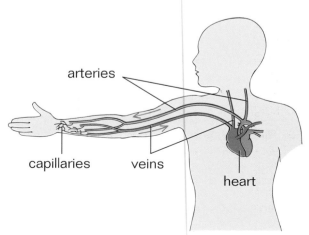

arteries

capillaries   veins

heart

▶ The heart

The heart is really two pumps side by side. One pump sends blood to the lungs, to collect oxygen. The other takes blood from the lungs and pumps it round the rest of the body.

blood collects oxygen

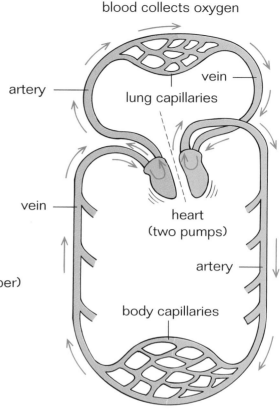

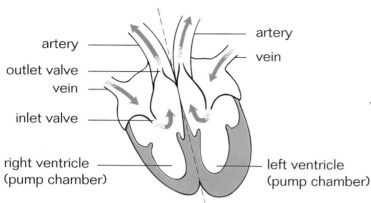

Each pump has two **valves** and a chamber called a **ventricle**. When your heart **beats**, the chamber gets bigger, smaller, bigger, smaller.... and so on. This pulls in blood through one valve and pushes it out through the other.

blood delivers oxygen

1 *white   red   plasma*

  Copy these sentences. Fill in the blanks, choosing words from those above:
  _____ blood cells fight germs.
  _____ blood cells can carry oxygen.

2 Here are three types of blood tube:

  vein   capillary   artery

  Write down which type does each of these:
  a Carries blood away from the heart.
  b Carries blood back to the heart.

3 The diagram on the right shows how blood circulates round the body.
  Copy the diagram. Then write in these labels:

  heart   oxygen collected here
  oxygen delivered here

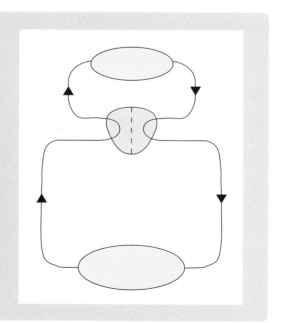

2.9 The lungs and breathing

▶ The lungs

The cells of your body use up oxygen. At the same time, they make carbon dioxide (and water) which they do not want. The job of the lungs is to put oxygen into the blood, and remove carbon dioxide (and some water).

The lungs are two spongy bags. They are filled with millions of tiny air spaces.

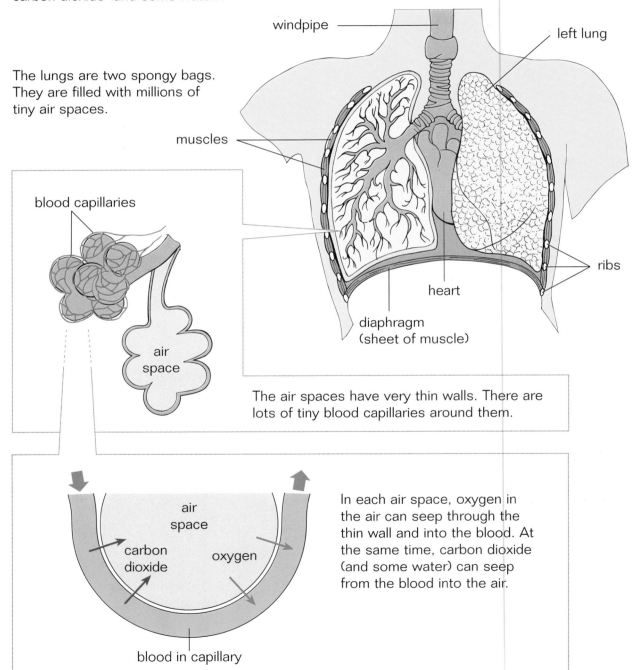

windpipe

left lung

muscles

blood capillaries

ribs

heart

diaphragm (sheet of muscle)

air space

The air spaces have very thin walls. There are lots of tiny blood capillaries around them.

air space

carbon dioxide

oxygen

blood in capillary

In each air space, oxygen in the air can seep through the thin wall and into the blood. At the same time, carbon dioxide (and some water) can seep from the blood into the air.

▶ Breathing

As you breathe in and out, your lungs get bigger and smaller. Some of the old air in your lungs is replaced by new. There is an **exchange** of carbon dioxide and oxygen.

Breathing in

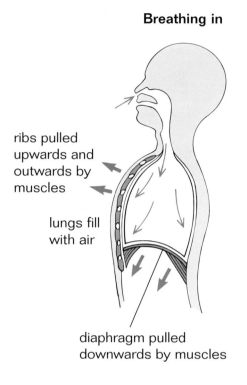

ribs pulled upwards and outwards by muscles

lungs fill with air

diaphragm pulled downwards by muscles

Breathing out

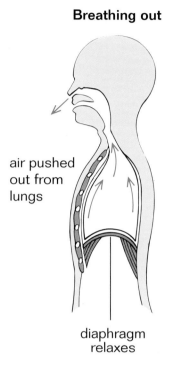

air pushed out from lungs

diaphragm relaxes

If you are running, you burn up food faster. So you must take in more oxygen and get rid of more carbon dioxide. That is why you have to breathe faster.

1 *rib   lung   heart   diaphragm   windpipe*
   Copy the diagram on the right. Fill in the blanks using the labels above.

2 *diaphragm   air   water   blood   lungs   ribs*
   Copy these sentences. Fill in the blanks, choosing words from those above:
   When you breathe in, your ____ move upwards and outwards, your ____ moves downwards, and your ____ fill with ____. In your lungs, the tiny air spaces are surrounded by ____ capillaries.

3 In your lungs, what gas goes into the blood?

4 In your lungs, what gas comes out of the blood?

5 Explain why you breathe faster when you are running.

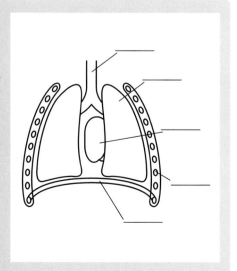

Making human life

A baby grows from a tiny cell in its mother. The cell is made when a tiny *egg* inside the mother is fertilized by a *sperm* from the father.

▶ Puberty

This is the time when a girl can first become a mother, and a boy can first become a father. For girls, the age is often 12-14. For boys it is often 14-16. But later than this is quite normal.

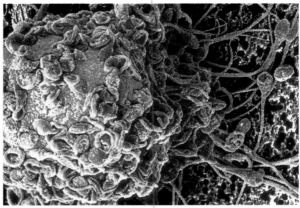

Sperms around an egg, magnified 1000 times

▶ A woman's sex system

Ovulation About every 28 days, a woman releases an egg from one of her *ovaries*. This is called *ovulation*. The tiny egg moves down the *egg tube* and into the *uterus* (womb).

Lining growth The lining of the womb thickens, and blood capillaries grow in it. The womb is now ready for a fertilized egg.

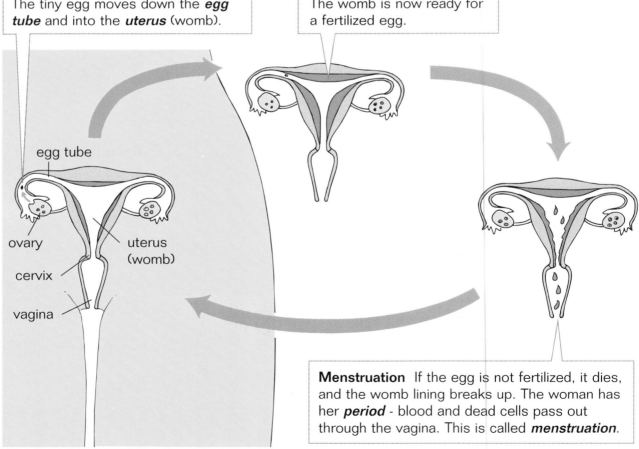

egg tube

ovary

uterus
(womb)

cervix

vagina

Menstruation If the egg is not fertilized, it dies, and the womb lining breaks up. The woman has her *period* - blood and dead cells pass out through the vagina. This is called *menstruation*.

A man's sex system

A man makes sperms in his **testicles**.

Before sperms leave his body, they are mixed with a liquid. Sperms and liquid are called **semen**. Semen comes out of the man's penis.

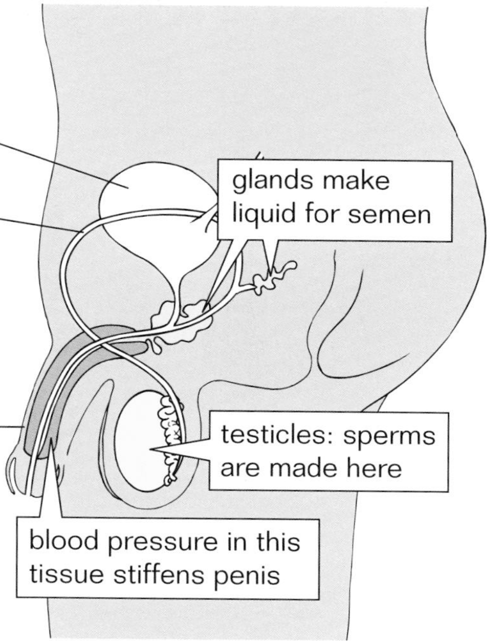

Fertilization

When a man and woman have sex, the man's penis goes stiff and is put in the woman's vagina. Then semen shoots out of his penis. There are millions of sperms, but only one can fertilize the egg.

Birth control

Parents may want a small family. If so, they may decide to use **contraception**. Here are some of the methods:

bladder

sperm duct

glands make liquid for semen

penis

testicles: sperms are made here

blood pressure in this tissue stiffens penis

Condom This is a rubber cover which fits over the man's penis. It traps sperms. It is only reliable if used with a cream which kills sperms.

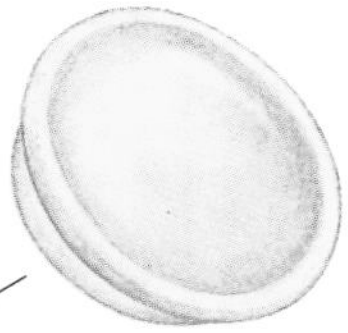

The pill The woman takes this every day. It stops her ovaries releasing eggs. It is reliable, but can cause heart, liver, and breast disease.

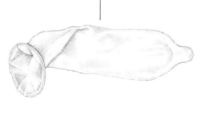

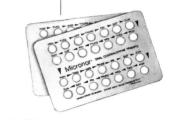

Diaphragm This is a rubber cover which fits over the woman's cervix. It stops sperms reaching the womb. It is only reliable if used with a cream which kills sperms.

Natural method The woman does tests to find out when ovulation is close, and does not have sex near that time. This method can be used by people who think that other kinds of birth control are wrong.

1 Copy these sentences in the correct order, starting with the one which tells you about *ovulation*:
   The woman has her period.
   If the egg is not fertilized, the womb lining breaks up.
   An ovary releases an egg, and the womb lining thickens.

2 *ovaries   testicles   fertilization   menstruation*
   From the above words, choose one for each of these:
   a Sperms are made in these.
   b Eggs are released from these.
   c A sperm joining with an egg.

2.11 Growing to be born

Actual sizes

Fertilized egg

Embryo

...at 4 weeks

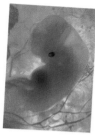

...at 7 weeks

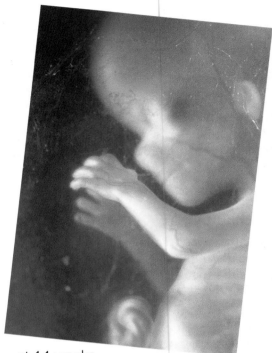

...at 14 weeks

▶ **From egg to embryo**

If a human egg is fertilized, it grows into a tiny ball of cells. This is called an *embryo*. It sinks into the lining of the womb and starts to grow into a baby.

▶ **The growing embryo**

After six weeks, the embryo has a heart and a brain. It lies in a bag of watery liquid which protects it from jolts and bumps.

The embryo cannot eat or breath, so it must get all the things it needs from its mother's blood. It does this through an organ called the *placenta*. This grows into the womb lining.

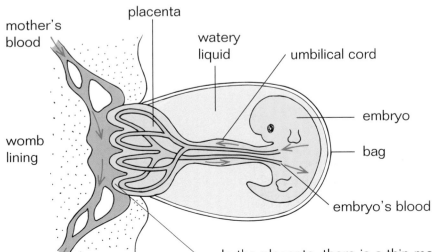

mother's blood

placenta

watery liquid

umbilical cord

embryo

womb lining

bag

embryo's blood

The embryo is linked to the placenta by an *umbilical cord*.

In the placenta, there is a thin membrane (sheet) between the mother's blood and the embryo's. The bloods do not mix, but food, oxygen, and other things can pass between them.

▶ Birth

This is what normally happens:

9 months before birth
> Fertilization.
> Embryo starts to grow.

A few days before birth
The baby turns head down.

Just before birth
> Contractions start - muscles round the womb squeeze up.
> The cervix starts to open.
> The baby's head passes into the vagina.
> The bag bursts and the watery liquid runs out.

Birth
> Contractions push the baby out.
> The baby's lungs fill with air. From now on, the baby must take in its own oxygen and food.

Just after birth
> Contractions push out the placenta (the 'afterbirth').
> A doctor or nurse cuts the umbilical cord. The remains of the cord will shrivel away to leave the 'belly button'.

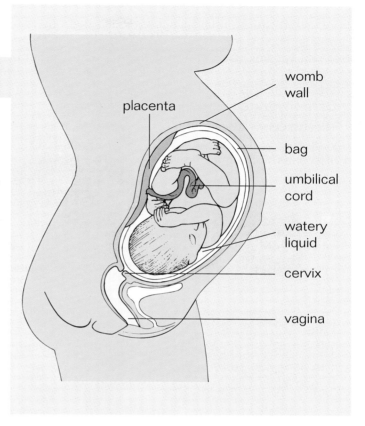

placenta · womb wall · bag · umbilical cord · watery liquid · cervix · vagina

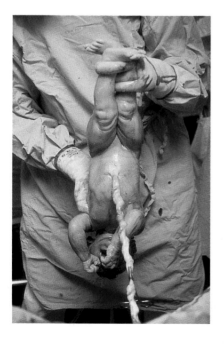

1 *umbilical cord   embryo*
   placenta   bag of watery liquid

   Write down which of the above things does each of these:
   a Protects a baby in the womb from jolts and bumps.
   b Links the baby to the placenta.
   c Grows into the womb lining so that things can pass between the mother's blood and the baby's.

2 Copy these sentences in the correct order.
   > The baby turns head down.
   > The umbilical cord is cut.
   > Contractions push the afterbirth out.
   > The embryo grows into a baby.
   > The embryo sinks into the womb lining.
   > Contractions push the baby out.

3 Explain how a baby gets its food and oxygen when it is in the womb.

The food you need

Food is a mixture of useful substances - carbohydrates, fats, proteins, fibre, minerals, vitamins, and water. A *balanced* diet is one which gives you the right amounts of all of them.

Carbohydrates

These supply about half of your energy. The body may also change them into fats.

Examples

Sugar in...
jams, cakes, sweets, fruit

Starch in...
potatoes, rice, bread, flour

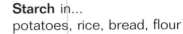

Fats

These are rich in energy. The body can store them to use later.

Examples

Butter, margarine, vegetable oil, lard, meat, cheese

Proteins

These are for body-building. You need them for growth and for replacing dead cells.

Examples

Meat, eggs, fish, milk, cheese, bread

Minerals

Your body needs small amounts of these.

Examples

Calcium (for making bones and teeth) from cheese, milk
Iron (for making blood) from liver, eggs, bread

Vitamins

Your body needs small amounts of these.

Examples

Vitamin A	**Vitamin B$_1$**	**Vitamin B$_2$**	**Vitamin C**	**Vitamin D**
Margarine, butter, liver, carrots, green vegetables, fish oil	Yeast, bread, meat, milk, potatoes	Milk, liver, eggs, cheese	Blackcurrants, green vegetables, oranges	Margarine, eggs, fish oil

Fibre

You can't digest fibre. But it is good for you because it helps food pass through your gut more easily.

Examples

Vegetables, cereals, bread

Water

You need about a litre of water every day - more if it is hot or you are very active.

Examples

Drinks, fruits and other foods with water in

1 *proteins   carbohydrates   fats   vitamins*
  Copy these sentences. Fill in the blanks, choosing words from those above.
     You need ____ and ____ for energy.
     You need ____ for growth.

2 Copy the chart on the right.
  The tick shows that bread has lots of carbohydrate in it. Put in more ticks to complete the chart.

3 Write down *two* foods with *calcium* in.

4 Write down *two* foods with *fibre* in.

5 Write down *two* foods with *vitamin C* in.

6 Copy and complete these sentences:
  a Your body needs calcium because......
  b Your body needs fibre because....

Food ▼	carbo-hydrate	fat	protein
bread	✓		
milk			
cheese			

2.13 Germs and diseases

▶ Microbes

Microbes are tiny living things that can only be seen with a microscope. There are billions in the air, soil, water, and our bodies. The harmful ones are called *germs*. They cause disease.

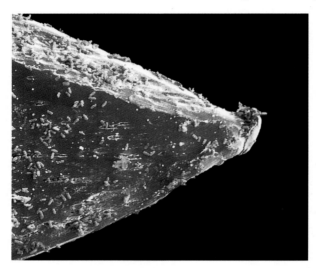

Bacteria on the tip of a hypodermic needle, magnified 400 times.

Bacteria and viruses are microbes:

Bacteria are living cells. They can *multiply* very quickly - until there are millions of them.

Diseases caused by bacteria - examples
Sore throats, pneumonia, food poisoning.

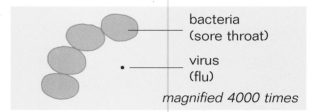

bacteria (sore throat)

virus (flu)

magnified 4000 times

Viruses are smaller than bacteria. They invade your cells and stop them working properly.

Diseases caused by viruses - examples
Flu, chicken-pox, colds

▶ Fighting disease

If germs get into your body, your white blood cells attack them. Some cells make chemicals called *antibodies* which kill germs.

If you have had chicken-pox, you probably won't catch it again. You are *immune* to it. That is because you already have antibodies for the disease, so you are ready for the next attack.

Medicines help fight disease:

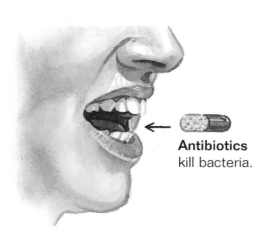

Antibiotics kill bacteria.

Vaccines have weak or dead germs put in them. Your white blood cells make antibodies for these germs. So, when the real disease strikes, your body is ready to fight it.

▶ Spreading germs

An invasion of germs is called an *infection*.
Germs can spread like this:

Droplets in the air When you cough or sneeze, you spray droplets into the air. These carry germs which other people breathe in.

Example
Catching flu or a cold.

Animals Insects may leave germs on food. Or they may leave germs in the blood when they bite.

Example
Blood-sucking mosquitoes spreading malaria.

Contact You can pick up some germs by touching an infected person or thing.

Example
Catching chicken-pox.

Dirty food and water Germs from toilet waste can get into food and water.

Example
Handling food after using the toilet.

1 *germs   infection   vaccine   immune   antibodies   antibiotics*
Copy these sentences. Fill in the blanks, choosing words from those above.
   a Harmful microbes are called ____.
   b An invasion of germs is called an ____.
   c If you are ____ to a disease, you won't catch it again.
   d Some white blood cells make ____ which kill germs.
   e A ____ has weak or dead germs in it.

2 Look at the diagram on the right. Write down *three* ways in which germs might get into the boy's body.

3 Explain why you should wash your hands after using the toilet.

Healthy living

To help your health, you need to do these things:

Eat sensibly

Take plenty of exercise

Avoid health risks

▶ Diet

- If you do not eat enough fruit and vegetables, you may not get enough vitamins and fibre.

- Too little fibre makes you constipated and may cause disease in the gut.

- Too much fat makes you overweight and may cause heart disease.

▶ Health risks

Smoking This causes heart attacks, blocked arteries, lung cancer, and difficult breathing.

Solvents These are in glue and paint. Sniffing them is very dangerous. It damages the lungs and brain.

Alcohol This slows your reactions. Heavy drinking damages the liver, heart, and stomach.

Drugs Some of these are *addictive*. When the body gets used to them, it cannot do without them.

AIDS

AIDS is a disease that can't yet be cured. It is caused by a virus called **HIV**.

People with the virus are **HIV positive**. But it may be many years before they develop AIDS.

HIV attacks white blood cells, so the body can't defend itself against disease.

HIV can only be passed to others in three ways:

- When two people are having sex.
- By blood-to-blood contact.
- From an infected mother to her unborn baby.

If a man wears a condom while having sex, there is less chance of HIV being passed on.

▶ Health before birth

A mother must look after her baby *before* it is born.

Smoking If she smokes, her baby may be born underweight.

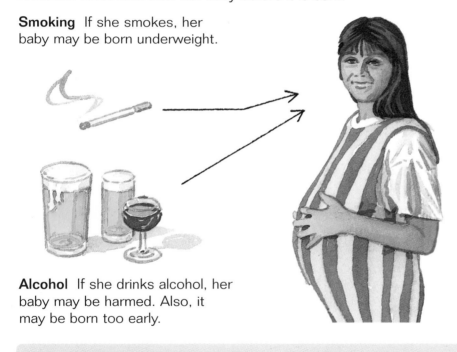

Alcohol If she drinks alcohol, her baby may be harmed. Also, it may be born too early.

German measles (rubella) If she catches German measles in the first three months of pregnancy, her baby may be born deaf, blind, or with heart trouble.

That is why girls are given injections to stop them catching German measles.

---

1 The sentences below have got the wrong endings.
  Write them out so that the correct parts go together.

Smoking is bad for you because...	...it helps prevent constipation.
A pregnant woman shouldn't smoke because...	...it contains vitamins and fibre.
Too much alcohol is bad for you because...	...they damage your lungs and brain.
Solvents are bad for you because...	...it causes lung cancer and heart disease.
Fibre is good for you because...	...her baby may be born underweight.
Fruit is good for you because...	...it damages your liver.

2 Explain why girls are given injections to stop them catching German measles.

Sorting and grouping

Look at these two animals.

They have some features which are *similar:*

They have some features which are *different:*

- One beak
- Two eyes
- Lots of feathers

- Length of beak
- Position of eyes
- Colour of feathers

Scientists use *similar* features to put things into groups.

The two animals are both in a group called **birds**.

Scientists use *different* features to tell things apart.

One bird is an **owl**. The other bird is a **gull**.

▶ Keys

Here are four insects:

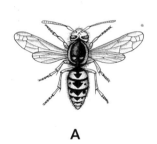

| A | B | C | D |

The table on the right is called a **key**.
Use it to work out the name of insect **A**.

Start at number 1.
See which description is the best match.
Go to another number if you are told to.
See which name you end up at.

Key

1	Wings	Go to **2**
	No wings to be seen	Earwig
2	One pair of wings	Housefly
	Two pairs of wings	Go to **3**
3	Wing larger than body	Butterfly
	Wing smaller than body	Wasp

Here are four plants:

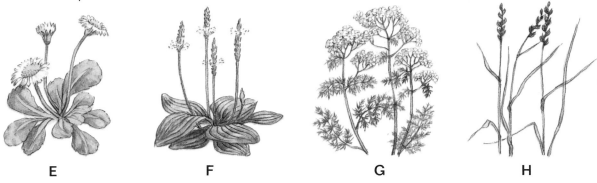

E   F   G   H

The chart below is another type of key. Use it to work out the
name of plant **E**.

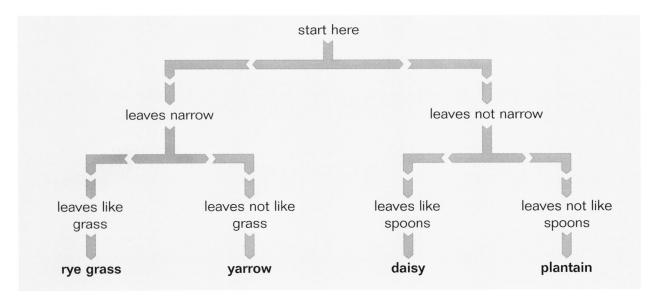

start here

leaves narrow   leaves not narrow

leaves like   leaves not like   leaves like   leaves not like
grass   grass   spoons   spoons

rye grass   **yarrow**   **daisy**   **plantain**

Start at the top.
See which description is the best match.
Follow that line to the next description.... and so on.
See which name you end up at.

1 Look at the two animals on the right.
  a Write down *three* features they have
    which are *similar*
  b Write down *three* features they have
    which are *different*.

2 Use the key on the left-hand page to work out
  the names of insects **B**, **C**, and **D**.

3 Use the key on this page to work out the
  names of plants **F**, **G**, and **H**.

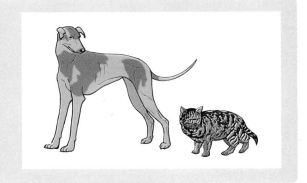

2.16 More sorting and grouping

Scientists think that all living things are related. They sort them into groups with similar features. The biggest groups of all are called **kingdoms**. You can see them on the next page.

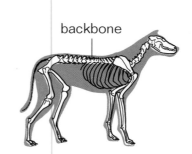

backbone

▶ Animals with backbones

In the animal kingdom, animals with backbones are called **vertebrates**. There are five main groups:

Fish

Fins
Covered in scales
Live in water
Gills for breathing
Lay eggs
Body temperature changes

Examples Shark, herring, cod

Reptiles

Covered in dry scales
Most live on land
Lungs for breathing
Lay eggs
Body temperature changes

Examples Crocodile, tortoise, lizard

Amphibians

Covered in moist skin
Live in water and on land
Adults have lungs for breathing
Lay eggs, usually in water
Body temperature changes

Examples Newt, toad, frog

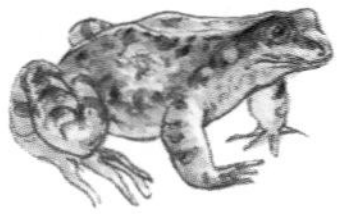

Birds

Covered in feathers
Lungs for breathing
Lay eggs
Steady body temperature

Examples Robin, penguin, blackbird

Mammals

Covered in hairy skin
Lungs for breathing
Most give birth to babies
and do not lay eggs
Mother makes milk for babies
Steady body temperature

Examples Cat, human, whale, mouse

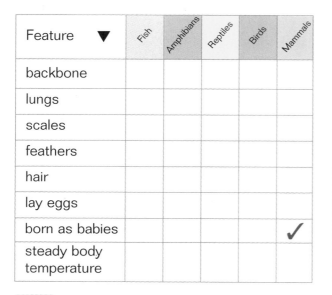

Feature ▼	Fish	Amphibians	Reptiles	Birds	Mammals
backbone					
lungs					
scales					
feathers					
hair					
lay eggs					
born as babies					✓
steady body temperature					

1 Copy the table on the left. The tick shows that most mammals have babies.

Put in more ticks to complete the table.

Put a big 'H' at the bottom of the column that humans are in.

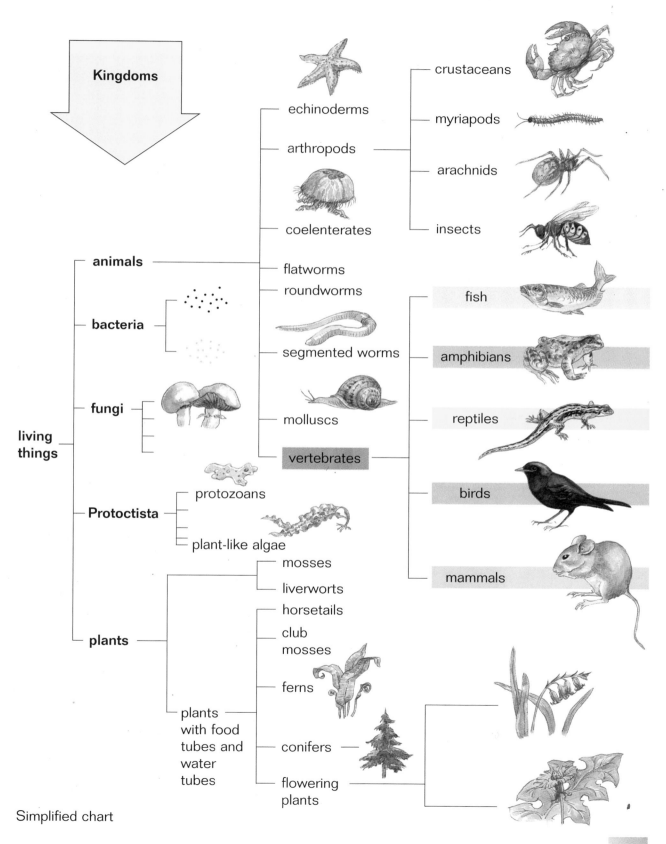

Kingdoms

crustaceans

myriapods

echinoderms

arthropods

arachnids

coelenterates

insects

animals

flatworms

roundworms

fish

bacteria

segmented worms

amphibians

fungi

reptiles

molluscs

living
things

vertebrates

birds

Protoctista

protozoans

plant-like algae

mammals

mosses

liverworts

horsetails

club
mosses

plants

ferns

plants
with food
tubes and
water
tubes

conifers

flowering
plants

Simplified chart

Living places

▶ Habitats

The place where an animal or plant lives is called its *habitat*. It is usually shared with other animals and plants.

A frog's habitat is in and around a pond, where it is wet and shady. A frog needs these conditions to stop its skin drying out.

Here are some of the *factors* which affect living things and their habitats:

Non-living factors

Climate Some places are hotter, wetter, or windier than others.

Days and seasons It is warmer and lighter in the day than at night. It is warmer in summer than in winter.

Landscape It is more sheltered in a valley than on a hill or the coast.

Soil Clay soils hold water. Sandy soils dry quickly. Some soils have lime in them. Others have acid. This affects how plants grow.

Living factors

Other living things

Plants stop other plants getting light and water.

Animals eat plants and other animals.

Humans take over land for crops. They dig soil and cut down trees.

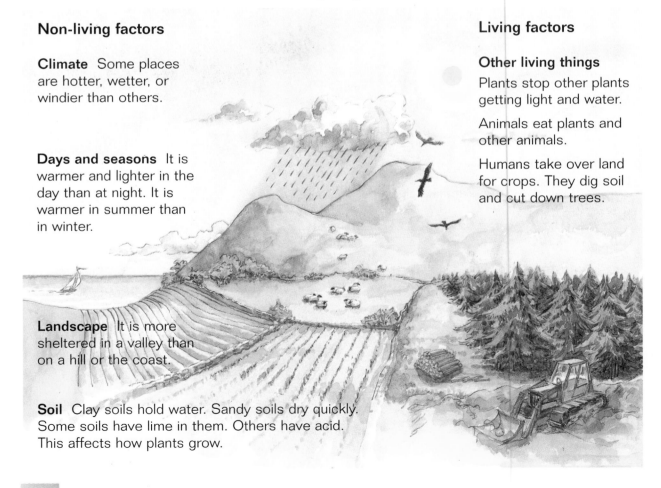

▶ Pollution

Pollution can harm living things and their habitats.
Humans are to blame for pollution.

Harmful gases These come
from power stations,
factories, cars, and trucks.

Factory waste Poisonous
chemicals may be dumped
into rivers or the sea.

Sewage This is often
dumped at sea. The germs in
it are harmful to health.

Fertilizers and pesticides These chemicals are put on
crops to help them grow. But if the chemicals run into
lakes and rivers, they harm the wildlife there.

Oil This sometimes spills from
tankers. It kills sea-birds and fish,
and ruins beaches.

---

1 Here are four animals:

human   polar bear   frog   camel

Write down the animal which does each of these:
a Lives in a wet, shady habitat.
b Lives in a cold, icy habitat.
c Causes pollution.

2 Write down *three* ways in which a river might become polluted.

3 Copy and complete these sentences with your own words:
a A plant can stop another plant growing because...
b An animal can stop a plant growing because...

Features for living

Animals and plants have special features to help them survive in their habitat. They are **adapted** to their way of life.

▶ **Surviving the winter**

This robin fluffs up its feathers when cold. The feathers trap air like a sleeping bag or duvet.

Many trees lose their leaves in the autumn. Without leaves, they need less water. So they can survive when the ground is frozen.

▶ **Camouflage**

Peppered moths are difficult to see against a tree. So they probably won't get eaten by a bird.

There is a leaf insect in this photograph. Can you find it? (See also Question 2)

▶ Catching food

The chameleon has a long tongue which it flicks out to catch insects.

The chameleon is also very good at camouflage. It can change colour to match its background.

This owl has special features to help it catch and eat its food (see Question 1).

1 Look at the owl in the photograph (above right). Write down the features you think the owl has to help it:
   a hunt at night.
   b grip small animals.
   c tear small animals apart.
   d keep warm.

2 Look at the photograph on the left.
   The leaf insect looks like a leaf. Explain why this helps it survive.

3 Look at the diagram on the right and the sentences below. They are about some of our human features.

   The sentences have the wrong endings. Write them out so that the correct parts go together.

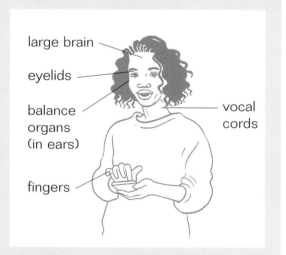

large brain

eyelids

balance organs (in ears)

vocal cords

fingers

We have eyelids...	...to stop us falling over.
We have fingers...	...so that we can speak.
We have a large brain...	...for holding and moving things carefully.
We have balance organs...	...to clear dust from our eyes when we blink.
We have vocal cords...	...so that we can think and remember, and understand our language.

Chains and webs

▶ Food chains

All living things need food. It gives them energy and the substances they need to build their bodies.

A *food chain* shows how living things feed on other living things. In the food chain below, the blackbird feeds on the snail, and the snail feeds on the leaf:

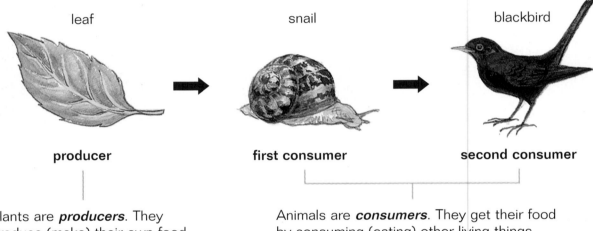

leaf	snail	blackbird
producer	**first consumer**	**second consumer**

Plants are *producers*. They produce (make) their own food.

Animals are *consumers*. They get their food by consuming (eating) other living things.

▶ Predators and prey

Animals which kill and eat other animals are called *predators*. The animals they kill and eat are their *prey*.

Here are some examples:

predator

prey

Predator	Prey
blackbird	worms insects snails
lion	zebra antelope wildebeest
wolf	reindeer moose
fox	rabbits mice birds

▶ Food webs

Many animals eat more than one type of food. So living things can be part of several food chains. The result is a **food web**. Here is an example:

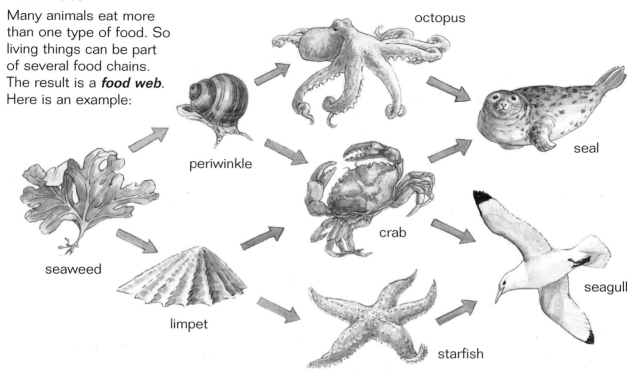

octopus

periwinkle

seaweed

limpet

crab

starfish

seal

seagull

▶ Pollution problems

If poisonous chemicals get into a food chain or web, they can kill lots of living things.

Look at the food web above. If poisonous chemicals are dumped at sea, they may be sucked in by *limpets*. So they will end up in the bodies of all these animals:

crabs   starfish   seals   seagulls

1

The diagram above shows a food chain. There is some information about the things in it on the right:
Copy the food chain. Fill in the blanks with these words:

caterpillar   thrush   cabbage   fox

fox feeds on thrush
caterpillar feeds on cabbage
thrush feeds on caterpillar

2 Copy and complete these sentences.
   In the food chain I have drawn, the producer is....
   In the food chain I have drawn, the consumers are....

3 Look at the food web at the top of the page. If *periwinkles* are poisoned by chemicals, what other animals will also get poison in their bodies? Make a list of them.

Looking at matter

▶ **Mass**

Mass is the amount of matter in something. It can be measured in **_kilograms (kg)._**

Small masses are measured in **_grams (g)._**

1000 grams = 1 kilogram

To find the mass of something, you can weigh it.

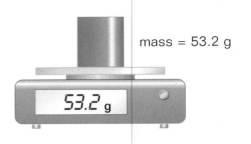

mass = 53.2 g

53.2 g

▶ **Volume**

Volume is the amount of space something takes up. It can be measured in **_cubic metres (m^3)._**

Small volumes are measured in **_millilitres (ml),_** also called **_cubic centimetres (cm^3)._**

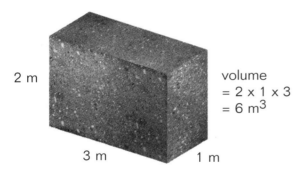

2 m

3 m   1 m

volume
= 2 x 1 x 3
= 6 m^3

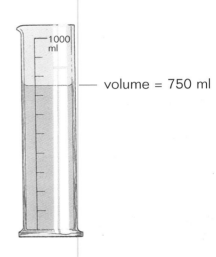

1000 ml

volume = 750 ml

You can work out the volume of a block like this:

volume = length x width x height

You can find the volume of a liquid using a measuring cylinder.

▶ **Density**

Steel has a higher **_density_** than water - it has more kilograms in every cubic metre.

Density is measured in **_kilograms per cubic metre (kg/m^3):_**

Densities

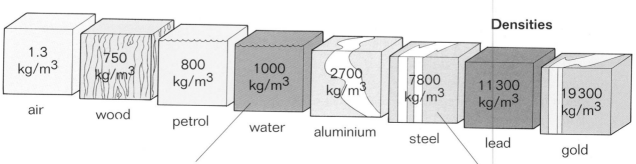

1.3 kg/m^3	750 kg/m^3	800 kg/m^3	1000 kg/m^3	2700 kg/m^3	7800 kg/m^3	11 300 kg/m^3	19 300 kg/m^3
air	wood	petrol	water	aluminium	steel	lead	gold

This means that there are 1000 kilograms in every cubic metre of water.

This means that there are 7800 kilograms in every cubic metre of steel.

Solid, liquid, or gas

Materials can be solid, liquid, or gas. These are their features:

Solid
- Has a fixed volume
- Has a fixed shape

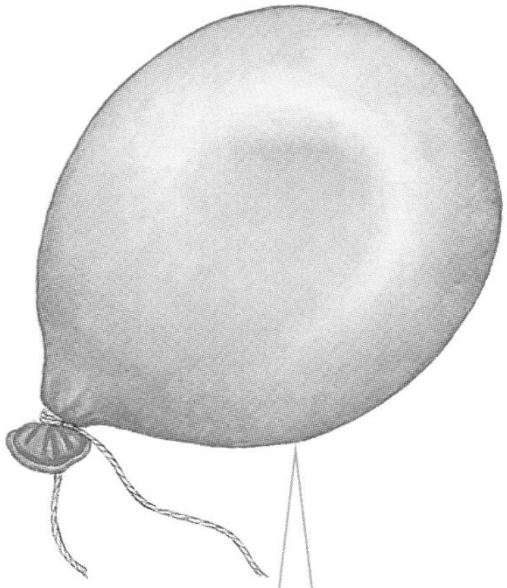

Gas
- Can flow
- Volume depends on container. (A gas fills its container.)
- Shape depends on container

Liquid
- Can flow
- Has a fixed volume
- Shape depends on container

Solids, liquids, and gases all have mass.
Gases are usually much lighter than liquids or solids.

1 Copy the table on the right. Put a tick (✔) or a cross (✗) in each box to show the different features of a solid, liquid, and gas.
   For example, if you think a solid has a fixed volume, give that box a tick (✔). If you think a solid can't flow, give that box a cross (✗).

Feature ▼	Solid	Liquid	Gas
fixed shape			
fixed volume			
can flow			

2 Look at the density diagram on the left. Write down the name (or names) of:
   a a liquid that is less dense than water.
   b two solids that are more dense than steel.
   c a gas with a low density.
   d a liquid which would have a mass of 2000 kg if you had 2 cubic metres of it.

3   *1   2   100   200   1000   2000*
   Copy the following. Fill in the blanks, choosing from the numbers above.
   a 1 kg = _____ g
   b 2000 g = _____ kg

3.2 Hot and cold

▶ **Changing state**

Water can be a solid (ice), a liquid, or a gas (steam):

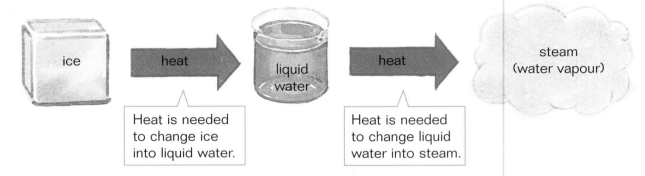

Heat is needed to change ice into liquid water.

Heat is needed to change liquid water into steam.

A change from solid to liquid, liquid to gas, or back again is called a change of **state**.

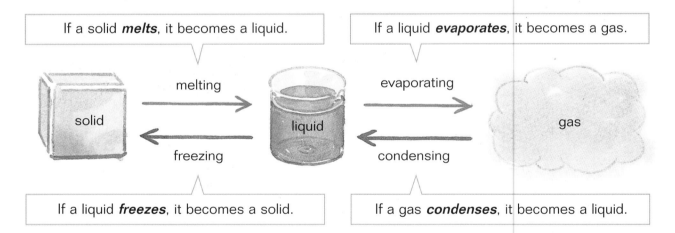

If a solid **melts**, it becomes a liquid.

If a liquid **evaporates**, it becomes a gas.

If a liquid **freezes**, it becomes a solid.

If a gas **condenses**, it becomes a liquid.

When water is cold, it evaporates very slowly.

When water is **boiling**, it bubbles, and evaporates very quickly.

The white cloud coming out of a kettle is steam which has condensed to form millions of tiny droplets. The real steam is invisible.

▶ Temperature

When something gets hotter, its *temperature* rises.

Temperature can be measured in *degrees Celsius* (*°C*) (sometimes called 'degrees centigrade').

On the Celsius scale, the numbers were specially chosen so that water freezes at 0 °C and boils at 100 °C.

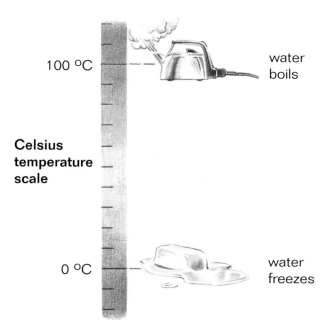

100 °C — water boils

Celsius temperature scale

0 °C — water freezes

▶ Expansion

If you heat a steel bar, it gets slightly bigger. It *expands* by a tiny amount. Most materials expand a little when heated.

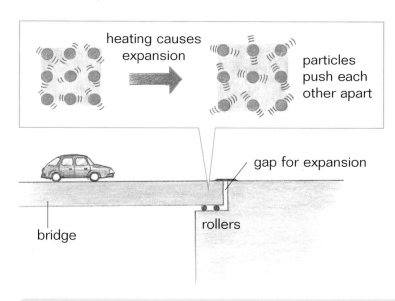

heating causes expansion

particles push each other apart

gap for expansion

bridge

rollers

Scientists think that all materials are made of tiny, moving particles, far too small to see with an ordinary microscope. Heating makes the particles move faster, so they push each other apart.

Gaps are left in bridges so that there is room for expansion on a hot day. Without a gap, the force of the expansion might crack the bridge.

---

1 Copy and complete these sentences:
  Water freezes at a temperature of....
  Water boils at a temperature of....

2 Copy these sentences. Fill in the blanks using the words on the right. (You can use the same word more than once):
  If a solid melts, it becomes a _____.
  If a liquid evaporates, it becomes a _____.
  If a liquid freezes, it becomes a _____.
  If a gas condenses, it becomes a _____.

  solid
  liquid
  gas

3 Explain why a bridge has a small gap left at the end.

3.3 Looking at materials

▶ **Properties of materials**

The features of a material and how it behaves are called its *properties*. Here are words for describing some properties:

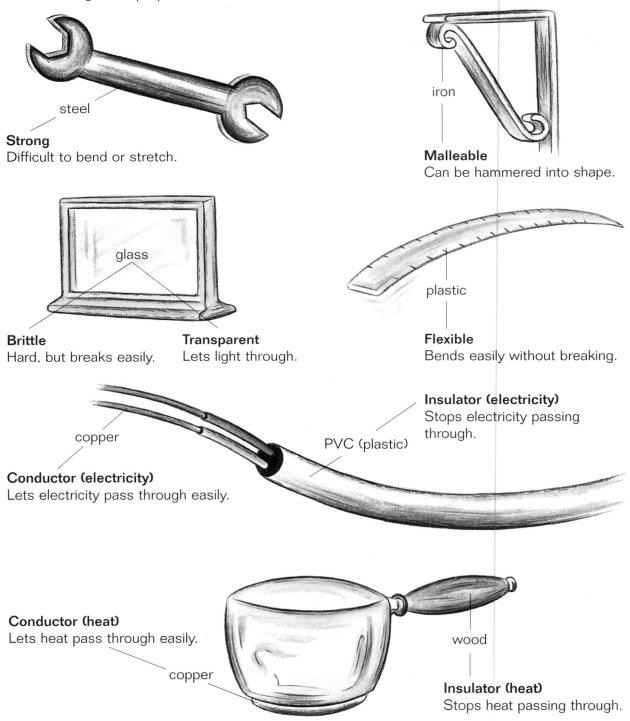

steel

Strong
Difficult to bend or stretch.

iron

Malleable
Can be hammered into shape.

glass

Brittle
Hard, but breaks easily.

Transparent
Lets light through.

plastic

Flexible
Bends easily without breaking.

copper

Conductor (electricity)
Lets electricity pass through easily.

PVC (plastic)

Insulator (electricity)
Stops electricity passing through.

Conductor (heat)
Lets heat pass through easily.

copper

wood

Insulator (heat)
Stops heat passing through.

▶ Useful materials

Here are five types of materials used for making things.
The properties are the ones they *usually* have.

Ceramics
- Made from clay
- Brittle
- Can stand very high temperatures.

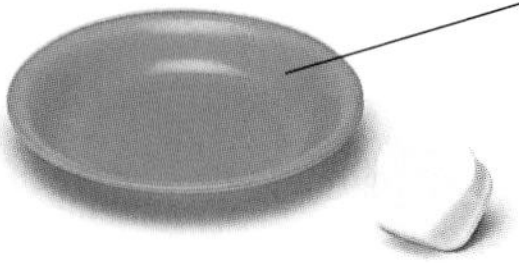

Plastics
- Synthetic (chemically-made)
- Melt easily
- Can be moulded when warm
- Flexible
- Good electrical insulators.

Glasses
- Made from sand
- Brittle
- Transparent
- Good electrical insulators.

Metals
- Strong and hard
- Shiny
- Difficult to melt
- Can be hammered into shape
- Good conductors of heat and electricity.

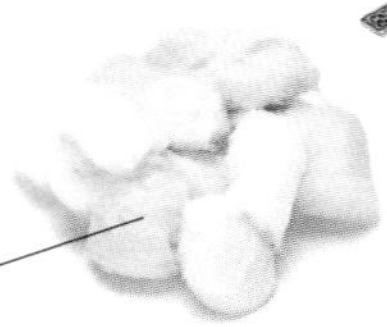

Fibres
- Materials made into threads.

1 *brittle   malleable   flexible   transparent   strong*

Write down a word for each of these, choosing from the words above:
   a Hard, but breaks easily.
   b Bends easily without breaking.
   c Lets light through.
   d Can be hammered into shape.

2 Copy the table on the right. Fill in the blanks by writing in a material with each property. (The first one has been done for you.)

3 *heat insulator   electrical insulator   transparent flexible   strong*

Choosing from the words above, write down the properties that a material should have for each of these jobs. (You can choose the same words more than once.)
   a Tow rope.
   b Table mat.
   c Cover of an electric plug.
   d Sides of a fish tank.

Property	Material
transparent	glass
flexible	
brittle	
conductor (heat)	
conductor (electricity)	
insulator (heat)	
insulator (electricity)	

3.4 Elements, atoms, and compounds

▶ Elements

Everything on Earth is made from about 90 simple substances called *elements*.

There are two main types of element: *metals* and *nonmetals*. Here are some examples, with their chemical symbols:

Metals	
Element	*Symbol*
aluminium	Al
calcium	Ca
copper	Cu
gold	Au
iron	Fe
lead	Pb
magnesium	Mg
potassium	K
silver	Ag
sodium	Na
tin	Sn
zinc	Zn

Nonmetals	
Element	*Symbol*
bromine	Br
carbon	C
chlorine	Cl
fluorine	F
helium	He
hydrogen	H
iodine	I
nitrogen	N
oxygen	O
phosphorus	P
silicon	Si
sulphur	S

Metals are usually hard, shiny, and difficult to melt. They are good conductors of heat and electricity. (For more on metals, see spreads 3.3 and 3.10.)

Examples

Copper

Aluminium

Nonmetals are usually gases, or solids which melt easily. The solids are often brittle or powdery. Most nonmetals are insulators - though carbon is a good conductor of electricity.

Examples

 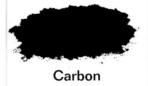

Sulphur   **Carbon**

▶ Atoms

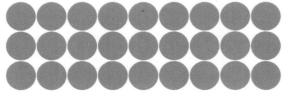

atoms in a bar of copper

The smallest bit of an element is called an *atom*. Each element has its own type of atom.

Atoms are very, very small. It would take more than a billion billion atoms to cover this dot!

▶ Compounds

Atoms can join together to form new substances, called **compounds**. These may be nothing like the elements in them.

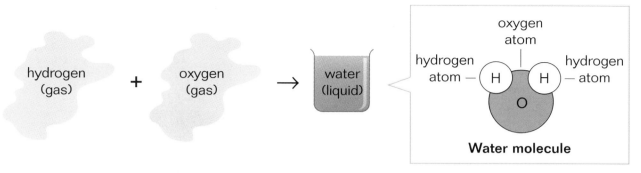

Water molecule

Water is a compound of hydrogen and oxygen. It is made when hydrogen burns in oxygen. But it is nothing like either of these.

The smallest bit of water is called a **molecule** of water. It is made of two hydrogen atoms stuck to one oxygen atom.

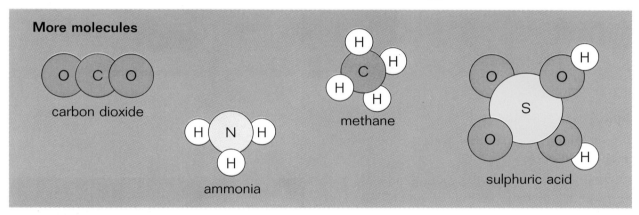

More molecules

carbon dioxide

ammonia

methane

sulphuric acid

Atoms don't really have colours. The colours here are to help you tell the atoms apart.

1 *nonmetals   metals   atoms   compounds   elements*

Copy these sentences. Fill in the blanks, choosing words from those above. You can use the same word more than once.

_____ are usually hard and shiny.

_____ are the smallest bits of elements.

_____ are good conductors of heat and electricity.

_____ are usually insulators.

_____ are made from more than one element.

2 Write down the names of the elements with these symbols:
   H   O   C   N   S

3 Copy the table on the right. Fill in the blanks by writing in the elements in each compound. The first one has been done for you.

Compound	Elements
ammonia	nitrogen hydrogen
water	
carbon dioxide	
sulphuric acid	

3.5 Mixtures and solutions

▶ Mixtures

One substance by itself is called a **pure** substance.

Most substances are not like this. They have other things mixed in. They are **mixtures**.

Mineral water may not be pure, but this does not mean it is dirty. Many of the minerals in it are good for you.

Distilled water
Contains: water

This is pure

Mineral water
Contains: water

+ small amounts of
  bicarbonates
  calcium
  chlorides
  sodium
  magnesium
  potassium
  silica
  sulphates
  nitrates

This is a mixture

▶ Alloys

A metal mixed with another metal (or nonmetal) is called an **alloy**.

Steel is an alloy of iron and carbon. It is mainly iron with a little bit of carbon mixed in. This makes it harder and stronger than iron by itself.

Steel
iron
+ carbon

Brass
copper
+ zinc

Stainless steel
iron
+ chromium
+ carbon

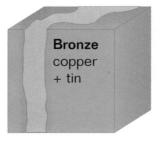

Bronze
copper
+ tin

Brass is an alloy of copper and zinc. Unlike pure copper, it keeps its shine and colour.

▶ Solutions

If you put sugar in water, the sugar breaks up into tiny bits which float away. The bits are so small that you cannot see them even with a microscope.

The sugar has **dissolved** in the water.
Scientists say that sugar is **soluble** in water.
The mixture of sugar and water is called a **solution**:

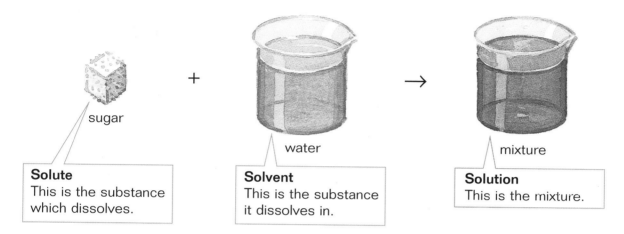

Solute
This is the substance which dissolves.

Solvent
This is the substance it dissolves in.

Solution
This is the mixture.

Water is not the only solvent. Here are some others:

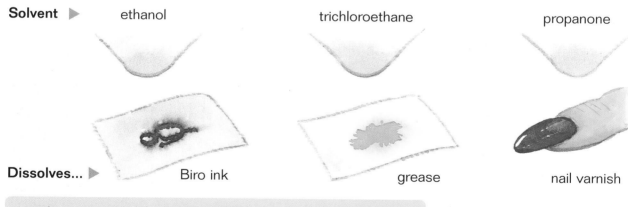

Solvent ▶ ethanol   trichloroethane   propanone

Dissolves... ▶ Biro ink   grease   nail varnish

---

1 *solution   alloy   pure substance*

Write down which of the things above means each of these:
  a One substance by itself
  b A metal mixed with another metal (or nonmetal).

2 *solvent   solute   dissolves   soluble   solution*

Copy these sentences. Fill in the blanks, choosing words from those above.
  When salt is mixed with water, the salt ____ in the water.
  Salt is ____ in water.
  The water is called the ____.
  The mixture is called a ____.

3.6 Separating mixtures

Here are some methods of separating mixtures in the laboratory:

Filtering

Example Separating sand from water.

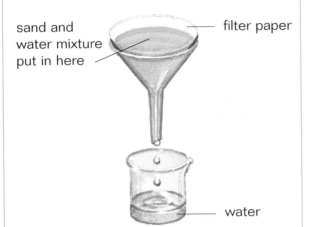

sand and water mixture put in here — filter paper

water

Pour the mixture into a funnel lined with filter paper. The filter paper lets the water through but stops the sand.

Dissolving and filtering

Example Separating sand from salt.

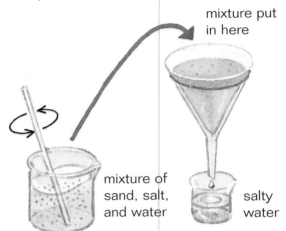

mixture put in here

mixture of sand, salt, and water

salty water

Mix the sand and salt with water, and stir. This dissolves the salt, but not the sand. Filter the new mixture. The filter paper lets the salty water through but stops the sand.

Evaporating

Example Separating salt from water.

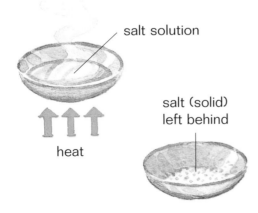

salt solution

salt (solid) left behind

heat

Heat the solution gently until all the water has evaporated. The salt is left behind as a solid.

Distilling

Example Separating water from ink.

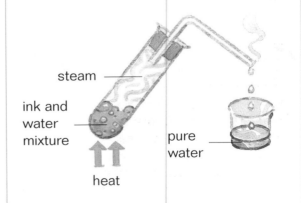

steam

ink and water mixture

pure water

heat

Boil the mixture so that it gives off steam. The steam is pure water vapour, with no ink in it. As the steam passes down the tube, it condenses into pure, liquid water.

Crystallizing

Example Separating copper sulphate from water.

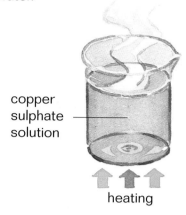

copper sulphate solution

heating

Heat the solution gently, so that some of the water evaporates.

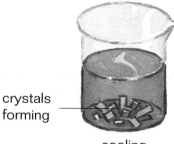

crystals forming

cooling

Leave the rest of the solution to cool. Copper sulphate crystals will start to form in it.

Chromatography

Example Separating inks of different colours.

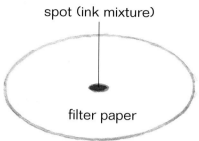

spot (ink mixture)

filter paper

Put a spot of ink mixture in the middle of a piece of filter paper and leave it to dry.

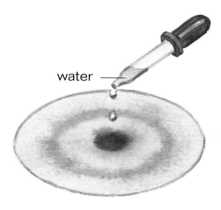

water

Drip water onto the spot. The ink mixture spreads through the damp paper. The different colours spread at different rates.

---

1 Here are some methods of separating mixtures:
*filtering   evaporating   crystallizing   distilling
dissolving and filtering   chromatography*

Write down which method you would use for each of these jobs (the information on the right may help):
a Separating sand and salt.
b Separating sand and sugar.
c Separating mud and water.
d Separating water paints of different colours.

2 A tea-bag is a filter. Write down what things you think it separates.

3 The bag in a vacuum cleaner is a filter. Write down what things you think it separates.

> Mud is tiny bits of soil floating in water
>
> Sugar will dissolve in water

3.7 Acids and alkalis

► Acids

There are acids in the laboratory. But there are natural acids in vinegar, sour fruits, and even in your stomach!

Acids dissolved in lots of water are called *dilute* acids. Acids dissolved in only a little water are *concentrated* acids.

When dissolved in water, acids are *corrosive* . They eat into materials such as carbonates and some metals.

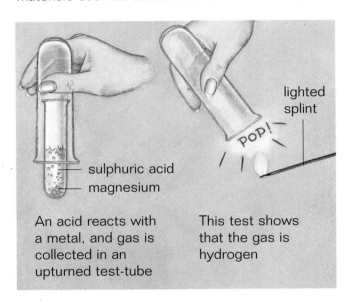

lighted splint

POP!

sulphuric acid
magnesium

An acid reacts with a metal, and gas is collected in an upturned test-tube

This test shows that the gas is hydrogen

Some natural acids

	contains....
lemon juice	citric acid
vinegar	ethanoic acid
fizzy drinks	carbonic acid
sour milk	lactic acid
nettle sting	methanoic acid
stomach juice	hydrochloric acid

Strong acids
hydrochloric acid
sulphuric acid
nitric acid

Weak acids
ethanoic acid
citric acid
carbonic acid

All acids contain hydrogen. When an acid eats into a metal, the hydrogen is released as a gas.

Acids which act quickly, and release lots of hydrogen, are called *strong acids*. Acids which act slowly are *weak acids*.

► Alkalis

Alkalis are chemicals which can *neutralize* acids. They can cancel out their acid effect (see the next page).

Strong alkalis
sodium hydroxide
potassium hydroxide
calcium hydroxide

Weak alkali
ammonia

Alkalis can be just as corrosive as acids. Their powerful chemical action is often used in bath, sink, and oven cleaners, like those in the picture.

▶ Neutralization

Neutralizing acids is called **neutralization**. Here are two examples:

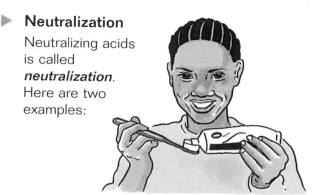

Sugar in your mouth produces acids which rot your teeth. Toothpaste is alkaline. It neutralizes these acids.

Acid in your stomach can become a bit too concentrated. Indigestion tablets release an alkali which neutralizes some of the acid.

▶ Testing for acids and alkalis

You can use **litmus paper** to test for an acid or alkali:

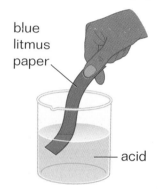

blue litmus paper

acid

Acids turn blue litmus paper red.

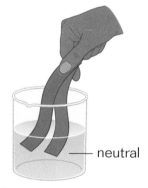

neutral

If a solution is **neutral** (neither acid nor alkaline), the paper doesn't change colour.

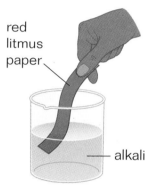

red litmus paper

alkali

Alkalis turn red litmus paper blue.

---

1 Copy the table on the right. Fill in the blanks, by writing 'acid' or 'alkali' in each space. The first one has been done for you.

2 Copy and complete these sentences:
  a An acid dissolved in lots of water is called a .... acid.
  b An acid dissolved in only a little water is called a .... acid.
  c If an acid eats into a metal, ... is released.
  d If an alkali *neutralizes* an acid, this means that........
  e If you dip litmus paper into a neutral solution, the paper........

	acid or alkali
Sour milk	acid
Turns blue litmus paper red	
Turns red litmus paper blue	
Always contains hydrogen	
Toothpaste	
Lemon juice	
Indigestion tablets	
Oven cleaner	
Vinegar	
Ammonia	

3.8 Changing materials

▶ Chemical change

When iron and sulphur are mixed and heated, they join to make a completely new substance, iron sulphide.

 +  heat →

iron (metal)   sulphur (yellow powder)   iron sulphide (black solid)

This is an example of a **chemical change**. Iron has **reacted** with sulphur. There has been a **chemical reaction** between the two. Here is a **word equation** for the reaction:

iron + sulphur → iron sulphide

▶ Signs of chemical change

If there is a chemical change:

One or more new substances are made
Iron sulphide is a compound (see 3.4). It is nothing like iron or sulphur.

The change is usually difficult to reverse
Changing iron sulphide back into iron and sulphur is difficult. Several reactions are needed.

Energy is given out or taken in
When iron reacts with sulphur, heat is given out.

Here are some examples of chemical change:

Once you have cooked eggs, you can't change them back again.

These chemical reactions give out energy as heat and light.

+ oxygen (in air) →

iron

rust (iron oxide)

If there is water around, a chemical change turns these..... ......into this.

▶ Physical change

If liquid water freezes, it becomes ice. This is an example of a **physical change**. If there is a physical change:

No new substances are made
Ice is still water, even though it is a solid.

The change is usually easy to reverse
Ice can melt to form liquid water again.

Here are some examples of physical change:

Liquid water can change into steam. When steam condenses, it becomes liquid water again.

Salt dissolves in water. But if you evaporate the water, you are left with the salt again.

1 *physical   chemical*

Copy these sentences. Fill in the blanks, choosing words from those above. (You can use the same word more than once.)

a In a ____ change, one or more new substances are made.

b A ____ change is usually difficult to reverse.

c In a ____ change, you end up with the same substance that you started with.

2 Copy the table on the right. Fill in the blanks, by writing 'physical' or 'chemical' in each space. The first one has been done for you.

	Change: physical or chemical
Cooking an egg	chemical
Ice melting	
Salt dissolving in water	
Baking a cake	
Iron going rusty	
Hot fat going solid when cooled	
Wood burning	

3.9 Burning

▶ Combustion

Combustion is another word for burning. It happens when substances react with oxygen in the air. When things burn, they give out energy as heat and light.

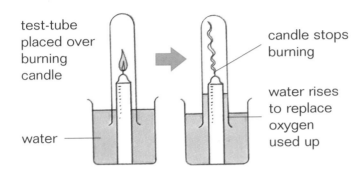

test-tube placed over burning candle

water

candle stops burning

water rises to replace oxygen used up

This experiment shows that about 1/5 of the air is used up when something burns. That is because about 1/5 of the air is oxygen.

Combustion

▶ Burning fuels

Petrol, coal, wood, and natural gas (methane) are all *fuels*.

Most fuels are compounds of hydrogen and carbon. When they burn, they make carbon dioxide and water, as on the right.

methane + oxygen → carbon dioxide + water

| atoms of: carbon hydrogen | atoms of: oxygen | atoms of: carbon oxygen | atoms of: hydrogen oxygen |

wooden splint

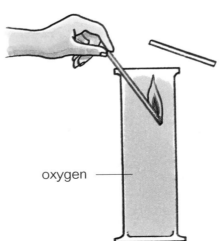

oxygen

Testing for oxygen Fuels burn more fiercely in pure oxygen than in air. You can use this fact to test for oxygen:

If a glowing wooden splint is put into oxygen, the splint will burst into flames.

► Fire!

The **combustion triangle** below shows the three things needed for burning. Getting rid of any of them stops the burning. So firefighters have three ways of putting out a fire.

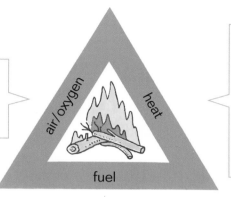

Cut off the air supply
For example Use a fire blanket, foam, or carbon dioxide gas.

Get rid of the heat
For example Cool things down with water.

Note Water is not safe for some fires. It conducts electricity and can give people shocks. Also, it can make burning fat or oil splatter and spread.

Cut off the fuel
For example Turn off the gas at the mains.

► Burning food

To get energy, your body 'burns up' food slowly, without any flames. This is called **respiration** (see 2.2). It makes carbon dioxide and water:

food + oxygen → carbon dioxide + water

► Testing for carbon dioxide

Carbon dioxide turns **limewater** milky. You can use this fact to tell that there is carbon dioxide in the air you breathe out.

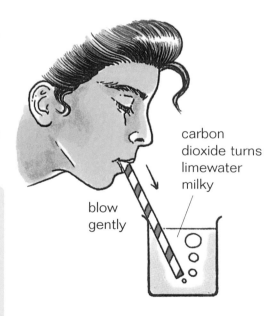

blow gently

carbon dioxide turns limewater milky

1 Here are three gases:
   oxygen   carbon dioxide   methane
   Write down which gas does each of these.
   (You can choose the same gas more than once.)
   a Puts out fires.
   b Is needed for burning.
   c Is made when most fuels burn.
   d Is used as a fuel.
   e Makes a glowing splint burst into flames.
   f Is made when your body 'burns up' food.
   g Turns limewater milky.

2 Write down the *three* things needed for burning.

3.10 More about metals

▶ Corrosion

The surface of a metal may be attacked by air, water, or other substances around it. This is called **corrosion**. Iron corrodes by going rusty. Steel is mainly iron. It can also go rusty.

The experiment on the right shows that air *and* water are needed for rusting. Dry air has no effect. Nor does water, if it has no air in it.

To stop iron and steel going rusty, they can be coated with paint, grease, plastic, or zinc.

Iron nail in.....

dry air

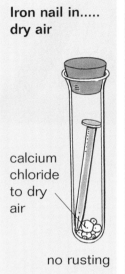

calcium chloride to dry air

no rusting

boiled water (air-free)

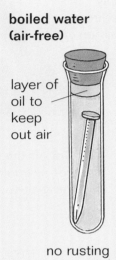

layer of oil to keep out air

no rusting

air and water

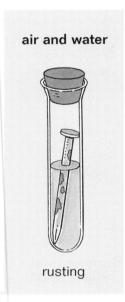

rusting

▶ Reactive and unreactive

Iron is a **reactive** metal. It reacts with other elements to form compounds. For example, it reacts with oxygen in the air to form rust.

Gold is an **unreactive** metal. It does not react with oxygen or acids. So it does not corrode however long it is left in the air or soil.

▶ Where metals come from

Most of our metals come from rocks in the ground. They are in compounds called **ores**. The metal has to be separated from its ore using heat or electricity.

Unreactive metals, such as gold, are found in the ground as small bits of the metal itself.

Metal	Aluminium	Copper	Iron	Gold
Useful properties	Light and strong, good conductor of electricity and heat	Very good conductor of electricity and heat	Can be made into steel, which is very strong	Doesn't corrode
Where found	 In ore called bauxite	 In ores such as cuprite	 In ore called haematite	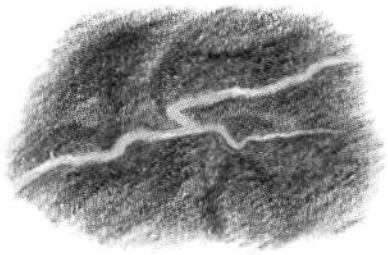 In rock, as a metal

To make steel, a tiny amount of carbon is added to pure, *molten* iron ('molten' means 'melted'). Steel is an **alloy** of iron and carbon. For more on alloys, see Spread 3.5.

1 Here are four metals:
   copper   aluminium   gold   iron
   Copy the following sentences. Fill in the blanks, choosing words from those above. (You can use the same word more than once.)
   a ____ is light and strong.
   b ____ is a very good conductor of electricity.
   c ____ is a very good conductor of heat.
   d ____ does not corrode.
   e ____ corrodes by going rusty.
   f ____ can be made into steel.
   g ____ is unreactive.
   h ____ is found in the ground as a metal, not an ore.

2 Write down *two* things which are needed for iron or steel to go rusty.

3 Write down *two* ways of stopping iron or steel going rusty.

Air

Air is not one gas. It is a mixture of gases.
The pie chart shows the main gases in air.

Oxygen

- Animals and plants need oxygen to stay alive.
- Oxygen is needed to make things burn.
- Oxygen affects some foods and makes them go off.

Carbon dioxide and other gases

- These are just a tiny fraction of the air. There is more about them on the next page.

Nitrogen

- Nitrates have nitrogen in them. Plants need nitrates for healthy growth.
- Nitrogen is combined with hydrogen to make ammonia. Ammonia is needed to make plastics, and fertilizers for farmers.
- Nitrogen helps preserve food in packets. Nitrogen doesn't make food go off.

- Very cold, liquid nitrogen is used for freezing food quickly.

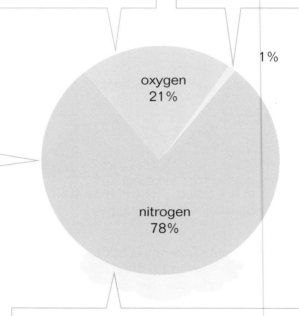

1%

oxygen
21%

nitrogen
78%

Water vapour

- Damp air has some water vapour in it. When water vapour condenses into millions of tiny drops, we see these as clouds and fog.

Carbon dioxide....

- Plants take in carbon dioxide for growth.

- Some fire extinguishers shoot out carbon dioxide. Things can't burn in carbon dioxide.

- Carbon dioxide is the gas that puts the fizz in fizzy drinks.

- Solid carbon dioxide is called 'dry ice'. It is much colder than ordinary ice. It is used for storing frozen fish and other foods.

...and other gases

- Argon is used to fill light bulbs. It stops the filament burning up.

- Helium is lighter than other gases in air. It is used to fill balloons.

- Neon is used in lamps that give a red glow.

---

1 On the right, there are the names of four gases:
Write down the gas that goes with each of these clues. (You can choose the same gas more than once.)
  - **a** There is more of this gas in air than any other.
  - **b** This gas is needed for things to burn.
  - **c** When this gas freezes, it becomes 'dry ice'.
  - **d** This gas is needed to make nitrates for plants.

2 Copy and complete these sentences. You must start each sentence with one of the gases on the right, then finish it with your own words:
  - **a** _____ is used to fill balloons because.....
  - **b** _____ is used in fire extinguishers because.....
  - **c** _____ is used to fill crisp packets because.....

3 The gases on the right are all part of the air. Write down the name of *one* other gas in air. Describe what it is used for.

carbon dioxide

oxygen

nitrogen

helium

Water

Here are some facts about water:

- Two-thirds of the Earth's surface is covered with water.
- All living things need water.
- Our bodies are two-thirds water.
- Water can be a solid (ice), a liquid, or a gas (water vapour).

▶ **The water cycle**

The Earth's water is recycled - it is used over and over again.
This is called the **water cycle**:

| The Sun heats the sea. Water evaporates. | The water vapour rises. It condenses to form clouds. A cloud is millions of tiny droplets of water (or ice). | Clouds release their water as rain (or snow). |

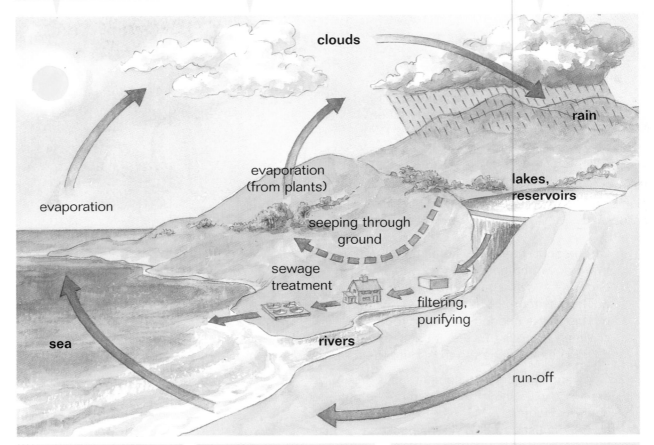

| Rain seeps into the ground, runs into streams and rivers, and flows back into the sea. | Plants take water from the soil. Some goes back into the air as vapour. | Reservoirs trap water for our homes. Waste water and sewage is put back into the sea (it may be purified first). |

▶ Freezing water

Water freezes at 0 °C.

When water freezes it expands. It takes up more space than before.

The force of the expansion can be huge.

This much water...   ...becomes this much ice

Here are some of the effects of freezing water:

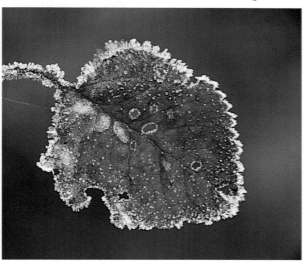

Water vapour condenses on cold ground or plants to form *dew*. When dew freezes, it is called *frost*.

Pipes burst when water in them freezes.

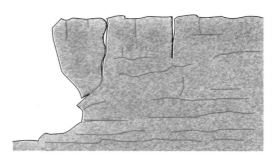

Rocks split when water freezes in cracks.

1 Write out these sentences in the correct order, starting with the one about the Sun:
   The Sun heats the surface of the sea.
   Water flows out to sea.
   Water evaporates from the sea.
   Rainwater runs into lakes and rivers.
   Rain falls to the ground.
   Water vapour condenses to form clouds.

2 Describe *two* ways in which water in the ground can get back into the air.

3 Copy and complete these sentences:
   Dew is formed when....
   Frozen dew is called.....
   When water pipes freeze, they burst because.....

3.13 Rock, stone, and soil

▶ Weathering

If rock or stonework is exposed (out in the open), it is weakened by the weather. This is called **weathering**.

The effects of weathering on stonework.

Sunshine heats some parts more than others. The expansion cracks the rock.

Rock splits when water freezes in cracks.

Rain is slightly acid. It eats into some rocks, such as chalk and limestone.

▶ Soil

Soil is mainly made from the rock underneath it. The rock gets broken up by rain, frost, and expansion caused by the Sun's heat.

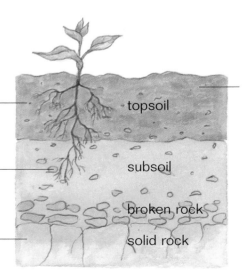

Soil is made from the smaller bits of broken rock.

Stones are the bigger bits of broken rock.

Under the soil, there is solid rock.

topsoil

subsoil

broken rock

solid rock

Topsoil has rotting plant and animal waste in it. This is called **humus**. It is rich in the minerals that plants need.

► The rock cycle

Materials from rocks are used over and over again. This is called the **rock cycle**. It can take millions of years. Here is one part of it:

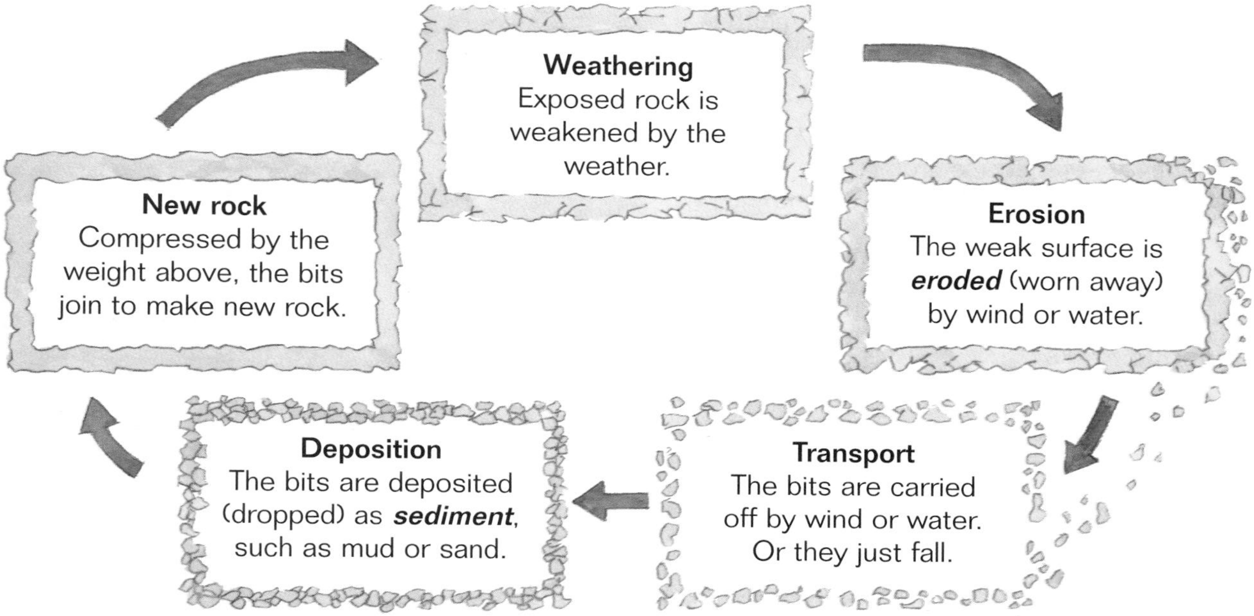

Weathering
Exposed rock is weakened by the weather.

New rock
Compressed by the weight above, the bits join to make new rock.

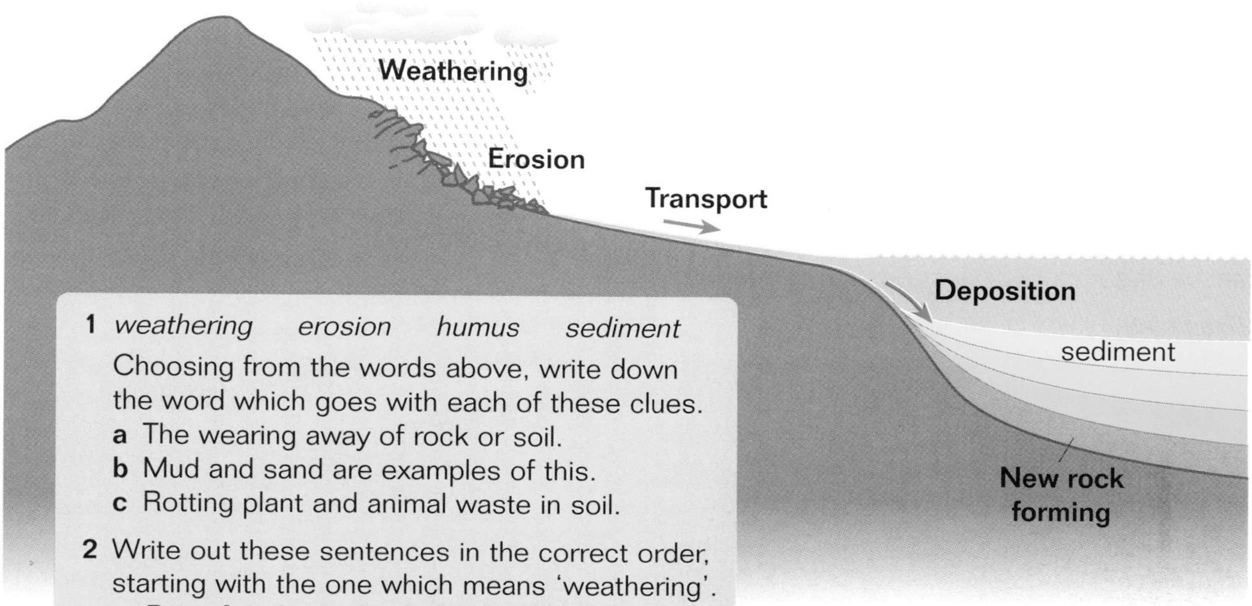

Erosion
The weak surface is *eroded* (worn away) by wind or water.

Deposition
The bits are deposited (dropped) as *sediment*, such as mud or sand.

Transport
The bits are carried off by wind or water. Or they just fall.

Weathering

Erosion

Transport

Deposition

sediment

New rock forming

1 *weathering   erosion   humus   sediment*
   Choosing from the words above, write down the word which goes with each of these clues.
   a The wearing away of rock or soil.
   b Mud and sand are examples of this.
   c Rotting plant and animal waste in soil.

2 Write out these sentences in the correct order, starting with the one which means 'weathering'.
   Bits of rock are dropped as sediment.
   Bits of compressed rock join together.
   Bits of rock are carried off by wind or water.
   Exposed rock is weakened by the weather.
   Bits of rock are worn away by wind or water.

Looking at rocks

The Earth is made of rock. Deep in the Earth, the rock is so hot that it is *molten* (melted). Sometimes, molten rock comes out of volcanoes, as in the photograph.

The Earth's surface changes slowly over millions of years. Rocks in the ground may be raised up and exposed. Other rocks may be buried.

There are three main types of rocks:

▶ Igneous rocks

These are made of tiny crystals. They are formed when molten rock cools and goes solid.

Examples

Granite This went solid underground. It was exposed when rocks above it were worn away.

Basalt This formed from molten rock which oozed out of cracks in the Earth.

▶ Sedimentary rocks

These are made from layers of sediment dropped by water, wind, or moving ice. The sediment is compressed by the weight above and sets like concrete. But this takes millions of years.

Examples

Sandstone This formed from bits worn away from other rocks.

Limestone This formed from the shells and bones of ancient sea creatures.

Metamorphic rocks

Deep underground, igneous and sedimentary rocks can be changed by heat or pressure. They become **metamorphic** ('changed') rocks.

Examples

Marble This formed from *limestone* when it was heated underground.

Slate This formed from *shale (mudstone)* when it was compressed underground.

Using rocks

We get minerals, such as diamond and gold, from rocks. The word 'mineral' really means anything useful that can be mined from the Earth.

The table shows some more uses of rocks.

Rock	Description	Examples of use
Granite	Very hard, sparkling	chippings, road stone building stone
Limestone	light colour	building/facing stone chippings in cement, concrete
Marble	light colour, hard, smooth	facing stone statues
Slate	hard, but splits into flat sheets	roofing tiles snooker tables

1 *igneous   sedimentary   metamorphic*

Copy these sentences. Fill in the blanks using the words above.
a Rocks formed from bits of rock or shell, dropped in layers, are called ____ rocks.
b Rocks formed when molten rock cools and goes solid are called ____ rocks.
c Rocks changed by heat or pressure are called ____ rocks.

2 Copy the table on the right. Fill in the blanks by giving one example of each type of rock and one use for that rock. (The name of one rock has been written in for you.)

Rock	Used for
igneous: granite	
sedimentary:	
metamorphic:	

4.1 Charges in action

'Electricity' is another word for **electric charge**.

The photograph shows electric charge in action.

▶ Charges from the atom

There are two types of electric charge. They are called **positive (+)** and **negative (-)**. They come from atoms.

An atom has equal amounts of negative (-) and positive (+) charge. So the charges balance.

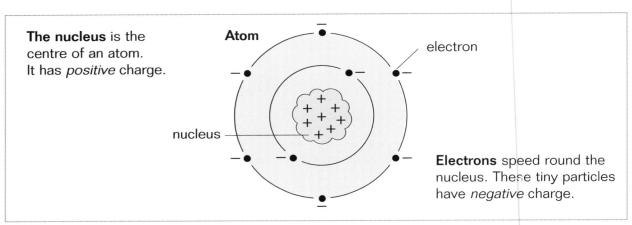

The nucleus is the centre of an atom. It has *positive* charge.

Atom

electron

nucleus

Electrons speed round the nucleus. These tiny particles have *negative* charge.

▶ From conductors to insulators

Electrons do not always stay with atoms. When you switch on a light, electrons flow through the wires. A flow of electrons is called a **current**.

Conductors let electrons flow through.

Insulators do not let electrons flow through.

Conductors		Insulators	
Good	*Poor*	plastics	glass
metals,	human body	*for example*	rubber
especially	water	PVC	
silver	air	polythene	
copper		Perspex	
aluminium			
carbon			

▶ Static electricity

You can charge up an insulator by rubbing it. People say that it has 'static electricity' on it.

If you rub a polythene rod with a cloth, the polythene pulls electrons from the cloth.

The polythene gains negative (–) charge.

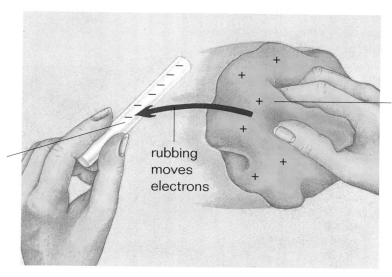

rubbing moves electrons

The cloth is left with positive (+) charge.

Rubbing doesn't make electric charge. It separates charges that are already there.

▶ Forces between charges

When charges are close, they push or pull on each other:

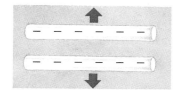

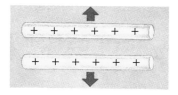

Like charges repel.

Unlike charges attract.

1 *positive   negative*

Copy these sentences. Fill in each blank with one of the words above. (You can use the same word more than once.)

The nucleus of an atom has a ___ charge.
An electron has a ___ charge.
A positive charge will attract a ___ charge.
A positive charge will repel a ___ charge.
A negative charge will repel a ___ charge.

2 Copy the table on the right. For each material, put in a tick to show whether it is a *good conductor* of electricity, a *poor conductor*, or an *insulator*. One tick has been done for you.

Material	Good conductor	Poor conductor	Insulator
air		✓	
copper			
glass			
plastic			
aluminium			
carbon			
water			

4.2 A simple circuit

This is called a **circuit**. The **battery** has two **terminals**.
It pushes electrons out of the negative (-) terminal,
round the circuit, to the positive (+) terminal.

When electrons pass
through the bulb, they heat
up a **filament** (thin wire) so
that it glows.

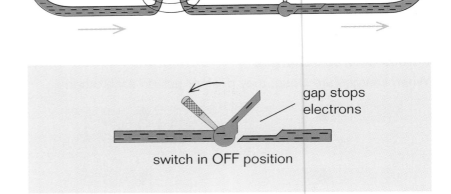

There must be a *complete*
circuit for electrons to flow.
If there is a break in the
circuit, the flow stops, and
the bulb goes out. Turning
the switch OFF breaks the
circuit.

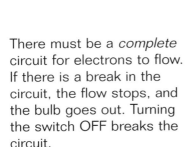

switch in OFF position

▶ **Spending energy**

The battery *gives* electrons
energy. The electrons *spend*
this energy when they flow
through the bulb. The bulb
sends out energy as heat
and light.

For more on energy, see
Spread 4.9.

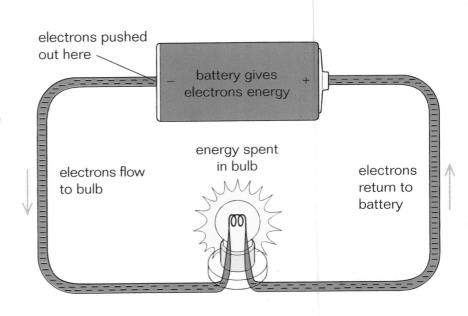

▶ Voltage

A battery has a **voltage** marked on the side. It is measured in **volts (V)**. A higher voltage means that each electron has more energy to spend.

To measure the voltage of a battery, you connect a **voltmeter** across its terminals.

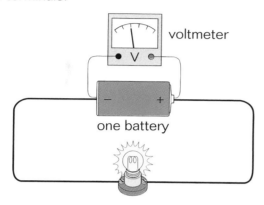

1.5 volt battery

▶ Current

Current is measured in **amperes (A)**. A higher current means a bigger flow of electrons.

To measure current, you connect an **ammeter** into the circuit.

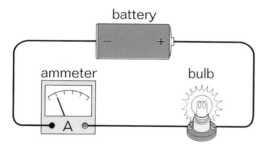

The ammeter can be put anywhere in this circuit, because the current is the same all the way round.

Putting in the ammeter doesn't affect the current.

---

1 *current   voltage   ammeter   voltmeter*

Copy these sentences. Fill in the blanks, choosing words from those above. (You can use the same word more than once.)

Current is measured with a meter called an ____.

____ is measured in amperes.

If there is a break in a circuit, there is no ____.

2 Copy and complete these statements about the circuit on the right:

Meter Y is called a ......
Meter X is called a ......
The reading on meter X is ......

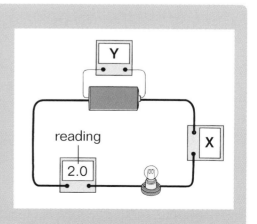

Batteries and bulbs

▶ **Adding batteries**

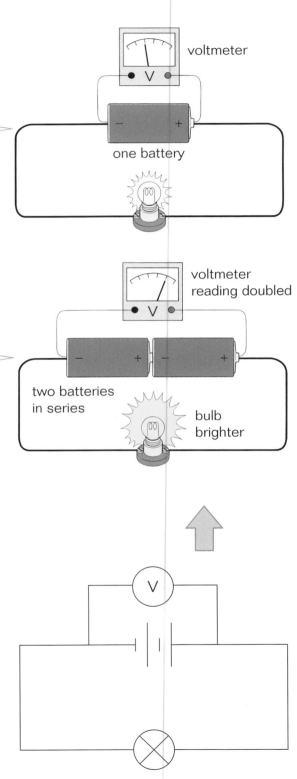

voltmeter

This circuit has one battery in it. The voltmeter is measuring the voltage across the battery.

A single battery is sometimes called a *cell*.

one battery

voltmeter
reading doubled

If *two* batteries are put in the circuit like this, the total voltage is twice what it was before. Also, the bulb glows more brightly because a higher current is being pushed through it.

When batteries are connected in a line like this, they are in *series*.

two batteries
in series

bulb
brighter

▶ **Circuit symbols**

Scientists and electricians draw circuits using *symbols*.

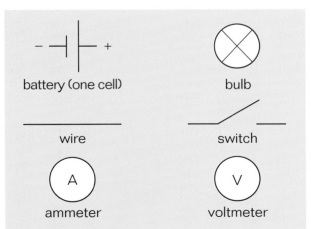

battery (one cell)

bulb

wire

switch

A — ammeter

V — voltmeter

The second circuit, drawn using symbols.

▶ Bulbs in series

This circuit has two bulbs in it. The bulbs are connected in *series* (in a line):

The bulbs glow dimly. It is more difficult for the electrons to pass through two bulbs than one, so there is less current than before.

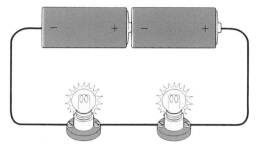

bulbs in series

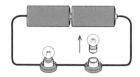

If one bulb is removed, the circuit is broken. So the other bulb goes off.

▶ Bulbs in parallel

This circuit also has two bulbs in it. The bulbs are connected in *parallel*.

The bulbs glow brightly because each is getting the full battery voltage.

Together, two bright bulbs take more current than a single bright bulb, so the battery will not last as long.

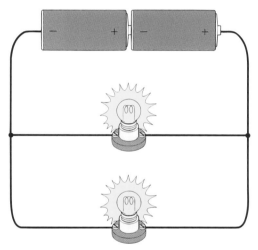

bulbs in parallel

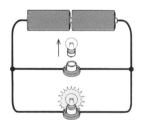

If one bulb is removed, there is still a complete circuit through the other bulb, so it stays bright.

---

1 Look at the circuit A and B on the right.
  a Write down which circuit, A or B, has the brighter bulb.
  b Explain why this bulb is the brighter.

2 Look at the circuits C and D on the right.
  a Write down which circuit, C or D, has two bulbs in series.
  b Write down which circuit, C or D, has the brighter bulbs.
  c Write down what will happen to bulb 1 if bulb 2 is removed.
  d Write down what will happen to bulb 3 if bulb 4 is removed.

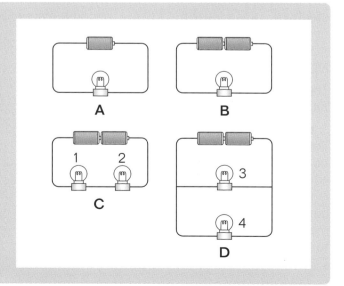

4.4 Magnets and electromagnets

Magnets

A few metals are *magnetic*. They are attracted to magnets and can be magnetized. Iron and steel are the main magnetic metals.

The force from a magnet seems to come from two points near the ends. These are the *north pole* (*N*) and the *south pole* (*S*) of the magnet.

When the poles of a magnet are brought close, you can feel the force between them:

Magnetic	Non-magnetic
iron	aluminium
steel*	copper
nickel	brass
	tin
* apart from	silver
stainless steel	gold

magnet (steel)

Like poles repel N ←→ N S →← N *Unlike poles attract*

Magnetizing iron and steel

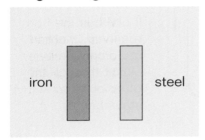

These pieces of iron and steel are unmagnetized.

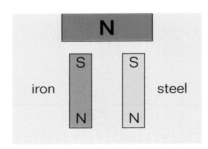

When a magnet is near, they become magnetized.

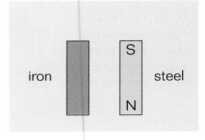

The magnet is taken away. Iron loses its magnetism. Steel keeps its magnetism.

Magnetic fields

The space around a magnet is called a *magnetic field*. The field pulls on anything magnetic.

You can use a *compass* to see which way the field is pulling. A compass is a tiny magnet which can turn on a spindle.

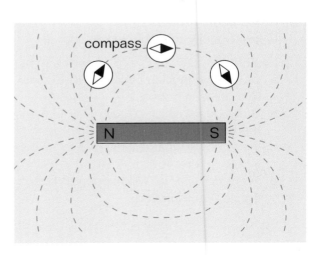

► Electromagnet

An electric current produces a magnetic field. This idea is used in an **electromagnet**.

The current in the coil produces a field. The field magnetizes the iron **core**. This makes the field much stronger.

When the electromagnet is switched off, the iron core loses its magnetism and the field vanishes.

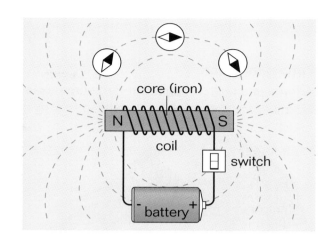

► Relay

A **relay** is a switch worked by an electromagnet. With a relay, you can use a tiny switch to turn on a big electric motor powered by mains electricity. The relay works like this:

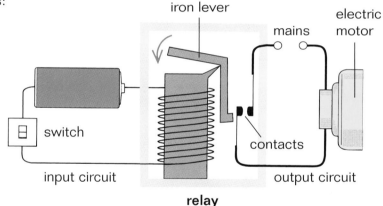

When you switch on the current in the input circuit, the electromagnet pulls on an iron lever.

When the iron lever is pulled down, it closes two contacts in the output circuit.

relay

---

1 *north   south*

Copy these sentences about magnets. Fill in each blank with one of the words above. (You can use the same word more than once.)

A north pole will attract a ____ pole.
A north pole will repel a ____ pole.
A south pole will repel a ____ pole.

2 Copy the table on the right. For each metal, put in a tick to show whether it is *magnetic* or *non-magnetic*. The first one has been done for you.

3 Write down the name of a metal which:
  a keeps its magnetism when magnetized.
  b loses its magnetism easily.
  c can be used as the core of an electromagnet.

Metal	Magnetic	Non-magnetic
nickel	✓	
iron		
aluminium		
copper		
steel		

4.5 Forces

▶ Forces in action

A force is a push or pull. Here are some examples of forces:

Friction This gives a tyre grip on the road when the brakes go on. There is more about friction in Spread 4.8.

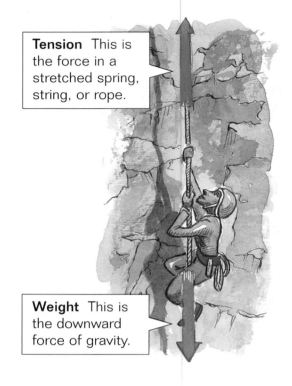

Tension This is the force in a stretched spring, string, or rope.

Weight This is the downward force of gravity.

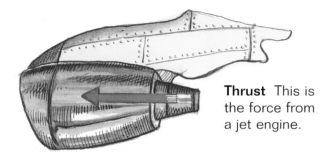

Thrust This is the force from a jet engine.

Air resistance This force tries to slow you down when you are cycling along.

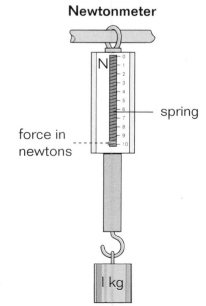

Newtonmeter

N

spring

force in newtons

1 kg

▶ Measuring force

Force is measured in *newtons* (*N*).

Weight is a force. So scientists measure it in newtons, just like any other force.

On Earth, a mass of 1 kilogram has a weight of about 10 newtons. The force can be measured using a *newtonmeter*.

► Balanced and unbalanced forces

A skydiver jumps from a helicopter. The forces on her are *air resistance* (upwards) and her *weight* (downwards)......

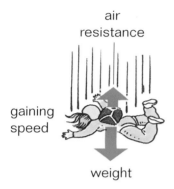

air resistance

gaining speed

weight

At first, the downward force is stronger than the upward force. The forces are **unbalanced**, so the skydiver **accelerates** (gains speed).

air resistance

steady speed

weight

Now, the forces are equal. They are **balanced**. Neither force wins, so she doesn't speed up, and she doesn't slow down. Her speed is *steady*.

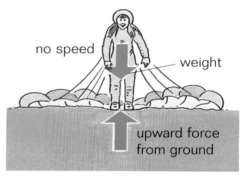

no speed

weight

upward force from ground

Now she is standing on the ground. The ground is compressed. It pushes upwards and supports her weight. The forces are *balanced*.

---

1 Here are five types of force:
   friction   air resistance   weight   tension   thrust

   Copy these sentences. Fill in the blanks, choosing words from those above.
   The downward force of gravity is called ____.
   The force between a tyre and the road is called ____.
   The force in a stretched rope is called ____.
   The upward force on a falling skydiver is called ____.

2 In the diagram on the right, there is an upward force of 6 N on the ball. Write down what the letter N stands for.

3 Copy the diagram on the right.
   Draw in a force arrow for the weight of the ball.
   Next to this force arrow, write down the size of the force (for example 1 N or 2 N or some other value - you must decide).

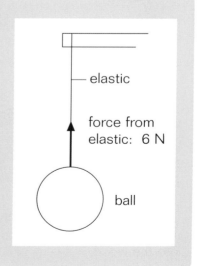

elastic

force from elastic: 6 N

ball

4.6 Pressure

You can't push your thumb into wood. But you *can* push a drawing pin in using the same force. That is because the force is concentrated on a much smaller area. Scientists say that the **pressure** is higher.

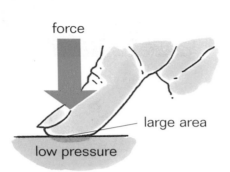

force

large area

low pressure

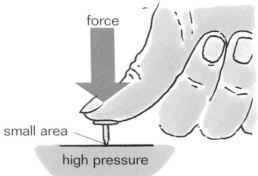

force

small area

high pressure

Spreading the force over a *large area* gives...

low pressure

This ski spreads the skier's weight, so the foot doesn't sink into soft snow.

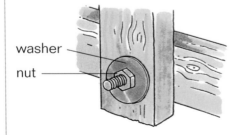

washer

nut

When you tighten the nut, the washer spreads the force, so the nut doesn't go into the wood.

Concentrating the force on a *small area* gives...

high pressure

When the studs on this boot are pressed down, they sink into the ground to give good grip.

A sharp blade concentrates the force so that cutting is easy.

Measuring pressure

Pressure is measured in **newtons per square metre** (**N/m²**).

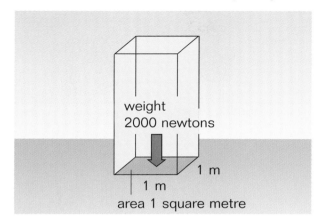

area 1 square metre

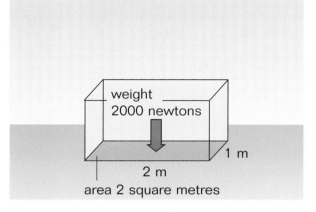

area 2 square metres

This block weighs 2000 newtons. So there is force of 2000 newtons pressing on 1 square metre of ground.

The *pressure* under this block is 2000 newtons per square metre.

This block also weighs 2000 newtons. But it is pressing on 2 square metres of ground. So there is a force of 1000 newtons on *each square metre*.

The *pressure* under this block is only 1000 newtons per square metre.

Tyre pressure gauges are sometimes marked in 'psi' (pounds per square inch).

The pressure in this tyre is 50 psi. That is the same as a pressure of 350 000 newtons per square metre.

1 Copy these sentences. Write either *high* or *low* in each blank space.
  a If a force is spread over a large area, the pressure is ____.
  b If a force is concentrated on a small area, the pressure is ____.
  c When you push in a drawing pin, the pressure under the point is ____.
  d When you wear skis, the pressure under them is ____.

2 Write down what 'N/m²' means in words.

3 Look at the diagram on the right.
  a Write down how many newtons of force are pressing on *each square metre* of ground.
  b Write down the pressure under the block in N/m².

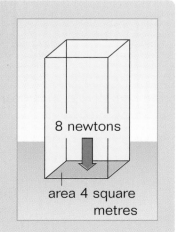

8 newtons

area 4 square metres

4.7 Turning forces

Forces can make things turn. They can have a turning effect.

On the right, someone is using a spanner to turn a bolt. The force has a turning effect on the bolt.

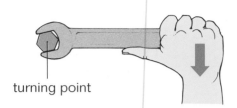

turning point

Here are two ways of making the turning effect *twice* as strong:

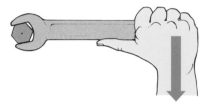

Pull with *twice* the force.

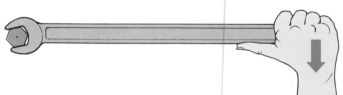

Use a spanner *twice* as long.

▶ Balance

The people below are sitting on the see-saw so that it balances.

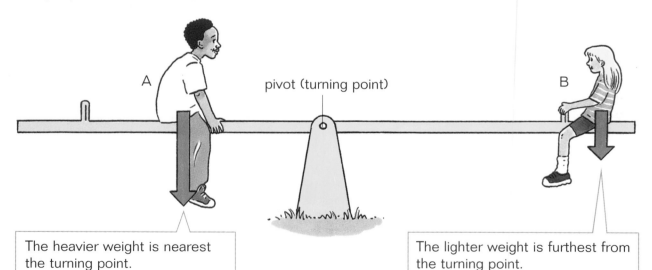

A

pivot (turning point)

B

The heavier weight is nearest the turning point.

It has a turning effect to the *left*.

The lighter weight is furthest from the turning point.

It has a turning effect to the *right*.

The turning effect to the left is the *same* as the turning effect to the right. So the plank balances.

► Centre of gravity

Every part of your body weighs something. Together, all these tiny forces act like a single force, your **weight**. This is at a point called your **centre of gravity**.

To balance like this, you have to keep your centre of gravity over the beam. Otherwise your weight will have a turning effect and pull you over.

total weight of different parts = weight of whole body

centre of gravity

balanced   not balanced

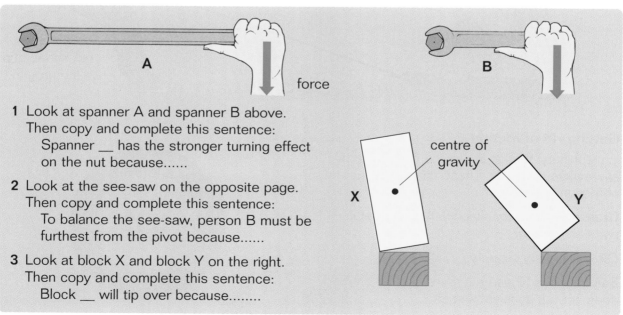

A   force   B

1 Look at spanner A and spanner B above.
Then copy and complete this sentence:
    Spanner __ has the stronger turning effect
    on the nut because......

2 Look at the see-saw on the opposite page.
Then copy and complete this sentence:
    To balance the see-saw, person B must be
    furthest from the pivot because......

3 Look at block X and block Y on the right.
Then copy and complete this sentence:
    Block __ will tip over because........

centre of gravity

X   Y

4.8 Moving and stopping

▶ Speed

The cyclist in the photograph has a **speed** of.....

15 metres per second

This means that the cyclist will move 15 metres along the track in one second.

Here are some speeds in miles per hour ('mph'), changed into metres per second:

30 mph   **70** mph

13 metres per second   31 metres per second

▶ Friction

This is the force that tries to stop things sliding past each other.
It can be a problem........   ......but it can be useful.

Friction makes it difficult
to drag a sledge over
the ground.

Friction gives
your hands grip
on the rope.

Friction gives
your shoes grip
on the ground.

▶ Getting rid of friction

In machinery, friction slows the moving parts and makes them hot. These things help get rid of friction:

Grease This is very slippery. It helps metal parts slide easily.

Oil is also very slippery.

Ball bearings These roll round so that a wheel does not rub against its shaft.

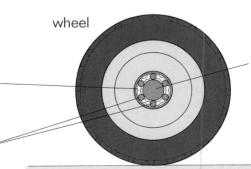

wheel

shaft

Smooth shape

Air resistance is a type of friction. It slows cars down and wastes fuel.

For less air resistance, a car needs a smooth shape so that it slips through the air more easily.

▶ Friction on a bicycle

Friction is a problem:

Air resistance This slows you down. With the wind against you, it slows you even more.

Bearings The wheels spin round on these. Any friction here slows you down.

Friction is useful:

Saddle Friction stops you sliding about.

Handlebar grips Without friction, your hands would slip.

Brakes When rubber blocks press against the wheels, friction slows the wheels down.

Pedals Friction stops your feet slipping.

Tyres Friction lets the tyres grip the road. Without friction, it would be like riding on ice.

---

1 Copy these sentences. Put a word or number in each blank:
   A car has a ___ of 20 metres per second.
   In 1 second, the car will move ___ metres.
   In 2 seconds, the car will move ___ metres.

2 Copy the table on the right. Fill in each blank to show whether the friction is *useful* or a *problem*. The first one has been done for you.

3 Look at the cyclist and bicycle in the photograph on the opposite page. Make a list of all the features which help get rid of friction (air resistance is a type of friction).

Example of friction	Friction: *useful* or a *problem*
Walking on ground	useful
Gripping handlebars	
Machinery going round	
Climbing a rope	
Skating on ice	
Putting on brakes	

4.9 Energy

You spend *energy* when you climb the stairs, lift a bag, or hit a ball. Energy is spent whenever a force makes something move.

Some things store energy.

This energy can be used to make other things move.

▶ Forms of energy

Kinetic energy This is the energy of moving things ('kinetic' means 'moving').

Potential energy This is stored energy. You give something potential energy if you lift it up or stretch it.

Chemical energy Foods, fuels, and batteries store energy in this form. Chemical reactions release the energy.

Heat energy (thermal energy) This comes from hot things when they cool down.

Light energy and **sound energy**

Electrical energy This is the energy carried by an electric current.

Nuclear energy This is energy stored in the nucleus of an atom.

▶ Measuring energy

Energy is measured in *joules* (*J*).

50 joules

Energy of a football when you kick it.

300 000 joules

Energy stored in a chocolate biscuit.

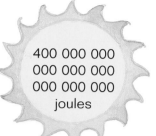

400 000 000
000 000 000
000 000 000
joules

Energy leaving the Sun every second.

▶ Energy chains

When you spend money, it doesn't vanish. Someone else spends it, then someone else..... and so on.

When you spend energy, it doesn't vanish. It changes into a different form, then a different form.......and so on, in an *energy chain*:

Law of conservation of energy

This law says:

Energy can change into different forms, but you cannot make energy and you cannot destroy it.

| chemical energy | → | kinetic energy | → | potential energy | → | kinetic energy | → | heat energy |

The body gets this energy from food.

When things bang or rub together, they heat up.

1 *kilograms   joules   forms*

Copy and complete these sentences, choosing words from those above.
   Energy is measured in ____.
   Energy can change into different ____, but it never vanishes.

2 Copy the table on the right. In each blank space, write in an example of something with that form of energy. The first one has been done for you.

Form of energy	Example
light	torch beam
kinetic	
chemical	
potential	

93

4.10 Storing and changing energy

▶ **Heat and temperature**

A high temperature isn't the same as lots of heat energy:

The sparks from this sparkler are at 1600 °C. But they hold so little heat energy, that they don't burn you when they touch your skin.

This molten (melted) iron is also at 1600 °C. It holds lots of heat energy, and is far too dangerous to touch.

▶ **Energy storers**

Some things are useful because they store energy:

In this toy, a spring stores energy when you wind it up. When it unwinds, it releases the energy and moves the toy.

This battery stores energy when you connect it to a charger. It delivers the energy as an electric current.

A hot water bottle stores enough energy to keep your feet warm for about an hour.

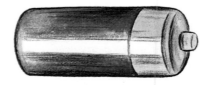

This battery isn't rechargeable. It is made from chemicals which already store energy.

▶ Storing the Sun's energy

Plants take in energy from sunlight (see Spread 2.2).

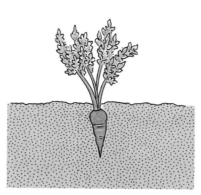

The energy is stored in roots and leaves as they grow.

Animals (like us) can get this energy by eating plants.

▶ Energy changers

Some things are useful because they change energy into a different form:

An electric kettle changes......electrical energy...  ...into heat energy.

A loudspeaker changes..........electrical energy...  ...into sound energy.

A gas ring changes................chemical energy...  ...into heat energy.

1 Copy these sentences. Write TRUE or FALSE after each one:
   A kettleful of boiling water has the same temperature as a cupful of boiling water, but it holds more heat energy.
   If something has a high temperature, it must have lots of heat energy.

2 *hairdrier   plant   candle   hot water bottle*

   Copy and complete these sentences, choosing words from those above.
      A ____ stores heat energy.
      A ____ stores energy from the Sun.
      A ____ changes electrical energy into heat energy.
      A ____ changes chemical energy into heat energy.

4.11 Energy for electricity

Our homes and factories need energy. Much of it is supplied by electricity. The electricity comes from *power stations*.

In a power station, the electric power is produced by a *generator*:

shaft

generator

cables

When this is turned.. ..power comes out here.

Turbine

▶ **Inside a power station**

Most large power stations work like this:

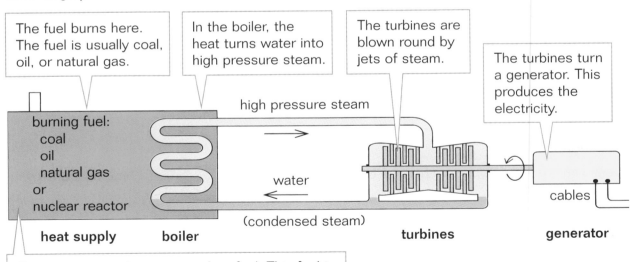

The fuel burns here. The fuel is usually coal, oil, or natural gas.

In the boiler, the heat turns water into high pressure steam.

The turbines are blown round by jets of steam.

The turbines turn a generator. This produces the electricity.

high pressure steam

burning fuel:
  coal
  oil
  natural gas
  or
  nuclear reactor

water
(condensed steam)

cables

heat supply   boiler   turbines   generator

Some power stations use nuclear fuel. This fuel is made from uranium. It doesn't burn. It gives off heat when its atoms are split in a *nuclear reactor*.

Pollution When a power station burns fuel, its chimney gives out invisible waste gases.

Carbon dioxide adds to global warming (the greenhouse effect).

Sulphur dioxide mainly comes from coal-burning power stations. It causes acid rain.

96

▶ Turning the generators

In the power station on the opposite page, the generator was turned by steam.

Here are some other ways of turning generators. None of them make polluting gases:

Hydroelectric power River and rainwater fill up a lake behind a dam. Water rushes down from the lake and turns the generators.

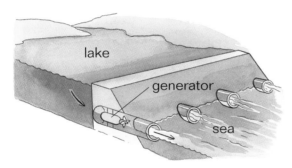

Tidal power The dam is across a river where it meets the sea. The lake fills when the tide comes in. It empties when the tide goes out. The flow of water turns the generators.

Wind power Huge windmills are blown round by the wind. There is a generator in each windmill.

1 Copy these sentences in the correct order so that they describe what happens inside a fuel-burning power station:
  The turbines turn a generator.
  The heat is used to make steam in a boiler.
  The burning fuel gives off heat.
  The generator produces electricity.
  Jets of steam blow the turbines round.

2 Five types of power station are listed on the right.
  Copy and complete these sentences. (You have to write in the types of power station which go with each one. You can choose the same type more than once.)
  The power stations that produce waste gases are....
  The power stations that do not produce waste gases are....
  The power stations that use the force of flowing water are....

> Power stations
>
> fuel—burning
>
> nuclear
>
> tidal
>
> wind
>
> hydroelectric

4.12 Energy supplies

▶ **Energy from the Sun**

Plants get their energy from the Sun.

Like other animals, we get our energy by eating plants - or by eating animals which have fed on plants. So all the energy for our bodies comes from the Sun.

energy

▶ **Fossil fuels**

Our main fuels are oil, natural gas, and coal. These are called *fossil fuels*. They formed from the remains of plants and tiny sea creatures that lived millions of years ago. So they store energy which once came from the Sun.

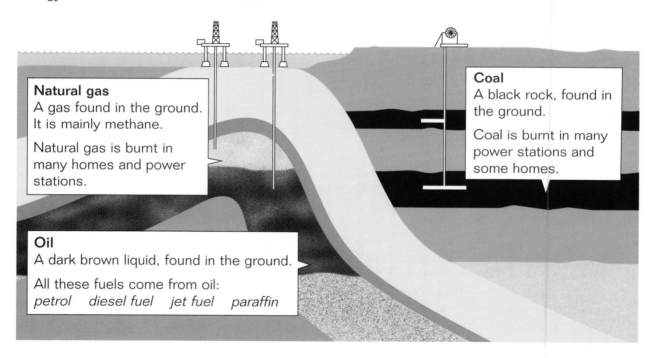

Natural gas
A gas found in the ground. It is mainly methane.

Natural gas is burnt in many homes and power stations.

Coal
A black rock, found in the ground.

Coal is burnt in many power stations and some homes.

Oil
A dark brown liquid, found in the ground.

All these fuels come from oil:
petrol   diesel fuel   jet fuel   paraffin

Our supplies of fossil fuels will not last for ever. The chart shows how many years they will last if we go on using them at the present rate.

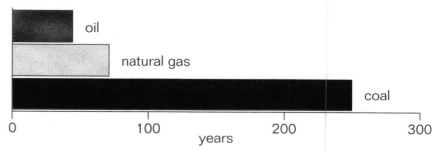

oil

natural gas

coal

| 0 | 100 | 200 | 300 |

years

▶ Biofuels

These are fuels made from plants, or from plant and animal waste.
Here are some examples:

Wood is the main fuel for many people in the world.

Alcohol can be made from sugar cane. In some countries, cars use it instead of petrol.

Methane gas comes from the rotting waste in rubbish tips and sewage works.

▶ Renewable or non-renewable?

Some energy supplies are *renewable*. They never run out because they can always be replaced.

For example
You can grow more trees to replace those cut down.

Renewable energy supplies	Non-renewable energy supplies
Examples hydroelectric energy tidal energy wind energy biofuels	*Examples* fossil fuels: coal oil natural gas nuclear fuel

Some energy supplies are *non-renewable*. Once they have run out, they cannot be replaced.

For example
Oil can't be replaced. It takes too long to form in the ground.

1 Copy these sentences in the correct order so that they describe how the energy in our bodies came from the Sun.
   Food energy is stored and used in our bodies.
   Humans eat plants.
   Plants take in energy from sunlight.
   The Sun radiates energy.
   Plants store energy in their roots and leaves.

2 Copy the table on the right.
   Write *yes* or *no* in each blank space to show whether each fuel is a fossil fuel or not, and whether it is renewable or not. One example has been done for you.

Fuel	Fossil fuel?	Renewable?
wood	*no*	
coal		
alcohol		
oil		
natural gas		

4.13 How the world gets its energy

Solar panels
These use the Sun's rays to heat water for the house.

Solar cells
These use the energy in sunlight to produce electricity.

The Sun
Deep inside the Sun, atoms change their nuclear energy into heat. The Sun radiates more energy than a million billion billion electric fires!

Energy in food
Our bodies get energy from food. The food may be from plants, or from animals which have fed on plants.

Energy in plants
Plants take in energy from sunlight. The energy is stored in their leaves and roots as they grow.

Biofuels from plants
Biofuels are fuels from plants and other 'living' materials. Wood is a biofuel. Alcohol is a biofuel made from sugar cane.

Fossil fuels
The main fossil fuels are oil, natural gas, and coal. They formed from the remains of plants and animals that lived millions of years ago. Power stations, factories, and vehicles burn fossil fuels.

Biofuels from waste
Methane gas comes from rotting waste and sewage. It can be burnt as a fuel. Waste paper and other rubbish can also be burnt as a fuel.

Batteries
Batteries store energy. Some are given energy by charging them with electricity. Others are made from chemicals that already store energy.

Fuels from oil
Petrol, diesel fuel, jet fuel, paraffin, central heating oil, bottled gas.

The Moon
The Moon's gravity pulls on the oceans and makes them bulge. As the Earth turns, each place has a high and low tide as it moves in and out of a bulge.

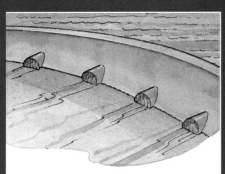

Tidal energy
As the tide comes in and goes out, the flow of water turns generators.

The atom

Some atoms have lots of nuclear energy stored in them. Changes in these atoms can release this energy.

Nuclear energy
In a nuclear reactor, uranium atoms release energy as heat. The heat is used to make steam for driving generators.

Geothermal energy
Deep underground, the rocks are very hot. The heat comes from radioactive atoms. It can be used to make steam for heating buildings or driving generators.

The weather
The Sun's heat makes winds blow across the Earth. It lifts water vapour from the oceans. Later, the water falls as rain.

Wave energy
Waves are caused by winds and tides. The up-and-down movement of the water can be used to drive generators.

Hydroelectric energy
Water rushes down from a lake and turns generators. Rainwater keeps the lake topped up.

Wind energy
For centuries, sailing ships have used the power of the wind. Today, huge windmills can turn generators.

Making sounds

▶ **Sound waves**

When a loudspeaker cone vibrates, it stretches and squashes the air in front.

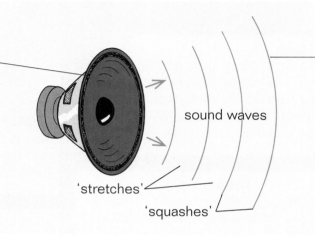

sound waves

'stretches'

'squashes'

The 'stretches' and 'squashes' spread through the air like ripples on a pond. They are *sound waves*. In your ears, you hear them as sound.

▶ **Features of sound**

Sound needs something to move through

Sound waves can travel through gases, liquids, and solids. But they cannot travel through a vacuum (empty space).

The air has been taken out of this jar, so you cannot hear the alarm clock.

Sound is made by vibrations

Here are some things that give out sound waves when they vibrate:

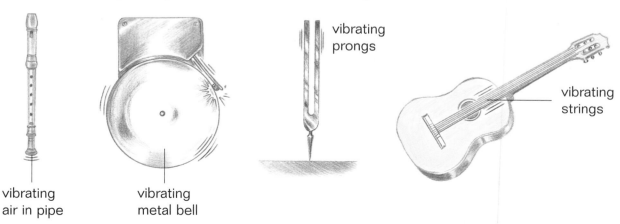

vibrating air in pipe

vibrating metal bell

vibrating prongs

vibrating strings

The speed of sound

In air, the speed of sound is about 330 metres per second. This means that sound travels the length of three football pitches in a second:

The speed of light is 300 000 *kilo*metres per second. So light is much faster than sound. That is why you see a flash of lightning before you hear it.

Sound on screen

oscilloscope

If you whistle into a microphone connected to an **oscilloscope**, you see a wavy line on the screen.

sound waves

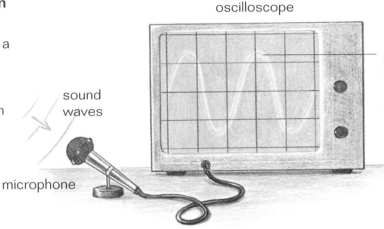

The wavy line is a graph. It shows you how the air next to the microphone vibrates backwards and forwards as time goes on.

microphone

1 Here are some words connected with sound:
   oscilloscope   vacuum   air   vibrations
   Write down the word that matches each of these clues.
   a Sound can travel through this.
   b Sound cannot travel through this.
   c This instrument shows sound waves as a wavy line on a screen.
   d Sound is made by these.

2 Copy these sentences and fill in the blanks. (The information you need is somewhere on this page.)
   The speed of sound in air is.........
   The speed of light is.........
   You see a lightning flash before you hear it because.........

Hearing sounds

▶ **The ear**

This is what the ear is like inside:

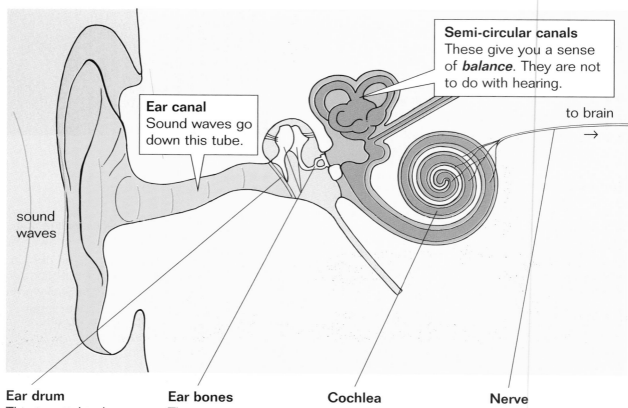

Semi-circular canals
These give you a sense of *balance*. They are not to do with hearing.

Ear canal
Sound waves go down this tube.

to brain
→

sound waves

Ear drum
This is a tight sheet of skin. Sound waves make it vibrate.

Ear bones
These pass on vibrations from the ear drum.

Cochlea
This picks up the vibrations and sends signals along a nerve.

Nerve
This carries signals to the brain so that you hear the sound.

▶ **Low or high**

When you listen to a musical instrument, the note may be

low...

...or high.

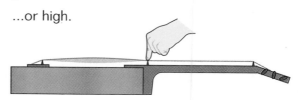

This guitar string is vibrating 200 times every second. So it is sending out 200 sound waves every second. Scientists say that the *frequency* is 200 *hertz* (*Hz*).

This guitar string is vibrating faster: 400 times every second. Its frequency is 400 hertz. To the ear, the note sounds higher than before. The note has a higher *pitch*.

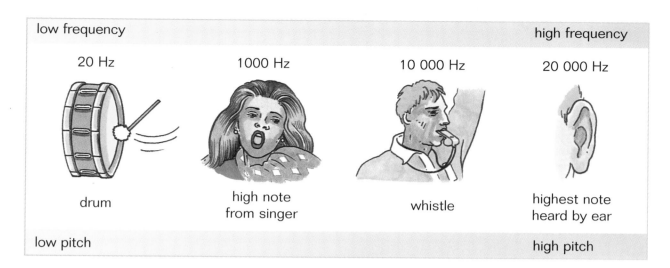

low frequency			high frequency
20 Hz	1000 Hz	10 000 Hz	20 000 Hz
drum	high note from singer	whistle	highest note heard by ear
low pitch			high pitch

▶ Quiet or loud

When you listen to a musical instrument, the note may be

quiet...   ...or loud.

This guitar string is making small vibrations. It is giving out a quiet sound.

This guitar string is making bigger vibrations. It is giving out a louder sound.

▶ Hearing damage

Very loud sounds can damage the cochlea and nerve so that the signals reaching the brain are very weak.

You should never play a personal stereo at high volume. Hours and hours of very loud music will gradually make you go deaf. But the change may be so slow that you do not notice it.

1 Copy these sentences in the correct order so that they describe how the ear works:
    The cochlea sends signals along a nerve to the brain.
    Sound waves go down the ear canal.
    The ear bones pass on the vibrations.
    Sound waves make the ear drum vibrate.
    The vibrations are picked up by the cochlea.

2 *higher   lower   louder   quieter*
    Copy these sentences. Fill in the blanks, choosing words from those above:
    If a guitar string vibrates faster, the note becomes ____.
    If the vibrations are bigger, the sound becomes ____.

105

4.16 Rays and mirrors

Light is a form of energy. In space and in air, it travels at a speed of........

300 000 kilometres *per second* ⟶

Light is the fastest thing there is. It takes less than a millionth of a second for light to cross a room!

▶ Rays and shadows

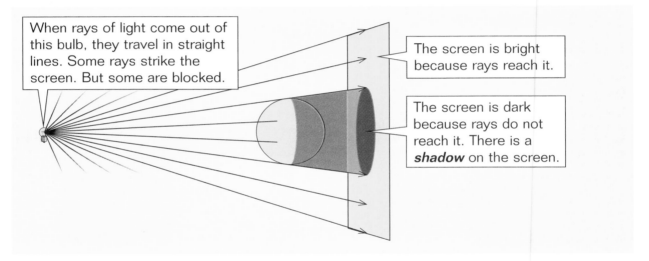

When rays of light come out of this bulb, they travel in straight lines. Some rays strike the screen. But some are blocked.

The screen is bright because rays reach it.

The screen is dark because rays do not reach it. There is a **shadow** on the screen.

▶ Reflecting light

You see things if they send light rays into your eyes.

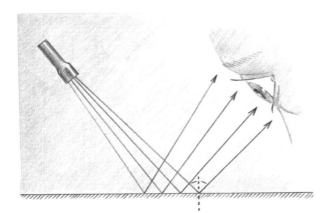

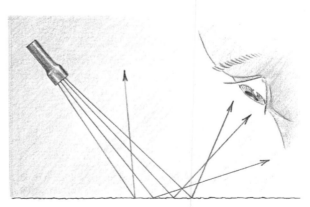

A smooth, shiny surface **reflects** light like this. Each ray strikes at an angle and bounces off at the same angle.

A rough surface reflects light all over the place. You see the surface because some of the light goes into your eyes.

▶ Image in a mirror

Light rays from this bulb are reflected by the mirror.

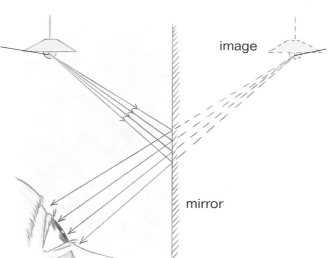

image

mirror

This person is looking towards the mirror.

The person thinks that the rays come from a place behind the mirror. So that is where she sees an *image*.

The bulb and its image are in matching positions. The image is the same distance behind the mirror as the bulb is in front.

When you look at something in a mirror, the image has its left and right sides the wrong way round.

Can you work out what the 'mirror writing' on the right says?

LIGHT TRAVELS FASTER THAN SOUND

1 Copy the diagram on the right. Draw in lines and shading to show where you would see a shadow of the ball.

2 Copy the diagram below. Draw in the rest of the ray to show how it will reflect from the mirror.
   On your diagram, show where the person will see an image of the pencil.

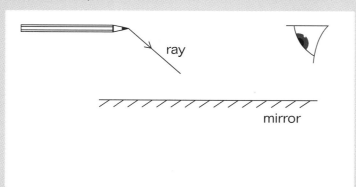

ray

mirror

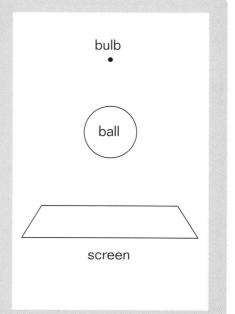

bulb

ball

screen

3 Copy and complete this sentence:
   When light shines on a piece of paper, you can see the paper because.....

4.17 Bending light

A *transparent* material lets light through, so you can see through it.

Here are some transparent materials:

 glass

 water

 clear plastic

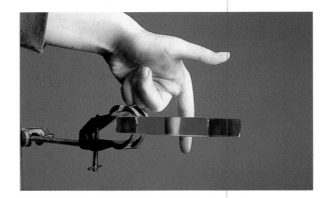

Transparent materials can bend light rays, as well as let them through.

▶ Refraction

The glass block in the photograph is bending light. The bending is called *refraction*.

This ray of light is going into a glass block. ———

When the light enters the block it bends *towards* this line. ———

When the light leaves the block, it bends *away* from this line. ———

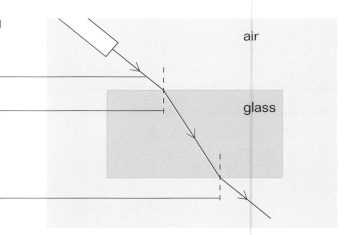

air

glass

▶ Deeper than it looks

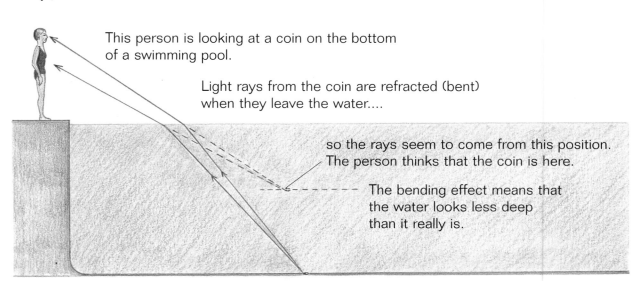

This person is looking at a coin on the bottom of a swimming pool.

Light rays from the coin are refracted (bent) when they leave the water....

so the rays seem to come from this position. The person thinks that the coin is here.

The bending effect means that the water looks less deep than it really is.

► Why light bends

Here is one explanation:

This roller-skater is moving towards grass. The grass will slow her down.

This skate hits the grass first. So it the first to slow down.

As one skate was slowed before the other, the skater moves in a different direction.

A light beam isn't solid like a skater, but slowing still affects it. When a light beam goes into glass, it slows down and moves in a different direction.

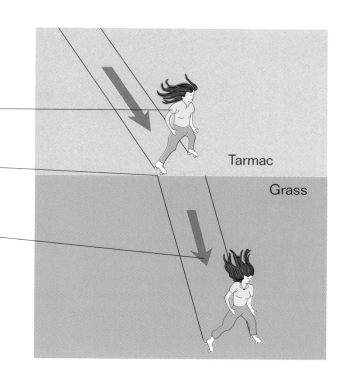

Tarmac

Grass

► Refraction in air

Light bends when it goes from hot air into cold air - or from cold into hot. That is why you get a wobbly view when hot air is moving about in front of you.

1 *reflection   refraction   transparent*
   Copy these sentences. Fill in the blanks, choosing words from those above.
   a If a material is ____, you can see through it.
   b Light bends when it goes into a glass block. The bending is called ____.

2 Copy the diagram on the right.
   Draw in the rest of the ray to show how it goes through the glass block.

3 Copy and complete this sentence:
   When light goes from air into glass, its speed.....

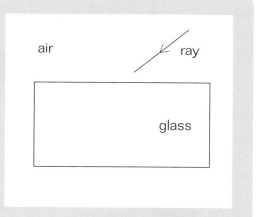

air   ray

glass

Lenses at work

Lenses bend light and form images. There are two main types:

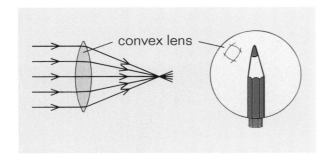 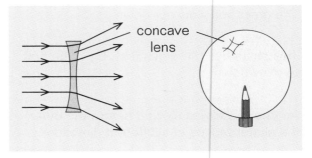

Convex lens This bends light inwards. It makes *very close* things look bigger. A convex lens can be used as a **magnifying glass**.

Concave lens This bends light outwards. It makes things look smaller.

▶ **Cameras**

With *distant* things, a convex lens brings rays to a **focus**. The rays form a tiny, upside-down image which you can pick up on a screen. This idea is used in a **camera**:

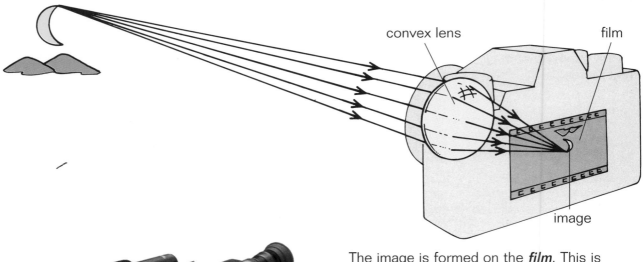

The image is formed on the **film**. This is coated with chemicals which react to light. To let in the right amount of light, you press a button so that a **shutter** opens and shuts very quickly.

◀ A **camcorder** (video camera) also has a convex lens in it. But instead of a film, it has an electronic plate at the back to pick up the image.

The eye

Like a camera, an eye uses a convex lens to form a tiny image at the back.

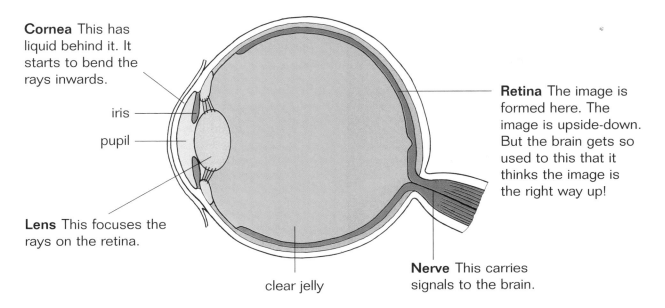

Cornea This has liquid behind it. It starts to bend the rays inwards.

iris

pupil

Lens This focuses the rays on the retina.

clear jelly

Retina The image is formed here. The image is upside-down. But the brain gets so used to this that it thinks the image is the right way up!

Nerve This carries signals to the brain.

Pupil This is the gap where the light goes in. It looks black because the eye is dark inside.

Iris This changes size so that the pupil lets in more light or less light.

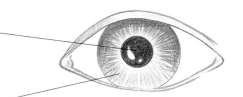

Eye in bright light

Eye when it is darker

---

1 Copy the diagrams on the right. Complete the rays to show where they go when they come out of each lens.

2 *convex   concave*

   Copy these sentences. Fill in each blank with one of the words above. (You can use the same word more than once.)
   In the diagram, lens A is a ____ lens.
   In the diagram, lens B is a ____ lens.
   A camera has a ____ lens in it.
   A ____ lens can be used as a magnifying glass.
   An eye has a ____ lens in it.

3 Copy and complete these sentences:
   In a camera, the image is formed on.....
   In the eye, the image is formed on.....

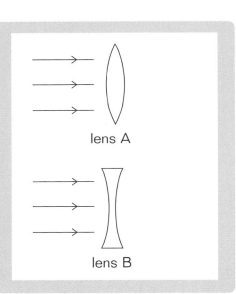

lens A

lens B

▶ **A spectrum**

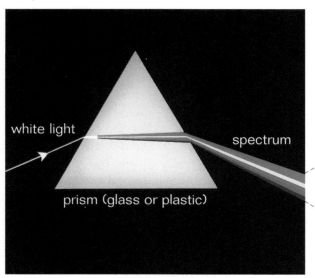

White light is not a single colour, but a mixture of colours. A **prism** splits them up.

The light is refracted (bent) when it goes into the prism, and when it comes out.

The refracted light spreads to form a range of colours called a **spectrum**:

red
orange
yellow
green
blue
violet

The spreading effect is called **dispersion**.

▶ **Making white**

The human eye doesn't need all the colours in the spectrum to see white. Red, green, and blue are enough. If beams of red, green, and blue light overlap on a white screen, they make white.

Red, green, and blue are called the **primary colours**.

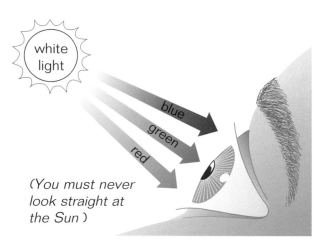

(You must never look straight at the Sun)

The Sun glows and gives out white light. So does a bulb. To the eye, the white light is the same as a mixture of red, green, and blue.

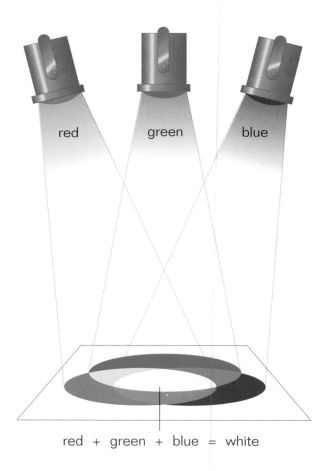

red + green + blue = white

▶ Why things look coloured

Most things don't glow. We see them because they reflect light from the Sun or a lamp. However, only some colours may be reflected. The rest are *absorbed* (taken away).

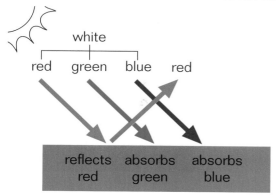

This patch reflects only red light. So it looks red. It absorbs green and blue.

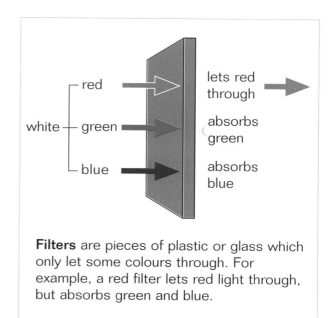

Filters are pieces of plastic or glass which only let some colours through. For example, a red filter lets red light through, but absorbs green and blue.

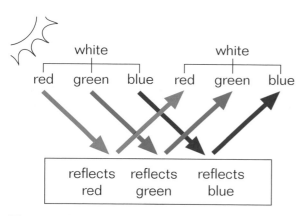

This patch reflects red, green, and blue, so it looks white. It absorbs no colours.

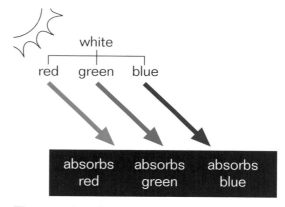

This patch reflects no light, so it looks black. It absorbs red, green, and blue.

---

1 Copy and complete these sentences:
   A triangular glass block is called......
   It can split white light into a range of colours called......

2 On the right, there is a list of colours. Write down the colour or colours which go with each of these statements. (You can choose the same colours more than once.)
   a When white light goes through a prism, this colour is refracted (bent) the least.
   b If these colours overlap on a white screen, they make white.
   c A red filter lets this colour through.
   d If something absorbs all the light striking it, it looks this colour.
   e A red book absorbs these colours.

white

black

red

green

blue

4.20 Sun and Earth

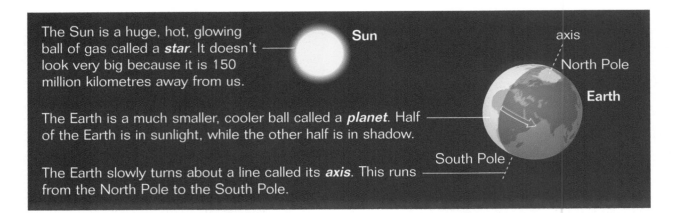

The Sun is a huge, hot, glowing ball of gas called a *star*. It doesn't look very big because it is 150 million kilometres away from us.

The Earth is a much smaller, cooler ball called a *planet*. Half of the Earth is in sunlight, while the other half is in shadow.

The Earth slowly turns about a line called its *axis*. This runs from the North Pole to the South Pole.

▶ **Day and night**

The Earth takes **one day** (24 hours) to turn once on its axis. As it turns, places move from the sunlit half into the shadow half. So they move from daytime into night.

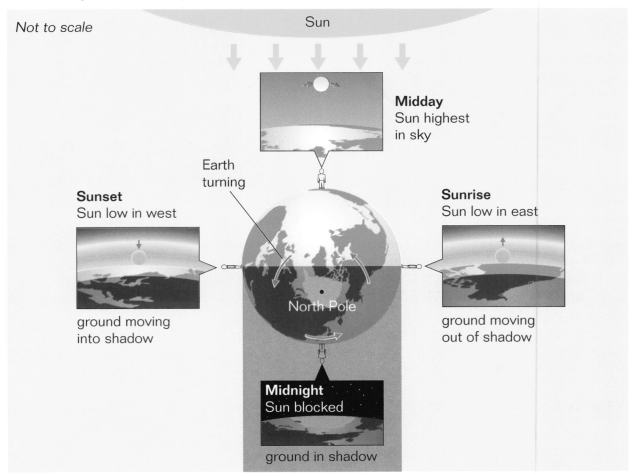

Not to scale

Sun

Midday
Sun highest in sky

Earth turning

Sunset
Sun low in west

ground moving into shadow

North Pole

Sunrise
Sun low in east

ground moving out of shadow

Midnight
Sun blocked

ground in shadow

The year and seasons

The Earth moves around the Sun in a big circle called an **orbit**.
The Earth takes **one year** (about 365 days) to orbit the Sun.

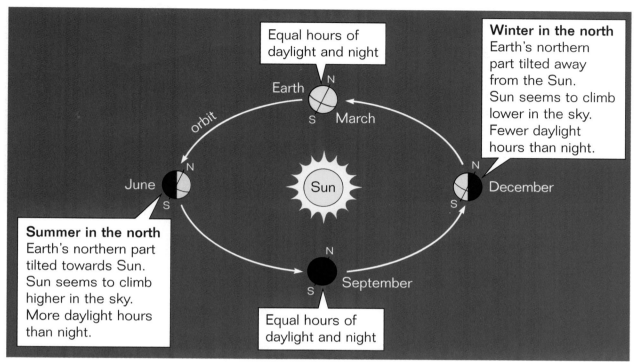

Equal hours of daylight and night

Earth

March

Winter in the north
Earth's northern part tilted away from the Sun.
Sun seems to climb lower in the sky.
Fewer daylight hours than night.

orbit

June

Sun

December

Summer in the north
Earth's northern part tilted towards Sun.
Sun seems to climb higher in the sky.
More daylight hours than night.

September

Equal hours of daylight and night

The Earth's axis leans by about 23°. This means that the Earth's northern part is sometimes tilted towards the Sun and sometimes away from it.

In June, the Earth's northern part is tilted towards the Sun. That is when the Sun seems to climb highest in the sky and there are most hours of daylight. So it is summer.

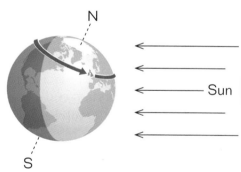

N

Sun

S

1 *24 hours   7 days   365 days*

Copy these sentences. Fill in the blanks, choosing times from those above. (You can use the same time more than once.)

There are _____ in one day.
There are about _____ in one year.
The Earth takes about _____ to orbit the Sun.
The Earth takes _____ to turn once on its axis.

2 a Copy the diagram on the right. Shade in the part of the Earth that is in shadow.
  b Write down whether it is *daytime* or *night* in Britain.
  c Write down whether it is *summer* or *winter* in Britain.

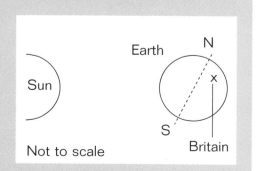

Sun

Earth

N

x

S

Britain

Not to scale

4.21 Orbiting the Earth

▶ Satellites in orbit

There are hundreds of satellites in orbit around the Earth.
Here are some of the jobs they do:

Communications satellites These pass on TV and telephone signals.

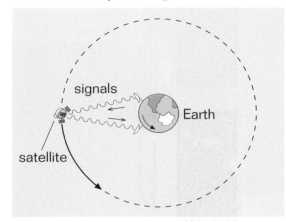

This satellite is in a **geostationary** orbit. It goes round at the same rate as the Earth turns. So it always seems to stay in the same place in the sky.

Weather satellites These send pictures down to Earth so that forecasters can see what the weather is doing.

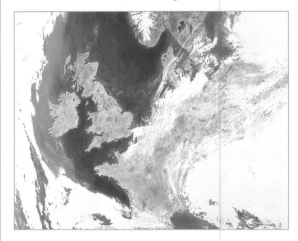

This satellite picture shows the weather over Europe.

Research satellites Some of these carry telescopes for looking at stars and planets. Above the atmosphere, they get a much clearer view.

This is the Hubble Space Telescope. It radios its pictures back to Earth.

Navigation satellites These send out signals so that a ship or aircraft can work out its position.

This receiver picks up signals from satellites, calculates its position, and shows the result.

▶ The Moon

The Moon orbits the Earth. It is smaller than the Earth, and has a rocky surface with lots of craters.

The Moon is *not* hot and glowing like the Sun.

We can only see the Moon because its surface reflects sunlight. We don't see the part that is in shadow.

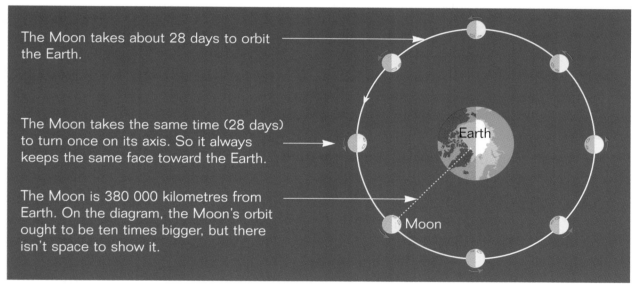

The Moon takes about 28 days to orbit the Earth.

The Moon takes the same time (28 days) to turn once on its axis. So it always keeps the same face toward the Earth.

The Moon is 380 000 kilometres from Earth. On the diagram, the Moon's orbit ought to be ten times bigger, but there isn't space to show it.

Earth

Moon

1 7   28   365   380 000

Copy these sentences. Fill in the blanks, choosing numbers from those above. (You can use the same number more than once.)
   The Moon is _____ kilometres from Earth.
   The Moon takes about _____ days to orbit the Earth.
   The Moon takes about _____ days to turn once on its axis.

2 *Earth   Moon   Sun*

Copy these sentences. Fill in the blanks, choosing words from those above. (You can use the same word more than once.)
   a We see the _____ because it is hot and glowing.
   b We see the _____ because it reflects light which came from the _____.

3 Write down *three* jobs that satellites are used for.

The Solar System

The Sun has lots of **planets** orbiting it. The Sun and its planets are called the **Solar System**.

This diagram shows how the sizes of the Sun and planets compare (the distances are not correct):

The inner planets These are mainly made of rock.

The asteroids These are thousands of tiny planets. The largest is only 1000 km across.

The outer planets Apart from Pluto, these are large and mainly made of gas. Saturn's rings are billions of bits of ice

Planet ▶	Mercury	Venus	Earth	Mars	Jupiter	Saturn	Uranus	Neptune	Pluto
Distance from the Sun in million km	58	108	150	228	778	1430	2870	4500	5900
Time for one orbit (y=year, d=day)	88 d	225 d	1 y	1.9 y	12 y	29 y	84 y	165 y	247 y
Diameter in km	4900	12100	12800	6800	143000	120000	51000	49000	3900
Average surface temperature	350°C	480°C	22°C	−23°C	−150°C	−180°C	−210°C	−220°C	−230°C
Number of moons	0	0	1	2	16	23	15	8	1

From Earth, a planet looks like a tiny dot in the night sky. Without a telescope, it is difficult to tell whether you are looking at a star or a planet.

We can see planets because they reflect the Sun's light. They are not hot enough to give off their own light.

▶ Orbits

This diagram shows how the sizes of the planets' orbits compare:

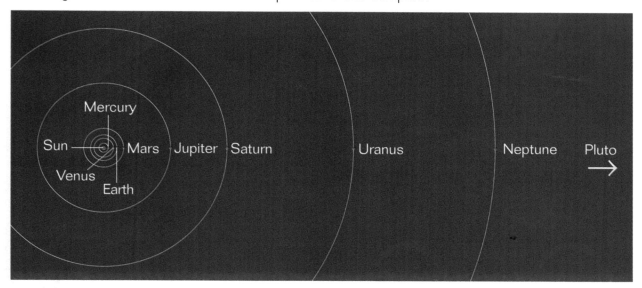

▶ Gravity in action

Gravity is a force.

The Earth's gravity holds us on the ground.

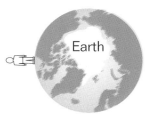

The Earth's gravity holds the Moon in its orbit around the Earth.

The Sun's gravity holds the Earth and other planets in their orbits around the Sun.

There is a pull of gravity between *all* masses. But to produce a strong pull, one mass has to be very large - like the Earth.

---

1 Copy and complete each of these sentences by writing in the name of a planet:

    The biggest planet is.....

    The planet nearest the Sun is.....

    The hottest planet is.....

    The planet furthest from the Sun is.....

    The coldest planet is.....

    The planet with most moons is.....

    The planet which takes the least time to orbit the Sun is.....

    The planet which takes the most time to orbit the Sun is.....

2 Write down the name of the force which holds the planets in their orbits around the Sun.

Summary

The spread number tells you where to find more information.

- Living things need food and air. They reproduce, react, make waste, grow, and move.
- Living things are made from cells.

2.1

- Plants make food in their leaves. To do this, they need the energy in sunlight.
- Plants make oxygen. Animals use it up.

2.2

- To make a seed, a male cell from a pollen grain must join with a female cell in a flower's ovary.
- Pollen grains are carried to other flowers by insects or the wind.

2.3

- In a plant, if a female cell is fertilized by a male cell, it becomes a seed.
- To start growing into a new plant, a seed needs water, warmth, and air.

2.4

- Blood carries food, water, and oxygen to cells in all the organs of your body.
- Your body has lots of organs. Each one has a special job to do.

2.5

- Your skeleton gives you support. It protects organs and lets you move.
- Your joints are moved by muscles.
- Muscles are controlled using nerves.

2.6

- In your gut, food is digested so that useful things can get into your blood.
- During digestion, food is turned into a liquid. This job is done by enzymes.

2.7

- Blood is a mixture of things.
- One side of the heart pumps blood to the lungs. The other side pumps it round the rest of the body.

2.8

- In the lungs, oxygen gets into your blood and carbon dioxide comes out.
- As you breathe in and out, old air is replaced by new.

2.9

- About every 28 days, a woman releases a tiny egg from one of her ovaries.
- The egg may be fertilized by a sperm from a man. If the egg is unfertilized, the woman has her period.

2.10

- A baby is born about 9 months after the egg is fertilized.
- In the womb, a baby gets food and oxygen from its mother's blood. It does this through the placenta.

2.11

- Food is a mixture of carbohydrates, fats, proteins, fibre, minerals, vitamins, and water. For a balanced diet, you need the right amounts of all of these.

2.12

- Bacteria and viruses are very tiny. The harmful ones are called germs.
- Germs can be spread by droplets in the air, contact with other people, animals, and dirty food and water.

2.13

- To help your health, you need to eat sensibly and take plenty of exercise.
- Smoking, alcohol, drugs, and solvents can all damage your health.

2.14

- Scientists put living things into groups by looking for features which are similar.
- A key is a chart which helps you work out the name of an animal or plant.

2.15

- Animals with backbones are called vertebrates.
- The five main groups of vertebrates are fish, amphibians, reptiles, birds, and mammals.

2.16

- The place where an animal or plant lives is called its habitat.
- Humans cause pollution which harms other living things and their habitats.

2.17

- Each type of animal or plant has special features to help it survive in its habitat. Scientists say that it is adapted to its way of life.

2.18

- Leaves are eaten by snails which are eaten by blackbirds. This is an example of a food chain.
- Plants are at the start of every food chain.

2.19

Summary

The spread number tells you where to find more information.

- Mass is measured in kilograms, or in grams. 1000 grams = 1 kilogram
- Volume is measured in cubic metres, or in millilitres.
- Materials can be solid, liquid, or gas. Liquids and gases can flow. Gases fill any container they are in.

3.1

- Heat is needed to melt ice.
- Heat is needed to change liquid water into steam (water vapour). The change is called evaporation.
- On the Celsius scale, water freezes at 0 °C and boils at 100 °C.
- Most materials expand when heated.

3.2

- The features of a material and how it behaves are called its properties.
- Most metals are strong, hard, and shiny, and can be hammered into shape. They are good conductors of heat and electricity.

3.3

- Everything is made from about 90 simple substances called elements.
- The smallest bit of an element is an atom.
- Elements can join together to form new substances, called compounds.

3.4

- One substance by itself is called a pure substance.
- Most substances are mixtures.
- An alloy is a metal mixed with another metal (or nonmetal).
- A solute dissolves in a solvent to form a mixture called a solution.

3.5

- There are many ways of separating mixtures. These include filtering, dissolving, evaporating, distilling, crystallizing, and chromatography.

3.6

- Acids are corrosive: they eat into some materials (for example, some metals).
- Alkalis are also corrosive.
- Alkalis can neutralize acids: they can cancel out the acid effect.
- An acid turns blue litmus paper red.
- An alkali turns red litmus paper blue.

3.7

- If there is a chemical change, the signs of this are:
  - new substance(s) made.
  - change difficult to reverse.
  - energy given out or taken out.
- In a physical change, like melting, you still have the same substance.

3.8

- For burning, these things are needed:
  - fuel (something to burn)
  - air (because of the oxygen in it)
  - heat.
- When most fuels burn, they make carbon dioxide and water.

3.9

- Rusting is an example of corrosion.
- Water and air are both needed for iron or steel to go rusty.
- Gold does not corrode. It is unreactive.
- Most metals come from ores which are found in the ground.

3.10

- Air is a mixture of gases. It is mainly nitrogen (78%) and oxygen (21%).
- Other gases in air include carbon dioxide, argon, helium, and neon.

3.11

- Water evaporates from the sea and forms clouds. These turn into rain which flows back into the sea. This is part of the water cycle.
- When water freezes, it expands. This can damage pipes and split rocks.

3.12

- The surface of rocks can be weakened by frost, the Sun's heat, and acid in rain. This is called weathering.
- Bits of broken rock can be worn away. This is called erosion.
- Bits of rock may be moved, buried, and crushed to form new rock. This is part of the rock cycle.

3.13

- Igneous rocks are formed when molten (melted) rock cools and goes solid.
- Sedimentary rocks are formed from sediment which has been dropped.
- Metamorphic rocks are formed when igneous or sedimentary rocks are changed by heat or pressure.

3.14

Summary

The spread number tells you where to find more information.

- Metals are good electrical conductors. Most other materials are insulators.
- Like charges repel; unlike ones attract.

4.1

- For a current to flow, a circuit must have no breaks in it.
- Voltage is measured with a voltmeter.
- Current is measured with an ammeter.

4.2

- Bulbs can be connected to a battery in series or in parallel. When in parallel, both get the full battery voltage.

4.3

- A magnet has two poles (N and S). Like poles repel; unlike poles attract.
- An electromagnet only works when there is a current through its coil.

4.4

- Force is measured in newtons.
- If something is staying still, or moving at a steady speed in a straight line, the forces on it are balanced.

4.5

- If a force is spread out over a large area, the pressure is low.
- If a force is concentrated on a small area, the pressure is high.

4.6

- A force has a stronger turning effect if it is moved further away from a turning point (pivot).

4.7

- If a car moves 10 metres in 1 second, its speed is 10 metres per second.
- Friction can be useful or a nuisance.

4.8

- Energy is measured in joules.
- Energy can change into different forms, but it can't be made or destroyed.

4.9

- Heat is not the same as temperature.
- Some things store energy. Some things change it into different forms.

4.10

- In fuel-burning power stations, heat is used to make steam. The steam turns turbines which drive the generators.
- In some power stations, the generators are turned by flowing water or wind.

4.11

- Oil, natural gas, and coal are fossil fuels. Supplies are running out.
- Energy from rivers, winds, and tides is renewable. It never runs out.

4.12

- Nearly all of the world's energy comes from the Sun.

4.13

- Sounds are made when things vibrate.
- Sound needs something to travel through. It can't go through a vacuum.
- Sound is much slower than light.

4.14

- Sound causes vibrations in the ear.
- Faster vibrations make higher notes.
- Bigger vibrations make louder notes.

4.15

- Shadows form when light is blocked.
- A mirror reflects light so that the rays seem to come from behind it. That is where you see an image.

4.16

- If light rays strike glass or water at an angle, they are refracted (bent).

4.17

- Concave lenses bend light outwards.
- Convex lenses bend light inwards.
- The camera and the eye use a convex lens to form an image at the back.

4.18

- A prism can split white light into a range of colours called a spectrum.
- We see most things because they reflect daylight (or lamp light). But they may only reflect some colours.

4.19

- As the Earth turns, we move from sunlight into shadow. That is why we get day and night.
- The Earth takes 1 year to orbit the Sun.

4.20

- The Moon orbits the Earth.
- Satellites in orbit can pass on radio and TV signals, watch the weather, and carry telescopes.

4.21

- The Sun has lots of planets in orbit around it.
- We can only see planets because they reflect the Sun's light.

4.22

Answers to questions on spreads

2.1
1 plants; cells; body; nucleus
2 a) Cat eating b) Flower dropping seeds
  c) Dog barking when you move
  d) Plant growing towards the light
3 nucleus (top left), animal (bottom left), cell
  wall (top right), plant (bottom right).

2.2
1 Leaves shaded in
2 sunlight; carbon dioxide, oxygen; oxygen,
  carbon dioxide; oxygen
3 Water goes in through roots, then moves up
  water tubes
4 Minerals go in through roots with water
5 Gases pass in and out through tiny holes

2.3
1 pollen (top left), nectar (bottom left), ovules
  (top right), petal (bottom right)
2 female; male; pollination
3 a) To attract insects b) Looking for nectar
  c) Pollen sticks to bee's body, bee flies to
  another flower, pollen sticks to this flower

2.4
1 fertilization; germination
2 Sentence order is 5th, 2nd, 6th, 3rd, 1st, 4th
3 Water, warmth, air
4 Seed falls slowly and is blown by wind

2.5
1 a) stomach b) lung c) heart d) kidney
2 Brain (in head); lung (in chest)
3 Food, water, oxygen
4 From kidneys (through bladder), from lungs

2.6
1 skull; ribs; backbone
2 a) teeth b) muscles c) nerves
3 calcium; ligaments; tendons

2.7
1 blood; digestion; enzymes
2 Sentence order is 3rd, 6th, 1st, 5th, 2nd, 4th

2.8
1 white; red
2 a) artery b) vein
3 Heart is in middle, oxygen is collected in
  lungs, oxygen is delivered to body

2.9
1 From top: windpipe, lung, heart, rib,
  diaphragm
2 ribs, diaphragm, lungs, blood
3 Oxygen
4 carbon dioxide
5 You have to 'burn up' food faster, so more
  oxygen needed

2.10
1 Sentence order is 3rd, 2nd, 1st
2 a) testicles b) ovaries c) fertilization

2.11
1 a) bag of watery liquid b) umbilical cord
  c) placenta
2 Sentence order is 5th, 4th, 1st, 6th, 3rd,
  2nd 3 Baby's blood gets food and oxygen
  from mother's blood, in the placenta

2.12
1 carbohydrates, fats; proteins
2 Ticks to show the following: carbohydrate in
  bread; fat in cheese; protein in bread, milk,
  and cheese
3 Cheese, milk
4 Vegetables, bread
5 Blackcurrants, oranges
6 a) ...it is used in making bones and teeth
  b) ...it helps food pass through gut more
  easily

2.13
1 a) germs b) infection c) immune
  d) antibodies e) vaccine
2 From sneeze, from dirty food, from dirty
  hands touching food
3 So that germs on hands won't get on food

2.14

1 Sentences:
1st on left goes with 4th on right;
2nd on left goes with 5th on right;
3rd on left goes with 6th on right;
4th on left goes with 3rd on right;
5th on left goes with 1st on right;
6th on left goes with 2nd on right

2 So that they won't catch German measles during first three months of pregnancy, as this would harm baby

2.15

1 a) Four legs, one tail, two ears b) Length of legs, length of tail, colour of fur
2 B is housefly, C is earwig, D is butterfly
3 F is plantain, G is yarrow, H is rye glass

2.16

1 Ticks to show the following:
all have backbones; all have lungs;
fish, amphibians, and reptiles have scales;
birds have feathers; mammals have fur;
fish, amphibians, reptiles, and birds lay eggs; mammals have babies; birds and mammals have a steady body temperature; also H is at top of 'Mammals' column.

2.17

1 a) frog b) polar bear c) human
2 By factory waste, sewage, and fertilizers
3 a) ...it stops it getting light and water
b) ...it may eat it

2.18

1 a) Large eyes b) Large claws
c) Sharp beak d) Feathers which can trap air 2 Difficult for it to be seen by animals that might eat it
3 Sentences: 1st on left goes with 4th on right; 2nd on left goes with 3rd on right; 3rd on left goes with 5th on right;
4th on left goes with 1st on right;
5th on left goes with 2nd on right

2.19

1 cabbage → caterpillar → thrush → fox
2 ...the cabbage; ...the caterpillar, thrush, and fox 3 octopus, crab, seal, seagull

3.1

1 Ticks and crosses to show the following: solid has fixed shape, fixed volume, and can't flow; liquid has fixed shape, no fixed volume, and can flow; gas has no fixed shape, no fixed volume, and can flow
2 a) petrol b) lead, gold c) air d) water
3 a) 1000 b) 2

3.2

1 0 °C; 100 °C
2 liquid; gas; solid; liquid
3 So that there is room for expansion on a hot day

3.3

1 a) brittle b) flexible c) transparent
d) malleable
2 Examples of materials (from top): glass, PVC (plastic), glass, copper, copper, wood, PVC
3 a) strong, flexible
b) heat insulator c) electrical insulator, strong
d) transparent, strong

3.4

1 metals; atoms; metals; nonmetals; compounds
2 hydrogen, oxygen, carbon, nitrogen, sulphur
3 Table: water is made from hydrogen and oxygen; carbon dioxide is made from carbon and oxygen; sulphuric acid is made from hydrogen, oxygen, and sulphur

3.5

1 a) pure substance b) alloy
2 dissolves; soluble; solvent; solution

3.6

1 a) dissolving and filtering b) dissolving and filtering c) filtering, or distilling
d) chromatography
2 Tea-leaves, liquid tea (mainly water)
3 Dust, air

3.7

1 From top: acid, acid, alkali, acid, alkali, acid, alkali, alkali, acid, alkali
2 a) dilute b) concentrated c) hydrogen
d) ...it has cancelled out the acid effect
e) ...does not change colour

3.8
1 a) chemical b) chemical c) physical
2 From top: chemical, physical, physical, chemical, chemical, physical, chemical

3.9
1 a) carbon dioxide b) oxygen c) carbon dioxide d) methane e) oxygen f) carbon dioxide g) carbon dioxide
2 air (oxygen), heat, fuel

3.10
1 a) aluminium b) copper c) copper d) gold e) iron f) iron g) gold h) gold
2 air, water
3 coating with paint, coating with grease

3.11
1 a) nitrogen b) oxygen c) carbon dioxide d) nitrogen
2 a) Helium, ...it is lighter than other gases in air
  b) Carbon dioxide, ...things can't burn in it
  c) Nitrogen, ...it doesn't make food go off
3 Neon, used in some lamps

3.12
1 Sentence order is 1st, 3rd, 6th, 5th, 4th, 2nd 2 By running into river, then sea, then evaporating; by going into plants, then evaporating
3 ...water vapour condenses on cold ground or plants; ...frost; ...water expands when it freezes

3.13
1 a) erosion b) sediment c) humus
2 Sentence order is 4th, 5th, 3rd, 1st, 2nd

3.14
1 a) sedimentary b) igneous c) metamorphic
2 granite (igneous) used for chippings; limestone (sedimentary) used in cement; slate (metamorphic) used in snooker tables

4.1
1 positive; negative; negative; positive; negative

2 Ticks to show the following: copper, aluminium, and carbon are good conductors; water and air are poor conductors; plastic and glass are insulators

4.2
1 ammeter; current; current
2 ...a voltmeter; ...an ammeter; ...2.0

4.3
1 a) B b) Because the voltage across it is higher, so the current through it is higher
2 a) C b) D c) It will go out d) It will stay bright

4.4
1 south; north; north
2 Ticks to show the following: nickel, iron, and steel are magnetic; aluminium and copper are non-magnetic
3 a) Steel b) Iron c) Iron

4.5
1 weight; friction; tension; air resistance
2 newton
3 Force of 6 N downwards from centre of ball

4.6
1 a) low b) high c) high d) low
2 newtons per square metre
3 a) 2 b) 2 N/m^2

4.7
1 A, ...it is longer
2 ...she is lighter than person A
3 Y, ...its centre of gravity is not over the table underneath, so its weight has a turning effect which will pull it over

4.8
1 speed; 20; 40
2 From top: useful, useful, problem, useful, problem, useful
3 Streamlined helmet, streamlined frame, streamlined wheels, crouching position

4.9
1 joules; forms 2 Examples, from top: torch beam, moving car, petrol, stretched spring

4.10
1 TRUE; FALSE
2 hot water bottle; plant; hairdrier; candle

4.11
1 Sentence order is 3rd, 2nd, 5th, 1st, 4th
2 fuel-burning; nuclear, tidal, wind, and hydroelectric; tidal and hydroelectric

4.12
1 Sentence order is 4th, 3rd, 5th, 2nd, 1st
2 'yes' and 'no' to show the following: coal, oil, and natural gas are fossil fuels; wood and alcohol are renewable

4.14
1 a) air b) vacuum c) oscilloscope d) vibrations
2 ...about 330 metres per second; ...300 000 kilometres per second; ...the light travels much faster than the sound

4.15
1 Sentence order is 2nd, 4th, 3rd, 5th, 1st
2 higher; louder

4.16
1 Two straight lines should leave bulb, touch ball either side, and reach screen; shadow area on screen is between these two lines
2 Ray should reflect from mirror at same angle as it arrives, then go into eye; image of pencil is below mirror, and in a position which exactly matches that of pencil above mirror
3 ...it reflects light into your eyes

4.17
1 a) transparent b) refraction
2 Ray should bend downwards slightly as it goes into glass (as in diagram on p108); ray should bend again as it leaves glass, so that its direction is parallel to the direction it first had (see also diagram on p108)
3 ...becomes less

4.18
1 Rays should be as in diagrams at top of p110
2 convex; concave; convex; convex; convex
3 ...the film; ...the retina

4.19
1 ...a prism; ...a spectrum
2 a) red b) red, green, and blue c) red d) black e) green and blue

4.20
1 24 hours; 365 days; 365 days; 24 hours
2 a) Right half of Earth should be in shadow (edge of shadow should be vertical) b) night c) winter

4.21
1 380 000; 28; 28
2 a) Sun b) Moon, Sun
3 Communications, navigation, watching the weather

4.22
1 Jupiter; Mercury; Mercury; Pluto; Pluto; Saturn; Mercury; Pluto
2 Gravity

Index

*The main topics are in **bold**.*

The WIDE-WORLD

CONTENTS

INTRODUCTION

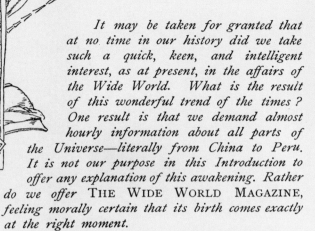

It may be taken for granted that at no time in our history did we take such a quick, keen, and intelligent interest, as at present, in the affairs of the Wide World. What is the result of this wonderful trend of the times? One result is that we demand almost hourly information about all parts of the Universe—literally from China to Peru. It is not our purpose in this Introduction to offer any explanation of this awakening. Rather do we offer THE WIDE WORLD MAGAZINE, feeling morally certain that its birth comes exactly at the right moment.

The key-note of the Magazine is struck in the motto on the cover—" Truth is Stranger than Fiction." This we hope to prove by personal narratives and actual photographs. Also on the cover you will read, " Astounding Photographs"—" Thrilling Adventures." Big words, these. Do the Contents of this first number justify such phrases? It is for our readers to judge.

There will be no fiction in the Magazine, but yet it will contain stories of weird adventure, more thrilling than any conceived by the novelist in his wildest flights. These will be the plain, straightforward narratives of well-known travellers, explorers, and others. As a rule, the photo. of each narrator will be reproduced, so that you may see for yourself what manner of man the story-teller is. And so wonderful will the pictures be found, so enthralling the letterpress, that the Magazine will be found to fascinate not merely serious men, but also women of all degrees and even the smallest children, who will learn many delightful lessons from its attractive pages. As to the pictures, these will be mostly direct reproductions from photographs ; and we think we may fairly claim for some depicted in these pages that they are the most amazing photos. ever seen. And the supply is practically inexhaustible, thanks to the far-reaching arrangements we have made in both civilized and uncivilized countries.

The enterprise is absolutely unique ; and the Conductors conclude this "foreword," in quiet assurance that THE WIDE WORLD MAGAZINE may safely be trusted to carry into every home, by means of the infallible camera and the responsible traveller, the almost incredible wonders of the Wide World.

"THE LION LEAPT OUT OF THE HUT INTO THE DARKNESS."

THE WIDE WORLD MAGAZINE

Out of the Lion's Jaws.

By ERNEST BROCKMAN.

The most appalling true narrative on record.

MY name is **Ernest Brockman**, and my present age twenty-eight. In May 1896, after having served the Chartered Company as postmaster and telegraphist in Mashonaland, I returned to England for six months' holiday. At the expiration of this period I went back to Africa, making straight for Beira, where, in December of the same year, I was introduced to Major Patrick Forbes, who represented Cecil Rhodes in Northern Rhodesia, and had charge of the telegraphs and general administration of that particular territory. The construction of the Trans - Continental telegraph wire—Rhodes's pet scheme, the "Cape to Cairo" telegraph — was being actively pushed forward, and Major Forbes suggested that I should join the working party at "the front," going direct to Chinde, at the mouth of the Zambesi.

I promptly acted on this suggestion, and some weeks later found myself one of a very large party of telegraph workers in the very heart of Central Africa. The great work was going on surely and rapidly. Yet it was practically unknown to people at home. We worked in sections or

ERNEST BROCKMAN.
From a Photo. taken a few days before the adventure.

gangs, each section being composed of 100 or 200 workers under the command of a man experienced in the work of telegraph construction. The first gang cleared the forest along the route where the wire was to be laid, the next gang dug holes for the poles, and the third section fixed the poles upright and placed the insulators in position. The section I had charge of was the last of all, and my duty was to test the wire after the ordinary work of the day was finished. I had to see that proper communication was maintained with our base at Blantyre, so that we could order up stores as required. Our object was to take the wire right up to Lake Tanganyika, whose northernmost point was about 700 miles from the extreme south of Lake Nyassa.

About the beginning of October last year I found myself fairly settling down to work in the telegraph camp, about thirty miles distant from Kota-Kota. My mate — the only other telegraphist at that place besides myself — was a stout - hearted Irishman, named Dan Morkel; and we had a gang of about fifty workers. Our camp was established in a small clearing in the great forest, about two hundred yards in circumference. This clearing was almost entirely encircled by oil palms, which stretched away on all sides for countless miles, interspersed at intervals with groups of rubber trees and prickly cactus. This open space also contained three regularly made brushwood huts. My friend Morkel occupied one of the huts, the second was used as a storage-house, whilst I was the occupant of the third. These huts were circular in shape, and about 10ft. in diameter. It is necessary here to say a word or two about the construction of the huts. Stout poles, 2ft. or 3ft. apart, were first of all driven into the ground to form the skeleton of the hut, and the walls were simply of matting, woven out of strips of shredded bamboo. There was, however, an inner coating of twisted grass, and a thatched roof of the same material.

My hut was near the centre of the clearing, and close by it was the telegraph wire on which we were working. A small wire ran right down into my hut, and was connected with a telegraph instrument resting on a cask that stood by my bedside. The cask itself contained our sugar, and was used by me as a table. My bed was composed of four bamboo stumps, with bamboo netting stretched between them, on which the mattress was laid, and I was provided with a couple of pillows and two or three blankets. Above the bed was a mosquito net, supported on bamboo poles at the corners, and enveloping me completely like a big square meat-safe. The bed, I should mention, stood close to the wall of the hut, almost opposite the doorway, which was merely a small opening, blocked up at night by a shield of grass and bamboo. My Lee-Metford rifle stood leaning against the sugar barrel, where I had placed it on retiring to rest. These details may be uninteresting in themselves, but they are, nevertheless, necessary to a complete realization of my terrible tale.

On the fateful day I arose soon after sunrise —say, about a quarter to six—and, as I had no very pressing business on hand, I went out into the forest round about for a little shooting, accompanied by two or three of the others. My luck was not very great, however, although I succeeded in potting a hartbeest; and I returned to camp about four o'clock, when I had tea with Dan Morkel in the open air. When the meal was over, we sat smoking before the big fire and continued to tell yarns until nearly ten o'clock. This gossip in front of the camp fire in the open air was our regular custom on fine nights. At this time the dry season was drawing to a close, and the

weather was not quite so warm as it had been. At a little after ten o'clock I began to yawn, so I rose to my feet and tried to peer out into the extraordinarily dense darkness of the night. I said good-night to my companion, and we each went off to our respective huts, intending to go to bed without further delay. I was not sleepy, however, and after getting into bed I commenced to read a copy of *Tit-Bits* that had reached me by the last mail. My reading lamp was the end of a candle, stuck in an old whisky-bottle, and placed on the sugar cask by the side of the telegraph instrument. I gradually dozed off and lost consciousness. The next thing I remember was waking suddenly up at about midnight and listening to the doleful howlings of the hyenas that surrounded the camp. These brutes were afraid to come too near; but as they didn't seem inclined to go away, I thought it would be a good idea to go out and see what effect a shot might produce amongst them. I drew on my coat and trousers, took my rifle, and went out into the darkness, where nothing was visible except the hideous yellow eyes of the hyenas gleaming amongst the forest trees. The silence of the night was strangely oppressive—so much so, in fact, that I thought of going across to Morkel's hut and asking him to come out and have a shot with me. I changed my mind, however, as he was not a keen sportsman, and went noiselessly over to my hut, when I fastened up the door again, and then slipped into bed. I couldn't have been there long before I fell into that sound sleep from which I was to have such a ghastly awakening.

It was around about two o'clock in the morning when I suddenly became conscious of something moving backwards and forwards, and up and down underneath my bed. Just as consciousness was growing clearer and stronger, a loud, long, and indescribable *sniff*, *sniff*, broke the stillness of the night. Though my experience of Africa was not extensive, I instantly realized that my death was at hand, and that *a man-eating lion was under my bed!* No other animal, as I knew perfectly well, would be bold enough to come right into my hut in this manner. Now, everyone will ask what were my feelings in this dreadful situation. Well, all I can say is, that every one of my faculties seemed to be utterly paralyzed with horror. Though perfectly conscious of everything that was going on, I was unable to utter a sound. My heart beat as though it would burst, and its tremendous throbbings almost suffocated me. I was almost fainting with terror at the thought of so fearful a fate. After a moment or two I became aware that the lion had got out from under the bed, and was sniffing his way along the edge, perhaps a little puzzled by the mosquito curtains. I then seemed to realize that I *must* do something, and instinctively, yet as noiselessly as possible, I huddled all the pillows and bed-clothes up over my head and face—actuated by the same instinct, perhaps, which prompts little boys and girls to dive under the bed-clothes when afraid of the bogey man.

No sooner had I done this than the lion, with a horrible *purr, purr*, grabbed me by the right shoulder, and dragged me out on to the floor,

"THE LION GRABBED ME BY THE RIGHT SHOULDER."

bed-clothes and all. The brute immediately commenced to suck the blood that streamed down my neck and chest, and every time I moved he bit the more savagely. As I raised my knees to get into a crouching, protective position, he gave me a little pat with his paws which nearly broke my leg, and inflicted a dreadful wound. After a moment or two of this awful experience on the floor of the hut the monster dropped me out of his mouth, placed one proud and massive paw on my chest, and then, throwing back his noble head, he gave one, two, three, four terrific roars of triumph and defiance.

As these mighty, reverberating sounds died away I could hear the terrible uproar outside.

Everyone was firing off guns like mad. I afterwards learned that the first thing each of them did was to swarm up the nearest available tree in order to get out of harm's way. It is necessary to bear in mind that a darkness prevailed in the clearing which might, in homely language, have been "felt." It seems that Morkel was awakened at the first roar, and, without a moment's delay, he got out of bed, put on his trousers and hat, and then sallied forth with his rifle, thinking that the lion must at least be very close to the camp, judging from the loudness of the roar he himself had heard. He made his way, or rather felt his way, over to my hut, doubtless wondering why I had not come out to meet him. He was guided partly by the loud excited cries and partly by the deep, hoarse growls of the fearful brute that had got me. When Morkel got to the door, he cried out, "Brockman, where are you? Speak to me, for God's sake!" I heard him, as indeed I had heard everything else, but was absolutely unable to utter a sound, though I was fully aware that my life depended upon it. Morkel must have worked round my hut, and seen the hole made by the lion, who simply pushed the poles on one side, and then tore out the mat walls, and crawled in under my bed. Then, of course, poor Dan realized what had happened, and he ran round to the other side, and kicked the door down.

All this time, the only thing I seemed to take an interest in was the loud sipping suck, suck, made by the lion as he drew my life-blood into his reeking jaws. I remembered, with a pang of regret, that I had not lived a model life recently, and I began to pray as I had never prayed before. As I prayed, I thought how curious it was that I should be lying there without the slightest sense of pain, with a man-eating lion chewing my flesh and drinking my blood. I *could* not realize the full horror of the thing. I had been lying on my back on the floor of the hut when Morkel kicked in the door. As he did so, the lion drove his terrible fangs into my right groin, and next moment, with another loud *purr-r-r-r*, he leapt out of the hut into the darkness—almost into Morkel's face (see frontispiece). As he ran with me he seemed to be twisting and jerking me round sideways, as though striving to get me on his back. You may imagine Dan Morkel's feelings as he groped around in the inky darkness, screaming out first to one and then to another to bring lighted bunches of grass, for God's sake. He found his way into my hut, and on feeling in the bed he placed his hand in a large pool of blood, which gave unmistakable information as to what had happened. The lion ran across the clearing with me for about thirty yards, and put me down under a big baobab tree, the situation of which is shown on the accompanying sketch-plan. He ran with a

I lay on my back at the base of the tree with the lion on top of me, occasionally gazing at me with his great, luminous, greenish-yellow eyes, which seemed to fill me with unutterable loathing and horror, so expressionless and cold were they, yet so diabolical in their ruthless cruelty. I ought to tell you that from the very first I had not ceased to wonder how it was that the lion didn't kill me outright—either by biting my head or tearing me to pieces with his terrible claws. I had seen lions kill oxen by driving their heads down between their legs and so breaking their necks, and I knew that if the monster who was drawing my blood in streams into his mouth only chose to kill me, he need only give me one little tap with his all-powerful paw.

But the lion seemed perfectly content and quiet with his prey. I felt his long, rough tongue scraping up my thighs and abdomen, and

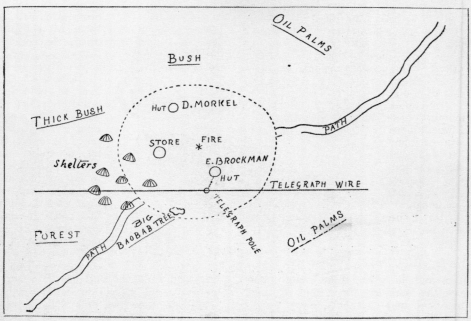

PLAN OF THE CLEARING.

springy leap, purring loudly as he went, for all the world like a contented cat. Even as he ran he was sucking violently, and as the flesh became dry in one place he let me half drop out of his jaws, and then bit savagely in another place, and commenced to suck again. The brute seemed to resent the slightest movement of my body. If I moved an arm he bit it viciously, and an uneasy jerk of my leg would be punished by a terrible scrape of the claws.

as it crept up higher and higher I felt little gusts of his horrible, stinking breath, which was so utterly loathsome that I thought I should faint, so intense was the disgust that filled me. I half turned my head away, but still the long, greedy tongue rose higher and higher towards my throat. Up to this time I had been reflecting, in a strangely calm manner, on the curious aspects of this frightful affair, precisely as though I were a disinterested outsider, instead of the dying victim of the man-eater. As I felt the lion's carrion-soiled jaws near my face and throat, however, I was seized with terror, and instinctively I threw up both arms, and thrust them far in between his jaws, and, indeed, almost down his throat. As I did so the monster snapped off three fingers of my right hand, and, horrible as it may seem to the reader, I actually left my arms and hands lying idly in the lion's jaws. "Thank God," I thought, "he is satisfied with sucking the bleeding fingers he has bitten off, and as long as I can keep him at arm's length with my hands in his mouth, I will have yet a few moments of life left for earnest prayer." And I prayed—God! how I prayed. Sometimes it seemed to me it was a little hard to die in this way, and I felt I didn't want to leave my bones in that horrible place. My life, however, was fast ebbing away, and later on I didn't seem to mind it so much. I grew fainter and fainter, and—so I am told—I kept moaning feebly, "Dan, Dan. Oh, why can't you shoot him, or do something? Oh, Dan, Dan, Dan."

Constantly my thoughts reverted to my people at home, and I felt bitterly sorry on their account, for I knew how horrified and shocked they would be at my terrible end. After thinking of these things I would resign myself to death and next moment, perhaps, I would have some kind of vague idea that I should be saved after all. I could distinctly feel each bite, because, although it caused not the slightest pain, yet, as the fearful fangs were driven into a fresh place in my thighs—the monster only chose the more fleshy parts—I was conscious of a strange numbness in that particular part. I kept murmuring to myself, gently, "Perhaps he won't kill me, after all— perhaps he will, though, the moment he has sucked that place dry. I wonder when he will commence eating me";

and then I reflected, quite in a serious sort of way, "He will find me very dry eating, after all the blood-sucking he has done."

During all this time people kept screaming, "*Nkanga, Nkanga!*" (the lion, the lion). Poor Dan Morkel was simply waltzing around the clearing in utter bewilderment and agony of mind. The appalling blackness of the night added a horror to the thing which no pen could describe. At last my friend did finally manage to obtain a couple of torches of dry grass, and by the lurid and uncertain light of these, Morkel was enabled, though very indistinctly, to see the lion standing over my prostrate body. He was an enormous, gaunt brute, over 10ft. in length, and with a luxuriant tawny mane that imparted to him a most majestic appearance. Dan told me afterwards that, as he approached with his gun, I was moaning or crooning softly to myself. Up to this time my unfortunate companion was afraid to shoot, lest he should kill me instead of the lion. He screamed out, "Keep cool, Brockman"—a funny admonition, this—"only keep cool, and I will do what I can for you!" As he approached, the lion took his fangs out of my groin, which was by this time a mere

"MORKEL LEVELLED HIS RIFLE AND FIRED."

pulp, and he faced about, growling and snarling horribly, and with one big paw on my chest. How Morkel kept his head at ten paces from the lion I don't know, but, anyhow, he levelled his rifle and fired. The lion immediately staggered back a few paces, clear of my body, for he had been hit fairly in the eye, and the ball, after touching his brain, had come out through the lower jaw, which it had broken badly. Morkel instantly proceeded to reload, but he was in such a desperate hurry that the lever of his rifle jammed, and he found himself practically helpless. Will it be believed that this desperate man, now fairly at his wits' end, rushed forward towards the lion and dealt him a terrific blow on the head with the stock of

wounds—*of which I had one-and-twenty!* My poor friend tells me that my naked body presented so shocking, so revolting a spectacle, my hands, groins, and thighs being chewed and bloodless, like paper pulp, that he nearly lost his reason, and became delirious. All that night, however, my heroic companion had sat by my bedside until daybreak, and well do I remember that with awakened consciousness came the first poignant shock of agony from my wounds. For many days and nights I suffered the torments of the accursed, taking not one atom of solid food, but only enormous draughts of brandy and champagne.

Now comes the horrible sequel of my story. Remember, at this stage I am hundreds if not

"HE DEALT HIM A TERRIFIC BLOW ON THE HEAD."

his rifle? This did the lion no harm, whereas Morkel's gun was literally crumpled up. My friend, however, at once implored someone to run over to the hut and get my rifle, and with this he killed the lion in two other shots.

It may be asked, what did I do when I felt myself free? It is important to remember that when Morkel's first shot rang out in the night air, the lion had been worrying, biting, and sucking me for about *thirteen minutes*. Well, the moment the brute retreated from me, I actually got up on to my legs and ran for twenty or thirty yards! Then I fell like a stone to the earth, and I remember no more until the next day, when I found myself in a warm bath, that had been prepared by Morkel to wash my

thousands, of miles from civilization, and even the nearest missionary doctor is far away from this remote spot. Without wishing to harrow you with unnecessary details, I may say that every one of my wounds mortified—no doubt owing to the poisonous filth that incrusted the man-eater's fangs. As I was rapidly growing more and more feverish, Morkel resolved to send me by lake steamer to Bandawe, where I could be attended by Dr. Prentice, of the Livingstone Mission at that place. This steamer was due to make its monthly call the following day at Domara, only a few miles from our camp. A messenger was therefore sent to intercept the captain, and ask him to make a call a little farther down the lake in order that I might be put on board. I was wrapped in blankets and laid on a plank, which in turn was placed transversely on a canoe. Just after we had started for the steamer, however, quite a "sea" arose on the lake, and the plank shifted to one side, so that if I had not been grabbed by one of the men in the boat, I should have been drowned! Is it not pitiful?

It took a day and a half to reach Bandawe, the weather being boisterous, and the water very choppy. A little hut was rigged up for me on deck, but I had a shocking time of it. When Dr. Prentice saw me at the mission station he told me that my case was utterly hopeless. My right leg, I was told, would have to go, but owing to my condition, it was deemed inadvisable to amputate it immediately on my arrival. Then there was no chloroform at the mission station and the ether had gone wrong through the climate, and therefore would not act. Thus I had to lie, conscious and screaming, in agony, while the doctor was cutting and carving away the mortified flesh from all parts of my tortured body. It is perfectly clear that my day had not come, for all

PHOTO. OF MR. BROCKMAN REPRESENTING HIM
AS HE CAME OUT OF THE HOSPITAL.

the bites in the thigh had missed the artery by about an eighth of an inch!

And night after night I went through the whole fearful business again. Ghastly, horrible nightmares took possession of me, and I would have gone raving mad were it not for the powerful opiates that were administered. A slamming door, the sudden appearance of a man before me, anything and everything, threw me into a perfect agony of terror, pitiful to witness. My mind and reason were all but gone, and I, who had been a giant of strength, was like a timid little child, a mere wreck of a man in mind and body.

The British South Africa Company have been very kind to me, for, of course, it isn't as though I had gone out hunting, when, naturally, I should have to take the risks incidental to sport of that kind. I believe mine is the only case on record of a man-eater taking an Englishman out of his bed at night. I still hobble about on sticks, and I often wake up in a cold perspiration, thinking I can hear the soul-destroying sniff, sniff of the man-eating lion beneath my bed.

THE OUTDOOR MAN
Equipment Guide

THE 'CAPTAIN' WILL BE PLEASED TO GIVE ADVICE AND ANSWER QUESTIONS ON CAMPING

The LAST DIVE

The job of the abalone diver is a hard one—and perilous. This is the story of one of them who wanted too much, and tried for too long. . . .

"We hauled him around and cut loose the tangle."

EIGHTY miles or so from Cape Town, along the coast, the road passes a little town called Hermanus Cape. It climbs a rocky hillside overlooking a man-made harbour, behind the huge breakwater, where waves come rolling in from storms three-thousand miles away.

From there, the ocean stretches away unbroken to the South Polar ice. The deep southerly currents run in close to the shore, rich in nutritive salts which promote a wide variety of marine growth, and still very cold. It is hardship to swim in those icy waters for any length of time.

I spent a couple of years on that coast among the free-living men, mostly young, who dive for perlemon, or abalone as you call it, from which comes most of the mother-of-pearl used in ornament.

Because the market varies, and the beds of shell shift, and are open to all who will dive for them, there is no large company interested in the operations. The men generally work two or three together from one boat, with an assistant to mind the equipment, and work the air pump, if you use a proper diving suit. Most of us preferred the greater mobility that goes with a free swimming aqua-lung

As told to J. Sawyer-Williams

By R. ROBERTSON

outfit. Whatever equipment you use, however, it's terribly cold.

Reaching the prize is no easy matter. First you must cruise until you find a shell-bed. That means long hours spent swimming about the bottom, thirty to sixty feet down, until you come on that magic, ever-thrilling sight—the perlemon shells, stretching away on the sandy or stony sea bed, among luxuriant and varied growths of weed, as far into the surrounding murk as the eye can pierce.

Having found them, you must get them up—and be quick about it, before someone notices your boat moored so long in one place, and comes along to "help you out."

You race to the surface, disregarding your crackling ears, and the twinges that you get from the effects of nitrogen deposition, the "bends," as it is popularly called, to which you become more prone as your hours spent undersea mount up, and which will probably retire you in the end, if it doesn't kill you first.

From your boat, your helper hands you a net bag, and you turn at once, to plunge down again, into the almost freezing water, and scurry about the sea-bed in a crazy, slow motion, until your bag is full, and you go to the surface once more, to hand it in to the boat. At once you take another bag, and return to the bottom to repeat the operation, as many times in a day as may be possible.

As the hours go by, you keep working, growing weary, but pausing only to change your air tanks. The bitter chill eats into your bones and you dream of the bright, sandy beach, and the open veldt, baking under the sun.

So you go down again and again, until at last you can do no more, and must drag yourself weakly over the side of the boat, to lie almost retching with exhaustion and chill misery on the bottom boards.

After a bit, when you can summon the strength to hold the cup, you take a little hot coffee from the vacuum flask, while the boat runs home to port—home to collect, and spend, your money.

It can be sixty, eighty, a hundred pounds a week—even more, if you hit a run of luck. The divers buy a good deal of "hard tack"—that is, hard liquor, Scotch, mostly. Not much of it is under ten years old.

What sort of men are they, who follow this painful, perilous trade? Young men, individualists, too restless, or too fiercely independent, and possibly, too quarrelsome, to fit into the pattern of organized life. They are men made restless by war, or by lack of war; those who hate authority, and who fear it, or the obligation to society to get along.

R. Robertson (right), and friend, with a jeep laden with shell for market. Slung on the back of the vehicle are the inflated inner tubes that serve as "resting-point" for the diver when he surfaces.

These men cannot work from nine to five, nor live, and count it living, on a weekly pay check. That is the impression that stands out in my mind, as I recall the faces round the table in the dining-room of the Marine Hotel, where we went in a little band, every Saturday night, to eat well, and drink better, together.

We were united, even when we quarrelled, by the bond of pride in our hazardous living. We understood one another.

THE DIVING GREENHORN

Van de Merwe was his name, Koos Van de Merwe—a short, sloping-shouldered, wide-browed country Dutchman, with a mop of dusty, brown hair, a suspicious manner, and a burning desire to improve his fortunes.

I understand that he'd been around town a long time, and had worked in the boatyard, I believe, but of course none of us paid him much attention until he blossomed forth in his own diving outfit.

A bunch of us were hanging around the boats, down in the harbour, on a day when it was too rough to go out, when we saw him come down the far end of the shelving beach, dressed in full diving-kit, tanks and all, and walk into the water. We didn't know who it was, what with the mask and goggles, probably shouldn't have recognized him anyway, but the kit was all new, so we guessed he was a greenhorn—that, and the way he went into the water, all tippy-toes—nervous, you know.

Well, he got into trouble immediately. We could see that he might offer us competition, but you can't let a man drown, so a couple of us doubled down there, and dragged him out with a belly full of dock water, and wheezing like a shot hippo.

We pulled off his mask, pumped him dry, and called him many kinds of a fool. In the end, some of us got together and taught him how to use his kit.

He didn't start at once, diving for shell. For a couple of months he was out every day, the boat yard being on short time, fooling about the shoreline and in the harbour, getting the feel of it, working up his nerve, I suppose, although he had plenty to start with. It took more nerve than sense to just put on a new kit and walk into the water like that, you know.

At the beginning, he thanked us for pulling him out and for what we taught him; he even bought a round of drinks at the hotel, I think; but after that, he didn't mix much.

Perhaps he felt that he wasn't wanted—he s p o k e English with a heavy up-country accent—or maybe he didn't find our free-living ways much in line with his Reformed Church background, for we were a well-travelled, cosmopolitan group. Everyone had at least been to Jo'burg—and our ideas were bound to be very different from his. Perhaps he just didn't see himself as a big-time spender; what the rest of us made, pretty well all went as fast as it came, one way or another.

I remember, on the evening that he did come to the hotel with us, he confided to me over the glasses that some day he would have a great farm, many cattle, a fine house, a radio-gram and electric light, and come to town in a fine great Buick.

"People will know who Koos Van de Merwe is, when they see him!" he claimed.

We all have our dreams. However, as time went by he tended to keep his own counsel, and restrict himself to a civil greeting, if he met one of us in the street.

One weekend he hired a man, and a boat, and headed out to the grounds with the rest of us. The following week, he quit his job, and from then on went diving regularly every day, with his assistant, who was in every way suited to him—a competent, wizened guy in his forties, whose previous boss had been killed by sharks the year before. Every morning, long before the rest of us were ready, these two would be out, chugging through the harbour mouth in Koos' weather-beaten dory, not wasting two extra words on one another.

So it went on all summer.

Really, he shouldn't have been diving at all. When he was learning, I could see this. For one thing, he had a sort of perpetual running cold—sinus, I suppose, or an allergy perhaps—but of course, anything that tends to irritate or obstruct the air passages that connect the sinus and throat and ears is bound

Anchored over a good bed, the divers shrug on their foam rubber suits and prepare to go down. Robertson may be seen on right.

to be ten times as bad under conditions of varying pressure.

When I saw him rubbing under the hinge of his jaw, where the Eustachian tube passes, and gaping and yawning desperately to clear the pressure from his ears, hawking and spitting, and all, I told him he'd best drop it—but he paid me no mind. Instead, he put in more time than anybody.

Starting early, he would quit late; the first out, he was invariably the last in. As regular as the clock, as dusk fell, and we were sorting our gear, he would come chugging up to the dock, and dourly unload the straining sacks of shell—as much as twelve-hundred in a day, sometimes. Always it was the result of really hard work. He hadn't the experience to find the best places easily.

Yet with all that money, he'd never spend a cent if he could help it—not the way we did, anyhow. For instance, we all had new boats and launches, but he kept the old dory that he had rented in the beginning, slow as it was. It stank, right up to the end; for, of course, it couldn't last, not the way he was doing it; but first, I must tell you about the car.

I suppose that in his own way, among his own people, he saw himself as a big wheel. Sometimes on a Sunday, if you were out early, before noon, you might meet him in the street, coming from Church.

He would be dressed in one of those long-coated black suits, the outlandish masterpiece of some country tailor; there would be a shoe-string tie, a wide hat set square on his head, and a pipe in his mouth.

A round-faced country girl in a cotton dress, a little pallid and pimply without make-up, would be hanging on his arm, seeing, and being seen.

Some evenings, too, he would put on his best, or second-best, a little outgrown, but equally splendid, and stand about by the stores, where the farmers gather when they are in town, talking slowly, with authority, hands in pockets, about the government, or the harvest.

TRAPPED BELOW!

After he'd been diving a couple of months, always doing pretty well, he took a few days off, put on that Sunday suit, and went down to Cape Town. When he came back, it was at the wheel of a bloated red-and-black American car, a couple of years old, but still looking pretty good, which some smart salesman down in the Cape must have sold him on hire-purchase terms.

After that, the few hours of the evening were spent on polishing it, or driving, never fast, up and down the main street, his girl beside him, both a little stiff, self-conscious, straight-faced—but secretly very pleased with themselves. With the diving good, and every day big hauls of shell, and big money coming in, I suppose he felt that he'd set foot on the end of the rainbow at last. As the big car sighed them along, they must have been very busy, re-working their dreams into plans, and dreaming anew.

Autumn was coming, and the weather turning a little cooler. Repeated squalls, making the little boats leap and buck like frightened horses, had added to our discomfort, and made us quit early. That was the day that Koos's Nemesis finally caught up with him.

A bunch of us were standing about on the pier after cleaning out the boats, when a man in a little fishing launch came by, and shouted that the "Afrikaans" was in trouble.

As soon as we heard, of course, half-a-dozen of us ran at once, and got into Dicky Ransome's launch. A nearly-new Chris-Craft, with twin Chrysler engines, it was the fastest thing on the coast.

Some of us had seen the old dory earlier on, over a poor bed we all knew of, not far from the harbour, so it was only a few minutes before we reached there. The little boat was dancing on three-foot waves, and the man in it leapt up and waved frantically, when he saw us.

We reversed the propellers a moment, then eased up to him slowly from down-wind. As we hovered a dozen yards off, Dicky got out the megaphone.

"Stay still, and tell me what's the trouble."

The man was leaping and gesticulating so wildly, that we were afraid he would be thrown by the motion of the boat. Now he steadied himself and shouted back.

" He go down three, or fo' hour' ago, never come up, never give no signal. Nobody come by, only just now."

We held a little conference, clinging to the gunwale of the heaving launch, spattered with spray.

"Look," said Dicky. "He's probably done for anyway; four hours is a long time, even if his tanks were full when he went down."

The thing was, of course, no one would care to be left like that. We talked it over, and in the end, although conditions were bad, we decided that a couple of us should go down and see. Since we had been diving from the launch, and had our suits on board with us, Dicky and I went.

Under water, the light was poor, since the sky had clouded over. We followed down the mooring rope, by which the dory was anchored, and to which, for some reason of his own, Koos had hitched a fish line, running in brass eyes, and connected to a bell in the bows of the dory, a type of signal we never used. We came to the bottom, where the small mud-anchor lay half-buried in the sand.

You couldn't see any distance, because of the bad light, and the seaweed that grew about there like a regular forest, twenty-feet high, but fortunately, that wasn't necessary Koos was only a dozen feet from the rope, caught up with some seaweed in a crazy tangle of stuff, all wrapped and snarled in the knobs and buckles of his air tanks.

As I got to him, I saw a little cluster of bubbles go up; he still had air to breathe. I saw, too, what it was that he had got tied up with.

SILLY FROM SHOCK

I have told you already that we take down one net bag, fill it, and return to the boat with it, to fetch another; well, he had a drogue of at least a dozen of them floating behind him, a thing we never did, just because of this danger. Underwater, things like these bags don't hang, as they do in the air; they float and drift with every move you make, and the passing currents, and can soon get tangled in your air valves, or anything else nearby; then you're stuck.

I suppose he found the changes of pressure, going up to the boat frequently, very painful, so he had rigged that bell, and had the man send him down a rope to haul up the bags, as they became full, thus saving his eardrums.

Of course, he could save time, too, this way, so that this, even more than the long hours he put in, had given him his big hauls. He could stay down there until his air was nearly used up, without having to surface at all.

When we reached him, hauled him around and cut loose the tangle, he didn't seem to

The divers " do the town " while their little ships
are tied up at Hermanus.

we cut in freeing him, until in the end we gave him a few, seeing that he wasn't right in the head, and had to be pacified.

He used to hang about the dock, messing around the boat, talking to anyone who'd listen, explaining that he'd had an accident.

" When I recover my health, I will go down again, next week, I expect."

As he spoke, he often would reach back vaguely over his right shoulder as if for the air valve. Often, too, so his landlady said, he would scream in his sleep, dreaming he was still down there, I suppose.

Of course, he never did go down again.

In the evenings, still, he would get out the car, not driving much—for his queerness had frightened off the girl-friend—but just sitting in it, or polishing the metal work.

"Getting it ready for the finance company to take away," some of the boys used to say, for of course it wasn't all paid for, and now it would never be.

recognize us ; from this, later, I got another insight into his character. It seemed that when he found he was trapped, he cut down his air to the barest minimum, to make it last until, he hoped, we would come looking for him. He cut it so low, in fact, that he was quite silly from anoxia, and shock too, I suppose, for accidents underwater, particularly the sensation of being trapped, are very frightening.

Most men, I know, forget themselves completely when some such thing goes wrong; they panic, spit out the mouthpiece of the aqua-lung, and breathe great gulps of sea water—and that's that. He was a pretty cool customer, really.

The sad thing is that all that cool self-control didn't do him any real good in the end.

Perhaps it was the shock, or the anoxia, but his wits seemed to be permanently affected by the experience. I'm inclined to accept the latter explanation.

As you know, particularly for old people, gas anaesthesia is not recommended, because it acts directly on the brain, reducing the oxygen supply, and speeding senile deterioration. My theory is that the long hours he spent down there on short rations of air had the same effect, although, as I've said, he was a relatively young man.

Whatever the reason, he no longer was normal in his behaviour. He took minutes to answer the simplest question, seemed always vague, walked about with his eyes, as it were, only half focused, as if in a fog.

He was irascible, too, attaching undue importance to insignificant things. For instance, he made a great fuss about the nets

RELIEF AT LAST

Another month or so went by. One Sunday night, after dark, we were driving back to town from Steembras Beach, twenty miles or so up the road.

Every town has its quota of girls who like a big spender, and sometimes we would load up a car with good food and drink, and drive up there with them for the weekend.

Now, on our way back from such a trip, jammed together, singing and a little drunk, in a big open car that was roaring through the cool, gusty darkness of the coast road, we spotted in the headlights the form of the big American car, a hundred yards off the road at a sharp bend, tilted on its side among the boulders.

Tyres howling, we swerved to a stop on the shoulder of the road, and tumbled out. Our noisy fun evaporated suddenly, as we struggled through the bushes towards the vehicle.

The car itself was empty, when we got there, and our driver went back and focused his spotlamp. In a little while we found Koos, sprawled in an unnatural posture among the stones, dead this time for sure—from internal injuries, so the coroner said.

His right hand was cocked over his shoulder, in the now familiar gesture, and on his face was a look of great relief, as if he had at last been able to treat himself to a real big gulp of fresh air.

Odds and Ends.

The accompanying photograph illustrates a remarkable feat which was performed recently by a one-legged motorist in the State of Oregon, U.S.A. He not only drove his automobile up the steep incline shown in the photograph, but actually allowed it to rush down again backwards, using no brakes whatever and, for a portion of the time, standing on the seat. Our snap-shot shows the car descending the incline at terrific speed by the force of gravity, the man guiding it backward.

Once a year the firemen in Japanese cities have an official parade and display. After this function is over the men break up into their respective sections and parade the streets, giving clever acrobatic performances *en route*, as shown in the photograph here reproduced. Some of the feats they perform on their light bamboo fire-ladders are marvellous, and all their performances are carried out with a dash and enthusiasm which is good to see. Their abilities as fire-fighters are highly spoken of by Europeans who have seen them tackling a blaze. We imagine that our readers will be interested in the cut and pattern of their trousers, which are, to put it mildly, unique.

The WIDE WORLD

THE MAGAZINE FOR MEN

JULY 1942

1/3

THE UNDOING OF BA TIN

Lost in Vesuvius.

By Dr. Z. E. Birasky, of Essec, Sclavonia.

Wherein is related how Professor Blondel, disregarding the warnings of the guides, persisted in going round the crater and walking on some partly cooled lava. The unfortunate savant fell through the thin crust and was destroyed in the fiery sea. One photo. shows the guides actually pointing out the terrible danger to the Professor.

MY dear friend Professor Blondel and I found ourselves one wet night in a café at Zurich: it was in April, 1897. Our conversation soon turned upon the adventures each of us had had. Professor Blondel was a meteorologist, and in pursuit of his researches he had travelled a great deal. It was some years since last we met, and now my friend related to me how he had visited Central Africa, India, and other regions in pursuit of his professional studies.

In the course of the evening the Professor said he was compelled, for the purpose of making some meteorological examinations, to ascend Mount Vesuvius, and as it was incumbent upon him to do this in the approaching season, he would have to be in Naples at the beginning of May. He remarked how pleased he would be if I would accompany him on this expedition, saying how much it would add to his enjoyment to have a companion. I returned no definite reply. However, M. Blondel, whom I was continually seeing after that evening, kept pressing me for my decision on the suggested journey, and having obtained a fortnight's leave, I went to the Professor on the 25th of April and told him I was ready to accompany him.

Accordingly, two days after this interview, we took the train and crossed the beautiful mountains of Switzerland into Italy, and, breaking our journey for a

THE AUTHOR, DR. Z. E. BIRASKY, WHO WAS WITH PROFESSOR BLONDEL WHEN HE WAS *From a]* DESTROYED. *[Photo.*

rest at Genoa, we arrived at the gay city of Naples four days after leaving Zurich. This was my first visit to the beautiful city. We engaged apartments at the Pension Suisse, just near the Bay, from whence we could see the famous volcano and also the smoke from its crater, as from the funnel of a steamer in the distance.

After a few days' sightseeing we decided to proceed with our ascent of Vesuvius; so one morning Professor Blondel went to see one of his friends, and on his return told me that at one o'clock in the afternoon we would leave by boat from the quay near our hotel. Accordingly, we started, having left word that we should, in all probability, return to dinner, but in any case we desired our host to have something ready for us, as on our return we should be very tired and hungry. We arrived at our destination after an hour's row, the distance being about four miles; and on landing we were at once solicited by many guides desiring to be engaged. Selecting three of them, we walked towards Resina, one of the small towns nearest to the shore.

The view of the volcano from here was, as compared with that from our hotel, was altogether different. The whole side of the mountain was covered with vineyards and gardens, in which the choicest of fruits are grown. From this point we could see on the summit the lavas of the various flows during the

THIS IS THE UNFORTUNATE SAVANT, PROFESSOR BLONDEL, WHO MET A FEARFUL DEATH IN *From a]* VESUVIUS. *[Photo.*

"CLOUDS AND SMOKE AROUND THE GLOOMY SUMMIT LIKE STEAM FROM BOILING WATER."
From a Photo. by Dr. Z. E. Birasky.

trees, and vines grew to perfection, and in which roses and camellias bloomed in profusion, we now found ourselves making our way through a black, sterile, and forbidding waste, utterly devoid of vegetation, and covered only with huge folds, waves, and unshapely masses of rough lava.

However, by-and-by we reached the crocelle, on the summit of which stands the hermitage of San Salvatore. As is the custom of all travellers making the ascent on foot, we had a rest here, and partook of refreshments. Here also is found a well of good water. The streams of lava which have at various times descended the mountain near the crocelle have flowed on either side of this ridge, and so its summit had hitherto afforded a safe site for a habitation ; whilst all around has been from time to time covered with a perfect sea of liquid fire. Attached to the hermitage there is a sanctuary containing an altar and the shrine of the saint whose remains lie beneath.

We remained here for an hour, as Professor

past thirty years. It is difficult to convey the scene to the minds of those who have not seen a volcano. A good comparison is to suppose that a sea of boiling pitch has been violently agitated by a storm, and then suddenly cooled —so quickly, however, as to retain when solidified all the roughness and irregularity which the surface had when liquid. The clouds and smoke around the gloomy summit give an appearance not unlike the steam arising from boiling water.

From Resina there is a railway which goes to the top of the mountain, but our desire (more especially that of Professor Blondel, who wanted to see Vesuvius as closely as possible, to explore every point, and take notes of his observations) was to proceed on foot. As we slowly made the ascent to the top, the view that presented itself was in most striking contrast to that which gladdened our eyes on the commencement of our journey. In the place of beautiful gardens, in which orange, lemon, almond, fig

"THERE IS A RAILWAY TO THE TOP, BUT OUR DESIRE WAS TO PROCEED ON FOOT."
From a Photo. by Dr. Z. E. Birasky.

Blondel wished to make some investigations. I should explain that on account of the commanding position of this ridge, and its comparative immunity from danger, it has an observatory, built by the King of Naples, for

"AN OBSERVATORY BUILT BY THE KING OF NAPLES FOR THE STUDY OF VOLCANIC
From a Photo. by]   PHENOMENA."   [*Dr. Z. E. Birasky.*

the purpose of facilitating the study and observation at close quarters of volcanic and earthquake phenomena. In this observatory there is a collection of the minerals found around Vesuvius, and this museum is shown to visitors by an intelligent and obliging custodian.

After this stay we commenced the ascent of the cone itself. This is the most difficult and laborious part of the whole climb—the looseness of the rough, angular lava masses, and the consequent uncertainty of footholds causing great fatigue. With the assistance and encouragement of the guides, however, coupled with constant exertion on our own part, we were at length enabled to reach the terrace at the summit. We were greatly excited by the proximity of the mouth of the volcano and the deeply interesting phenomena we were about to witness. So, naturally, in spite of the warnings of the guides, Professor Blondel pressed on to make the ascent of the new cone, and gain the very edge of the crater.

From this crater arose columns of vapour charged with sulphurous fumes. Stones and cinders of most irregular and various sizes were also discharged with loud subterranean noises almost every minute. These stones and cinders rise to a great height almost perpendicularly; and if there is not much wind, the greater number of them fall back again into the crater. As the vapour emerges from the sides of the pit it deposits sulphur and various salts, these covering the surrounding surface with variously and beautifully coloured incrustations.

Notwithstanding the oft-repeated warnings of the guides, I followed Professor Blonuel up the new cone, and gained with difficulty the edge of the crater; then together we peered into the terrible interior of the volcano. I shall never forget the sight—words utterly fail me to describe adequately the strange and awful scene that presented itself to my view. Rolling clouds of dense white fumes were seen covering the bottom and almost hiding from sight the sides; while, from the more distant part of the fiery and mysterious abyss, the cinders and stones before-mentioned were discharged with thunderous roars. No flames were to be seen, but on looking down the fumes were found to be illuminated as if by a colossal fire beneath.

On the opposite side of the crater the lava was in a liquid state, and vapour was rising from its glowing surface. The Professor, after examining closely and with great interest everything around us, wanted me to accompany him close to the liquid lava, but I firmly declined to do so, for to me the sight of it was awful enough without closer inspection. Heedless of the counsel of the guides, who strenuously advised him not to go—pointing out that the lava was in a molten state, and that he might slip and fall into it—Professor Blondel persistently determined to proceed, and actually started off. At the last moment one of the guides caught hold of him and passionately urged him not to attempt so foolhardy an adventure, adding that he and his fellow-guides, as natives of the district, knew the frightful danger which was before him, and felt sure he would perish in the attempt. And yet, in spite of these

"TOGETHER WE PEERED INTO THE TERRIBLE INTERIOR OF THE VOLCANO."
(A SNAP-SHOT NOW POSSESSING A MOURNFUL INTEREST—GUIDES POINTING OUT THE DANGER TO THE DOOMED MAN.)
From a Photo. by Dr. Z. E. Birasky.

entreaties and my protests, Blondel positively declined to abandon the attempt, and would not be dissuaded.

"He is going to certain death," said the guide who had addressed himself to me. "I would stake all I possess that this unfortunate signor will never return alive. Such a crazy adventure I have never heard of in all my mountaineering experience. My companions," he added, "join me in repudiating any responsibility for what your friend is doing." As for me, I was in a perfect agony of terror and helplessness. Professor Blondel was still proceeding, so I shouted out to him imploring him to return and not risk his life in such a mad attempt. I now felt certain the lava was too liquid on that side to support his weight. To my cries, however, he never responded, but pressed forward eagerly.

I cannot well describe how I felt at this time. Nothing that I could do would stop the doomed man. And such a hideous death . . . . crashing through the treacherous crust, not into icy water, but into living fire !

Anxiously I followed M. Blondel's every step through my glass until he had reached the very edge of the crater. By this time he appeared to be extremely fatigued, and was advancing slowly along the edge, until at last he approached the smooth, recently-formed lava, in which I felt sure he would sink, the surface being too soft to bear him. Still keeping my eyes fixed

upon him fascinated, I thought I should lose my reason. I wanted desperately to call out again to urge him to come back, but I was quite unable to do so. My throat was parched and contracted from the agony of that awful scene. I could only murmur that poor Blondel was lost—lost ! As I stood there helplessly, with all my limbs trembling in deadly fear, you may judge of the ghastly shock I sustained when I saw the unfortunate man sink slowly into the fiery lava, from which there was no possible escape. He uttered no sound that I could hear. I can, as I write this, see him as it were again before me, as he clasped his hands in horror and despair, and made desperate efforts to extricate himself. He appeared to call for assistance to help him out of the great expanse of liquid fire—but, alas !—all was in vain. He gradually sank beneath its dread surface, and was swallowed up like a stone that is thrown into deep water.

This heart-rending scene, which lasted only a few minutes, seemed positively to paralyze my faculties. I did not know what to do for some time. All my senses seemed to leave me, and I could not move from the spot whence I had witnessed my dear friend sinking into the sea of fire. My thoughts ran on what he must have suffered in those last moments, and how the unfortunate man should have turned back as he found the vapours grow more suffocating and the lava more treacherously soft.

I see again before me that joyful and courageous Blondel who had yielded up his life in scientific pursuits. For, of course, he would never have gone to the other side of the crater but for his determination to make some meteorological examinations—to carry out his original plans upon which he had started. He had set his mind on solving some problem, and no risk was great enough to deter him. Poor Blondel !

After this terrible disaster, and as soon as I had recovered myself a little, I hastened to make the descent of Vesuvius, leaving for ever in its bottomless pit the remains of my poor friend. Then, taking at the foot of the mountain the road leading to Naples, I made my way to the hotel with all possible speed, and there found awaiting me the refreshments ordered by my late companion. I was, of course, too distracted to eat, and hastened to telegraph to the family of the late Professor what had befallen him. Returning to the hotel, I packed my luggage and returned home by the midnight train.

The mighty, ninety-foot bandsaw screamed through the heavy logs ; faster and faster the blade revolved, and the men of the timber mill went apprehensively about their work. Then, with shattering suddenness, the giant saw split asunder, reared and flayed like a vengeful serpent and scythed across the mill . . .

BANDSAW

MOST thrilling real-life adventures occur in the Great Outdoors—in the jungles, forests, deserts, mountain ranges and ice wastes, and I've had my share of these during years of worldwide travel. Yet one of my most nerve-racking experiences occurred in the Small Indoors—to be precise, in a little sawmill on the bank of the South Thompson River in central British Columbia.

My job was not a particularly enviable one. There had been no competition for it. The pay was twenty cents an hour for ten hours a day, six days a week.

But I was young and strong, and got on very well on pay which in Canada, nowadays, would be considered mere "peanuts." Being unskilled, I was pushed around to any part of the mill from which refuse had to be shifted.

On the day that the mill crew went berserk, I was helping a buddy to sling heavy slabs of waste wood into a conveyor which bore them to the riverside destructor, locally called the "burner."

This crazy day began like most others, without any hint of what was in store. The morning passed normally, with everyone sweating under the impetus of Carl King the topsawyer who, as usual, set a hot pace as if trying to break his own record of cutting a hundred and twenty thousand lineal feet of lumber within the ten hours.

Conditions were vastly different in the afternoon, and, but for a miracle, I would not be alive today to record the event that struck terror into the heart of every man on that sawmill deck.

However, the calamity of that hot afternoon is best understood if readers take a brief preview of the ordinary working conditions.

The logs were borne upward from the river to the raised sawmill deck by an endless bullchain. They were then hurled in turn, by steel mechanical arms, on to a steam-carriage. The huge arms and carriage were operated by Carl King, who stood in the sawyer's box working the levers and foot-pedals.

To his right, was the big glistening saw that tore each log into whatever timbers and boards were required. It was a double-cutting bandsaw, ninety feet long, over a foot wide, and set with teeth about two inches apart. It could best be described as an endless ribbon of steel, tightened on two large fly-wheels. One of these wheels was overhead, the other below the level of the mill-floor. When they were speeding at full revolutions, the saw appeared as a continuous streak of lightning. It was, in fact, held in position only by the precise adjustment of those two smooth, whirring fly-wheels.

Carl had to use all his expert judgment in preparing for, and then making, the day's cut. If the saw became slowed and jammed in a log, an expensive delay could occur—if nothing worse.

Carl King, the "High Priest" of the double-cutting bandsaw, worked fast, with brilliant judgment and the utmost delicacy. Two men, the dogger and setter, rode on the carriage. Carl held their lives in the hollow of his hand. By hauling on levers, Tom Sweeney the dogger, jammed the steel "dogs" into each log to hold it fast. His mate "Red" McCrum then set the log for the initial cut, acting on instructions conveyed by Carl's rapid hand signals.

The steam-carriage was movable, both forward and backward, on narrow-gauge rails. The bandsaw ripped off the first long strip of bark with a falsetto scream and a shower of sawdust ; then it began cutting the log into boards, each of which dropped in turn on to "live" rollers. The operation and speed of the carriage were entirely Carl King's responsibility. By light manipulation of a small lever, he controlled this tremendous machine and cut the lumber with a precision and rapidity that made him the highest-paid key-worker in the mill.

The boards next went to an "edger" machine, equipped with circular saws for cutting them to narrower widths. The edgerman was "Lofty" Reede, whose predecessor had been killed at the start of the season. Somehow a huge board had been fed in askew. The whirring saws caught it and hurled it back with the force of a battering ram against his stomach. The sawmill had shut down for an hour as a gesture of respect.

Two buddies, Jud Mawson and Ted Haynes, worked the trim-saws to which the boards were conveyed from the edger. These circular saws trimmed the ends squarely to required lengths.

By

W. E. STANTON HOPE

AMOK

The bandsaw split asunder, and reared like a vengeful serpent.

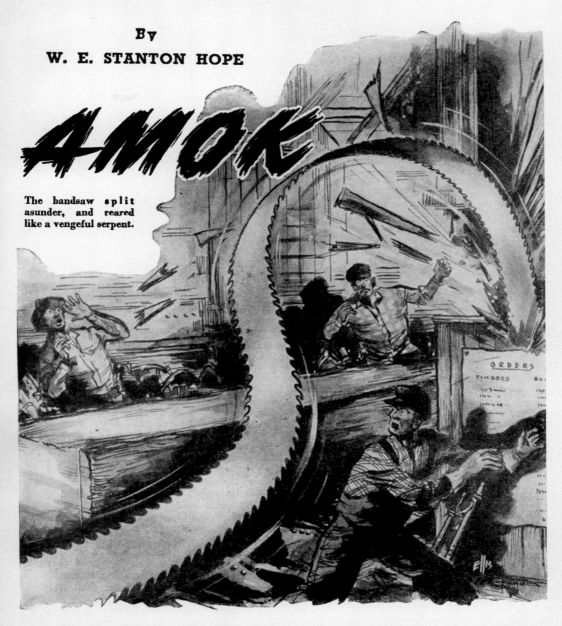

Not far from their trimming table was a small bandsaw, called the re-saw, which was operated by Jake Christiansen, who had come to Canada from Sweden as a child. Jake was deputy to Carl King, the fast-cutting top-sawyer who, on his best form, drove us all to demoniacal excesses of work. We frequently cursed Carl but we were always confident in his skill.

We became inured to the odd flying wood-knots and damp sawdust, which were not sucked through the zinc pipes of the blower system to the boiler-house furnaces.

We were inured, too, to bruises and cuts, and the deafening din and vibration of the mill.

But we were not used to Jake in the rôle of top-sawyer, except on the few occasions when he operated the steam-carriage with Carl standing by, watchful as a hawk.

The mill at full blast was a dramatic sight. The management recognised this and an overhead observation gallery had been built. It extended from where the logs entered the building near the big bandsaw, to a place overlooking the planing department on a lower floor. People from Kamloops and tourists from the Pacific Slope were encouraged to come along to watch the tremendous processes of transforming logs into all the varied wood products used for building purposes.

A 40-foot log rides up the bull-chain from the river into the mill, there to be cut to the required shape and size by the bandsaw.

On infrequent occasions, visitors came to the observation gallery accompanied by a clerk from the general office. They were briefed in advance, but learnt little from the guide during the leisurely tour. The mighty orchestra of the mill precluded that. Jake Christiansen, who was something of a romantic with musical leanings, likened it to a fiendish rendering of Tchaikovsky's 1812 Overture, the saws producing weird discords against a background of booming tones from the planer machines, and the explosive clatter of wood fragments in the blower pipes supplying the percussion in lieu of kettle-drums.

We, who had worked in the mill for many weeks, were able to identify the individual sounds. We knew instantly if anything was amiss by certain changes of tone. When such changes occurred, nerves grew tense because the atmosphere of the mill was always charged with some threat of danger. And, too often, this danger materialized in a casualty caused by a broken pulley-belt or other sudden mishap.

Visually, the most sinister thing in the sawmill was the double-cutting bandsaw, a mere silver streak to the eye when it was running at full speed. Jake Christiansen was fascinated by it. He revered the big saw and regarded it as possessing some supernatural power. He envied Carl King the power associated with the head-sawyer's unique position. Otherwise, he appeared to have only one other great interest.

A few weeks earlier he had gone to town on a Saturday night to see a one-night-stand show at the local drill hall, known on such occasions as the Grand Theatre. Between acts

he had sauntered across the road with Jud Mawson and a few others to the Sundae Parlour. There, for the first time, he had seen the soda-fountain attendant, Sheila Daley, daughter of the proprietor. Since then, it was said, Jake had avoided the saloons and spent his few leisure hours pretending to like maple nut sundaes better than Canadian rye.

Of course, he had plenty of competition. His shy attempts at courtship appeared to make no impression. The girl was equally pleasant to all customers. "Sure," she said frequently, "one of these fine days I'll be coming along to see you all lounging around in that old mill of yours."

Well, she did come, with a small party from a social club, and it happened to be on the fateful afternoon when the mill staged a drama more starkly horrifying than anything ever offered by the local theatre.

During the morning Carl King fell ill with colic. He was taken to hospital in the mill buggy and did not return after the mid-day break. This meant that Jake had to take the top-sawyer's place for the rest of the day.

If he had been handed a thousand dollars, Jake couldn't have looked more pleased and excited. The understudy was about to take over the star rôle, if only for a few hours. He stepped jauntily to the sawyer's box, and began the afternoon's cut with meticulous care. The manager draped himself over the wooden observation gallery and watched for half-an-hour. Then he left for the office in a separate building, resigned to a lower output but satisfied that Jake would jog along competently.

The bandsaw had to be changed two or

The bandsaw slices its way through a forest giant in a Canadian sawmill.

three times a day, for naturally the teeth became blunted. When a change was made, the worn saw was taken off the fly-wheels, and delivered to the head filer and his minions for sharpening. The fly-wheels were moved automatically farther apart to tighten the new saw on them. Then the machinery was started up again, and the cut resumed.

There was no need this afternoon to make an early change, and Jake carried on work with commendable caution. At least a dozen ninety-foot double cutting bandsaws were included in the mill's equipment. But it was always *the* saw to Jake—"Old Lightning," he called it affectionately—a living, god-like entity to which the giant logs were sacrificed.

Now, standing-in for Carl, he treated his steel idol with due respect. Whenever the bandsaw registered a slightly deeper and more ominous tone, Jake slowed the steam-carriage. This eased the pressure of the log against the saw which quickly regained highest speed in a triumphant crescendo of sound.

Yet the brooding sense of danger, never entirely absent, was intensified. More variation in the booming song of the saw had something to do with it. Mostly it was a psychological effect, I guess. We were used to Carl setting the pace and were more trustful of a talent we knew. The tension built-up and we relaxed only when, after about an hour and a half, Jake decided to change the bandsaw.

Resumption of work was leisurely, in marked contrast to Carl's invariable speed-up to compensate for the few unproductive minutes. No one objected to Jake taking it easy. We got no more pay for the tearing, sweated labour that Carl imposed on us.

The going was easier than during the first period of the afternoon. Then another short delay occurred, more unexpectedly. The loggers down on the river boom had temporary difficulty in sorting a few logs and getting them to the mobile bull-chain. Jake wiped sweat from his forehead with hands encased in buckskin gloves, and had time to look around. He glanced upward, and I saw him start in surprise. His leathery face reddened deeply. I followed his gaze. A small party from a social club in town had just appeared on the observation gallery. Among them was Sheila Daley—the local beauty who presided at the soda-fountain of the Sundae Parlour.

Jake began to fidget as if his boots were full of sharp splinters. He could hardly wait to get cracking again. That was the effect that one glance at Sheila Daley had on him.

Directly the logs began coming to the sawmill deck, he proceeded to give the liveliest display hitherto. The logs were slammed on to the steam-carriage and Tom Sweeney and "Red" McCrum responded instantly by force of habit acquired under Carl King's demanding régime. A touch on a lever, and Jake moved the log to the roaring bandsaw which ripped the timber apart amid spurting sawdust.

We began to sweat in the old familiar way. Things were much the same now as when Carl was in the sawyer's box. We soon noticed, though, that the saw whined and growled more often than usual when a Douglas fir or hemlock arrived on the carriage. The variation in the voice of the saw jangled our nerves.

My buddy and I seized long strips of water-soaked bark and waste wood from among the lumber that came rushing along the rollers from the saw. We dragged them off and hurled them into the conveyor that took them to the burner, performing massive juggling feats and dodging to avoid each other's "line of fire."

All operations were speeded up. It was a lively spectacle for the visitors, and I reckoned Jake was fully aware of the dramatics and pleased with his own prowess in setting a hot pace. He couldn't see the observation gallery now, but that girl with the dancing Irish eyes was right there in his mind.

There was no hope of our getting another easy period while he was in this elevated mood. Such zeal disturbed us mentally. Only recently there had been talk at the boarding-house of an incident down on Puget Sound. A substitute top-sawyer had mistakenly accelerated a steam-carriage, and sent it crashing out of the sawmill, killing both the dogger and setter. There were times, during Jake's hot spell, when it seemed he might emulate the feat.

The whole place thundered and throbbed as cut timbers and boards were spewed from the big saw to pour through the other processes of the mill. Everyone, I felt, was working in a state of abnormal tension. Furthermore, the recent tragedy at the edger machine was fresh in mind, and this helped to increase our uneasiness.

Every now and again my spine tingled at some novel screech or whine from the bandsaw. Jake Christiansen was overdoing it a bit. A show-off! Here was his chance to impress that blue-eyed blonde—something he could never do when, among other millmen, he had his elbows on the counter of the Sundae Parlour.

No one signalled to Jake to slow down. "Lofty" Reede and the other Canuck machinists had an obstinate pride. They had never demanded a favour from Carl King in his fiercest mood, so they would certainly not kow-tow to a "Scandiwegian sidekick." Not on your life!

We all knew, however, that by making the cut at such high speed, the comparatively inexperienced Jake was taking a chance. His exuberance and his cockiness bred suspense and a growing sense of impending disaster. . . .

SCREAMS AND SPARKS

Yet when the calamity occurred, it came as a shattering surprise. The bandsaw, showering sawdust with a booming note, signified "all's well." Then, an instant later, all hell broke loose. A metallic scream pierced the thunderous rhythm of the mill. A blinding shower of sparks shot upward as if a firework had ignited within the half-cut log. The bandsaw split asunder. It reared like a vengeful serpent. Jake recoiled, horror-stricken. The dogger and setter flung themselves backward from the steam-carriage and crashed full-length behind the narrow-gauge track.

My work-mate threw himself under the conveyor. I stopped and stared like a fool. For a split-second the bandsaw was curved upward to an incredible height—a quivering Sword of Damocles poised menacingly. The rending of timbers mingled with human screams. In its upward leap from the spinning fly-wheels, the saw had sliced through supports under part of the observation gallery. That part of the gallery was sagging and Sheila Daley, lagging behind the rest of the visitors, clung desperately to the handrail above the sawn-off struts.

Dry sawdust showered over me. More sparks flashed as the saw twisted convulsively and tore across the iron levers of the steam-carriage. In sudden frenzy of fear I vaulted over the conveyor and dropped prone on a cushion of damp dust and bark strips.

"Lofty" Reede, the edgerman, beat the foreman to an emergency alarm, and signalled the engine-room for an immediate shut-down. But no human intervention could take the life

Almost contemptuous of the proximity of the vicious bandsaws, a filer takes his "break" before giving them his attention.

out of the saw, no longer a band but an elongated strip of steel armed with razor-sharp teeth, and thin stiletto points at the ends.

MOMENTS OF HORROR

It came racing almost parallel with the conveyor and ripped splinters from the floor in its vicious passage.

It screamed across the sawmill deck and ripped slivers from the conveyor's wooden side, not far from where my buddy and I were flattened among the damp refuse.

It seemed an unending n i g h t m a r e, although the whole episode could not have lasted more than a matter of moments. The end came with a crash, as if a thunderbolt had hit the place. I saw nothing of that last explosive feat of the runaway bandsaw, but visitors on the sound part of the observation gallery had a grandstand view. They were among the few who were watching when the bandsaw raced across the trimming table and struck the mill wall.

Nails went flying; a sheet of corrugated iron slammed outward like a door—and the bandsaw went streaking through the gap. It fell in the drying yard twenty feet below the sawmill deck, spun convulsively and, with a final shudder, became still.

Men scrambled up, asking questions no one could answer, and expressing some mighty lurid opinions of Jake Christiansen, the substitute sawyer. We looked round dazedly, expecting to see a few mutilated corpses strewing the place. The saw had heavily scarred the floor, benches and metal bases of machinery, but happily there were no human relics on that fantastic trail. Our relief was marred, however, as a shout from Jud Mawson cut through the confusion of voices. He had jumped on the trimming table, and was peering through the hole made by the saw in its last fling.

"Jeez! It's got Sammy!"

Sammy! That was Sam Wong, an old Chinaman who had served previous seasons as an oiler under the mill, and this year was rated "maintenance man" with no arduous duty.

Jake leapt forward with outstretched arms as she plunged from the wrecked gallery.

We charged up between the silent trimsaws to peer out. Sammy in his faded overalls lay sprawled on the ground, his head resting in blood-stained sawdust. The big saw was coiled near him with several of its formidable teeth missing.

"That Scandiwegian swab! He's killed him."

Jud spat out the words with a venom that seemed foreign to his genial nature.

A couple of men from the box mill ran to Sam Wong and examined him. The manager and clerks from the general office hurried to the scene.

"Must ha' cut through his head," said Ted Haynes.

But the fellows on the ground reassured us. When the saw had fallen and twisted round in its last spasm, it had ripped jagged bits of rock from the soil. One of these had struck the old man above the ear and made an ugly wound. Luckily, it was nothing worse than a dent, needing an overnight s t a y i n hospital.

Now we had time to assess the damage near the sawyer's box. The dogger and setter had escaped with bruises sustained in their fall from the steam-carriage. They and "Lofty" Reede, the edgerman, were standing near Jake Christiansen who was laid out flat, his face the colour of old putty. Kneeling beside the fellow was Sheila Daley, showing no sign of her ordeal on the broken part of the gallery, other than a torn dress.

We went across in a straggling mob to where Jake's lank body lay.

"What's wrong wi' him?" Jud demanded.

"Lofty" poured ice-water on the sawyer's head.

"Aw, he's fainted," he said. There was a trace of contempt in his tone. The girl looked up at once.

"Sure, and maybe yourself would faint if you'd been so badly hurt," she retorted, very hotly.

She had a first-aid box beside her and was bandaging Jake's left shoulder, which had been torn by jagged wood broken from the observation gallery.

Jake opened his eyes, raised his head after a pause and looked round at the group in bewilderment. The colour flooded back to his cheeks and his brain began to function.

"Sammy!" he croaked. "The saw—it killed Sammy!"

Apparently, he had made light of his own injury, and then had had the grace to faint on hearing Jud's impetuous shout about Sammy having been fatally injured.

"Naw, he's only hurt some," Ted Haynes snapped. "But no thanks to you he didn't get his ticket."

Others growled protests about Jake's "reckless" way of making the cut and blamed him for the accident. But "Red" McCrum and Tom Sweeny, who had been examining the log on the carriage, called us over.

A chunk of rock was embedded deeply in soft wood under the bark. The bandsaw had hit that rock, and Jake could not be faulted, except that possibly the saw might not have broken had he been taking things more easily. That, however, was problematical.

Now and again, pieces of rock got under the bark when a felled tree crashed to the ground in the forest. Logs were examined carefully before being rafted on the river to be sent down to the sawmill, and usually such foreign objects were promptly detected. It was just bad luck that the impetuous Jake should get a dangerous log on the carriage during his initial solo trial as top-sawyer.

Some of the workers still reckoned he could have averted a situation that might well have spread death wholesale over the sawmill deck. But that was not Sheila Daley's opinion. In her view, he was completely vindicated. If she thought he had been a show-off, she evidently regarded his working zeal as a compliment to her presence. Furthermore, she saw him as a heroic figure despite his fainting fit.

The reason, as we soon learnt, was that when the weakened part of the observation gallery sagged and fell, Jake had leaped with outstretched arms to catch her as she came down with it and plunged over the gallery rail. Undoubtedly, he had saved her from a severe fall at grave risk (she considered) to himself.

The manager took a poor view of the whole affair. When Jake Christiansen came out of hospital a day or two later, the re-saw job had been filled. There was only the offer of a humbler one in the drying yard which Jake indignantly refused. Shortly afterwards, though, the girl's father engaged him as a "soda-jerk" at the Sundae Parlour—a mighty lucky break for him and a unique opportunity to win an attractive wife.

Jud, and a few others who might have been in the running, took it philosophically. We reckoned it was safer for all to have him in the Sundae Parlour than in the sawyer's box, and thereafter we suffered Carl King's fast-cutting spells rather more gladly.

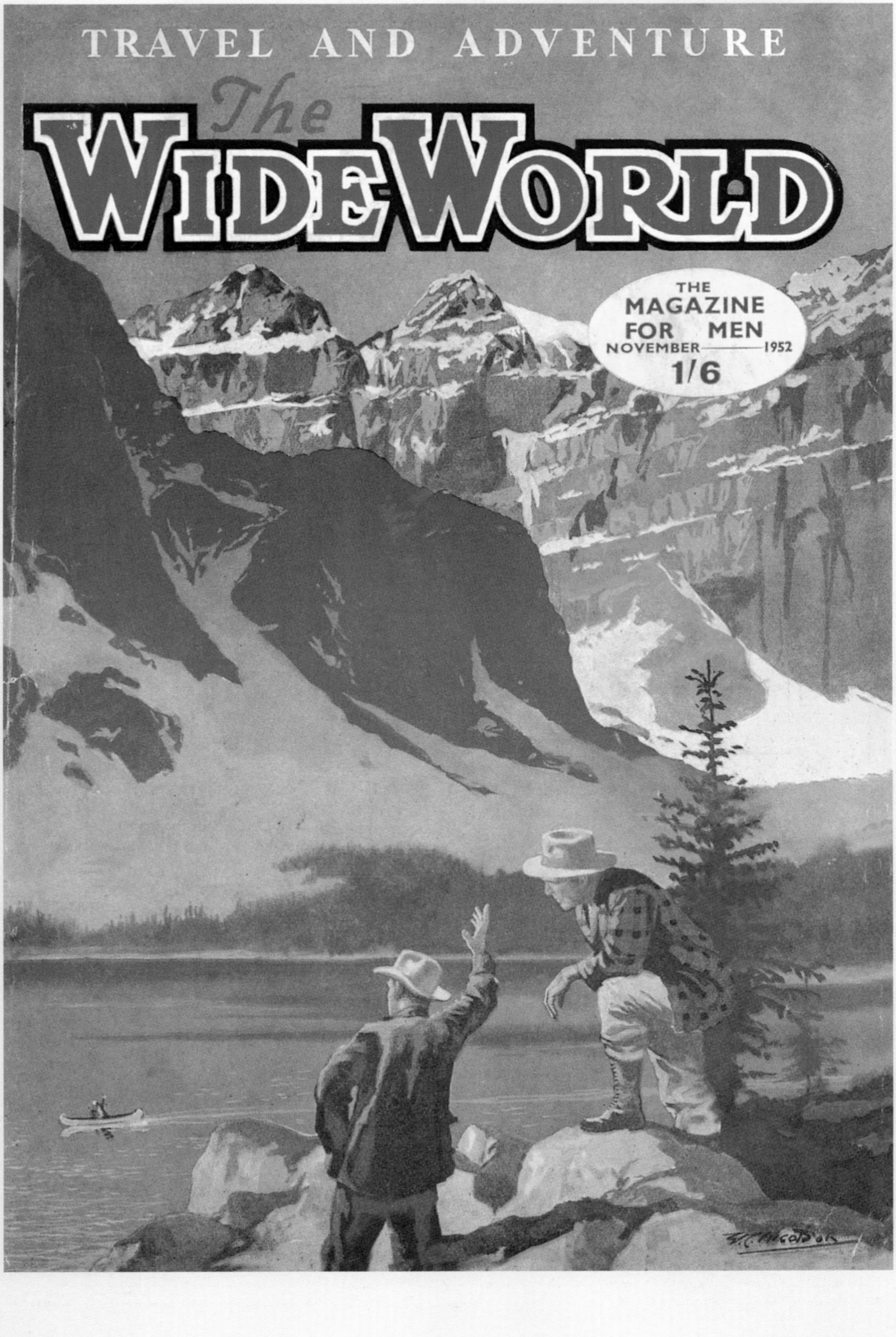

TRAVEL AND ADVENTURE

The
WIDE WORLD

THE
MAGAZINE
FOR MEN
NOVEMBER — 1952
1/6

*From America comes
the Water Trotter,
claimed to be the
world's safest vehicle.*

WONDER BUBBLE

WAYNE E. WILSON, an engineer of the General Electric Company in Pennsylvania, USA, has recently invented, constructed and patented a really strange vehicle.

He calls it a "Water Trotter," and, from a distance, it looks like a bubble in the ocean, or an out-of-space machine.

According to the inventor, it is the world's safest vehicle for use on water, although it is so new that time has not yet afforded trials under abnormal conditions. Means of propelling it are being kept secret.

Its configuration provides over 800 lb. excess buoyancy when positioned with an entrance port in the water, and over 2,000 lb. in the normal operating position—the weight of the average user being relatively so small as to have no significant effect on these margins.

Thus, it is practically "proof" against swamping, and the user cannot fall out.

Even under the extremes of possible (but unlikely) puncture and ensuing panic by the user, the structure still would not sink, because its configuration automatically traps over twice as much air as is needed for floatation.

Sinking can be caused only by two or more punctures.

The plastic material, called "Tenite Butyrate" is 3/16 in. thick, and is so tough that it is comparable to boot leather in many respects, and the structure is capable of taking as much abuse as a ping-pong ball.

Being transparent, the part above the water line affords observation for orientation, while the surface in contact with the water provides for observation beneath without interference.

Thus, the wonders of submarine life and landscape can be observed at the user's leisure (unless the water happens to be too muddy) without danger from attack, exhaustion or drowning.

Operation is so simple, that no experience is needed to enjoy the "Water Trotter" and it can be handled by anyone from ten to a hundred years of age.

Two lockers are provided, to carry refreshments or personal belongings, and rest and relaxation can be enjoyed simply by reclining on the bottom. Fishing can be done through an entrance port by tipping the vehicle to the entrance position.

With co-ordination, it can be used successfully by two people at the same time, but it is primarily a single-operator device.

Since it keeps its passenger dry, it can be used with comfort in water and weather far too cold for comfortable swimming.

Wayne E. Wilson and, above, his Water Trotter.

A Fall of Three Thousand Feet!

By Professor Charles Wolcott.

The well-known New York aeronaut tells the fearful story of his fall from the clouds in Venezuela. Our readers cannot, we think, fail to be interested in the amazing narrative of Mr. Wolcott's miraculous recovery after sustaining the shocking injuries detailed herein.

IN the fall of 1895, having closed a very successful season in New England, I prepared to sail for South America; I had a winter's contract with the Venezuelan Government. Arriving in New York City, I learned that my assistant (whom I had given a short leave of absence) could not join me in time for the boat which sailed next day. However, as I expected to spend several weeks in Venezuela before commencing my engagement, he could easily arrive in time by sailing on the next steamer, nine days later. So I deposited his fare with the steamship company, and when the "Red D" steamship *Venezuela* (now the U.S. troopship *Panther*) sailed next day, I was a passenger. With me went my dog aeronaut "Pedro," a thoroughbred English bulldog, which had accompanied me in many a lonesome voyage among the clouds. After a pleasant but uneventful voyage of seven days we arrived at La-Guayra. From there to the Venezuelan capital, Caracas, is a railway journey of but a few hours' duration. Arriving at the latter place I was soon comfortably installed in one of the several good hotels of which the city boasts.

That night I met several native friends whom I had known in New York, and arrangements were made for my entertainment during the weeks of my supposed idleness. For one thing, mountain lions were numerous within a dozen miles of the city, and a week of hunting was decided on by way of a start. I have always been an ardent hunter, and was somewhat disappointed when my agent informed me next morning that my contractors, having learned of my arrival, desired me to commence my performances at once. The fact that I had left my assistant behind was no fault of

From a] THE PARACHUTIST AND AUTHOR, PROFESSOR CHAS. WOLCOTT. *[Photo.*

theirs, and as I had no reasonable excuse for delay I sent word that I could be ready in twenty-four hours after arriving on the grounds. I thought I could easily pick up a man to assist me for a few trips, or until my regular assistant turned up.

I was informed that I was wanted on October 28th at Villa-de-Cura, the capital of the State of Miranda, to assist in the celebration of the birthday of Simon Bolivar, the liberator. That afternoon I received my orders, which, being interpreted, read, "Leave Caracas to-morrow morning, at 6.30. German railway to Cagua; then by express to Villa-de-Cura. Deliver the inclosed package to the Governor, General Andrada." This was rather meagre information, but thinking a more definite understanding could be had at Cura, I started. After a tedious ride of nearly ten hours in a poorly ventilated, ill-smelling, little, narrow-gauge coach, I arrived at Cagua, where I learned, to my amazement, that the "express" to Villa-de-Cura consisted of several large two-wheeled carts, each drawn by six wicked-looking mules, and escorted by several mounted men armed with Winchester rifles. This was a mode of travel hardly to my liking, but it was that or nothing, so I had to put up with it. The overland trip, though interesting, was extremely tiresome. My driver volunteered the cheerful information that people seldom attempted the journey by night; and even in the daytime the presence of an armed guard was necessary, as wild beasts and highwaymen were always in wait, to pounce upon the unwary traveller. And as we wound our way through miles of wild tropical jungle, I could see no reason to doubt the truth of his statement. Late that night we arrived at the little city of Villa-de-Cura. I had been advised to stop at the American House, and so to the American House I went.

I spent an entire day in getting together the material for the inflation of the balloon—which was a hot air one ; and in looking over the possible landing-places, I found but one really dangerous place to descend, that being a large lagoon or dead lake, that stretched away for a mile or more across the plain, and was filled with decayed vegetation, which would make swimming impossible. As I looked the place over, I realized that to make a descent in such a place would be as much as a man's life was worth, no matter how strong a swimmer he might be. A native who lived near by told me the lagoon was infested by alligators and huge serpents, and that many cattle had been lost by wading out a short distance from shore.

The next morning (October 28th) dawned clear and beautiful. The crowd had increased during the night, until the streets were almost impassable. On arriving at the place from which the ascension was to take place, I found my paraphernalia surrounded by an immense crowd, and my native assistant in an adjacent wine-shop. All that day, until 5.30 p.m., the time of the ascension, I was annoyed and my work impeded by a multitude of crowding, hustling, shouting, curious, and excited natives. My helper was of no assistance whatever, I having all the work to do, while he was explaining the science of aeronautics to his many friends. You see, he was an important man that day. At last, however, I was ready to commence the inflation, and, taking my assistant inside the balloon, I gave him instructions and then left him. As the great balloon breathed in the hot air, and slowly grew larger and larger, the excitement among the spectators became intense —even comic. My assistant became frightened,

"I WAS INSTANTLY BORNE ALOFT."
This Photo. was taken on the identical occasion referred to.

crawled hastily from inside the balloon, and positively refused to return, thus doubling the work for me. Calling a policeman, I explained to him that it would be necessary for me to go inside the balloon for a few moments to arrange the sand-bags and furnace-cover before leaving the ground, and that I desired him to keep the crowd back from my paraphernalia. Whilst I did this I suppose he tried to do as I requested, but finding himself unequal to the task he called in the assistance of some twenty or more cavalrymen, who rode their horses round and round the now rapidly filling balloon, trampling upon and hopelessly entangling the lines of my parachute, which had all been nicely arranged and attached by a small rope to the top of the balloon.

When I again came from inside the balloon everything was ready for the start, and so, quickly running to the trapeze-bar, I gave the word, " Let go all." I was instantly borne aloft, high above the heads of the shouting multitude. I had commenced my acrobatic work on the trapeze-bar when, chancing to look upward, I noticed the tangled condition of my parachute, which hung at the side of the balloon and was connected with my trapeze-bar by a small rope running to the corresponding bar of the parachute. I immediately turned my attention to repairing the damage, but as I could reach only to the bottom of the entangled cords I made but little headway. I cursed all South American republics and their crazy peoples. At this time I was fully 6,000ft. high. It was rapidly growing dark on the earth, but from my elevated position I could plainly see the sun over the mountains. I had reached my maximum height, and in another moment was gradually descending. Realizing the impossibility of getting my parachute in proper condition for the leap before the balloon descended, and thinking I had only to wait until the balloon, losing its buoyancy, would slowly and safely drift to the earth, I turned my attention to looking down and picking out my probable landing-place. Judge, then, of my horror, when I saw that it would undoubtedly be near the centre of the dreaded lagoon previously mentioned! I was already nearly over the edge of that noisome, alligator-infested lake, and was yet fully 3,600ft. high. A skilled aeronaut learns to think quickly. I knew that to descend in that dead lake was to meet a certain and terrible death. Should I jump? Well, the pressure *might* cause the parachute to open and the ropes to untangle themselves. It was an awful chance, but the only one, and taking a firm grip on the iron ring of the parachute and throwing one leg over the bar, I leaped into space.

For the first few seconds my descent was similar to hundreds that I have made during my aeronautical career; but I soon realized the fact that I was falling at a frightful rate of speed. For the first time in my life I thought I was facing certain death, and wondered if I would not have done better to have taken my chances with the balloon. I looked far above me and saw the balloon, which had overturned and was vomiting out dense masses of black smoke. I wondered if it would fall in the lake and be lost. I remembered a dear friend in New England who had advised me to give up this trip and remain in the States. I could plainly hear the shouts of the people, many of whom were following the course of the balloon. I remembered stories I had read of people falling great distances and losing consciousness, and dying before they reached the earth; I wondered what could possibly have given rise to that impression. I could hear the wind as it shrieked through the tangled cordage of my parachute, which had now failed me for the first time. I could feel the hissing wind cut my face like a knife. I knew I had fallen thousands of feet, and as the mad rush continued I could see the earth apparently flying up to meet me with terrible rapidity. An agony of helplessness came over me. I think I know all the sensations a man feels who falls to his death—right up to the point of unconsciousness. I don't suppose I felt the physical fear that would have seized almost anyone but a balloon man. Still, I made up my mind to die.

But when scarcely 200ft. from the earth the parachute lines became loosened —the canvas cracked and swelled. I swayed dizzily. For an instant I thought I was saved, but the awful pressure of the atmosphere proved more than the parachute could stand. Though my fall was stopped for an instant, the cloth burst in a dozen places, with reports as sharp as rifle-shots. The cords broke like thread, and again I was falling. I now braced myself to meet the shock, and next moment struck fairly on my feet on the grassy plain—I actually *heard* my person strike the solid earth. The parachute had opened enough to save my life. I was unable to move, but knew I was terribly injured. I was dimly conscious of what was transpiring around me. I heard the mounted soldiers order the crowd away, and, when they would not obey, they charged them with drawn swords, riding their horses over me. I saw the flying hoofs above my head, and wondered that they did not step on me. Only one shoe of the flying feet struck me, cutting a small gash in my head. I knew when I was picked up and carried to a small bamboo hut near by and laid on a soldier's blanket. Then I must have lost consciousness, for when next I remember it was dark. I was still lying on the ground, and with the exception of my head and right arm I could not move a muscle. My faithful dog had found me during the night, and now lay with his head on my face, howling

mournfully. It is simply impossible for me to describe my sufferings during the long hours of that terrible night. Most of the time I was conscious, and wondered how long I could hold out. Morning came at last, however, and just as day was breaking I heard someone singing. Attracted doubtless by the barking of my dog, a native woman who was on her way to the town came to the door of the hut. After gratifying her curiosity by answering many questions, and assuring her that I was positively alive, and that the dog would not injure her (a native of Venezuela is never in a hurry), I succeeded in obtaining her promise to deliver a verbal message to the proprietor of the " American House," she flatly refusing to go direct to the Governor. Then, after hours of waiting and suffering, the Governor came, accompanied by his bodyguard and a physician. The surprise and sorrow of General Andrada at seeing me in such a condition were certainly genuine. I had been reported dead, and he was about to give orders for my burial, when a soldier informed him that a woman had brought the report that I was still living. Procuring a doctor, he at once came to my assistance, and assured me he would do all in his power to aid me. He asked where I wished to be taken. I told him I had been informed that the only good hospital in the republic was at Caracas, and I thought I could get proper medical attendance there. He fully agreed with me regarding the hospital; but the physician, who, during our conversation, had been examining me, stated that it would be simply impossible to have me moved that distance—that nearly every bone in my body had been broken. Furthermore, that he was surprised at my having lived through the night; that I certainly would *not* live to cover half the distance to the railway. Finally, he concluded that it would make but little difference any way, as I had left but a few hours more of life at best. I, however, assured the Governor that, as I had already lived fifteen hours since the accident, I would certainly live to get through. If he wished to assist me at all, I said he could best do so by arranging for my transportation as far as the railway station at Cagua. While willing to accede to my request, he insisted on my knowing what my chances were, and informed me that during the night the usual South American insurrection had broken out, and that even now the city was threatened. I cursed all these Republics again. But he could furnish me with an escort, which, perhaps, would have no difficulty in passing the insurgent lines. The chances were a hundred to one that I would never live to reach the railway; yet, if I insisted, he would do all he

could for me. I did insist, and that afternoon, at three o'clock, I was taken by my escort, which consisted of twenty mounted soldiers, with their captain; six men to carry the stretcher (improvised from a canvas-cot); and a mule cart for my baggage. Just before starting the Governor called the captain to the side of my cot, and in my hearing gave him his orders. He should order his men to carry me as carefully as possible, by the most direct route in the direction of Cagua; and he was to keep on stopping when necessary, until either the station was reached or I no longer lived. In case of my death before the station was reached, my body was to be left wherever we might be. The soldiers were then to hasten back to Villa-de-Cura, as the town was sadly in need of every man capable of handling a gun. Then, after wishing me good luck and God-speed, General Andrada gave the order to march. Thus, twenty hours after the accident we started, my dog barking joyously as if he, too, was anxious to be off.

It is impossible for a pen of mine to describe the horrors of that journey. The route lay across the plains of Miranda. The tropical sun shone down upon my unprotected head with merciless force. Night found us in the foothills of the Andes, but brought no relief— up steep hills and over rough roads, until I thought each step would close my precarious lease of life. But still we plodded on, stopping only for a few moments when we reached the great Cagua jungles. If we passed any insurgents on the road, I did not see or hear them. The insects, however, were positively ferocious, and wild beasts howling close by made the night hideous. Once a mountain lion, attracted, the soldiers said, by the smell of blood, which still flowed from the wound on my head, screamed in the bush so near to us, that the soldiers were alarmed, and fearing an attack formed in a circle round my cot. My dog, too, bolted under cover with a howl; but a moment later the lion was heard stealing away through the bush in the opposite direction, and then the heart-breaking march was resumed once more. If anyone had told me that a human being could live to endure such horrible suffering as I experienced that night, I would not have believed it. Each step seemed to add to the torture, and I begged the captain to leave me and return, as I preferred to die rather than continue the journey. But the captain would reply: " You heard the Governor's orders?"

It was daylight when we reached the Cagua River; and at 9 a.m. we arrived at the station, where I was left on the platform. The captain and soldiers bade me good-bye, and started on the return trip. The sun shone down pitilessly, and I soon began to feel the tortures of thirst; no one came near me, however, for some time. Then the low growling of my dog caused me to look up, and I saw a little native girl standing by my cot. Though seemingly frightened, she asked me in her native tongue if I was sick and why I was there alone. I told her I was indeed sick, and asked her to get me a drink of water; whereupon she hastened away and soon returned with a battered tin cup filled with coffee, which was still hot. I drank it eagerly, and never was a drink more appreciated by me. Fearing to be again left alone, I coaxed the child to me, and taking her hand tried to detain her, but becoming frightened she broke away and I saw her no more. After what seemed many hours the station-master arrived and asked me gruffly what I was doing there and what I expected was to become of me. I replied that I wished my cot placed in the baggage-car of the train for Caracas, as I was unable to move and was trying to reach the hospital at that place. He said he could *not* put the cot in the baggage-car, as that was intended for baggage only; and if I expected

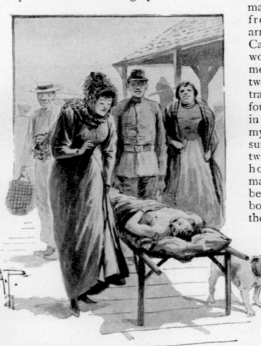

"SHE ASKED ME IN A KIND VOICE IF SHE COULD DO ANYTHING FOR ME."

to go on that train I must go in the passenger coach, where I would be allowed a regular seat for a regular first-class ticket. As he walked away I thought my last chance was gone, and bitterly regretted that I had not taken the Governor's advice and remained at Villa-de-Cura. Soon other people began to arrive and gather round my cot. Among them was a lady, who looked at me in surprise. And, indeed, I must have presented an awful appearance, being still clad in acrobatic silks and covered with blood and dirt. This lady asked me in a kind voice if she could do anything for me. I explained the situation to her as well as I could, and informed her that my only chance for life was to get to the hospital at Caracas. She quickly called one of her servants and bade him send the station-master to her at once. To him she explained that she was the wife of the Vene-

zuelan Secretary of War, and that I was to be put on that train at any cost. The man meekly promised to see what he could do, and was cautioned by the lady to *see quickly*. Then, ordering one servant to bathe my face and head in cool water, and sending another for a bottle of wine, she bade me keep heart, and said she would see that I got to the hospital at Caracas all right. She would, she said, telegraph to her husband to have arrangements made for my removal from the train on its arrival at the city of Caracas, so that no time would be lost in getting me to the hospital. At twelve o'clock, noon, the train arrived, when it was found there was no room in the baggage-car for my cot. For the modest sum of one hundred and twenty-five dollars in gold, however, the station-master allowed my cot to be placed in an empty box car—into which, by the way, a crate of live chickens was subsequently thrown. This station-master was not a native, but a German-American, who spoke English well, and who had formerly lived in New York. He volunteered this information him-

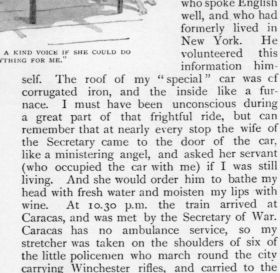

self. The roof of my "special" car was of corrugated iron, and the inside like a furnace. I must have been unconscious during a great part of that frightful ride, but can remember that at nearly every stop the wife of the Secretary came to the door of the car, like a ministering angel, and asked her servant (who occupied the car with me) if I was still living. And she would order him to bathe my head with fresh water and moisten my lips with wine. At 10.30 p.m. the train arrived at Caracas, and was met by the Secretary of War. Caracas has no ambulance service, so my stretcher was taken on the shoulders of six of the little policemen who march round the city carrying Winchester rifles, and carried to the hospital, a distance of several miles. Vargas Hospital does not have a surgeon on duty at night, and so I was taken to the operating-room in order to be in readiness as soon as they came in the morning. This was also in case of my death during the night, when they would not have so far to carry my body, the same room being near the morgue. I remember but little of that night. I seemed to be beyond further suffering. I was afterwards informed by one of my watchers that I talked incessantly all through the night, and begged them not to inform my friends in the States that I had met with an accident. The next morning, at ten o'clock, just *sixty-four hours after the accident*, the hospital surgeons gathered round my cot. I had accomplished my purpose, and lived to get

having a terrible time with the *yellow fever!* The days passed, and, contrary to all expectations, I lived and grew stronger. The visiting surgeon, Dr. Acosta, informed me that my injuries consisted of the following, which I am sure my readers will let me term an appalling diagnosis : Both ankles crushed, both knees crushed and broken, right thigh broken, right hip broken and socket crushed, pelvis broken clean across, every rib on left side torn from the spine, four ribs on right side broken, and spinal column dislocated in one place and positively fractured in another !

This diagnosis was, later, pronounced correct

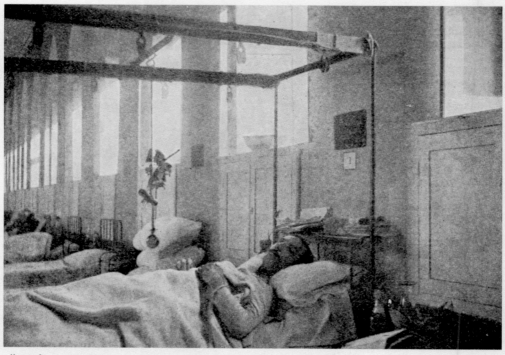

From a] MR. WOLCOTT LYING IN VARGAS HOSPITAL, CARACAS. [*Photo.*

into the doctors' hands. Nature would stand no more. The pain seemed to leave my body. Breathing became difficult. Then came oblivion. Two weeks later I regained consciousness, to find myself on a cot in the surgical ward. Wax candles were burning at my head and feet. A sweet-faced Sister of Mercy was standing at my bedside, holding a crucifix before my face. Seeing that I was conscious, she asked me in French if I were a Catholic. I replied "No," and she said, "It makes no difference—rest." The surgeons came soon after, and seemed surprised and pleased that I was conscious. They informed me that I had been

by the best surgeons of New York City, and verified by full-length X-ray photographs. I might write many pages descriptive of the six months I spent in Vargas Hospital. I will only say, however, that I slowly got stronger, nursed with loving tenderness by the Catholic Sisters of Mercy, who, although they could not bind a wound skilfully, knew the art of comforting, and would not allow a patient to suffer if they could prevent it. Most of the patients of that ward were brought in—some from long distances —suffering from wounds made by gun-shot, knife-thrust, or snake-bite. Occasionally a leper was found among them ; but these were removed as soon as possible to the leper colony, situated farther up among the mountains. Vargas Hospital is supported by the Government. The attending surgeons were all well-educated men, well up to their business. Many of them are graduates of the best medical colleges of the U.S. or France. But having no modern appliances and a limited amount of supplies, they were seriously handicapped. I have known the death-rate to be 3 per cent. a day for months.

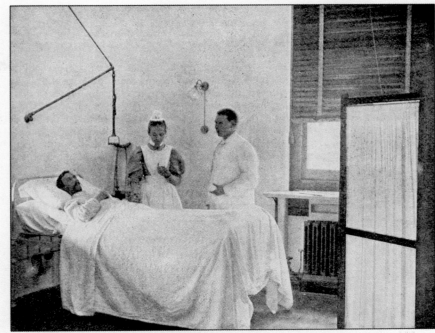

MR. WOLCOTT IN ST. LUKE'S HOSPITAL, NEW YORK, WHERE THE GREAT OPERATION WAS PERFORMED.

They did little for me in a surgical way, and plainly told me that I might live for some time—perhaps for years—but would for ever be paralyzed from the waist down. Of course, I suffered a great deal, but nevertheless managed to derive a certain amount of amusement during my sojourn there. I at one time had a class of eight men and boys, whom I taught English; some of them became quite proficient. Many American residents visited me, and I was regularly supplied with newspapers and periodicals by friends in New England. As I grew stronger I determined to try and get to New York, where I knew I could obtain the best treatment with the latest appliances, for I thought I might possibly recover. It was against the advice of the surgeons that I left, but I had made up my mind; and in six months and two days from the time I entered Vargas Hospital I was placed on an inflated rubber bed and taken to the railway. The rain was falling in torrents at the time, and when I arrived at the depôt I was soaking wet. General Thomas, the American Minister, furnished me with a private car, and, accompanied by the Secretary of the Legation, I made the trip to La-Guayra, and was soon on board the steamship *Venezuela*. The officers gave me a warm welcome and made me as comfortable as possible.

Seven days later we arrived in Brooklyn, and in a few hours I was comfortably installed in the beautiful new Saint Luke's Hospital, on Morningside Heights, New York City. My case attracted the attention of many of the principal surgeons outside the hospital staff, and was discussed far and wide; and the Metropolitan papers printed columns regarding my accident. After many consultations, it was at last decided that an operation alone could relieve me of paralysis; and after four months' medical treatment and careful nursing I was pronounced strong enough to be operated upon. In the presence of fourteen of the world's most prominent surgeons, the spinal column was chiselled into and the vital cord exposed for a distance of nine inches. Pressure was found and removed. As an operation, it was a success, and I was afterwards informed that it was the first operation of the kind ever successfully performed. Five months later I was able to walk with the aid of crutches, and left the hospital—just one year one month and one day after the accident. I am still in the aeronautical business, but my physical condition compels me to let paid assistants make the trip to the clouds.

THE
SHEER
FACE
OF
HELL

Alone, Walter Bonatti set out to climb the half-mile of near-vertical rock that was said to be unconquerable · □□□□□ By DAVID LAMPE, Jr.

BONATTI began his second attempt to climb the virgin wall of rock on the morning of August 16, 1955. The first time, two years before, he had taken two Alpine guides, but they had all turned back after spending a terrifying night on a narrow ledge with rocks the size of freight cars rocketing past them.

No one had ever successfully scaled this half-mile of sheer rock, and every other climber in the world had written it off as impossible ; but the twenty-five-year-old Walter Bonatti was determined to try again—this time, alone.

That morning Bonatti and his three companions, Italian engineer Paola Ceresa and two Alpine guides named Berardini and Géry, had climbed up nearly 10,000 feet of the mountain, and were finishing their breakfast in a tar-paper-roofed hut called the Charpoua Refuge. Above them loomed the peak guides called the Wall of Hell.

Shortly after eight o'clock, Bonatti stood up, adjusted his gear, shook hands with his friends, and left the hut. Alone now, he trotted at a steady pace across the *Mer de Glace*, that jagged, treacherous ice field that looked like an ocean frozen in mid-storm. He kept moving, knowing that if he stopped, he could not keep his feet. His friends watched until Bonatti disappeared over the high stone crest known as the *Corniche*.

At the base of the wall, Bonatti stopped. He peered up at the grey stone pinnacle of the 12,245-foot mountain called the *Petit Dru*.

The most dangerous climb in the French Mont Blanc Range, the highest European range, it jutted straight up for 2,300 feet above his head—nearly twice the height of the Empire State Building.

He took a deep breath and began to climb. Gingerly clutching for hand and *(continued overleaf)*

Bonatti gambled with death to write history in the French Alps.

footholds, he inched slowly up the glassy face.

When he reached a point where there were no places to take hold, he stopped and hammered a piton (a 4-inch aluminum-alloy spike) into a crack, took one of the steel snap-links he'd looped in a chain at his waist, and knotted the end of the nylon rope to the link. He then pulled himself up and stood on the spike, and began inching upward.

When he had crawled up another 20 feet, he drove in another piton, and snap-linked his rope to it. By driving them every 20 feet, he knew that if he lost his grip, he could not fall more than that distance—unless the weight of his falling body pulled the piton out of the crack.

Another 20 feet . . . another piton and snap-link. When he had laid a vertical course of 10 spikes, each roughly 20 feet apart, he lowered himself on the rope to the bottom piton where he'd hung his clumsy rucksack.

He guyed the pack to the doubled nylon rope, then hammered loose the bottom piton. Then up to pull out the next spike. The next . . . and the next . . . until he was back at the top of the course. Then he hauled up the pack, hung it on the remaining piton and began repeating the long tortuous process.

By mid-afternoon he'd climbed nearly 500 feet; but now a smooth rock protruded, forming an uncracked ceiling above him. No crevasses for pitons or wooden wedges. No way up.

Patiently he had to lower himself, his ropes and pitons back down as tediously as he'd ascended. Daylight was almost gone when he returned to the Charpoua Refuge. He had wasted an entire day and had gained nothing except the knowledge that he would have to attack elsewhere on the Wall of Hell.

By walkie-talkie, Ceresa 'phoned Walter's bad news to Montenvers, the French town at the base of the *Petit Dru*; then the four men ate, and went to sleep.

In the morning, to lighten his load, Walter cut his food down to a chunk of bread, four small cheeses, three cans of meat, some sugar and a bottle of brandy diluted with water. Near the food he stowed a bottle of rubbing alcohol.

His kit included 79 pitons, 15 snap-links, six-wooden wedges with rings attached, an ice hammer and a rock hammer, two 40-metre nylon climbing ropes and two shorter, thinner, silk ropes, and three sets of stirrups (rope ladders with aluminium-alloy rungs).

Bonatti was up early, impatient to start. "I'll see you at the top," he said with a faint smile. "You can come up the easy side."

Then he was gone, trotting again across the *Mer de Glace*.

The others watched until Walter had begun to climb, and then began descending the mountain to Montenvers. They could watch him from there by telescope. Later, if he seemed to be reaching the top, they could climb up Dru's easier east wall and meet him at the summit. Bonatti could climb down the other side—if he ever reached the crest.

The temperature was way below freezing, but Walter wore no gloves; he had to keep his sensitive fingers free to find hand-holds. Course after course of pitons and wedges all day.

Sometimes he chimneyed up crevasses, pressing his back against one slick wall, his rubber-cleated boots on the opposite wall, sliding his back upward a little bit, then raising his feet, then sliding his back again.

Dragging his dangling, ungainly rucksack, he conquered inches. Once he had to climb outward to clear the protruding roof of a 30-foot bottomless chimney.

Toward late afternoon, his rope froze stiff as wire cable. He had to stop and coil the nylon around himself to dry it with body heat till the rope would slide through the snap-links again.

Still in the *Flammes de Pierre* at dusk, he found a ledge just barely wide enough to stand on. In Montenvers pinpoints of light flickered. There was no room on his ledge to sit, let alone lie down, but it was the only flat spot he'd reached all day.

From the deep cut where his ledge was, the base party wouldn't see his flashlight signal. So he arranged his gear, drove a piton into a fissure overhead, looped rope coils around his body and fastened himself to the piton.

Slung against the mountainside papoose-fashion, he tried to sleep off the melancholy that climbers feel as the solitary nights begin.

Snow fell all night, and landslides tumbled cabbage-size rocks past Walter's ledge. Stones bruised and pummeled him, and gashed his knapsack, but this time he did not give up.

At sunrise, Walter shook the icy crystals from his blue anorak, the thick, cotton jacket that he wore over his sweater. He stretched, then unfastened the ropes. Snow was still falling.

In Montenvers, Ceresa, Berardini and Géry began climbing back to the *Mer de Glace*. Later, from the Charpoua Refuge, they reported on the walkie-talkie that they saw Walter higher on the face, climbing steadily upward.

That day, Walter's climb was easy till he reached an icy corner he had to get around. Laboriously he chopped grips for his hands

---

' Slung against the mountainside, he tried to sleep off the

This is the hazardous route Bonatti planned to follow from Charpoua Refuge across the *Mer de Glace* and up to the peak of the *Petit Dru*.

and then his feet, working carefully so as not to slip off the wall.

Time sped. When he realised it was late in the afternoon, he was at the bottom of a 100-foot wall—as smooth as the side of the Washington Monument. He knew he had to scale it before dark, so he began pounding in courses of pitons, gradually hoisting himself up the slabs.

By the time dusk came, he had climbed to a point about 715 feet above the *Mer de Glace*. This may not sound high, but it was higher than any man had ever climbed before on the Wall of Hell.

Even so, there were still over 1,500 feet to go. He kept going until it was dark, then he flashed a weak signal back to the Charpoua Refuge.

"Everything is all right," he signalled.

He then tapped a piton into the mountainside and roped himself to it, falling asleep hanging over a 2,300-foot chasm.

It was 15 degrees below zero; but when he loosened his ropes in the morning he felt

rested. Above was the only route he could follow—a deep, ice-lined chimney.

He forced his body into the cut, raised his feet, slid his back up the icy wall and began chimneying. The ice stung the blisters in the palms of his hands. His back was stiff and sore. But he kept going; pausing to rest would cost strength, and relaxing would make him lose purchase, so that he'd plummet downward.

At 50 feet he found a small ledge and rested till his senses focused and his ears stopped pounding. No time for hunger. Time only to drag himself and his rucksack up through the chimney. He had gained only 250 feet that day.

After roping himself to the place where he would sleep, he opened his pack to eat. The bottle of rubbing alcohol had broken, ruining the bread and cheese. He'd already eaten the canned meat, so now there was no more food except the diluted brandy—and most of that was already gone.

(continued overleaf)

melancholy that climbers feel as the solitary nights begin '

THE SHEER FACE OF HELL

(continued)

As he fell asleep, again roped to the mountainside, a storm broke. Lightning crashed and flickered all around him. The anorak, damp when he'd slipped it on, was frozen stiff. The sky was black, and no lights were visible from the valley. His flashlight batteries were too weak to signal.

The following day dawned clear and cold. Through telescopes Montenvers' crowds picked out Walter's thick red socks and his blue anorak. Sometimes he'd disappear in a crevass, then reappear. Coldness stung the scratched, blistered palms of his leathery hands.

Towards afternoon, he began scaling the *Placche Rosse*—those reddish slabs that seem almost to lean outward from the mountainside. Pitons . . . wedges . . . snap-links . . . inch by inch upwards . . .

From their telescopes the watchers wondered where Walter got his stamina.

Walter roped himself to the mountain for another foodless night of sub-zero snow and rain. Now his flashlight worked dimly again and he signalled, "Everything well."

He spent his fourth night of painfully trying to sleep, hanging over the void—but within 1,000 feet of *Dru's* summit.

His fifth day dawned clear, blue, cold.

Hours to gain yards. The last 100 feet over those rocks were next to impossible.

Early afternoon. A small monoplane buzzed near him. At first he thought it was a passenger 'plane, but it hovered within a hundred feet, circled, then slid away on the *Petit Dru* updraft.

Bonatti was too busy climbing the deep crack to try to signal the pilot. The huge red stones were beating him. He climbed down from a dead-end vertical crack, rested his rucksack, and inched along a narrow shelf. A breeze could have blown him from the ledge.

Rounding the corner, he saw a solution— but a desperate one. Groping to the right along the rock wall, he drove a piton into a crack. Below the spike was a clean drop of thousands of feet. Walter gathered his gear for the next move.

Walter tied the end of the nylon rope to the piton; then lowered himself about 15 feet down the rope. Hanging in space, he made a sort of lasso with the other rope. There was nothing below him but misty air and a faraway valley.

A firm-looking rock crag jutted out above, maybe 20 feet to his right. He tried to lasso it. His rope missed. He tossed the lariat again—and missed again. Several more tries —his seventh or eighth perhaps—and the rope caught.

Again he jerked the lasso. It seemed to be secure. The crag protruded about 15 feet.

He planned to swing to a rock nearly 50 feet across the chasm to his right.

From the stronger telescopes in Montenvers people were terrified when they saw what Bonatti was going to do.

Clutching the lasso, Walter went back up the dangling rope. At the top he opened the snap-link carefully and worked the lasso through it. He closed the link over the pair of ropes. Next he untied the first line and hung it coiled across his chest. He was then hanging on the lasso that threaded through the snap-link.

Again he opened the link to pull the lasso free of the piton—then he took a deep breath and let go.

Like a pendulum he swung out across the gap, reaching out with one free hand. Arching toward the rock face, he grasped—and missed. He hadn't swung out far enough.

He floated back and lurched out a second time. Still not enough momentum.

He coasted back, then lurched again at the rope. That time he made it. He clawed at the rough rock wall and pulled his body onto it from the void.

His foothold firm, he whipped the slack lasso until its loops came free of the crag. After coiling in the rope, he rested till his giddiness left.

More chimneys and courses of pitons. At dusk not even sign of a ledge to rest on. So he spent his fifth night hanging on a rope sling—nothing supporting his feet or his gear, in space over a 3,600-foot abyss, held by a single 4-inch spike hammered only an inch into the mountainside!

Exhaustion, hunger and anxiety kept him from sleeping.

Daybreak. All Montenvers was watching Walter through telescopes. On the east face of *Dru,* the other three climbers tuned in their walkie-talkie at 8 a.m.

"Montenvers calling Rope Charpoua. Where are you?"

"We're on the *col* called Brèche," the voice of one of the climbers crackled. "Bonatti can't see the top yet. He's about 300 yards from it. He's higher than us, up in a corner hanging by a rope—over a 2,000-foot drop. We're in yelling distance. He says his hands are now completely raw."

The tiny transmitter clicked off.

Another transmission at 9 a.m.

"Rope Charpoua calling Montenvers. Bonatti is now in full sunlight and beginning to climb again—awfully slowly. He says he feels sure of himself, but we'll stay here awhile, and then go up to the top to try to lower him some food."

The next message was passed at 10 a.m.

"Montenvers calling Rope Charpoua. Any news?"

A pause, then came a frightening answer.

"He's climbing up an oblique chimney, but we don't know how he can get out. He's heading for a dead end. Have a look in your telescope, and tell us if he ought to exit toward the right or left."

Through the telescope, Roger Toussaint, a famous Alpine guide, could see Walter's caterpillar-like progress. The rock face looked like polished red marble. No cracks for pitons. Toussaint picked up the walkie-talkie.

"We can see him," he said. "Tell him we think he ought to turn left and try and pass over that west face. Tell him it looks like tough going, but better than climbing to the right."

At 10.20 a.m. another signal was sent.

"Rope Charpoua calling Montenvers. We passed on your message. Now we just hope he understood. We're leaving for the summit to lower ourselves to him on the double rope. He has only 150 feet to go, but you can see what it's like. We're worried. We'll call you at 2.30 this afternoon."

People on the hotel terrace fought for a squint through the telescope. Whenever Walter disappeared in chimneys, there were gasps. When he reappeared—relieved sighs.

The next message was passed at 2.30 p.m.

"Rope Charpoua calling Montenvers. We're at the top and can see Bonatti. He's in trouble. From now on we want you to call every half hour."

Walter was really in trouble. His hands were dark with blood that oozed and congealed in the torn palms. His face was stiff with exhaustion and tension. And there was that awful rock brow! It didn't look so bad through the telescopes, maybe, but it was the worst overhang he'd faced—jutting out nearly 15 feet.

He lashed together two sets of stirrups and began swinging outward on them, until he trapezed up and could grab the wind-polished edge of the overhang. The blood made his hands slippery.

Below was the drop, deeper than ever. He worked frantically, driving pitons, trying to hang onto the horizontally-looped ladder with his legs.

At 3.0 p.m. there came another signal.

"Montenvers calling Rope Charpoua. Come in Rope Charpoua!"

There was no answer.

Walter was still on the stirrups, driving in pitons. His torn hands stung and his knapsack tugged at his tired shoulders.

At 3.30 p.m.: "Montenvers calling . . ."

No answer again.

Bonatti was still on the stirrups, his body horizontal, trying to pull himself over the boulders as his pack still tried to tug him down. The pitons were hard to hold, and his hands were too weak to grip them. He dropped several and they tumbled lazily earthward.

"Montenvers calling Rope Charpoua. Come in, Rope Charpoua!"

Silence. That was at 4 o'clock.

Italian newspapers kept telephone lines open from Montenvers to Rome. In a Monza tenement Walter's widower-father, a labourer, sat tensely at a radio. Walter's mother had died, suddenly, in 1951, while listening to the news of his progress on the Grand Capucin, another treacherous Alpine wall.

On the Montenvers hotel terrace the Italian contingent kept their walkie-talkie turned on full blast—just in case.

At the telescope, a German guide suddenly yelped and threw his hat into the air. The Italians mobbed him, screaming questions, but they couldn't understand a word of his babble. One of them grabbed the telescope, his hands shaking as he tried to focus it at *Dru's* summit.

Finally it came clear—a tiny figure, arms raised, showed at the very top of *Dru*.

At 4.45, Rope Charpoua called. "This is Walter! I'm at the top of *Dru*! I'm very happy! Happy that I can eat and drink! I'm eating a chicken! I've got to eat! Call back at five o'clock."

At precisely 4.47 in the afternoon of August 22, 1955, Walter had closed the books on the last of the Alps' virgin climbs. He had accomplished the impossible.

Italians speak of him now as they once spoke of Caruso and Nuvolari. They tell you "Walter Bonatti has taken the mountain of his life."

Probably he will never try *Dru* again. But there are always other mountains. ▲▲▲

Bonatti (centre) with his two French mountaineering guides, Berardini and Géry.

The WIDE WORLD

THE MAGAZINE
FOR MEN
JANUARY, 1929
1/-

OVER NIAGARA IN A BALL!

Over Niagara Falls in a Rubber Ball!

By
Orrin E. Dunlap

of Niagara Falls, N.Y.

For many years, as regular readers are aware, Mr. Dunlap—the historian of Niagara Falls —has regularly described in our pages every sensational "stunt" performed at Niagara. The great cataract seems to have a fatal fascination for all sorts of foolhardy adventurers, many of whom have paid with their lives for rash attempts to brave its perils. Here is the story of the latest Niagara sensation—a young man's daring trip through the rapids and over the hundred-and-sixty-eight-foot Canadian Fall in a big rubber ball!

THERE are approximately one thousand eight hundred million human beings on the face of the globe, and of all these people Jean Albert Lussier is the only one who, at this writing, has gone over the Falls of Niagara and lives to tell the story of how it feels to be tossed and tumbled about in the rapids of the Upper Niagara River and then dropped over the brink of the mighty Horseshoe Fall into the gorge below. Nevertheless, Lussier was not the first person to perform this feat. That honour belongs to another—and a woman at that. She was Mrs. Annie Edson Taylor, who, on October 24th, 1901, startled the world by shooting the Horseshoe Fall of Niagara in a barrel and coming out alive.

Mrs. Taylor was forty-three years old on the day she made the trip, and she rode the waves of the rapids and plunged over

Fastening Lussier up inside his big rubber ball. The opening was sealed by means of two water-tight lids.

the great waterfall in a barrel of Kentucky oak that was four feet six inches high, twelve inches in diameter at the top, and twenty-eight inches in diameter at the bilge and bottom. A two-hundred-pound anvil was attached to the base of the barrel to keep it upright as it floated.

The barrel, with Mrs. Taylor inside, passed over the brink of the Fall at 4.23 p.m., and she was taken out at 4.40 p.m. She died penniless on April 29th, 1921, and is buried in Oakwood Cemetery, Niagara Falls, N.Y.

Just nine years and nine months after Mrs. Taylor conquered Niagara, "Bobby" Leach, born in Bristol, England, but who came to Niagara Falls from Watertown, N.Y., also went over the Horseshoe and came out alive. Leach made his voyage in a barrel of steel, which floated on its bilge, and the date of his trip was Tuesday, July 25th, 1911.

Leach crossed the brink at 3.10 p.m., and was picked up a few minutes later in the gorge below, in a state of utter collapse. His body was frightfully bruised, his jaw broken, and both knee-caps were smashed. He lay in a hospital for twenty-three weeks, but for all that he was delighted to have conquered Niagara. By the irony of fate Leach later slipped on a piece of orange peel in Christchurch, New Zealand, injuring one of his legs so badly that an operation was necessary, and he died there on April 28th, 1926.

Bristol, England, also contributed the next Falls adventurer in the person of a barber named Charles G. Stephens, aged fifty-eight, who sought to go over the cataract in a barrel of Russian oak, painted black and white in zebra stripes. It was on the morning of Sunday, July 11th, 1920, that Stephens and his barrel were towed out on the river from a point near Chippawa, Ontario, Stephens being the first man to start from the Dominion side of the stream.

Fearing that the authorities might seek to prevent the trip, the barber was cast adrift, at the mercy of the currents, at 8.10 a.m., and at 8.55 o'clock he swept over the brink. The barrel went to pieces, and the body of the unfortunate Stephens was never found. His right arm, torn off at the shoulder, was later picked up and identified by tattoo-marks.

In 1912–13 Jean Albert Lussier was working at St. Catharine's, Ontario, and saw Leach and his steel barrel. Lussier didn't think much of that barrel as a means of shooting the Falls; he conceived the idea

The sphere poised on the brink of the Horseshoe Fall, just before making the hundred-and-sixty-eight feet plunge to the river below.

he could make a much better and safer craft wherein to go over Niagara. The idea and the ambition grew with him.

In 1916 he was employed in a factory making rubber tyres for automobiles, and it occurred to him that a ball made of fabric and rubber, reinforced by steel strips, would withstand the buffetings of Niagara better than any barrel ever made. After sundry experiments he finally built a sphere of this kind in the works of the Mohawk Rubber Company at Akron, Ohio.

Lussier's ball weighed seven hundred and fifty-eight pounds, and was six feet in diameter. In colour it was bright red. There were two steel frames, an outer and an inner one, the latter surrounding the compartment in which Lussier rode. Outside each of the steel frames were thick layers of rubber and canvas, while between the outer and inner frames were thirty-two air-compartments. These " pockets " were designed to offset any bumps the ball might receive in its headlong journey through the upper rapids and over the Fall.

In the centre of the big globe was a compartment twenty-four inches round, widening out to thirty-six inches at the bottom to accommodate Lussier's feet. In this cavity Lussier rode on a seat, with fabric straps round his head, body, and legs, the straps about his legs having a downward pull so that he would not plunge on to his head if the ball turned over.

Surrounding him, when he made his voyage, were about a dozen cushions, so that he was apparently well protected from injury. On the so-called " bottom " of the ball a hundred-and-fifty-pound iron weight was placed to keep the sphere from rolling, if possible. Lussier claimed that the ball cost him between five and six thousand dollars, which seems a very large sum to pay for such a contrivance.

Previous to the trip it was announced that Lussier planned to have his strange craft dropped into the river from an aeroplane which would fly from a distant point in order that the authorities might have no chance to prevent the performance.

Actually, however, the ball was brought from Akron, Ohio, to Niagara Falls, N.Y., on a truck, and early on the afternoon of the appointed day it was placed in the river at La Salle, an up-river district about five miles from the Falls proper. From there the big red globe was towed by a launch out to the Canadian channel of the river. The Canadian side was selected because there the stream runs deeper than on the New York side, and to be set afloat in the Canadian channel meant a greater possibility of going over the Horseshoe Fall than the American Fall.

A trip over the latter would mean certain death, owing to the rocky " talus "

at the foot of the cataract. To succeed, the ball, with its human freight, must pass over the Horseshoe, and nearly in the centre of the brink at that, for there the emerald-green torrent plunges in great depth sheer to the river below.

It was no joy-ride " stunt " that Lussier was planning. Once set adrift, he was alone and completely helpless, at the mercy of the currents of a swift river that tosses madly over a full mile or more of dangerous reefs ere the brink of the Fall is reached.

Directly the ball was set free, no human agency could direct its course; the treacherous waters would hurl it onwards just as they chose, each minute rushing it closer to that awful drop of a hundred and sixty-eight feet into the gorge below. And then, unless the plunge took place within a very small area, the man inside the globe was going to inevitable destruction. Small wonder that the authorities do their best to discourage such foolhardy attempts!

All being in readiness, Lussier left the launch and clambered into the " passenger compartment " of the ball, in which he was doubly sealed by two lids in order to prevent leakage of water. Then the launch towed him farther out into the river and, reaching the danger-point for boats, set the globe adrift.

Meanwhile, on the New York side of the river, a vast multitude was celebrating Independence Day—a national holiday.

Lussier's ball floating out from the foot of the cataract. A boat is seen going out to tow it ashore.

Lussier being lifted out of the ball. He was somewhat dazed, and had sustained several slight injuries, but speedily recovered.

The city was crowded with visitors, and the stream of humanity found its way across to the Canadian side, so that thousands of people were sightseeing in the neighbourhood of the waterfalls and the gorge. When it was reported Lussier was coming downstream and going over the Fall, the riverbanks became black with great crowds, all anxious to witness this extra " thrill."

The launch hurried back to shore, and the big red ball rolled on with the current. Lussier's ambition was about to be gratified ; he was on his way to that terrific drop. The authorities were powerless to stop him now ! Every moment brought the ball nearer the Fall, and it was soon seen that it was behaving wonderfully well in the leaping waters. It was evident, too, that Lussier's luck was " in," for the sphere was heading to sweep over the brink at the point where the water runs deepest.

On past the reefs it voyaged safely ; then it passed into that beautiful stretch where the stream runs smoothly before plunging into the canyon. A minute later, exactly at 3·20 p.m., the ball swept over the brink of the Fall and dropped down, down, down, to the foam-lashed bosom of the river below.

The waiting thousands held their breath. Standing there in different countries, with an international border-line

between them, the people almost moaned in distress as the big globe tumbled in full view on that bright July day. Instantly every eye was strained to watch for it to emerge from beneath the mighty wall of water that rolled over the precipice.

Suddenly the ball bobbed into view again, and as it was seen to float away on the lower river everyone wondered if the daring fellow inside was still alive, or whether the tossing in the rapids and that terrific hundred-and-sixty-eight-foot drop over the cataract had battered the life out of him.

Up the river came the steamer *Maid-of-the-Mist*, laden with passengers clad in rubber coats as a protection from the spray. From the Canadian shore William (" Red ") Hill put out in a small row-boat, intent on the recovery of the ball. The current swept the big globe nearer and nearer, and soon Hill had attached a line to a wire handle on its side. With the ball in tow the boat made for the Canadian shore and effected a landing in front of the abutment of the upper arch bridge. Quickly the globe was slit open, and Lussier was found crouching in his compartment.

At first he appeared rather dazed, but speedily recovered in the fresh air. He was bleeding from wounds on his left temple, and there was a scratch on one arm, but otherwise he was quite uninjured ; he had made the trip over the Horseshoe in better condition than any of his predecessors. The ball itself, however, was badly battered, and its symmetry was completely gone, great dents appearing on all sides. Still, it was intact and had behaved well during the arduous trip, though somehow or other it had shipped about two gallons of water.

Lussier was taken from the globe at 3.50 o'clock, and after his slight injuries had been attended to he went aboard a small boat and was rowed to the Canadian *Maid-of-the-Mist* dock, a few hundred feet upstream. Here he ascended the inclined railway to the top of the bank, where he entered an automobile and was driven to the New York State side of the river. There he met several relatives, who were overjoyed at his success. Motion-pictures had been taken of his voyage and also of the work of building the ball, and other photographs were taken of his arrival and departure from his hotel.

Lussier was greatly elated at his success, especially as he had been a prisoner in his ball a much longer time than either Mrs. Taylor or " Bobby " Leach in their barrels.

At some point in the trip, it was discovered, three of the air-chambers in the ball were broken, and Lussier explained that this mishap caused the bruises on his temple. He claims to have made the drop over the Fall head-first, and says that when the sphere landed in the lower river it rebounded several times, giving him a most extraordinary sensation. The water immediately at the foot of the cataract is so surcharged with air that it lacks buoyancy, and so it may well have been there that the air-chambers collapsed.

" In twenty years' time, maybe," Lussier predicted, " people in search of a thrill will be making trips over the Horseshoe regularly. I shall make another trip myself—if I am paid for it. After my former experience I feel confident I can build a much better ball than the one I used."

Lussier's success apparently filled his brain with visions of limitless wealth. As he talked, he seemed to visualize streams of golden dollars flowing into his coffers. So did Annie Edson Taylor, but she went to a pauper's grave. " Bobby " Leach, too, was not without dreams of affluence, and chased the wealth he longed for nearly round the world, to die at last in a far-away country, among strangers. In an interview Lussier is quoted as saying that he wants three hundred thousand dollars and expenses to repeat his feat.

Now a dollar is appreciated just as highly at Niagara Falls as in any other part of the world. Three hundred thousand dollars is three hundred thousand dollars on both sides of the river, where the respective Governments maintain free parks, open to all mankind for ever, in order that the sublime spectacle of the Falls may be viewed without charge. Just how Lussier thinks anybody could possibly get an adequate return by investing a fortune in a repetition of his performance is difficult to understand.

People who live far away from Niagara Falls may imagine there is a speedy influx of wealth to the dare-devils who stage " stunts " of this kind, but it is not so. The writer has met practically all the men and women who have risked their lives in various ways at Niagara, but in not one single instance did any of them gain affluence, or even a moderate access of fortune.

These people come to Niagara, attempt their " stunts," and either lose their lives or succeed in accomplishing whatever foolhardy feat it is they set out to do. In the latter case, they come back to earth, so to

Lussier as he appeared after he left the ball.

speak, full of grandiose expectations that are never realized. In a few days—a very few days —they are practically forgotten, and before long someone else eclipses their performance.

Meanwhile the Falls remain, a permanent background to the fleeting notoriety that attends the rash folk attracted, mothlike, by the majestic cataract. Fools may come and fools may go, to paraphrase the poet, but Niagara rolls on for ever.

Travellers' Tales

Giant Clam Test

Hans Haas and his wife Lottie are famous for their underwater exploration and photography. They have successfully braved many of the traditional killers of the deep—sharks, rays, octopuses and others. In " Danger is Their Business " (Cassell 9s. 6d.), a book which dramatically describes the lives of people who dare death for a living, Marjorie and Edward Ward tell of an experiment which Haas carried out in order to test the reputed menace of giant clams :

"They are huge shell-fish weighing over 100 lb. and measuring up to six feet across. Haas [seen in our picture] had heard many gruesome stories of how divers had stepped unwittingly into the open jaws of these monsters, which had then closed on their legs in a vice-like grip from which no amount of struggling would free them.

"Haas found this hard to believe and determined to try an experiment. In a draper's shop in Cairns he managed to buy a plastic leg used for displaying nylon stockings. To strengthen it he filled it with plaster and took it with him on his next diving expedition. He found the clam again and pushed the leg into the open jaws. The great clam closed instantly. Haas began pulling on the leg. The harder he pulled the tighter the clam gripped. Then he left the leg for a few minutes and tried to take the clam unawares. But the moment he touched the leg again the clam tightened its grip. He tried prizing at the shell with a harpoon and hacking at the ' hinges ' of the immense shells. But nothing had the slightest effect. In the end he fastened ropes round the clam and hauled it and the leg up to the surface, where at last he was able to force it open."

A Fight With a Leopard.

By Ivan Calvin Waterbury.

The story of a terrible struggle—a death-wrestle between an unarmed man and an infuriated leopard. For the first time in the history of big-game hunting the combat terminated in favour of the man, who, although terribly wounded, left his opponent dead on the ground. How human muscle and pluck triumphed over brute force is graphically told in the narrative.

 URING the zoological expedition sent to Africa in 1896 by the Field Columbian Museum of Chicago, the taxidermist of that institution, Mr. C. E. Akeley, killed a leopard in fair fight, using no other weapons than his bare hands. This remarkable victory of human muscle and pluck over brute strength and ferocity was won in the hinterland of British Somaliland; and the way it happened was as follows.

While hunting antelopes alone in a sandhill district, Akeley shot a hyena and left it lying, for the time being, in a thicket that covered a steep-banked islet formed by a river and the forks of a brook. On returning to the same spot at sunset, he found that the carcass had been removed. The tracks leading away seemed to be those of a small lion, and the man eagerly followed the spoor along the half-dried brook-bed to the head of the island, hoping to get a shot at the king of beasts. He was taking chances in a most reckless fashion, for darkness would soon be upon him, and in his zeal he did not even pause to refill the magazine of his Mannlicher, in which only one cartridge remained. He merely carried an extra cartridge in his hand.

There was no need to follow the traces far. Suddenly Akeley heard a rustle, followed by a low growl, from the edge of the underwood at the top of the high bank opposite him. Looking across, he could dimly see the shadowy outline of some large animal, he could not tell what, crouching on the alert beside what he took to be the stolen carcass of his hyena. Promptly the taxidermist raised his rifle and fired at the pair of gleaming eyes, but the light was too poor for snap-shooting, and with another growl the creature sprang out of sight unwounded.

The next instant, to Akeley's surprise, the bushes parted and a full-grown leopard leaped down into the wash-out and turned to attack him. Akeley saw that no dread of firearms would keep the infuriated cat from making an onset, and he realized with alarm the predicament into which his own lack of caution had precipitated him. Only a score of yards of sand and a little pool separated him from the maddened beast, and his rifle was empty. In a twinkling he turned and ran, at the same time pushing the solitary cartridge he held into his gun. But it was too late to mend his mistake. A slight splash in the pool behind warned him that he was hotly pursued, and he turned and fired wildly just as the great cat flew viciously at his throat. His bullet shattered one of the brute's hind legs, but did not break the force of the animal's leap through the rifle-smoke. By

MR. C. E. AKELEY AND THE LEOPARD WITH WHICH HE HAD HIS TERRIBLE FIGHT FOR LIFE.
From a Photo. taken shortly after the encounter.

sheer luck, however, as the lifted rifle was knocked aside the breech of the weapon got in the way of the terrible jaws, which just missed the man's throat, but locked about his upper right arm in a grip of steel.

Akeley is anything but a powerful-looking man, being only of middle height and very slender, weighing barely a hundred and forty pounds. At that time, moreover, he was not in the best of health, but in spite of the shock of the leap and

before he could withdraw the limb from that living vice. Coat-sleeve and shirt-sleeve were torn off and remained in the gnashing, foaming mouth, but the naked, bleeding right arm, though somewhat numbed, was not disabled.

Throttling then with both hands, Akeley drove the madly-struggling creature over backwards. The hind-quarters turned in the fall, so that the sound hind leg became pressed against the soft ground. Still the choking continued, while the

"AS THE LIFTED RIFLE WAS KNOCKED ASIDE THE BREECH OF THE WEAPON GOT IN THE WAY OF THE TERRIBLE JAWS."

the pain of the bite, he kept his footing and seized the snarling leopard's throat with a left-handed grip, at the same time springing with his heavy boot upon the cat's sound hind leg. In his choking grasp, which momentarily tightened, the brute gasped, coughed, and gurgled, though it did not relax its hold, snapping and tearing the flesh frightfully all the way down the captive arm with its gleaming fangs. With the sustained strength of desperation—though every movement gave him exquisite torture—Akeley freed his arm little by little at each jerk of the champing, blood-flecked jaws, which bit him deeply in the biceps, the forearm, the wrist, and the hand,

deadly fore paws, armed with their terrible claws, were held wide apart and useless by the hunter's knees. With set teeth and staring eyes Akeley maintained his grip with both hands, conscious of only one thing—that if he relaxed his hold even for an instant he would be promptly torn to pieces. With panting breath and quivering muscles he held on, till he no longer felt on his face the hot, fetid breath. A few moments more and the lithe, contorted body gave a convulsive shudder and became limp.

But the life-and-death struggle was not yet over. Kneeling on the leopard's stomach and holding the fore legs helplessly apart with his

"AKELEY DROVE THE MADLY-STRUGGLING CREATURE BACKWARDS."

convulsively this way and that, the brute tried to reach the throttling hands with teeth that gleamed like curved ivory daggers.

Would this nightmare combat *never* end?—the tortured man asked himself. Feeling his over-taxed strength gradually giving out, he felt desperately for the brute's ribs with his knees, and one by one broke half-a-dozen of them. One rib, in snapping, pierced the leopard's lungs, and this hastened the end. The big cat's body grew limp again, the heart left off beating, and for the first time in history one of the great jungle felines succumbed in fair fight to a weaponless man.

Akeley rose to his feet exhausted, trembling, and bleeding, and scarcely able to realize how he had accomplished the feat. His wounds were terribly painful, and, under the circumstances, very dangerous. Yet, notwithstanding his exhaustion, he contrived to reach camp, though he had to leave his trophy to secure later. Dr. D. G. Elliot, commander of the expedition, undoubtedly saved him from death by immediately bathing the venomous wounds with diluted corrosive sublimate, binding them up next morning with antiseptics and oiled silk. The wounds were healed in a week, and the plucky taxidermist bagged many more specimens of big game during the same expedition; but for over a year his right arm pained him in performing certain processes of his work.

elbows, the gasping taxidermist, hardly able to comprehend his victory, loosened his grip on the animal's throat for a short breathing-spell. Almost immediately, however, he marked a flash of new light in the glaring golden eyes and felt the stir of returning energy through the dappled skin. Once more the hunter grabbed for the leopard's throat, only just in time, and the battle went on as before—man against beast, brain and muscle against brute force.

But for the softness of the sand the great cat could have wriggled its body free and brought to bear the deadly claws of the sound hind foot, which, as things were, only worked its way deeper into the yielding soil. In vain, writhing

FIELD COLUMBIAN MUSEUM
CHICAGO

9th April 1906

The above account is true and personally know.

D. G. Elliot

Commander of Field Museum
E. African Expedition

THE AUTHENTICATION FURNISHED BY DR. ELLIOT, THE LEADER OF THE EXPEDITION, AS TO THE TRUTH OF THIS STORY.

Four miles
above the earth
he ejected
from his plunging
jet fighter
—to find his
parachute
in shreds

I FELL 20,000 FEET

By Pilot Officer BRIAN CROSS

Royal Auxiliary Air Force

AT 10.01 on Sunday morning, 5th December, 1954, the voice of the ground controller crackled in my earphones, vectoring me and Pilot-Officer Bill Woollard, in our Royal Air Force Meteor turbo-jets, into target position.

We throttled eastward, encountered the two other Meteors that had been flying with us and were now our targets in the training exercise. It was just routine, 500-mile-an-hour Sunday flying. Weather clear. Slight ground haze. Mist over the English Channel.

Five days a week I repair telephones in London. I fly jets on weekends.

I'd been airborne 26 minutes, still felt my tanks heavy with jet fuel. We intercepted the targets and I made a clean run on them, then heeled into a dive.

My Meteor's Mach indicator was climbing. Mach-point-seven, it read —seven tenths the speed of sound.

I banked downward to around 28,000 feet. The cockpit was snug, pressurized for about 16,000 feet, and my summer-weight flying-suit and tropical helmet kept me warm enough. My head was clear, and the drop in altitude didn't make my eardrums pop.

Oxygen equipment working fine. Controls, positive. Everything okay.

In that dive I glanced at the Mach indicator just long enough to see it going up. Looking through *(continued overleaf)*

the windshield, I noticed the checkerboard fields coming toward me in a gentle spiral. Then a moment of panic—I was in a Mach dive, twisting earthward too quickly to pull out of the spin!

I knew I must put on the brakes in a hurry. I forced the lever, shoving open the air brakes. Then I waited for the comb-like flaps to buck against the rushing air. No time to look out at the wings. My speed would be lessened with a jolt.

I braced myself, but no jolt came.

Instead, the fields spun faster as the Mach indicator needle rose. I was spinning earthward at 560 miles an hour. It wouldn't take more than a few moments for me to bore a hole through the sky and then into some East Anglian sand flat.

Easing back the throttle, I centred the control stick, and waited for the Meteor to pull itself out of the spin—out of the Mach dive—back to level.

The Mach indicator needle climbed. Mach-seven-point-six . . . seven-eight . . . seven-nine. *Mach-eight.* Eight-tenths the speed of sound!

I felt an insistent shuddering, beginning at my wing tips and vibrating the cockpit as the ship found itself nearing the rim of the sound barrier—"Mach buffeting," we call it.

Fields below me were beginning to whirl like a roulette wheel. Through the thin ground-mist, visibility was about 15 miles. I could make out the metallic sea off to the side, green fields, the ochre, sandy coastline . . . all coming up to meet me.

'Nearly half the parachute was missing. Some of the shroud lines were torn and whole sections gone.'

My altimeter showed I had dropped from 28,000 to about 20,000 feet in seconds. The Mach indicator still kept forcing forward. No time to watch instruments. No time now to call ground control. No time to yell, "Mayday!", the airman's SOS.

I hit the canopy release and the plexiglass bubble blew away, letting in whistling, hissing air that blasted my face, tried to pull back my cloth helmet, tried to blow off my oxygen mask and headphones.

Everything happens in a hurry in a jet. I had taken about 20 precious seconds to get the cockpit cover free. Now I had to move quickly —had to get out while there was still time.

I reached for the ejection-seat handle overhead, but the cutting wind blew my hands away from the grip.

Carefully I made another, better-calculated pass with both hands, first along the sides of the cockpit, then in a sort of breast-stroke gesture upwards, trying to keep wrists and elbows together where they would be able to shield my chest against the next blast.

The wind tried to part my arms as I groped, my palms nearly level with my face, inching carefully toward the handle.

My gloved fingers clutched the icy metal bar. I tugged downward awkwardly, trying to lower the spring-loaded curtain that would protect my face and at the same time set off a charge that would catapult me, seat and all, clear of the 'plane.

I jerked hard but nothing happened. I tugged again. The second pull did it.

I felt a "kick in the pants" . . . and I shot out of the Meteor, helplessly somersaulting over and over.

Now everything would be automatic. The pilot 'chute would burst free, fill and then pull out the big silk. There would be a stiff jerk at my thighs, whipping and slamming at my shoulders, and the parachute would open. Then I would drift lazily to earth.

I let go of the ejection-seat bar and its wildly-flapping canvas tore past my face, ripping off my helmet and oxygen mask. The oxygen line and helmet flapped and dangled from a hook on my chest. The oxygen bottle was secure in the escape pack hanging behind me.

As the pilot seat automatically fell away from me I instinctively straightened my body.

I had no sensation of falling, no sensation of speed—only the wind. Too much wind. The jerk I awaited didn't come.

I looked up, expecting to see the glistening white umbrella unfurling high above me. Instead I saw only a trailing bunch of silk. The webbed canvas straps above me were busily twisting themselves together. The 'chute was streaming long, like a candle, above me. It hadn't opened out!

Hurtling downward, feet first, I was now scared—really scared. In training lectures on ejection-seat technique we had been told a little about what to do in cases like this. Remembering those lectures, I grasped the canvas risers and tried to untwist them. They were so snarled and bunched up that I could touch the shroud lines, which normally would have been far out of reach. Quickly I parted the nylon strands. At last the jolt came.

The harness jerked at my thighs, hit my shoulder blades. The parachute sorted itself out.

I looked at my chest and saw blood spots, probably from cuts on my brow and nose from the moment when the ejection-seat release curtain had snicked off my helmet and oxygen mask. Then I glanced down. My left shoe was gone, and a brown stain of blood covered half my sock. No time to worry about that.

I could feel the 'chute full of air. Below

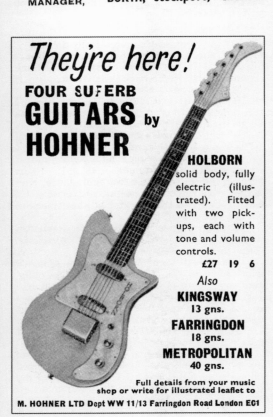
I FELL 20,000 FEET

me, the Meteor was corkscrewing, still in its earthward Mach dive. Maybe it would touch ground before me after all!

Then I glanced up—and I was horrified. Nearly half the parachute was missing! Some of the shroud lines were torn away and whole sections were gone.

About two-fifths of the parachute was just a gaping hole, grey sky showing through it.

I glanced down again, saw my Meteor spiralling still faster. I was glad to be out of it, even if I was swinging on only half a parachute.

My flying suit was too thin, but there wasn't time to be cold.

Again the air began whistling past me faster than I thought it should. Looking upward I could see why. The parachute was no longer a bulging canopy. The air had spilled out of it. It had "candled" again!

My body was gently twisting, and the limp parachute risers were braiding themselves, so I reached up to try to tug them apart.

Finally I let go of the risers, too weak to fight them any more.

Suddenly, my body snapped and jolted and I looked up to see that the parachute had straightened itself out, had billowed and was supporting me again.

I should have tried to steer my 'chute, but things were happening too quickly. I didn't want to spill out the little bit of precious air that supported me. Instead, I hung on, hoping the 'chute would do likewise.

Below me, the Meteor gently stopped revolving and flattened into a neat dive. The 'plane and I were both over the water by then. The ship levelled for a moment, then bellyflopped into the sea. The shock broke it to bits and the pieces sank, leaving only an oil slick and some struts showing above water.

Slowly my body started turning again, and the wind started rushing up more quickly. I glanced upward. The torn parachute had candled a third time!

Very soon I'd hit, I knew, with a spine-cracking thump. Maybe I should have unclipped my escape kit and let it fall into the water—anything to make myself lighter—but there was no time for that, no time for anything else.

As I spun, the risers and shrouds entangled themselves. I reached up and pulled outward at the rough canvas straps, trying desperately to force them apart. The parachute *had* to open.

I succeeded! The harness suddenly caught me and jerked at my tense muscles, as the parachute opened again.

I FELL 20,000 FEET

I tried to relax, tried to make myself limp for what I knew would be coming in seconds.

I stared upward, still fascinated by the shock-torn 'chute. The hole must have been ripped by the high speed of my dive when I baled out at around Mach-point-eight. No sheets of silk could be expected not to rupture with that much air blown into them all at once.

When things like this happen to you, they say, your whole life flashes past. My twenty-one years didn't. I was too preoccupied with the possibilities—every last one of them bad.

So far, I'd been lucky enough. In less than three minutes I'd lost a 'plane in a Mach dive, had my 'chute first tear, then refuse to open, then candle twice but reopen both times. Now I'd just break a couple of legs—maybe break my back, too. Still I was alive, and there was much to be said for that. When my 'chute hadn't opened the first time, I was all set to consider myself a complete write-off.

My body no longer spun. I was still glancing up worriedly at the 'chute when I felt something whisk across my back.

Suddenly, my view was blanked off by a wet, milky whiteness that foamed past my face, enveloped my body. My back was skidding across something gritty, something I couldn't identify.

Then I knew I was under water. I had landed!

Kicking, thrashing, I tried to swim upward. As my head popped above the water, my feet touched sand. I was offshore in just three feet of water—very icy water.

Something was dragging at my body, and I remembered that I hadn't had time to shed the parachute before I hit the water.

I punched the quick-release wheel, and the torn silk drifted away. There was a wooden tower jutting up from the water several hundred yards away, and I tried to move towards it.

My legs held me erect, but my left foot ached when I tried to wade on it. Soon I was shivering violently, and my teeth chattered uncontrollably.

I inflated the dinghy that had been in the escape kit strapped behind me, and climbed aboard—taking half the ocean with me.

I'd landed in three feet of water all right, but I was nearly a mile from shore.

The dinghy's baling bucket was collapsible; it folded up each time I tried to use it. For awhile, I used my hands to slosh water out of the yellow rubber boat, but I couldn't keep it up very long.

The socks and gloves in the escape kit were wet, but I put them on anyway.

If it was impossible to bale out the dinghies, we had been told, the next best thing would be to pull over the rubberized storm covers, and let body heat warm the water inside the raft.

Just as I was doing this, Bill Woollard's Meteor, the one that had been flying with me, swooped low.

To save his fuel, Bill had shut off one engine, but he must have had only about seventy gallons left by then—practically dry for a jet.

As Bill circled back to the RAF base at North Weald, I fired one of the six flares from the escape kit at him, and then I sat back and waited.

For a while, I drifted. I didn't have the energy to try to get anywhere in particular. I decided I must be somewhere off Shoeburyness, a coastal town forty miles from London.

In the haze overhead, I could hear the slow, uneven drone of a piston-engine 'plane. I fired a flare to show where I was, and an Albatross amphibian came down through the clouds—an American Air Force 'plane.

I lit another flare, and the 'plane headed back up through the mist. I fired a third flare, and then a fourth at it.

As the Albatross made another run over me, I fired my last flare.

Fifty yards from me, the amphibian touched water and taxied in my direction. Its left rear hatch was already open, and three airmen stood waiting.

One of the Yanks threw me a rope, but I missed it. The wind and current carried me around to the other side of the Albatross.

As the airmen fumbled to open the hatch on the 'plane's right, I began drifting toward the idling starboard propeller, which was about a foot above the water. The pilot looked out, saw me, and revved his engine. It blew me back toward the open hatch.

As the Albatross took off, I was bundled on a stretcher and given first aid. Eight minutes later, I was in an ambulance, and within fifty-three minutes of my ejection, I was in a bed in the hospital at the American air base at Manston.

Captain George C. Williams, Jr., navigator of the 9th Air-Sea Rescue Squadron Albatross, came to the hospital to see me.

There had been, Williams said, a heavy wind blowing out to sea all that morning. Had my 'chute opened immediately, and had I gone down normally, I'd have been blown so far out to sea that nobody'd ever have been able to spot my raft.

Ironically, the torn 'chute, though it nearly killed me, had saved my life!

No write-off, I had only slight cuts on my brow, nose and right knee, and a chipped bone in my right foot. I was away from my job for several weeks, but I was aloft in a new Meteor, doing my weekend stint, just two months later. ▲▲▲

JUNE 1962 2/-

WIDE WORLD

THE TRUE ADVENTURE MAGAZINE FOR MEN

TREASURE AT ARM'S LENGTH

SEE INSIDE

FOREWORD

Although it is more than twenty years ago, I still have a vivid recollection of sitting with my companions under a rock at 21,000 feet in the upper basin of the East Rongbuk Glacier, while Kempson read aloud from the diary of the man whose body we had just found on the moraine a few yards away. It had been lying there for more than a year, and now it was as if the man himself was speaking to us, revealing his secret thoughts. Outside our shelter there was complete silence as the snow fell in large fluffy flakes.

As I listened to the strange, intimate story, I soon had little doubt of the writer's sincerity. The motive behind his wild venture was unusual. It was obvious that he had little liking for the mountains, and he certainly claimed no spiritual uplift in their presence. At the same time I did not feel that he was striving for personal glorification. He believed that he was guided by some kind of divine inspiration to deliver a message to humanity. His implicit faith in his destiny seems to have been with him to the last. This being the case it is obviously futile to judge his project from a mountaineering standpoint. Nor have we any touchstone by which to judge his arrogance, so clearly revealed in his diary ; for this characteristic may well be essential to his kind of faith. We cannot fail to admire his courage.

ERIC SHIPTON

I'LL CLIMB

MAURICE WILSON was born in Bradford, on April 21, 1898. He was the youngest of three sons born to Mark and Sarah Wilson, and his childhood was happy, with a humdrum, unexciting sort of happiness.

The day after his eighteenth birthday he enlisted as a private in the 5th Battalion of the West Yorkshire Regiment. He was nominated for a commission and in October, 1917, went with his regiment to France as a second lieutenant. His regiment was plunged almost at once into the fourth battle of Ypres ; many of his friends were wounded and many killed.

For conspicuous gallantry in sticking to his machine-gun post during a heavy mortar attack, Wilson was awarded the Military Cross. But by the time his award came through, he was in Manchester, in the Western General Hospital. While leading an Allied counter-attack on the outskirts of Meteren a burst of bullets splayed across his left arm and chest, and he was carried, dangerously near to death, to an Advanced Casualty Station. For ten days he was too ill to move ; but his splendid physique pulled him through and he was eventually moved to Manchester.

Wilson's struggle back to health was a long and painful one. Indeed, his arm never properly healed and was to trouble him for the rest of his life—though he took great pains to conceal this and few people knew of the hours of torment it gave him.

Demobilized in July, 1919, Wilson returned to Bradford. He was a restless, unsettled and

64

A truly amazing record of magnificent courage, un-swerving resolution and tremendous endurance begins below. It is the story of Maurice Wilson, an amateur mountaineer with one purpose in life—to prove an ideal by climbing mighty Mount Everest alone. His left arm practically useless, his age, inexperience and indifferent health all against him, Wilson nevertheless would not be deterred. His epic story has no parallel in the history of mountaineering.

EVEREST ALONE!

MAURICE WILSON

By DENNIS ROBERTS

vaguely unhappy man. Life in Bradford did not satisfy him. He moved to London, and then to America and New Zealand, taking a bewildering variety of jobs, none of which particularly appealed to him. For ten years he wandered in search of contentment before returning to London where he hoped to start life anew.

But three months after his return from New Zealand, Wilson's health began suddenly to deteriorate. He lost weight and developed a racking cough. He took his troubles, not to a doctor, but to a faith healer. Treatment consisted, very simply, of two things only: faith and fasting. Wilson fasted for thirty-five days, drinking only small quantities of water. He followed the advice of the healer implicitly and within a couple of months was completely cured.

Once his fast was over, Wilson spent a couple of months recuperating in the Black Forest: here, in a little café in Freiburg, he came across, quite by chance, an old newspaper cutting of the 1924 expedition to Mount Everest; and this cutting set him thinking.

At this time, in the autumn of 1932, Wilson was feeling a new man, both physically and mentally. He had put on two stones within a couple of months, and he had lost his cough and his feeling of depression. He felt, literally, as though he had been born again. He was convinced, rightly or wrongly, that his recovery had been due to divine help. He had followed his mentor's instructions to the letter; he had fasted for thirty-five days then prayed to God to make him a new man. And

God, it seemed to him, had done exactly that.

Here, he was convinced, was a panacea for all the malaise of the world. Yet he knew very well that it was a panacea which the world would not readily accept. It was too unorthodox. He could proclaim his new-found faith in the press, from a pulpit or from a soap-box, and the world would dub him a crank. The only chance of making people listen to him was to give them some striking and sensational demonstration of the practical effectiveness of such beliefs.

Reading of the dangers and apparently insurmountable difficulties that had faced the mountaineers, Wilson asked himself if he truly believed that fasting and divine faith could accomplish *anything*. No sooner had he asked himself than he knew his belief was indeed pure and absolute. And he realized what he must do. *He resolved to climb Mount Everest alone!*

It was a fantastic idea, and in it were all the elements of tragedy. For Everest could not be climbed, by any man, alone; yet it was not in Wilson's nature ever to give up. He had made up his mind and nothing would stop him from making the attempt.

His first need, he realized, was to find out all he could about the mountain he was challenging; and in the next couple of months he studied every book and map on Everest that the London libraries could lend him.

From the accounts of earlier expeditions Wilson should have learned two lessons. Firstly, that a possible way to the summit via the East Rongbuk Glacier and the North Col did in fact exist; and, secondly, that to follow this route was beyond the capabilities of any single man, even a highly-skilled mountaineer. But of the two lessons, he learned only the first. Nor did the tragedy of the 1924 expedition appear to drive home the point that if the summit of Everest was beyond the reach of a party of highly skilled mountaineers, it was also beyond the reach of a lone, inexpert climber—no matter how great his courage, no matter how immovable his faith.

The accounts of the 1924 expedition were the last Wilson was to read about an actual attempt to climb Mount Everest, for eight years were to pass before the Dalai Lama gave permission for another expedition to pass through Tibet. He and his advisers deplored the disasters and the loss of life that had taken place in 1922 and 1924, and they returned to their traditional policy of isolation from the rest of the world.

PLAN TO CRASH-LAND

But in 1932 the Dalai Lama gave way before the friendly pressure brought to bear on him by the India Office and the British Political Agent in Sikkim, and gave permission for a fourth expedition to Everest. At once preparations were set under way to enable a party of British climbers to leave England early in 1933 under the leadership of Hugh Ruttledge. This party did, in fact, attempt Mount Everest the year before Wilson; but he never saw their reports or spoke to any of the members.

The information available at the time to Wilson was scanty and incomplete, but nevertheless, after reading the whole of the known literature on Everest, Wilson might well have come to the conclusion that in trying to climb the mountain alone he was attempting the impossible. But a full realization of the dangers and difficulties involved served only to increase his determination. "Nothing," he wrote, "can stop my trying to climb Mount Everest. Obviously I think I can do it, or I shouldn't be going to try."

His first practical problem was how to get within striking distance of his objective. This question Wilson solved in a typically forthright manner. "No strings of Sherpas and yaks for me," he told his friends. "No tiring myself out before I ever get there. How shall I manage it? I'll fly." The fact that he had never been up in an aeroplane before, let alone piloted one, did not seem to worry him!

"Suppose," he said to his friends, "I fly by myself to Everest, and crash-land on the lower slopes. Then it will be a straight, short climb to the top."

His friends pointed out that there were two small points he seemed to have overlooked: he couldn't fly and he couldn't climb.

Wilson smiled patiently. "I know," he said. "But I can learn."

*   *   *

The period between the two world wars forms a romantic era in the history of aviation. For these were the years when men and women unfettered the shackles which had so long bound them to the earth, and pitted their skill, courage and tenacity against a new element which they now challenged for the first time—the air. The decade 1925-35 was perhaps the golden age of aviation; for lone adventurers in these ten years blazed new routes around the globe. Frail machines quested the sky in far-flung corners of the world; many of them crashed in ocean or jungle or desert or mountain range; but many more reached their destination and names such as Jim Mollison, Jean Batten and Alan Cobham became household words.

Maurice Wilson had never flown before, but having set his heart on travelling to Everest by plane, he entered wholeheartedly into the spirit of men's new-born challenge to the air and quickly became an enthusiastic, if not very skilful, pilot. His first step was to buy a plane. He studied the reports of famous flights, he talked to pilots, and he visited the factories of the leading aircraft companies.

It was only after much careful thought that he decided which type of aircraft would be best suited to his purpose. It was a de Havilland Gipsy Moth that he eventually settled on, a biplane, with a 55-100 horsepower engine. He could not easily afford a new machine, so he decided to buy a second-hand one. He was a shrewd enough business man to make a good buy, and after answering several advertisements he finally purchased a 1930 Gipsy Moth, with the serial letters G-ABJC.

It was typical of Wilson that he bought the plane before he had learned to fly; an action which underlined both his determination and his egotistical self-assurance. A week after he took delivery of the Moth, Wilson joined the London Aero Club.

The Club in those days

The plane tore through a hedge, cartwheeled over and ended up on its nose.

had its headquarters at Stag Lane, one of the de Havilland aerodromes near Edgware, Middlesex. Here Wilson came, week after week, for his initial flying instruction. But before his lessons had even started he aroused the curiosity of the club members by painting the words " EVER-WREST " on the nose of his aircraft. When questioned, he gave a carefully prepared statement.

" I intend," he said, " to fly to the lower slopes of Everest; land there, probably at about 14,000 feet, and then continue on foot. I know I shall be taking a big chance, but I shall pray for a safe landing." The more experienced pilots of the club smiled pityingly; their new member was putting a good deal of faith in his machine, not to mention in his own unproved ability as a pilot.

The Chief Flying Instructor at Stag Lane, Nigel Tangye, had heard a good deal about Wilson, and he decided to take him on as one of his own pupils.

There quickly developed between instructor and pupil a very real friendship. Tangye realized, however, from their earliest flight together, that Wilson would never make a good pilot. Of all the qualities needed to fly a plane it soon became obvious to Tangye that his eccentric pupil possessed only two: courage and determination. Even during the first lesson Tangye could see that Wilson was going to be a problem child.

" No! No! No! " he cried. " Don't be so violent, man! Make your movements slowly and smoothly. Not like a butcher hacking up the scrag-end! "

Day after day, week after week, the same heartfelt plea rose into the sky above Stag Lane, as Wilson hurtled the unfortunate Tangye around the winter sky. Wilson's flying instruction proved nerve-racking for the instructor and costly for the pupil.

To qualify for his " A " Certificate, a pilot had only to complete three hours' solo flying, and an average pupil was ready to fly solo after eight or ten one-hour sessions. But Wilson flew with Tangye for more than nineteen hours before the latter could trust his pupil to

take up a plane alone. And even so, the first take-off and landing was a sorry affair, the plane first swinging out of wind and then coming down with a series of frog-like bounces.

"You want to fly to India," said Tangye, as ten minutes later they walked away from the hangars, "but you'll never do it unless you learn to handle your plane more gently."

Wilson's lips tightened. "I'll manage," he said. "I'll fly to India alone or die in the attempt."

That, thought Tangye, was more than probable.

But as the weeks went by and the bond of friendship, based on mutual respect, began to grow between them, Tangye tried his hardest to dissuade Wilson from his attempt on Everest. It was not so much that he disapproved of the idea; he simply thought, with some justification, that Wilson was hardly likely to reach India alive. To fly five thousand miles in an open biplane, over some of the most desolate country of the world, would be an achievement that any experienced pilot might be proud of. For an inexpert pilot with only a handful of solo flying hours, it seemed a venture that could end only in disaster.

The weeks lengthened into months before Wilson got his "A" Certificate. This was a step in the right direction, but it certainly did not mean that he was now an expert or even a competent pilot. This Wilson realized, and he made a determined effort to improve. His solo hours mounted rapidly. He took to arriving at Stag Lane only a little after dawn, and people living near the 'drome breakfasted to the sound of his Gipsy Moth circling erratically overhead.

Tangye made a last effort to dissuade Wilson from his flight, the details of which he was now starting to plan.

"I tell you," the instructor said, "you're taking on a job that's quite beyond you. Give it up before it's too late."

"That I'll never do!" cried Wilson defiantly, and with a breezy "Cheerio!" he was off across the tarmac, his hobnail boots clattering defiantly.

WILSON PREPARES

Wilson began to buy equipment for his days on the mountain. And the careful and methodical nature of his purchases showed that his assault was not the hastily conceived and ill-executed project that some were later to dub it. His tent and sleeping-bag, for example, were of the "improved" type, made specially for the Ruttledge expedition, which, incidentally, was now on its way to Everest. His clothing was light but warm. Two of his last purchases were a height recorder, which he said would provide proof of his ascent, and a light camera. The latter had an automatic shutter which when set would allow him fifteen seconds to move into the picture. By using this he hoped to photograph himself standing on the summit.

His attitude towards the use of oxygen was eminently sane. He had read about the difficulties in breathing experienced by members of

earlier expeditions, and he considered it possible that a man would not be able to breathe enough of the rarefied air at 29,000 feet to keep alive. He therefore decided to take oxygen with him, and had special lightweight equipment made which weighed under fourteen pounds.

"About oxygen," he wrote, "I simply don't know. I shan't use it unless I absolutely have to. But I'm taking it with me in case."

His preparations were by no means confined to flying lessons and the buying of equipment. He went into strict training. In his hobnail boots he walked, much to the amusement of the club members, round and round the perimeter of Stag Lane. He was never seen in their Club House.

"I don't need a drink," he told Tangye. "I'm an apple and nuts man!"

And he did indeed embark on a strict and lengthy diet.

ROCK-CLIMBING REHEARSAL

His training consisted in the main of long and vigorous walks. He walked several times from London to Bradford in considerably less than five days. He thought nothing of walking fifteen miles in a single evening.

In February he made a serious effort to learn to climb; but here his preparations fell pathetically short of what was obviously required. He went for five weeks to the Lake District and later to the Welsh Mountains; but he seems to have made no serious attempt to acquire even the fundamentals of a mountaineer's basic technique. He spent most of his time on long hikes, with a little screen scrambling and rock climbing thrown in. Even the most elementary principles of snow climbing—such as step-cutting and the use of crampons—were a closed book to him. He did a little rope work, of the variety used by a lone climber, but as he intended to make his assault alone, ropes, in the generally accepted rôle of safeguarding the members of a party, were obviously of no use to him.

March saw him back in London, making a few final modifications to his plane.

It was about this time that the Press began to take a serious interest in his approaching flight and longish articles about him and his fantastic quest began to appear almost daily in the national papers. Photographs of Wilson, always in hobnail boots, leaning nonchalantly against his "EVER-WREST" invariably went side by side with the articles.

Early in April he gave the Press something fresh to write about. Quite by chance he met one evening two reporters, coming out of the Tube at Piccadilly. They noticed he was limping, though very slightly.

"What have you been up to?" one of them asked.

"My limp?" said Wilson cheerfully. "I got that when I made my parachute jump."

"When was that?"

Wilson looked at his watch. "Not quite twenty minutes ago."

The reporters looked at each other. "And

Wilson stands proudly by his faithful Gipsy Moth, " EVER-WREST."

"How long do you plan to take over the flight?" Wilson was asked.

"Only a fortnight," he replied. "That'll be more than enough."

Mid-April saw him about to fly north to bid good-bye to his family; but he suddenly went down with tonsilitis. This was a sad blow to his plans; for he had hoped to reach Everest early in May and make his assault at once, before the monsoon broke at the end of the month. It looked now as though his attempt might have to be postponed for a whole year. Wilson, however, fasted and prayed and at the end of a week declared himself perfectly fit.

On Sunday, April 23rd, he made final plans for his departure the next day, and that morning took off from Stag Lane to fly to Bradford where his family were awaiting him to say good-bye.

It was during this flight, on the very eve of his departure, that the inevitable happened.

why," one of them asked, "did you make the jump?"

Wilson smiled. "Just to test my nerve," he said.

And there, as far as he was concerned, the matter ended. But a couple of days later he was warned by the Air Ministry against making unauthorized jumps over London.

The modifications to "EVER-WREST" took longer than Wilson had bargained for. The first necessity was for a special long-range fuel tank to be fitted into the passenger's cockpit. This was done at the de Havilland workshops. Then Wilson—who at least seemed to have a fair appreciation of his own ability in landing —thought that a heavier and stronger undercarriage ought to be fitted. At last the modifications were completed, the plane was thoroughly overhauled, and Wilson settled on a definite date for his departure—Friday, April 21st, his birthday.

He bought a series of large-scale maps covering his proposed route; and these he studied in detail, noting the danger areas and marking up the aerodromes at which he hoped to refuel.

It was a flight of some 5,000 miles, much of it over difficult terrain. For a man with fewer than two hundred hours of solo flying it seemed a highly dangerous and almost impossible venture.

When "EVER-WREST" took off late that Sunday morning from the aerodrome at Stag Lane, her four-cylinder engine seemed to be running well; but at three in the afternoon as the plane was approaching Brighouse, only a few miles from his destination, it began to cough and splutter. Wilson tried to gain height, but—typically—jerked the stick back too roughly and the plane stalled. "EVER-WREST" spun helplessly toward the Yorkshire moors.

By the time Wilson had brought her under control she was flying at less than 800 feet; then the engine stopped coughing and cut out completely. Wilson searched the moors anxiously for a place to try a forced-landing.

As luck would have it, a large field, with only a handful of cattle in it, was almost directly below him, and Wilson circled this as "EVER-WREST" rapidly lost height. His attempt at a forced-landing would have made Tangye's hair stand on end! Wilson miscalculated almost everything; he came in cross wind, and undershot the field by a good fifty yards. The wheels of "EVER-WREST" tore through a hedge, the plane cartwheeled over, and ended up on its nose in a small country lane.

Wilson was lucky not to be killed; but as chance would have it, he was not even scratched, and simply hung there upside-down suspended from his safety-harness, while he mentally assessed the damage to his plane. There he was found by a small boy who jumped off his bicycle and asked politely:

"Can I help you down, mister?"

He undid the safety belt and Wilson tumbled to the ground. He was still ruefully inspecting the damage when ten minutes later a Press photographer arrived. The newspapers next morning were full of pictures of Maurice Wilson standing, with apparent pride, beside his crashed plane.

That night " EVER-WREST " was hoisted on to a lorry and taken the two hundred miles to London ; she was in the de Havilland repair shop by 7 a.m. the next day. Here the patient and long-suffering Tangye inspected the damage, which was considerable. It would take at least three weeks, he said, to make her airworthy.

Wilson was bitterly disappointed, for this delay meant the almost certain postponement of his plans. But he decided to leave for India as soon as the plane was ready. Even though he might not be able to climb Everest that year, at least he would be on the spot and could do some useful reconnaissance.

In the meanwhile, the two Westland planes of the Houston Air Expedition had flown over Everest; and the land expedition led by Hugh Ruttledge had established its base camp. Wilson watched anxiously as the assault on the mountain reached its climax. It would steal much of his thunder if Ruttledge met with success. But, judging by the reports that came through, Ruttledge was progressing only very slowly in the face of appalling difficulties.

At last " EVER-WREST " was ready, and a new departure date was fixed; Sunday, May 21st.

Somewhat belated efforts to stop the flight were made at the last minute by the Air Ministry.

Wilson was disconcerted, for he realized that without official co-operation the hazards of his flight would be substantially increased; but he had no intention of giving up his plans.

" The gloves are off," he told reporters. " I'm going on as planned. Stop me? They haven't got a chance ! "

A last-minute telegram forbidding his flight he tore up.

* * *

Sunday, May 21st, was cold but fine. Soon the sun shone brightly out of a sky that was clear and azure-blue. It was a perfect day for flying.

It was not an auspicious take-off. The crowd clustered along the tarmac were horrified to see " EVER-WREST " hurtling across the airfield not up-wind but down. In the excitement of what should have been a moving and dramatic moment, Wilson had forgotten one of the basic rules of flying. He tried to take off with the wind behind him. The plane gathered speed, but it seemed an age before the tail lifted. Even then the Moth was practically on the airfield perimeter before it became airborne. But at last it rose into the air, missed a hedge by less than a couple of feet, and then climbed slowly to 2,000 feet. Then it headed south-south-east, into the morning sun. Gradually it dwindled in size until it became a mere pin-point in the bright morning sky. At last it disappeared.

The crowd on Stag Lane airfield slowly broke up. Many of them had an uneasy feeling that they would never see Wilson again.

Wilson's flight to India was a minor epic in the history of aviation; a feat all the more remarkable because it was carried out not with the co-operation of the authorities but in the face of their every effort to stop him.

It is difficult for us today to realize that only some twenty-five years ago to fly solo to India was a considerable achievement. To see Wilson's flight in its true perspective we must be able to picture both his plane and the meagre facilities for long-distance flying that were then in existence.

His aircraft was a light two-seater, the passenger's cockpit being fitted with a twenty-gallon petrol tank and the pilot's cockpit being open. Its wing span was only thirty feet, and its cruising speed a little over eighty-five miles per hour. The range—without the extra fuel tanks—was slightly less than four hundred miles; its endurance—again without the extra tanks—was considerably less than five hours.

These figures could of course be improved on by a careful and skilful pilot, using extra tanks and taking advantage of local conditions. But, even so, few men would have cared to fly the Moth for distances of over five hundred miles or for longer than six hours.

And if Wilson's aircraft seems to our modern eyes a frail and primitive machine, then the conditions under which he flew it must seem even more archaic. For the vast and complex organization now known loosely as "flying control" was practically non-existent in 1933. The use of radio, the benefit of accurate weather forecasts, and the thousand-and-one aids to bad-weather flying that pilots now take for granted, none of these could come to Maurice Wilson's aid.

Another benefit to modern pilots that was not available to Wilson is the system of servicing and refuelling that now functions automatically on most aerodromes. In Wilson's day the number of airports at which a plane could undergo routine inspection and overhaul was strictly limited; and the fact that "EVER-WREST" received only two such inspections during five thousand miles added much to the danger of Wilson's flight; and the petrol he tipped into the long-suffering plane often came out of rusty old containers, nor was it always of a sufficiently high octane.

During most of Wilson's flight then, we must picture him muffled up in the cramped and open cockpit of "EVER-WREST," listening anxiously to a never-too-happy engine-beat, steering a rough compass course and peering doubtfully at the unfamiliar terrain that, mile after mile, fanned out in front of him.

The early phases of the flight were comparatively uneventful and it was not until he touched down on the sunbaked landing strip at Tunis that his troubles really began.

He found the facilities for refuelling were not to his liking at Tunis. Curiously enough, although the airstrip was quite a large one, he had difficulty in finding anyone who spoke English and to whom he could explain his needs. He therefore took off at once and headed north-west for Bizerta, only a few miles distant, where a larger airstrip had recently been built. He touched down safely, if not very expertly, and taxied over to the dispersal point.

As he clambered out of "EVER-WREST," a police car came racing across the 'drome and pulled up beside him in a cloud of dust. Three armed policemen tumbled out, told Wilson he was under arrest and pushed him into the back of their car. They drove in silence to the police station. Here Wilson waited for half an hour; then the same three policemen came in, told him to get into the car again and drove him back to "EVER-WREST."

"We are sorry," said one of them, "but you are not permitted to stay here."

The armed police grabbed
him and pushed him to-
wards their car.

"Suits me," said Wilson, "I never intended to stay."

"It would have saved us much unnecessary trouble," said the man coldly, "if you had told us that before."

It seemed pointless to argue.

"Can I refuel my plane?" asked Wilson mildly.

"No!" said the policeman, "you may not."

Wilson realized that any argument would probably land him in a Bizerta cell, so he clambered into his plane, returned to Tunis, refuelled "Ever Wrest" himself from a stock of rather rusty-looking drums and set course, with considerable misgivings, along the Tunisian shore.

The north coast of Africa is one of the bleakest, most barren areas of the world; mile after mile of monotonous desert, with little outcrops of rocks, occasional patches of scrub, and vast areas of drab, colourless sand. For long distances it is quite waterless and quite uninhabited. A forced landing here would have meant almost certain death, and Wilson listened with more than usual anxiety to the steady engine-beat of his Moth. It sounded, at first, reassuringly smooth. But after he had left Gabes some dozen miles astern and was nearing the Libyan border, it began to roughen and cough; soon a violent knocking began to jar through the whole plane.

Wilson quickly throttled back, turned through 180°, and, slowly losing height, headed back for Gabes. He landed safely, and as he was taxying across the airstrip, his engine gave a final splutter and cut.

"Your fuel had water in it!" a mechanic later told him. "You're lucky to be alive."

The rest of his flight over Africa was monotonous, but mercifully uneventful.

He landed at Cairo exactly a week after leaving Stag Lane. He was right on schedule.

"So far, so good," he wrote in a letter home. But his real test was still to come.

Wilson had been told, when he first worked out his route, that he would need a permit to fly over Persian territory. He had applied for this permit, and five weeks before his departure from Stag Lane he was officially notified that it had come through. The permit would, he was told, be waiting for him in Cairo. But when, from Cairo airport, he telephoned the British Legation to ask where he should pick up the document he received an unpleasant surprise.

The phone was first answered by a clerk who seemed to know all about his inquiry.

"Oh yes, Mr. Wilson," came the reassuring words, "I think there's something here for you."

Then suddenly the line went dead, and when Wilson was re-connected it was to an older man that he spoke.

"I'm sorry, old man," he was told, "I'm afraid there's no permit for you here. If there's any way I can help," the voice added sympathetically, "just let me know."

This was a set-back Wilson had never bargained for. He spent twenty-four hours in Cairo, being passed on from one government department to the next. He tried to be reasonable, he tried to bluster, but the result was always the same evasive answer, and the suggestion that some other official might be in a better position to help him.

It came to him that the disappearance of his permit might well be a deliberate attempt to halt his progress. Certain government departments might, he knew, be more than a little embarrassed were he to arrive suddenly in India; they might imagine that by withholding his Persian permit they could stop him.

But when Wilson had told reporters, "Stop me? They haven't got a chance!" his boast had been no idle one. He began to plan an alternative route, though a glance at the map will show that this was no easy task; for the six hundred thousand square miles of Persian territory lay sprawled directly across his route; to skirt them to the north he would have to fly over the Caspian Sea and the towering Elburz Mountains, while to the south lay one of the hottest and most desolate areas of the world—the Persian Gulf and the East Arabian desert.

He decided he would push on to

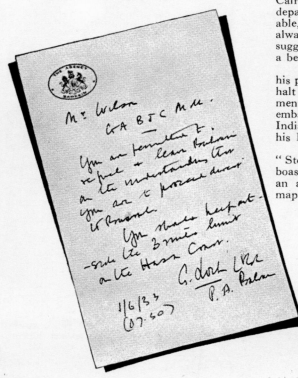

This was the vital fuel chit which enabled Wilson to resume his flight from Bahrein after he had run into trouble with the authorities.

The forbidding mountainous coast of the Persian Gulf, which the lone aviator skirted on his flight from Bahrein to India.

Baghdad, close to the Persian border, and there try again to find the mislaid permit, though he felt certain in his own mind that it was languishing—and not by accident—in some official's pigeon-hole.

At the Cairo airport "EVER-WREST" was given a thorough inspection and servicing—her last for some months—then Wilson flew the thousand-odd miles to Baghdad in a single day, with brief calls at Suez, Gaza, Bethlehem and Gadda *en route*. The last part of his journey, across the Trans-Jordan plateau, was particularly difficult; mile after mile the desert upland stretched out before him, with scarcely a single distinguishing feature; but Wilson's compass flying was, by this time, extremely accurate and he arrived safely at Baghdad half an hour before sunset.

Here he again made inquiries about his permit, and when it became obvious that this would not be forthcoming, tried to obtain a fresh one. But it soon became clear that permission to fly over Persia would never be given. If he landed there, even to refuel, without a permit, he would be arrested; so there was only one thing to do; change his route and fly round the formidable barrier.

His first necessity was maps, and he soon found that these were about the only thing in Baghdad it was almost impossible to buy! He eventually ran to earth a tattered school atlas and a survey sheet for the north-western section of the Persian Gulf. He worked out that Baghdad to Basra was three hundred miles, and Basra to the Island of Bahrein (a British Protectorate in the Persian Gulf) four hundred miles. Each of these "legs" was of quite a

reasonable length, and his spirits rose. Then, almost by chance, he heard that the airstrip at Basra was closed.

He was faced now by a flight of seven hundred miles, a distance very close to his plane's maximum range, and the second part of it over some of the most desolate country in the world. And for the last two hundred miles he had no map. A less courageous man would probably have turned back; but Wilson was now to show that streak of obstinate courage—some would call it rash stupidity—that was later to reach its full flowering on the upper slopes of Everest.

He took off from Baghdad and headed south-south-east. If he lost his way, even for twenty minutes, he would be faced with the prospect of an unpleasant, blistering death on the Persian shore.

Wilson worked out that the flight would take a little over nine hours; he therefore made an early start and was airborne at 7.30 a.m., less than an hour after sunrise. His track at first was easy to keep to, for it criss-crossed over the loops of the Tigris flood plain. Beneath him stretched a maze of canals and irrigated paddy fields, and away to starboard the sun glinted dully on the slow-moving River Euphrates. But after about a hundred miles the Tigris wound away to the left and the Euphrates to the right, and Wilson felt very much alone.

Soon he passed over the ruins of Narfer, on the fringe of Lake Hor-al-Afaq, and he realized he had drifted a little off course. He checked his compass and altered course 5° to port; and soon the great swamp of the Basra delta fanned out before him; an hour later he could see, far ahead, the sheen of sunlight on the Persian Gulf. He passed over Basra at eleven-twenty and knew that he was not yet half-way to the Island of Bahrein.

Over the shore of the Gulf the heat struck him like the banked-up flames of a blast furnace. His face, already tanned a deep bronze, now seamed into tiny painful cracks; and soon the golden shore line began to dance with fantastic mirages. Hour after hour he flew on, twelve miles off-shore and parallel to the Arabian Desert. The sun beat down, searing into his eyes and sending dull shafts of pain across the back of his neck. The water was a dull metallic blue; utterly without movement, utterly without trace of life; it lay as if ironed flat by the molten heat waves of the sun.

PETROL REFUSED

It was like a journey without end; and as the seventh hour passed slowly into the eighth, Wilson felt himself becoming light-headed with fatigue. Then, after eight-and-a-half hours' flying, he saw a faint shadow, very far ahead, darken the waters of the Gulf; and twenty minutes later he landed on Bahrein's newly-built and sun-drenched airstrip.

He staggered to bed at once with a splitting headache, but told the mechanics to refuel his plane that evening.

" I'm taking off again," he said, " at dawn."

Wilson had yet to learn that the arm of Authority is long. The next morning his fuel tanks were still empty and he was told that he had been refused petrol on the instructions of the British Consul.

With some justification Wilson felt that the authorities had over-reached themselves. His plane was airworthy and his pilot's certificate in order. He had, in the first instance, asked for all the necessary permits for his flight and had been told officially that these would be available. When one permit had failed to materialize as promised, he had, at considerable personal risk, flown by an alternative route. He had committed no crime and had broken no law. What justification, he asked, had the airport authorities for refusing him petrol? Did they expect him and his plane to stay stranded on Bahrein for ever?

Getting a good deal of sympathy, but no petrol, at the airport, Wilson called on the British Consulate. Here an official told him that he was forbidden to continue his flight since he had no permit to fly over Persian territory.

" But I haven't flown over Persian territory," Wilson pointed out. " Nor do I intend to!"

The official smiled suavely. " What type of plane are you flying, Mr. Wilson? " he asked.

" A Gipsy Moth."

" And what is the maximum range of this particular plane? "

" About seven hundred and fifty miles."

" Exactly, Mr. Wilson! Apart from Baghdad, where you've just come from, there is no airstrip within seven hundred and fifty miles of Bahrein that is not in Persian territory. We know, you see, where you must be heading."

Wilson threw up his hands in despair. " Can I take a look at your map? " he finally asked.

" With pleasure."

Wilson studied the large-scale map of the Persian Gulf that hung on the office wall; he memorized its scale and its details, while the official, smiling smugly, leant over his shoulder. As he turned away Wilson jotted down half-a-dozen figures on the cuff of his khaki shirt. An idea began to form in his mind.

Now Wilson was not by nature a deceitful man. But neither was he a man to lay down meekly under what he thought to be injustice. Rightly or wrongly, he thought that the authorities were treating him unfairly—" They tried," he wrote later to Enid Evans, " to do the dirty on me "—and he considered he had every justification for trying to outwit them. With a show of resignation he said he would accept the official's ruling. He asked him his advice and the two men, that afternoon, went out together for tea.

" What do you think I should do? " Wilson asked.

" If I were you," the reply came quickly, " I'd fly to Bushire—that's the nearest Persian drome. You could land and ask them for a permit there."

Wilson hid his anger. He knew very well that once he landed in Persia, with the permit not actually in his possession, " EVER-WREST " would be impounded and he himself imprisoned.

" I suppose you're right," he said with a smile. " Will you write me out a fuel chit? "

" Yes, of course, old man. Call in to-morrow for it."

" And perhaps you'd loan me some maps? "

" Can't let you take 'em away. Why not make copies? "

" That would do fine."

VITAL PERMIT

Next morning Wilson called early at the Consulate and an official wrote out the following chit:

MR. WILSON   G-ABJC   MOTH

You are permitted to refuel and leave Bahrein on the understanding that you proceed direct to Bushire.

You should keep outside the three-mile limit of the Hasa Coast.

P. A. Bahrein.

And while this was being written, Wilson made hurried notes from the map that hung on the Consulate wall. It was a large map and extended westward into Iran and eastward into Baluchistan. The official failed to notice that Wilson took most of his details from the extreme south-eastern corner.

Once he had the fuel chit, Wilson hurried back to the 'drome, and an hour later, at a little after 10 a.m., he was ready to leave. The official was there to see him off.

I'LL CLIMB EVEREST ALONE!

" Bye-bye, old man," he called out as Wilson taxied past him.

Wilson wished he could have seen the official's face as, once he was airborne, he turned the nose of his plane, not northward for Bushire, but due east for Baluchistan and Everest.

And so began the last and most amazing stage of his flight to the borders of India. While in the Consulate, Wilson had noticed on the wall-map that a newly-built airstrip was marked at Gwadar, a small Baluchistan town a few miles beyond the Persian frontier. He had jotted down on his cuff the scale of the map, and later he worked out that Gwadar was a little less than eight hundred miles from Bahrein—only just beyond the Moth's effective range.

He had no map; the track he would have to fly along lay almost entirely over the sea and out of sight of land; and if—as seemed very probable—he ran out of petrol and crashed, there would be little chance of his survival.

Wilson decided to take the risk.

He took his petrol permit to the airstrip, and while the plane was being refuelled he talked one of the native mechanics into selling him a small extra drum which he hid in" EVER-WREST'S " front storage locker. Then he took off.

The distance he had to cover was in fact seven hundred and seventy miles, the exact range of " EVER-WREST " taking her extra fuel drum into account. There was no room for the slightest margin of error.

Wilson flew almost due east. For nearly five hours, out of sight of land, he flew over the burnished waters of the Persian Gulf. He saw nothing, except once a handful of native dhows, apparently becalmed on the glass-like sea. Hour after hour he flew on.

Suddenly, for no apparent reason, the engine began to cough, then it cut out completely. Wilson was flying at two thousand feet. His mind flashed back to his engine failure in England; the fields of Yorkshire had been beneath him then, but now it was towards the vast emptiness of the sea that his plane began to fall. He checked his fuel-cock and engine switches; then began to carry out the drill for restarting an engine at height.

Already he was down to fifteen hundred feet. He put the nose still further down. The wind sighed through the struts, and as, for the first time, he pulled " EVER-WREST " out of her dive, the engine gave a single staccato cough, then again there was silence.

It seemed that only a miracle could save him. He was now down to less than one thousand feet. For what he knew would be his last attempt, he pushed the nose down .

(To be continued)

MAN AND HIS NEEDS

A MONTHLY CAUSERIE OF MATTERS CONCERNING MEN

By *The Captain*

BELL CRISIS

The old saying about shoemakers' children is probably a basic truth, for although I've been recommending what I believe to be modern and sensible products for years, it took a recent crisis at home to make me do something intelligent about a long-standing nuisance.

Ever since we've occupied our present house, the bells—front-door and side-door—have been on the mains-fed circuit.

This has meant that the same bell, in the centre of the house, rings when either bell-push is used.

Therefore, no one indoors knows whether the caller is waiting at the front door, or at the side door, which happens to be some distance from the front door. The waste of time and annoyance that this has caused hardly bears thinking about.

However, one morning the postman had to wait for a reply, because somebody had insufficiently stamped a letter. He rang—and the bell went on ringing indefinitely. Eventually, I stopped it by taking out the fuse for the bell circuit.

Later, the local electrician arrived. Nothing was wrong with either bell-push, or with the bell itself. Lengthy research proceeded, and eventually the gloomy verdict was reached. Some-

where in the internal reaches of the bell circuit, wires that shouldn't touch were in permanent union, and the whole circuit needed re-wiring !

This was something to be feared, of course. Just where in the walls or under the floor the bell circuit ran, was unknown. Equally unknown was the amount of damage to decorations that re-wiring would cause. One part of the house likely to be affected had just been redecorated !

I am ashamed to reveal that it took me quite a time to think out the obvious and simple solution—to abandon a doorbell system on the mains, and to have independent bells on each door.

Within 24 hours, I had had a battery-operated chiming bell fitted to the front-door, and a wind-up mechanical bell fitted to the side-door. The original front-door bell push still operates the new bell there. Thus, there was no need to re-wire, and no longer any uncertainty about which bell is being rung—and the whole job had cost under 40s.

SOCKLESS READERS

When I wrote about socks a few months ago I put quite a lot of business in the way of the G.P.O. WIDE WORLD readers seem to have a lot of ideas about socks, and I shall henceforth remember that this is a specially controversial item in men's clothing.

The most remarkable contribution to the socks post-bag was a letter from J. Irvine, of

Liverpool, who disposes of socks altogether. He tells me that the best advice I can give is to tell readers "to give up wearing these atrocities."

This reader buys hand-made, leather-lined boots; when they are new, he rubs a little hard soap on his feet and this leads to a high polish inside the boots which, he says, is retained until they wear out. What he saves on socks pays for the boots!

LADDER SAFETY

Having once been the witness of an accident with a ladder—as a result of which the unfortunate victim will always be lame—I may be more conscious than the average man of the danger of ladder-slip, but ladders can, and do, slip. A new device for increasing the security of the long, single ladder, i.e., not a pair of step-ladders, is, therefore, well worth the considera-tion of anybody who often uses one.

It is a ladder brace that hooks firmly on to the fifth or sixth rung of the ladder. Not only does the brace help to obviate the risk of ladder-slip, but it enables the ladder to be used at sharper working angles without increasing the risk of slip. The cost is 52s.

ANKLE DEEP IN EASE

The sports outfitter Lillywhites offers the very thing for warmth and comfort at the end of the day's sport—or work.

Enjoying the name of Slipper-sox, it is snugly-fitting footwear, comprising chrome leather soles and sock-like uppers.

These woollen "tops"—hand-knitted—feature bright multi-colours that will happily grace any foot and hearthrug during the winter months. Even the proudest dog-lover will be reluctant to trust his pet with these slippers of ease, which cost only 25s. 6d. per pair.

SHIRTS, CASUALLY

Coming back to clothes, I've been particu-larly interested in the Italian-designed sports-shirts made by "Mentor," which has intro-duced the "T.T. Club" casual sports shirt this year. It has a one-piece front that buttons neatly just below the open collar-neck, it hangs superbly, and is available in a variety of colours and check patterns. Sleeves can be long or short—the fabric is Sanforized cotton. For the younger man—and the not too conservative older man as well—a sports shirt that combines comfort with fashion. Unusual (at present) without looking outlandish.

EXHAUSTIVE CLEANER

A non-electric vacuum cleaner for cars should appeal to motorists. It works off the exhaust pipe on the venturi principle. A T-piece connection is made with the open end of the exhaust and the outgoing gas stream creates a suction in the attached hose.

The new cleaner will fit all diameters of exhaust pipe and has a twelve-foot hose. The extractor will remove all dust and even cigarette ends and gravel, and is particularly effective in reaching those normally inaccessible areas of a car's interior. Extra lengths of connecting hose can be supplied if required.

The price—£3—seems quite reasonable and I shall be happy to supply the makers' name and address.

Address all communications for this department to "The Captain," c/o THE WIDE WORLD MAGAZINE, *Strand, London, and send stamp if a reply is required.*

" I'LL CLIMB EVEREST ALONE "

Part II

In a fantastic attempt to conquer mighty Everest alone, Maurice Wilson set out from England in a tiny aircraft which he planned to crash-land on the mountain's lower slopes. After a hazardous and nerve-racking solo flight he reached Bahrein, refuelled and took off for India. Over the Persian Gulf his engine failed and he found himself plunging towards the burnished waters below. Only a miracle, it seemed, could save him. . . .

DESCENT FROM DANGER

By DENNIS ROBERTS

THE tiny plane plummetted towards the vast expanse of sea as Wilson wrestled with the controls. He heaved back the stick in a last effort to restart the engine, less than a hundred and fifty feet from the ocean and death. The plane came out of the dive, the engine coughed once, then twice, then to Wilson's immense relief, surged into life again. EVER-WREST skimmed low over the water, then rose in a steady climb towards the safety of the sky.

"I prayed," Wilson afterwards wrote, "and my prayer was answered."

After a little over five hours he saw a narrow rock of low-lying land jutting out across his path. Wilson sighed with relief. It was the Ras-el-Jebe peninsula, which divides the Gulf of Persia from the Gulf of Oman. Here he was able to check both his track and the progress he was making. He found he was exactly on course, but ten minutes behind schedule. Doggedly he pushed on. Soon, once again, he was out of sight of land.

He was flying over the Indian Ocean now, his course very gradually converging with the south-east Persian shore; soon he saw the shadow of its outline, fifty miles distant on his port bow.

After seven hours in the air Wilson began to suffer agonies from cramp. He was a big man and EVER-WREST'S cockpit was small. He could not stretch out his legs to ease the pain without putting pressure on the rudder and swinging EVER-WREST off course. Soon the sweat of his agony was added to the heat sweat which had already soaked his khaki shirt and shorts. After a little the pain wore off, but Wilson was left exhausted.

After eight hours he would have welcomed back the cramp to overcome his utter weariness. He had to fight now against a terrible drowsiness that gradually seeped into him. Several times his eyes closed, and he nodded off at the controls, and EVER-WREST veered off course. Once he pulled her out of a screaming dive less than two hundred feet above the sea.

After nine hours he could see ahead of him the grey haze of impending night. Darkness falls quickly in the tropics, and Wilson knew that yet another hazard would soon be threatening him. He checked his petrol and realized there was very little left.

Then, after nine hours and ten minutes in the air, he saw fanning out ahead the coast of India. He flew low over the mangrove and paddy fields, and twenty minutes later saw the white buildings of Gwadar airstrip, outlined by long shadows, standing like a mirage in the path of the setting sun.

As he came in to land his engine began to cough. There was not enough petrol in his tank to cover an upended sixpence, and ten minutes later it was quite dark.

* * *

It had taken Wilson a little under a fortnight to cover the five thousand miles to India; a great achievement for a man with so little flying experience.

Yet his adventures had, in fact, only just begun; and he was to overcome many and even more formidable obstacles before he finally set foot on Everest.

That first night in India he ate a huge meal, then went to sleep in the open; and the next day he began his flight to Purnea. His eyes were red and sore after his ordeal of the day before, and for the next week he took things very quietly, flying in easy stages from one airport to the next—Karachi, Hyderabad, Jodhpur, Allahabad, and finally Lalbalu, a military aerodrome only nine miles from Purnea.

Twice more he was refused petrol, apparently on Government orders. Once he flew to a neighbouring 'drome and refuelled there, and the other time he persuaded an Irish hotel keeper to show him where the airport's fuel was stored. He refuelled EVER-WREST himself, during the night, leaving the correct money beneath a stone at the entrance to the fuel store.

It was getting on for the middle of June when Wilson landed at Lalbalu. During the last few days of his flight across India the Press had again caught up with him, and wherever he landed Wilson was interviewed and photographed. Now that, in the face of all official forecasts, he had reached India alive, his fantastic quest began to be taken far more seriously.

Soon after Wilson landed at Lalbalu he received a visit from the local Chief of Police and the two men formed an instant liking for one another; but the latter had received certain very definite instructions and he eventually came to the point and served Wilson with an official notice, ordering the Yorkshireman to bring EVER-WREST into Purnea and then restraining him from further flying. When Wilson asked the reason for this, he was told, unofficially, that the authorities intended to make quite certain he never flew into Nepal without the necessary permit.

Wilson made constant appeals to the British and Nepalese authorities for permission to fly over Nepal to Everest and at last he was told he could fly to Raxall, on the border of Nepal, where his case would be considered.

The monsoon had broken now; and Wilson had to fly in heavy slanting rain, with the cloud base down to four hundred feet. It took him twenty-four hours to cover the two hundred miles to Raxall; and he might just as well have stayed in Lalbalu, for though the authorities must surely have realized that the breaking of the monsoon precluded any attempt on Everest, no permit was forthcoming.

Wilson persisted in his request for permission but time after time he was refused. In the end an official told him, "No! You can't fly over Nepal, and if you telephone ten times a day for the next ten years the answer will still be 'No'!"

Wilson was bitterly disappointed. He studied the approaches to

The pony missed its footing and slithered towards the edge of the five-hundred-foot precipice.

Everest with the greatest care, and came reluctantly to the conclusion that without crossing Nepalese territory, there was no way of approaching the mountain by air.

Since there seemed no possibility of flying to the foot of Everest, and since he had only "twenty quid left in the whole wide world," he decided to sell his aircraft and make for Everest overland. It was a hard decision to make, for the Moth had never failed him, and Wilson had developed a sentimental affection for the plane which had carried him safely a third of the way round the world. He received many offers for EVER-WREST which had now, of course, become famous, and eventually he sold her for five hundred pounds to a man he particularly liked—a planter named Cassells.

FORBIDDEN ROUTE

At the end of July Wilson set out for Darjeeling—the starting-off point of all Everest expeditions. He had, as yet, no definite plans ; but at the back of his mind was the feeling that, having been forbidden the direct route via Nepal, he could only hope to approach Everest from the flank, via Sikkim and Tibet. Arriving in Darjeeling he applied for a permit and was bluntly refused. He therefore began to make preparations in secret and his first step was to find a guide.

Here it seemed that fate played right into Wilson's hands ; for he was introduced one evening to Karma Paul, a 35-year-old Tibetan. He had served in the 1922, 1924 and 1933 Expeditions and he told Wilson a great deal about the approaches to Everest.

As winter approached, Wilson's plans began to crystallize. He lost hope of obtaining official permits to travel through Sikkim or Tibet, and he began to map out a route which he could follow, disguised as a Tibetan priest. He knew that priests were able to travel without permits, and he hoped that he would in a few months' time have learned enough of the Tibetan language to pass a casual inspection. To make doubly sure that he was not caught by the police and brought ignominiously back, he decided to travel entirely by night.

Towards the end of October Wilson applied for permission to join a small party, who were planning a ten days' tour of the Sikkim foothills and, much to his surprise, permission was granted. It was on this trip that Wilson caught his first glimpse of Everest.

At first he thought it was a cloud, then he realized it was too still, too unchanging in its outline. Even as he watched, the sudden glow of dawn swept over the upper reaches of the sky ; the nearer mists dissolved and a great semi-circle of peaks was suddenly unveiled, their summits warmed red by the titanic conflagration of dawn. And the summit of Everest rose majestically behind them all, and when the clouds again rolled back it was the last to disappear. The Goddess Mother of the World was waiting.

By the end of the trip Wilson had covered over one hundred and eighty miles, and he realized with some dismay that he was far from being one hundred per cent. fit. Back in Darjeeling he put himself on a strict vegetarian diet ; taking only one meal a day. He also started on the long walks that had been a feature of his training in England. Then, towards the end of the year, he embarked on a three weeks' fast ; he would, he said, rebuild his body anew, so that he would be worthy both physically and mentally of his supreme test.

Early in January, 1934, Wilson began making definite plans for a dash to Everest some time in March. Once he reached the mountain he planned to lay-up at the Rongbuk Monastery until the weather was good enough for his assault to begin—"some time late in April, I expect."

He sought guides, and managed to trace three Sherpa porters—Tewang, Tsering and Rinzing—who had taken part in the Ruttledge expedition of the year before ; he still planned to make the actual ascent of Everest alone, but he appreciated that porters would be invaluable in guiding him to the base of the mountain and carrying his provisions and equipment at least as far as the Rongbuk Monastery.

The three Sherpas wanted, if possible, to stay together, and Wilson accordingly engaged them all. Nor could he have made a wiser choice, for they proved trustworthy and hard-working. And, what is more, a bond of mutual regard and even affection came to make their relationship a peculiarly happy one.

Wilson acquired a vast collection of maps covering the approaches to Everest and over these he and Tewang pored, hour after hour, until Wilson felt certain that they knew the little-used track they had decided to follow so well that they could find it even in the dark. It was a route that lay mostly over the high, windswept Tibetan plateau, a route that would tax his endurance to the uttermost.

JOURNEY IN DISGUISE

He bought a small but sturdy Sikkim pony, which he intended to ride along the easier stretches. When the authorities asked what the pony was for, he said he was riding it at a tiger shoot to which a friend had invited him. And, as a further red herring, he paid the rent for his rooms six months in advance.

He enlisted the help of the Sherpas in perfecting his disguise. His flying and mountaineering kit he packed carefully into two thirty-pound packs, which the Sherpas were to carry until he could travel without disguise.

In the very early morning of March 21st, 1934, Maurice Wilson, in his elaborate disguise, slipped quietly out of Darjeeling and made for his secret rendezvous with Tsering on the last stage of his journey of no return. Before his departure he wrote in a last letter to England : "Man proposes and God disposes, though in my case I think He did both. I have the distinct feeling of knowing that I shall return ;

EVER-WREST, Wilson's tiny Gipsy Moth biplane, pictured in India after completing the epic flight of more than five thousand miles.

though if things turn out otherwise I've at least had some kick out of life. And if I had my life to live over again, I wouldn't wish it any other way."

Tewang and Rinzing had left earlier; this was to lessen the chances of four men travelling together being spotted by the authorities. A meeting place had been fixed in the forest some twenty miles beyond Darjeeling, and here the party reassembled at noon.

They kept to their original plan; resting through the day and travelling only by night. The route they planned to follow was shorter but more difficult than that taken by Ruttledge the year before—following the Tista Valley almost to its source among the foothills of Kangchenjau. This route wound its way among the heart of the great Himalayan peaks. Kangchenjunga rose some twenty miles to the west; Pauhunri and Kangchenjau less than half that distance to the east; while the shoulder of Chomio (22,400 feet) would have to be actually traversed. It was an exacting route to be chosen by a man with no mountaineering experience; and yet Wilson planned to cover a fair part of it by night.

On the first day they nearly ran into a police patrol. Progress, otherwise, went smoothly and on March 23rd they passed Gangtok. From now on the valley began to climb due north and very steeply. The going became far harder. In a couple of days they climbed from five thousand to twelve thousand feet.

On March 24th they covered sixteen miles in seven-and-a-half hours; good progress for climbing along an ill-defined track. Once in the darkness their pony missed its footing, and slithered almost to the edge of a five-hundred-

foot precipice; once they had to ford an ice-cold mountain stream, with the water swirling fast up to their armpits; and once they were caught, at the top of a small pass, in a minor blizzard of sleet—stinging rain and hard-packed granules of snow.

It was on March 27th that they crossed their first patch of snow, at the top of a 13,000-foot pass, a little to the east of Kangchenjunga. From now on the snow was never very far away. It was bitterly cold at night, though the days were hot. In due course the party gave up travelling by night, and on their last day in Sikkim they rose at seven-thirty and after breakfast climbed solidly for five hours. A little after noon they crossed into Tibet.

Wilson was jubilant. "Now in forbidden Tibet," he wrote in his diary, "and feel like sending Government a wire: 'Told you so.'"

In early April they were well into Tibet, but on April 3rd they suffered nightmare experiences of cold and pain, driving sand and utter exhaustion and, above all, of the screaming fury of a relentless north-west wind.

They ran into a blizzard of driving sleet and whipped-up sand. They covered half-a-mile in three hours. The pony bolted; they caught it and drove themselves on. They rested two hours for lunch, in the half-shelter of a great slab of rock, then they pushed forward.

As they climbed an unusually steep slope the wind rose to gale force and they had to hurl themselves against a stinging, almost blinding wall of sand and snow which the wind tore up and drove almost horizontally across the level plain. Within a few minutes their clothes were caked with sand and melting snow, and their eyes smarted as though they had been pricked by red-hot needles.

Then, after two hours, came a little relief; they dropped into a shallow valley and just before sunset the wind began to die away. But once it was dark and the encircling rim of peaks glinted sharp-outlined against the night sky it became very cold. At midnight Wilson's thermometer registered forty-eight degrees of frost; the cold was like that of interstellar space.

April 4th dawned, still bitterly cold, but fine; and it seemed at first as though the wind itself had been frozen into stillness. But the lull was short-lived. As Wilson and the Sherpas climbed out of the valley the wind once again came screaming down at them, tearing madly out of the west-north-west, directly into their faces. Dark masses of snow and sand, ripped off the plateau, darkened out the sun; and they could only crawl slowly and half-blindly forward into the teeth of the raging inferno. They inched painfully towards a narrow cleft in the plateau.

When they reached it the wind was tremendous and they could only crawl forward on hands and knees. But they had passed the worst now; and at last Tsering, speechless with exhaustion, pointed to a nearby ridge which fringed the Yaru Valley. Once over that, Wilson gathered, they would find at least a trace of shelter. Making a supreme effort they staggered towards the ridge.

It took them an hour to cover three hundred yards, but at last they scrambled down into the wide, U-shaped valley with its merciful promise of shelter. And the lower they descended the less furious the wind became, until by evening they were able to approach Kampa Dzong in comparative comfort.

In the last week of his trek to Everest Wilson averaged some twenty miles a day, and this at a height of over 15,000 feet.

Finally, on Thursday, April 12th, he wrote in his diary:

"Saw Everest this morning from 17,000 feet ridge. Looked magnificent. Eastern half in snow plume. . . . Two nights from now shall be at Rongbuk where I hope to fast for a couple of days to get ready for the big climb. Am already planning for future after the event. I *must* win."

Two days later Wilson and his party reached the head of the Rongbuk Valley. At first they climbed along the shelves of what looked like gigantic moraines, but which were in fact age-old river terraces. Then the valley narrowed; the hills closed in around them, and soon a south wind, ice-cold from the snows of Everest, began to drive in erratic stinging gusts into their faces.

Wilson's first sight, at close range, of Everest was spectacular. At one moment he and the Sherpas were walking along a rough, snow-covered track, in a valley which seemed to lead to nowhere in particular; then suddenly a corner was turned and there lay the Rongbuk Monastery, its massive walls utterly dwarfed by the magnificent mountain which rose fewer than twenty miles distant at the head of the Rongbuk Valley.

Wilson's trip across the roof of the world had been accomplished in fewer than twenty-five days, in which time he had covered three hundred miles of hazardous and treacherous territory.

Two days after his arrival at the Monastery Wilson began his ascent. He rose at dawn, dressed carefully, shouldered his forty-five pounds of kit and set out along the gently sloping Rongbuk Valley. He soon passed the site of Ruttledge's Base Camp at some 16,500 feet. Mid-day saw him plodding steadily on toward the dull grey moraines, with the heat of the sun sending rivulets of perspiration trickling from under his arms.

He had climbed eight miles and well over 1,200 feet by 3 p.m. and decided he would pitch camp now, in good time. He was at 17,600 feet. Wilson passed a comfortable night and set off again at eight o'clock the next morning. After about an hour he came across the remains of Ruttledge's Camp I at 17,800 feet.

Ahead of him rose the fantastic East Rongbuk Glacier, its foreground consisting of low banks of moraine which thrust their grey tongues into the gleaming ice of the glacier itself. Beyond and above this foreground the grey of the moraine disappeared, the seracs

The Head Lama of the Rongbuk Monastery —sanctuary for many Himalayan mountaineers.

and pinnacles of ice—some of them a hundred feet high—crowded closely together, until they merged into one vast, tumbling, ice-green sea, that rose in wave after fantastic wave to the foot of the North Col.

It was a scene of great beauty and impressive grandeur; but it can hardly have reassured Wilson, who saw ahead of him the first mountaineering problem he had ever met.

To Wilson, who literally fled down the lower slopes of Everest after his first assault had failed, the Rongbuk Monastery was a welcome sight.

Whatever he may have felt, the glacier was there; there was no way round it, so obviously it would have to be climbed.

Wilson set out along one edge, trying as far as possible to follow the lead of the moraines. It was arduous rather than difficult climbing, but Wilson's inexperience led to his making of it extremely heavy weather. Trying to pick his way among the towering pinnacles of ice he lost all sense of direction, and by mid-day was well and truly lost.

He regained his direction and pushed resolutely on. It was exhausting work and Wilson felt incredibly weary and sick. Any mountaineer could have told him that he was suffering from glacier lassitude, and that an hour's rest on higher ground would have afforded at least a temporary relief. But Wilson, in his pathetic ignorance, could only push wearily on.

It was no mean achievement for him on this second day to have again climbed some twelve hundred feet before pitching his tent for the night.

The next day Wilson reached the site of Ruttledge's Camp II half-way up the glacier at a height of 19,800 feet. He had hoped to press on to Camp III but a sudden heavy fall of snow and the onset of darkness forced him to make camp for the night. He knew now that there was little hope of fulfilling his promise to himself and reaching the summit on his 36th birthday, which was now three days away. As darkness fell he found himself battling against a terrible weariness which threatened to steal over him before his tent was up. He had, however, sufficient will-power to make camp efficiently before it was too late. He crawled into his sleeping-bag and settled down

for what turned out to be a cold, miserable night.

On April 19th, Wilson set off again. Soon, to add to his troubles, it began to snow ; but he struggled on, hour after hour, following one false lead after another, constantly slipping on the ice, but somehow always managing to avoid the half-hidden crevasses, any one of which could well have ended his fantastic assault.

It was three o'clock before he pitched camp. In six hours he had covered three-quarters of a mile and climbed two-hundred-and-fifty feet. His diary is briefly expressive: "April 19th, Thurs. Another hellish day! About an hour after struck camp it started snowing and hasn't stopped yet. . . ."

For the first part of the next day, which dawned bitterly cold and deceptively clear, Wilson made good progress, in spite of his fairly frequent halts ; but then, once again, it began to snow and the storm eventually increased to a full blizzard. Wilson was forced to pitch camp. He was at about 20,500 feet, only a couple of miles from Camp III.

In the evening, as he lay alone in his blizzard-swept tent—sleeping higher, probably, than any other man in the world—Wilson, for the first time, began to have doubts about the success of his venture. He was already in a somewhat precarious position. The whole success of his expedition now hung on his reaching Camp III and its supply dump, before his own meagre and inadequate supplies ran out.

At dawn the next morning he looked hopefully out of his tent, but he saw it was still snowing hard. And it continued to snow, day after day, with persistent and relentless fury, until Wilson found his store of food had

Desolate, blizzard-swept and forbidding—the mighty East Rongbuk Glacier.

dwindled practically away and the numbing cold had eaten deep into his being and would not be driven away.

Hour after hour, day after day, he sat in his storm-swept tent, listening to the roar of the blizzard that tore and thundered down the glacier. Twice he thought that the weather was going to clear; and twice he struck camp and struggled on a few hundred yards, only to be overtaken by another blizzard in which no man in the open could live.

HAZARDOUS DESCENT

His birthday, April 21st, saw him still 8,500 feet from his goal, snow-bound in the glacier trough. On the fourth day of the blizzard, Wilson realized, at last, that he would have to retrace his steps and lie up at the Rongbuk Monastery until the conditions improved.

He had to wait another twenty-four hours before the weather cleared sufficiently for him to make a start. A little before 3 p.m. on Monday, April 23rd, Wilson struck camp, leaving all his surplus equipment. Then, carrying only a skeleton load containing his tent, flea-bag and the last of his rations (barely enough for forty-eight hours), he fled—there is no other word for it —down the glacier.

He frequently lost his footing, and crashed heavily down on to smooth, unyielding protuberances of ice. At some risk and considerable discomfort he decided to glissade down some of the gentler gradients. Once he found himself, utterly out of control, sliding straight towards a narrow crevasse which split the glacier slope between two unstable buttresses of ice.

As he slithered towards the gaping chasm in the ice, Wilson knew he had only one chance to avoid plunging to his death. He swung his ice axe into the slope, praying that it would "bite" and hold. More by luck than judgment the blade of the axe sank deep and he felt himself jerked to an abrupt halt less than ten yards from the crevasse.

At 10 p.m. on April 24th, Wilson staggered towards the Rongbuk Monastery. He was dazed and delirious, injured and snow-blind; but he was alive. He had descended the glacier in exactly 31 hours, including a halt to pitch camp and snatch a few moments of sleep.

It would have been a creditable feat for a fit and experienced mountaineer to have descended five thousand feet down Everest in a single day; for a man of Wilson's condition —with swollen eyes, constricted throat, wrenched ankle and half-paralysed left arm— it was an almost incredible achievement: an ordeal which would have sapped the strength of any normal man.

Yet that very evening, as he lay exhausted in his tent, he began, while Rinzing and Tewang heated a bowl of soup, to enter up his diary. "Next time," he wrote, in a barely legible scrawl, "I'll take more supplies with me. I'll not give up. I still *know* that I can do it. . . ."

A man with more judgment and less courage would, at this stage, have admitted defeat. But the magnitude of his self-appointed task served only to spur Wilson on. The ascent of Everest would, he now realized, be a truly superhuman task: a task the fulfilment of which would be certain proof of his own Divine Inspiration. "Weren't we told," he wrote, "that faith could move mountains? If I have faith enough I *know* that I can climb Mount Everest."

Yet although he still seemed to think that God would guide him up the mountain, he planned his second assault with all the care and thoroughness his meagre circumstances would allow. As he lay in the monastery, weak and lethargic, his bloodshot eyes still throbbing with pain, he talked to Rinzing and Tewang and together they laid plans for their next attempt. Tsering had earlier been taken sick with a stomach complaint and was still too ill to accompany them.

It was agreed that the Sherpas would climb with him as far as Camp III, just below the ice-fall guarding the North Col. They would carry between them enough supplies to establish a well-stocked camp, and here they would lie up until the weather seemed set fair and Wilson, alone, could make "a last dive for the summit."

But for several weeks his plans for a second assault hung fire; for his recovery took longer than he expected.

READY TO TRY AGAIN

He stayed in bed for four days, sleeping and eating by turns; then on the fifth he got up for a couple of hours in the late afternoon. He felt terribly shaky and lethargic, and was glad to get back into his sleeping-bag. His feet were still swollen, and his left arm and left eye both throbbed painfully. But towards the beginning of May his recovery become more rapid.

Soon he began again those long walks which had played so large a part in his original training programme. He took pride in the fact that after a week he could "average fifteen miles a day and not feel the least bit tired." It did not seem to occur to him that he could have spent his time far more profitably in learning to use his ice-axe and crampons.

After being delayed by his Sherpas succumbing to illness, Wilson finally fixed a definite date for the start of his second attempt —Saturday, May 12th.

He paid far more attention this time to the question of supplies. He bought vast quantities of dates, and baked himself a sack of special biscuits, consisting mainly of brown bread, flour and oats; these he optimistically decided to keep for use "above Camp V, as they are so much lighter and handier than bread."

He divided their equipment into three packs—forty-five pounds for Rinzing, thirty-five pounds for himself, and twenty-five pounds for Tewang who was far from one hundred per cent. fit. He also took more climbing equipment, ropes, ice-axes, etc., as well as sun goggles and white cream to alleviate glacial sunburn.

TIRED OF DELAY

One of his last actions was to give Tewang a deed of assignment for the pony, making him promise that he would not sell it, but would use it for his ride to Lhasa. He also gave him a letter which was, in the event of his death, to be handed on to the authorities in Darjeeling. This letter asked that the three Sherpas should be exonerated from all blame in accompanying him on his forbidden journey.

That evening—May 11th—walking back to his camp, he saw Everest shrouded in mist and looking "very wild." But Wilson was tired of delay, and wrote "in any event we're off to-morrow, come what may. Shall be glad to get the job over."

And so in May, 1934, the last inevitable acts of the drama were played out on the northern face of Everest.

As soon as it was light on Saturday, May 12th, Wilson, Tewang and Rinzing left the monastery and set off purposefully towards the head of the Rongbuk Valley. Ahead, framed by the early morning mist, Everest's sheer cliffs of ice-draped rock seemed to rise out of the sky itself; but soon the sun broke through, the mists cleared and the mountain was clearly revealed in all her majesty.

It was a lonely, desolate world they were entering and it was bitterly cold. The sun seemed to have lost all warmth. Nevertheless, Wilson covered his face with anti-frost and anti-violet-ray cream, and for seven hours the three men climbed steadily up the lower slopes. Soon they passed Ruttledge's base camp and began to work their way along the moraine ledges of the main Rongbuk Glacier. Wilson was determined to waste no time, and urged the Sherpas forward. "We must," he said, "reach Camp I tonight."

(To be continued)

ODDS AND ENDS

THE GREAT MILESTONE CONTROVERSY

SOME years ago, in all innocence, we published a photograph of a milestone in Bermuda recording a distance of 3,076 miles from London. We casually inquired, at the time, whether anyone could beat it, and a reader promptly sent along a picture of a stone in Zanzibar—one of the " sights " of the island—indicating that it is 8,064 miles from London. This photograph duly appeared in our pages, but ever since, from all parts of the world, we have been bombarded with pictures of the same milestone, each and every correspondent apparently being convinced that he is the only person who has ever set eyes upon the pillar ! So far as we can judge, this Zanzibar example is a world's record in the way of milestones, but now and again, in the steady stream of " Zanzibars," there comes to light another " four-figure " stone. Here, for instance, is a photograph of a stone at Wankie, in the coalfields of Southern Rhodesia, about seventy miles from the famous Victoria Falls, recording the respectable mileage of 7,702 to London. Perhaps it is tempting Fate, but once again we ask—leaving the inevitable Zanzibar out of the question !—whether any WIDE WORLD reader can beat it.

White baboons did the trick

The Argus Correspondent

GEORGE, Saturday.

PLAGUED by a troop of baboons, Mr. J. F. Richardson of Rustoord, near Kammanassie, hit on the idea of painting two baboons white to scare the others.

He and his son built a wire cage and trapped two baboons Next they took two long poles with chains and loops and managed to place these over the baboons' heads. The baboons were led against the wire of the cage and painted white from outside the cage.

When the troop paid one of its regular visits (there were almost 150, including many youngsters), the cage door was opened and two now-white baboons sped out with all haste to rejoin them.

Their anxiety to be reunited was matched by the anxiety of the troop to avoid the apparitions, and they galloped away as fast as they could.

Since then — this was about three weeks ago — not a single baboon has raided the Richardson farm, nor have the two white ones been seen again.

The WideWorld

THE
MAGAZINE
FOR MEN
SEPTEMBER———1951
1/6

Maurice Wilson, a man of tremendous courage and resolution, set out to climb Everest alone. He failed, but his failure was in many ways a triumphant one, for he possessed the spirit which makes men great. He was past his physical prime when he first set foot on Everest ; he had an injured arm and no mountaineering experience, but nothing could damp his spirit, nothing would make him give up.

This concludes " I'll Climb Everest Alone," the inspiring, dramatic story of an incomparably brave man.

THE FINAL

TEWANG, still weakened by his illness, struggled gamely on. He never uttered a word of complaint, but Wilson could see that the journey was already sapping his strength.

Wilson himself was going remarkably well. His earlier attempt had obviously helped his acclimatization, and the ascent of 2,300 feet in a day caused him no trouble at all. Rinzing seemed equally fit.

It was soon after three o'clock that they reached the site of Camp 1, and pitched their tents under a moraine ledge at the approaches to the East Rongbuk Glacier. Within half an hour the sun had dipped behind the long arete of the North Peak and it grew bitterly cold. As Rinzing prepared the evening meal, Wilson and Tewang sat huddled together for warmth in the Sherpa's tent.

Hot tea soon restored their spirits; but later that night the cold seemed to penetrate more keenly than ever before into their tents. Wilson had to wear mittens while he brought his diary up to date. " My pencil is like ice," he wrote. At ten o'clock he got out of his sleeping-bag and looked at the thermometer; already it was recording over eighty degrees of frost. He felt reasonably warm but sleep that night eluded him.

The next day they again made good progress. Rinzing appreciated that on his first attempt Wilson had failed to eat sufficient hot, nourishing food—at altitudes of over twenty thousand feet it is quite impossible for a man to exist for long on his bodily heat alone—and this time he insisted on preparing a hot breakfast. While this was being cooked and the two Sherpas took turns at working the bellows, Wilson did a little reconnaissance and hit on a good lead. They started off at 8 a.m., and were soon climbing at a speed which put Wilson's previous efforts in the shade. The Sherpas proved invaluable in picking exactly the right route and in helping Wilson along the few difficult ledges. This day too they climbed a little over 2,000 feet, reaching Camp II at 3 p.m. and settling there for the night. " Gorgeous day," wrote Wilson. " Weather perfect—cold but sunny and no sign of the

monsoon. Here we are at Camp II after what seemed like a spring walk compared to my last effort."

Monday, May 14th, was another fine day: and a day, too, of excellent progress.

They had breakfasted and struck camp by eight o'clock, and the Sherpas showed Wilson the easiest route—the one used by Ruttledge —into the great glacier troughs. Well before noon they were pushing strongly upward among the great seracs and pinnacles that rose, up to one hundred feet in height, all round them.

As morning passed into afternoon they began to suffer from the inevitable glacier lassitude, Tewang especially had to make frequent halts to regain his breath ; but towards the head of the trough the gradient eased off and the going became, if anything, a little easier.

Wilson had given his cork-insulated boots to Rinzing, and was wearing the Sherpa's felt-lined ones ; he found that in these he could keep his footing more easily. Nevertheless he several times fell heavily on the polished surface of the ice—he badly missed the crampons which he had lost the day before. Over the few difficult places he cut inexpert but effective steps with his ice-axe ; it amazed him how much effort it required to dislodge even a few splinters of the tough, rubbery ice.

Soon after noon they passed the site of Wilson's highest camp on his first assault, and an hour later the trough began to peter out among the upper reaches of the East Rongbuk Glacier. Here the wind and the flying snow came tearing down on them—in sudden contrast to the almost warm and stagnant air of the trough. They were at 21,000 feet. Only a little way ahead lay the desolate and wind-swept site of Ruttledge's Camp III.

Bowed low against the wind, the three men struggled forward into one of the most breath-taking vistas in the world.

Quite suddenly the long northern buttress of Changtse (the North Peak) fell away behind them, and the upper slopes of Everest herself, hitherto hidden, rose suddenly and steeply before them ; six thousand feet of snow-encrusted slab and avalanche-swept couloir, and

ASSAULT

By DENNIS ROBERTS

It took them a couple of hours to cut steps up the forty-feet slope : their progress was reduced to a panting crawl.

beyond, the white, rock-strewn cone of the summit trailing its plume of windswept snow far into Nepal. At last the upper slopes of Everest were tangible, clearly revealed, no longer the fabric of dreams and visions. There, for Wilson to see, was the way to the summit, and in the bright, clear atmosphere it looked comparatively near. Wilson at that moment must surely have had visions of success.

But his dreams of the future were quickly shattered by the reality of the present. Their immediate concern was to pitch camp and give the exhausted Tewang some sort of shelter, for the Sherpa was clearly in much distress ; his breathing was fast and irregular, and he was doubled up with stomach cramp. They helped him towards the site of Camp III, half-way between the head of the glacier and the beginning of the great ice-fall which rose 1,500 feet above them to the shoulder of the North Col. It was the only level site that was reasonably free from the danger of avalanches which daily cascaded their millions of tons of ice down the approaches to North Col. Here among the moraine boulders and snowdrifts, at about three o'clock, they set up their two tents, and into one Tewang collapsed, utterly exhausted.

The approaches to the North Col consist of a steep, broken ice fall which rises some 1,500 feet from the upper reaches of the East Rong-buk Glacier to the crest of the col itself. As the ice fall is continually being pushed forward and downward, its slopes present a different appearance from year to year. The two expeditions of the 1920's, and the Ruttledge expedition, all found it a difficult obstacle to surmount—and these expeditions included some of the finest ice-climbers of the first half of the century. Yet Wilson, who could hardly cut an efficient step, was apparently quite undaunted.

To his left lay a series of precipitous ice-cliffs, each some hundred to two hundred feet in height, rising one above the other, with narrow shelves between. The face of most of them was sheer, clean-cut and quite unclimbable, while some had great overhanging bulges which threatened at any moment to avalanche into the East Rongbuk Glacier. Ahead, in the direction of the route followed in 1924, lay a clean-swept slope of ice rising steeply to the base of a 400-foot precipitous cliff; the slope itself was perfectly climbable, but at its foot lay the tumbled debris of many an avalanche, and the cliff at its head made it an obvious cul-de-sac.

Only to the right—in the general direction of the 1922 route—did the ice fall appear to be even remotely climbable. Here, the lower slopes were steep—steep enough to necessitate almost continual step-cutting; but they were kept free from avalanches by a great crevasse half-way up the fall which split it horizontally, and was wide enough to engulf all avalanches coming down from the upper slopes.

FORMIDABLE CLIMB

The crevasse, however, did not appear to be bridged; and whether it could in fact be crossed was something only a detailed on-the-spot inspection would disclose. Beyond the crevasse the slopes eased off a little, but the last fifty to a hundred feet seemed to consist of a sheer ice cliff, almost vertical, which would have to be taken by frontal assault. There seemed, however, at one point to be a chimney reaching almost to the top. Above this last ice cliff lay the North Col where Camp IV, at some 23,000 feet, would have to be established.

As Wilson wrote that night in his diary, "Summit and route to it can be seen quite clearly now. Only another 8,000 feet to go."

But what a formidable 8,000 feet they were!

Rinzing managed to make some rather lukewarm tea, and once they had finished this he suggested to Wilson that they make their way to Ruttledge's store-dump, which he felt

certain was only a few hundred yards distant. It says much for the fitness of the two men that at eight o'clock that night they ventured out on the windswept glacier to search for Ruttledge's supply-dump. After about ten minutes they lost each other in the pitch darkness, and Wilson returned to his tent. He was still thawing out his feet, half an hour later, when there was a heaving and grunting outside and after a moment Rinzing came staggering in.

THROUGH WIND AND DARKNESS

He had carried a forty-pound provision box for several hundred yards through the wind and darkness that engulfed the glacier. And he stood, licking his lips, while Wilson forced open the wooden crate. Out came a veritable stream of delicacies—honey, butter, cheese, anchovy paste, cream and chocolate biscuits and tins of soup and meat. Wilson was delighted.

It was, however, too late and too cold to think of cooking that night. So they contented themselves with chocolate biscuits and Wilson promised them an orgy the following day. And the three men settled down to sleep.

The next day, May 15th, was again fine. But Wilson, who had slept poorly, decided to lie up for the day before attempting the ice-fall. In his excitement the night before he had forgotten to level off the floor of his tent and he had spent most of the night rolling down on to an unpleasantly sharp boulder that lay alongside the tent wall.

After a day of rest, during which Wilson discarded any thought of dieting and sampled most of the previous expedition's stores, the three men felt ready to tackle the ice-fall early the next morning. Rinzing was especially energetic; and, delighted at the pleasure the food-boxes gave Wilson, he fetched another.

The next day Wilson wrote:

"May 16th. Wed. Weather rotten. Still at Camp III."

And five days later they were still pinned down to their exposed and windswept site by the blizzards which raged continuously about the northern face of Everest.

It seems that the weather in 1934 was especially bad on Everest. It was a year of extremes, with one or two perfect days followed by prolonged blizzards of unusual fury. Such a blizzard now enveloped Camp III.

Day after day the three men remained huddled together in their tents, which the wind threatened hourly to pluck up and hurl down the East Rongbuk Glacier. At least they had plenty of food, but the dull continuous roar of the wind and the numbing cold must have gradually sapped their strength.

At first Wilson's entries in his diary were long and optimistic—if sadly out of touch with reality; but gradually they became shorter and tinged with something like despair.

"May 17th. Thurs. It's snowing like the devil, and I can see less than 200 feet. Had bit of a head, but shall start to-morrow if

The tantalizing target of Wilson's tremendous endeavour—the higher slopes of Everest as seen from Camp III.

weather O.K. Have decided not to take short cut to Camp V as at first intended as should have to cut my own steps up the ice-fall; that's silly when there should already be handrope and steps leading to old Camp IV." (It seems that Wilson seriously expected the steps cut by Ruttledge over a year ago to be still intact.)

"*May* 18*th. Fri.* Nothing to do all day. It's still snowing and blowing like the D. Went to see how the boys were getting on at 3 p.m., but was soon glad to get back to sleeping-bag."

"*May* 19*th. Sat.* Another couple of days and it will be 12 months since I said cheerio to you all. How time flies. Weather still too windy and far too much drift snow to start off to-day, so am just sitting or rather lying quiet. Feeling bit better after long lay up out of sun."

"*May* 20*th. Sun.* Snow stopped and sun out but wind still v. bad. These violet rays are terrible. Have thick blanket strapped over tent, but can still feel them through my balaclava helmet."

"*May* 21*st. Mon.* Had enough bed the last few days for a year. Terrible when you can't put your head down for aching nerves. Weather better. We start again to-morrow."

And the next day, almost a year after he had left England, Wilson started on the penultimate stage of his lone assault. He had slept badly on the night of the 21st and woke feeling cold; he found himself shivering as he waited for Rinzing to brew up the tea, and took twenty minutes to lace up his climbing boots.

He breakfasted as the pale light of dawn came flooding coldly over the rim of North Col. Then he looked outside the tent and saw the crest of Everest, snow-plumed and seeming deceptively near. The wind had dropped, and as the sun came streaming over the eastern peaks he began to climb, very slowly, towards the ice-fall.

Rinzing had promised to come with him until it was noon to show him the approximate route used by Ruttledge; and to start with the two men made reasonable progress up the lower slopes. But soon the gradient steepened, the ice became broken into monstrous blocks and seracs, and the newly fallen snow masked the host of minor crevasses that split the face of the ice in all directions. Wilson looked about in vain for traces of the track hewn out by Ruttledge; the steps had been destroyed and the rope guides swept away. An hour after breaking camp they began to cut steps.

Wilson was so inexpert at this that he had to ask Rinzing to lead, and he watched the Sherpa carefully to see how the steps were made. After twenty minutes he took over the lead, but soon found that the additional effort of step-cutting quickly sapped his energy— probably his lack of skill meant that his exertions were far greater than those of an experienced mountaineer. Soon they came to an especially steep slope of some sixty degrees, crowned by a number of unstable-looking seracs. Their progress was reduced to a panting crawl.

It took them a couple of hours to cut steps up the forty feet of slope; but at last they emerged on to a narrow ledge among the grotesque seracs and pinnacles. At one end of the ledge a steep little couloir led upwards towards the great crevasse.

It was after noon and Rinzing told Wilson he could come no farther, as darkness would fall before he could make the descent to Camp III. They shook hands and the Sherpa began to retrace his steps. Soon he had vanished from sight, and Wilson felt very much alone.

He worked his way among the seracs to the foot of the little couloir; it looked, from close to, even steeper than he had feared. It was two o'clock now, and realizing he could hardly climb it that night, Wilson decided to pitch camp. It was difficult to find a spot level enough to set up his tent, and he was tempted to make use of the open space at the foot of the couloir.

There, however, the ground had been worn smooth by the passage of countless small avalanches, which periodically came sweeping down the couloir and then, after some fifty feet, cascaded over the steepening cliff. He decided—wisely—to prefer the discomfort of the seracs to the danger of the avalanches, and eventually managed to wedge his tent, at a somewhat alarming angle, between two reasonably stable pinnacles.

He was exhausted; and now he was alone he began once again to neglect his health. He could not be bothered to prepare a proper meal, but ate only some chocolate and dry biscuits before crawling into his sleeping-bag. He wanted desperately to sleep, but sleep did not come easily. Surely that night he must have been haunted by the spectre of impending failure; he had planned to reach the col by nightfall, but he was only some third of the way there. And tomorrow he would be alone.

May 23rd dawned mercifully fine. He was up early and cooked himself a good breakfast of hot stew; but he was surprised to find how long everything took. He woke at six; but it was seven-thirty before he had cooked breakfast, and after nine before he had struck camp.

DANGEROUS REFUGE

The sun's rays were surprisingly warm on his back as, a little before ten o'clock, he stood looking up at the couloir. Wilson hoped that the milder weather did not herald the approach of the monsoon. From higher up on the shoulder of Everest he could hear the distant roar of avalanches, and he dreaded being caught by one in the couloir. He knew it was near here that in 1922 seven porters had been killed by avalanching snow. He began, slowly, laboriously and inexpertly cutting steps up the edge of the couloir, avoiding the centre which he saw was liable to avalanche. And as morning passed into afternoon he must have realized the hopelessness of his task.

For his headway was pitiably slow and cost him great effort. Every few minutes he had to stop and gasp for breath. Once his foothold gave way and he slid back for twenty feet, starting a small avalanche, which, as he watched it, gained in bulk and momentum and went cascading down the ice-fall until, far below, it shot down and outward on to the East Rongbuk Glacier.

It took him three hours to climb the couloir. Then, still cutting steps, he traversed the slope that led up sharply toward the great crevasse. He pitched camp in a poor position on a shelf, tilted at twenty degrees, in the middle of the windswept slope. A blizzard would have blown him straight on to the glacier, now nearly a thousand feet below. But he was lucky.

FEAR OF FROSTBITE

The night was calm, though terribly cold. At 4 p.m., too exhausted to prepare a meal, he fell into his sleeping-bag. "Just," he wrote, "going to have a few minutes' shut-eye." When he woke it was dawn and he was bitterly cold.

There had in the night been fifty-seven degrees of frost and Wilson feared he must surely have frostbite. But after a couple of hours he found he could move both fingers and toes, and it was clear that he had somehow escaped it. He had, however, a headache, and a sore throat which two cups of lukewarm tea did little to alleviate. He ate a small quantity of snow, and then at 9 a.m. started off again.

His first obstacle was the crevasse.

He approached it cautiously, which was just as well, for it proved to have an unstable lower lip and looked quite bottomless. It averaged some thirty feet in width, and its walls were sheer, pale blue at the top, merging into royal blue, deep blue and indigo as it plummeted into unseen depths. Wilson worked his way along it, keeping to the left where the crevasse seemed to narrow slightly. After about an hour he came to an unstable-looking snow-bridge.

Snow-bridges present a tricky problem even to the experienced mountaineer; there is no certain way of gauging their strength. Wilson tried for a couple of hours to find an alternative route over the crevasse. There was none. He sat down and ate his lunch—five dry biscuits.

Then, because postponement of the issue was obviously no solution to it, he knelt down and prayed and when he had finished he got up and began to walk across the bridge. And the bridge held.

When he reached the other side he found a not-too-difficult slope, which he traversed with the cutting of only a few steps for some hundred and fifty yards. Then, at about noon, he reached the foot of the last ice cliff, guarding the comparatively easy slopes to the North Col. Another two hundred feet and he would reach the col. He looked in vain for some crack in the apparently unscalable face: sixty feet of ice and rock, not only vertical but actually in some places overhanging.

He remembered the chimney he had seen from Camp III, but in his preoccupation with

The formidable north face of Everest.

How far up he got we shall never know—probably not very far. But the fact that he failed to climb it is not really important; what matters is that he went on trying. The odds are that an experienced mountaineer could probably have climbed the chimney in about an hour—though even this is by no means certain as it may not have been on the exact route used by Ruttledge, or if it was, its composition may have altered.

In any case it was, for Wilson, an insurmountable obstacle; every difficulty he had so far met with he had overcome. But here was a barrier that courage and determination alone could never break. By the end of May 24th, when he stumbled into his tent, still at the foot of the chimney, he must have known with terrible certainty that he would never climb Mount Everest alone.

The next day, having neither drunk nor even eaten anything hot for over twenty-four hours, he set out again. But he was too weak to climb more than a few yards above his tent.

He realized that he was now faced with the same three courses as on the East Rongbuk Glacier a month before. He could climb up the chimney until he fell to his death; he could stay in his tent and wait for death to come to him; or he could go back, and try to persuade the Sherpas to accompany him still higher.

Wilson had still sufficient sanity to realize that only the last course afforded him the slightest hope of reaching the top of Everest. It seems from his diary—which from now on becomes slightly incoherent and extremely difficult to read—that he hoped to return to Camp III, rest there for a couple of days and then persuade Rinzing to carry supplies for him up to Camp IV; he evidently had sufficient faith in the Sherpa's mountaineering skill to believe that the two of them could between them climb the chimney on to the slopes of North Col.

And so at about ten o'clock Wilson began his second flight from Everest; a flight even more incredible than the first.

In less than five hours, weak and unskilled as he was, he slipped and slithered his way down fifteen hundred feet of extremely difficult ice. Twice he fell badly, and rolled over and over until the soft snow checked him. Each time he struggled quickly to his feet, rubbing the pain from his ribs; they might for all he knew have been broken; he had no time to find out; he only knew that somehow he must reach Camp III before nightfall.

He came to the crevasse, and the snow-bridge looked even frailer than before; but once again it held. He found his steps down the couloir, and half-scrambled, half-fell down them.

crossing the crevasse, he realized he had worked away from it. He started to hack his way along the foot of the cliff, apparently oblivious to the danger of avalanches, and at last, more by luck than judgment, found himself working toward the chimney.

That night, when he pitched camp at its foot, he was at a height of only a little under 23,000 feet. Once again he was too exhausted to cook a meal. Nor did he choose a good site for his tent—it would in all probability have been impossible to find a " good " site on the ice-fall, but Wilson was too weary to find even a passable one. He set up his tent at an angle of thirty-five degrees and scooped and hacked away the snow and ice to prevent his rolling down the ice-fall in his sleep.

He spent a miserable night.

The dawn of May 24th saw him crawl very slowly out of his tent and prepare his breakfast, " took two hours for damned water to boil." He used his matches as an improvised candlestand, and they soon became useless—saturated with grease. Wilson realized he now had no means of making either heat or light. But he refused to give up.

For seven hours he tried to climb the chimney.

In the twilight haze he could pick out far below him, the tents of Camp III. He saw the Sherpas stumbling upward to meet him, and almost sobbing with relief he fell into Rinzing's arms and was carried into his tent. A bowl of hot soup and then, quite literally, half-dead with exhaustion, he fell asleep. And he slept for thirty hours.

He woke at 11 p.m. on Saturday, May 26th, and his Sherpas had a hot meal ready and waiting. Their kindness and their obvious anxiety touched Wilson deeply; but when they spoke of returning to Rongbuk he simply shook his head.

"I didn't come back," he said, "because I'd given up—I came back because I want you to come with me to Camp IV."

Up to now Wilson's battered little diary has provided a fairly complete account of his day-by-day progress on to the upper slopes of Everest. But for the last days of his life the diary entries are short and pitiably incoherent; thus of his third attempt to climb the mountain we can gain only a blurred fragmentary picture.

We know that on Saturday and Sunday he remained resting in his tent. His diary simply reads:

"*26th Sat.* Stayed in bed.
27th Sun. „ „ „"

and we can imagine him, most of the time asleep, curled up in his bag, while the Sherpas in their tent a few yards away cooked food and probably reflected on the hopelessness of their position; and the wind tore and thundered around them incessantly, and the cold and inhuman desolation sapped away the very desire to live.

It must by now have been obvious to Wilson that if he went on alone, it could only be to his death; and he must therefore have used all his eloquence to try to persuade the Sherpas to accompany him at least to the top of the ice-fall. And by the night of Sunday, 27th, he apparently believed that his eloquence had taken effect, for he wrote next morning in his diary: "*28th Mon.* Tewang wanted to go back, but persuaded them go with me. This will be last effort, and I feel successful. . . ."

But in actual fact either he had misunderstood the Sherpas or else his mind had begun to wander—it is quite common for those who stay too long at high altitudes to suffer from delusions—for Tewang and Rinzing soon made it abundantly plain that under no circumstances would they go a step farther.

Tewang indeed was in no shape to continue; it would be as much as he could manage safely to descend, let alone ascend, the mountain; and Rinzing, who had climbed to over 27,000 feet on the previous expedition, knew enough about the upper slopes of Everest to realize that even if they climbed the ice-fall the summit would still be utterly beyond them.

Both the Sherpas, men born and bred in the high hills of the Himalaya, men whose judgment was far more balanced than that of Wilson, said emphatically that it was impossible to push on farther. It was too late, they said; in a few days the monsoon would break; they pointed out that they were all too weak (Wilson was partially snow-blinded and suffering from exhaustion and lack of oxygen); they had not enough porters, they said, or enough climbing equipment to force a way up the ice-fall and establish on the col a well-stocked camp; and, last but by no means least, they knew that Wilson lacked the technical mountaineering skill to lead the ascent safely.

With every justification, the Sherpas pleaded with him to abandon his attempt. With every justification, they refused to climb even another fifty feet.

And some time during that afternoon of Monday, May 28th, it must have become plain to Wilson that Tewang and Rinzing would indeed come with him no farther.

"Faith," he had once written, "is not faith that wavers when its prayers remain unanswered." Did he still, he must now have asked himself, hold fast to his original belief? Now that it seemed as though God had deserted him, now that all his theories seemed about to be disproved, did he still believe that he could climb Mount Everest alone?

His was the sort of faith that remains inviolate in the face of all adversity, and he began that night to make preparations for his last attempt.

He rummaged about among his kit until he found the "flag of friendship"—the silk pennant on which his closest friends had signed their names before he left London. He decided to take it with him. He also put into his rucksack the oxygen equipment and the bare minimum of supplies; he knew he would have to travel light, and he took with him food for only seven days; he reckoned if all went well he could climb the mountain in four or five days, and the exhilaration of success would sustain him on his descent.

He had a hot meal that Sunday night at a little before six-thirty; then as he struggled into his sleeping-bag, there came over him the strangest feeling; he became convinced that someone was by his side. The only sound was the tearing roar of the wind. The two Sherpas lay resting in their tent. Yet still Wilson felt

Alone and very slowly, he began to climb up the ice-fall. The Sherpas watched him go, knowing that they would never see him again.

an extra "someone" in the party. "When I reached the ledge I felt I ought to eat something to keep up my strength. All I had brought with me was a slab of Kendal Mint Cake. This I took out of my pocket and, carefully dividing it into two halves, turned round with one half in my hand to offer my companion. . . ."

That night Wilson slept reasonably well, and the next morning—Tuesday, May 29th—he was up early and as soon as it was light he went across to the Sherpas' tent.

It was chillingly cold and a long banner of snow streamed from the summit of Everest. The wind was very strong, and after covering even the few paces to the porters' tent, Wilson found himself gasping for breath. He came straight to the point. He told them he was determined to make a last attempt. Would they, he asked, come with him? Again Tewang and Rinzing refused; under no circumstances, they said, would they climb another step.

There was, in later years, some talk of the Sherpas having deserted Wilson; but both the word and also its implications of disloyalty are quite out of place. For only if they had made with their leader a joint suicide pact could the Sherpas have been reasonably expected to throw away their lives by joining in so foredoomed a venture.

It was a sad little drama that was, early that morning, played out to its inevitable climax in the porters' tent. The more Tewang and Rinzing pleaded with Wilson to return, the more obstinate he became. When at last he realized he would never get them to change their minds, he must have known in his heart what the end of his quest would be; but he ended the argument by saying simply:

"Wait here for ten days. Then if I don't come back, return by yourselves."

He went out, packed up his tent, his sleeping-bag and his few pieces of equipment. Then, alone and very slowly, he began to climb up

that he was not alone. "Strange," he wrote, "but I feel that there is somebody with me in tent all the time."

And before this feeling is attributed to an unbalanced state of mind, it should perhaps be remembered that Frank Smythe had undergone a similar experience on the upper slopes of Everest the year before, an experience that he writes about very vividly. "All the time," he tells us, "that I was climbing alone, I had the feeling that there was someone with me. I felt that were I to slip I should be held up and supported as though I had a companion with me with a rope."

Sir Ernest Shackleton had the same experience when crossing the mountains of South Georgia after his hazardous open-boat journey from Elephant Island, and he narrates how he and his companion felt that there was the ice-fall towards the slopes of the North Col.

The Sherpas knew that they would never see him again, as they watched him go. He did not get very far. Just how much he suffered in those last days is something that will never be known ; and this perhaps is as it should be, for the Calvary of a brave man is something strictly personal between that man and his God. But the half-dozen lines in his diary and the reports of the Sherpas when they returned later to Kalimpong give the bare facts.

Day after day, with the weather rapidly worsening, the Sherpas clung to their precarious foothold at the approaches to the North Col. Only when the monsoon broke, over a week after Wilson had set out, did they return sadly to the Rongbuk Monastery.

It was in July that the first rumours of Wilson's death began to filter through to the outside world. His three Sherpas had returned to Kalimpong ; here they were interviewed, interrogated and cross-examined for week after week, and though their story contained a number of inconsistencies, it did at least seem to establish the certainty of Wilson's death.

When the evidence had been correlated, filtered and checked, it did not amount to much ; it could only be surmised that Wilson had perished in that dangerous region at a height of about 23,000 feet.

The only other source of information is the last few entries of Wilson's diary. From this scanty material we can piece together the broad outline of the last three days of his life.

This picture of the mighty mountain was taken from Camp II by a member of the 1935 Reconnaissance Expedition, soon after Wilson's body was found.

*   *   *

Early on the morning of Tuesday, May 29th, we can picture Wilson as again he left Camp III and struggled about half-way up the ice-fall, carrying with him three loaves of bread, two tins of oatmeal and a small Union Jack. He must have been very weak, and the wind that day was high ; but he crawled on, inch by painful inch, until he reached a spot some little way above the great crevasse. There, utterly exhausted, he had to give up. It was failure once again. He retraced his steps and camped that night below the crevasse, probably only a little higher than Camp III.

On May 30th he was too weak to leave his sleeping bag and too weak, too, to scrawl more than a single faint line in his diary, "Stayed in bed."

Then on Thursday, May 31st, he set out for the last time. The sun was shining brightly as he packed up his tent and sleeping-bag ; but its rays, at 21,500 feet, held little warmth. Nevertheless it was fine, and Wilson wrote that morning in his diary: "Off again, gorgeous day." These were his last words. He tried to write more, but the message appears only as an incoherent scrawl.

Another day of battling with the seracs and crevasses of the ice-fall brought an end to his lone assault on Everest. That evening, again utterly exhausted, quite alone, and with the numbing cold of death already seeping into him, he stumbled down to the foot of the fall. There he pitched his tent, only a few hundred feet above Camp III.

Probably he hoped to rest there for another day, before renewing his assault. But the flame of his life was now burning low, and some time that night, or very early the next morning, he died—we can only hope in his sleep—of cold and exhaustion and exposure.

Everest had conquered the man, but not his spirit. That surely was borne up, seven thousand feet, to where the long plume of wind-torn snow began to stream south-eastward across the border of Nepal. And perhaps he was welcomed there by Mallory, and other men, who gave their lives in search of an ideal.

A year was to pass before men again set foot on Everest. Then, early in July, 1935, a party led by Eric Shipton arrived at the foot of the mountain. Their object was reconnaissance rather than a full-scale assault. And with them, for his first encounter with Everest, came a young Sherpa named Tenzing. At Rongbuk they were blessed by the Head Lama, who spoke warmly of the man who had, a year before, disappeared on the upper slopes of the Goddess Mother of the World. Then the party pushed on up the East Rongbuk Glacier.

On July 9th Shipton found the body of Maurice Wilson.

He was lying at the very foot of the ice-fall, only some few hundred yards above Camp III. His tent had been swept away by the fury of the monsoon and winter storms; and all that remained of it were the guy-lines, held down by boulders. Wilson was dressed in his windproof clothing: with his rucksack by his side.

There was now a sense of tranquillity about the mountain. The storms had, for the moment, died away. The glacier and ice-fall were still free of snow, and the scene gave no hint of the struggle for life that had taken place here eleven months before.

Shipton held a simple funeral service.

Maurice Wilson's body was buried in a ten-foot snow crevasse; as Shipton said later, "When we tipped it in, it completely disappeared. There was no hole where it fell, just plain white snow." A cairn was raised over the grave, and Shipton collected Wilson's diary and brought it back to England.

So ended the most incredible story in all the eventful history of Mount Everest; a story compounded in almost equal part of tragedy and heroism.

It was his attempt to prove a fantastic theory that led Maurice Wilson to make his lone quixotic challenge. He was past his physical prime when he first set foot on Everest; he had an injured arm, he had no mountaineering experience, yet he tried to climb the highest mountain in the world alone. And, after overcoming the most incredible obstacles, he reached a height of some 22,000 feet. There his quest ended in a wilderness of ice and snow and tearing wind that wore out his body but never damped the flame of his spirit.

Yet did Wilson really die in vain? Must he be remembered only as a pitiable failure? It is true that if we judge him by results, or by his technical skill, Wilson was no great mountaineer. He never in all his life climbed a single worth-while peak. But his spirit was that of Mallory. He failed to conquer Everest; but he never failed himself, or mankind, or his ideal. He possessed, in spite of all his faults—his recklessness and foolish pride—the spirit that makes men great.

No four words could tell more clearly a man's character than those pencilled, very faintly, as the last entry of Maurice Wilson's diary: "Off again, gorgeous day."

The last, poignant pages in the diary of a courageous man—Maurice Wilson—whose lone Everest attempt was a magnificent failure. The final entry reads: "Off again, gorgeous day."

The Professor in the Bear Trap.

By Otto Frank.

This extraordinary narrative of personal adventure will, we think, attract a good deal of attention. The well-known Austrian savant, Professor Ernst Schmidt, commissioned by his Government to survey some mountains in Bosnia, was actually caught in the jaws of a powerful bear trap chained to a beech-tree. His long imprisonment, the dreadful agony of his leg, the visit of the bear, the desperate struggles to get free, and by what strange expedient this was finally brought about.

IN the world-remote wooded mountains of Bosnia bears are very numerous to this day. There Mr. Bruin finds an abundance of the berries and other fruits which his heart loves. On the approach of winter, which is usually very severe in Bosnia, he will, in a sheltered spot, prepare himself a nest of twigs, leaves, and moss, in which to lie dormant through the coldest part of the year. During that time he takes no food, but lives literally on his own fat ; so that when he comes out in spring he is a sorry spectacle—thin and haggard, and therefore a dangerous customer to meet. Driven by hunger, he then seeks for food, and when there is a scarcity of vegetables — as may well happen early in the year— he seeks after flesh. When once he has tasted this he becomes a beast of prey in the true sense of the word. Success makes him bold ; he goes farther and farther afield, finally invading the habitations of men and robbing the stable or cow-house of some villager.

Of course, the Bosnian peasant does not quietly put up with that sort of thing, but tries his best to become still more nearly acquainted with the ungainly brown robber, in order at once to stop his thieving and to secure his valuable skin. Oddly enough, bears almost pedantically keep to one beaten track ; and so the peasants take great trouble to find out the robber's wonted way, and having succeeded, they place right in the middle of the path an extremely strong iron trap. The chain attached to this trap is then fastened round a tree—or if there be none near, to a large and heavy log of wood.

These bear traps are commonly placed far away from all spots visited by man ; and scrupulous care is taken to cover both trap and chain with moss and leaves, so as not to excite the bear's suspicions. Now to our story.

Professor Ernst Schmidt, whose portrait I am able here to reproduce, had been commissioned by the Austrian Government to survey the mountains to the south-west of Sarajevo, in order to prepare a geological map thereof. Now of necessity this work compelled the professor to penetrate to many different points in order to obtain specimens and ascertain the nature of the stratification ; he also wanted to study the Bjelasnica Mountains, the highest peaks of which are over 6,000ft. above the sea. Accordingly, one morning very early he left the railway at Tarcin, and wandered up the highly romantic Lepenica Valley. Having reached the sources of the Lepenica River, he struck into the mountains in an easterly direction, with the intention of reaching Pazaric, on the Sarajevo-Konjica Railway, the same night.

THIS IS PROFESSOR SCHMIDT, THE YOUNG AUSTRIAN SAVANT WHO SPENT SEVENTY HOURS IN THE BEAR TRAP.
From a Photo. by Gebastianutti & Benque, Trieste.

Professor Schmidt wore an ordinary tourist's suit, with laced boots and leather leggings. He carried in his knapsack a havelock or overcoat, besides food enough for the day, consisting of cold meat, a flask of wine, some eggs, bread, etc. He also had a coarse bag to hold his specimens, and a moderate-sized hammer, with which from time to time he broke off bits of rock after the manner of geologists. The professor possessed a good general knowledge of the Bjelasnica Mountains, having already made several excursions in them ; but, nevertheless, he had provided himself with a good map of the district and a compass.

He had a hard day's work cut out for him. A tour in the Bosnian Mountains is difficult enough under any circumstances, as in places they are very steep and full of crevasses ; and Professor Schmidt, in order to attain his object, might not always take the easiest way. At times, indeed, he was forced to climb the face of an extremely steep rock; at others, to penetrate almost impassable thickets, such as are common in the forests of these mountains. Consequently, it was no wonder that early in the afternoon, when he turned back, he was very tired—especially considering that he had to carry a heavy bag of stones with him. But yet that did not deter him, on the descent, from stopping now and again to examine the ground—on which occasions, by the way, the bag got fuller and heavier. At last he had almost reached the Krupar Valley, whence an hour and a half's walk would take him to the railway station. In his left hand he held the bag, which already dragged along the ground, and in his right he grasped his alpenstock. Just as he was in the act of quitting the thick beech forest and entering a meadow, Dr. Schmidt suddenly felt a terrific blow on his left leg, and instantly he was hurled full length on the ground. On rising, he was astounded to find that *he was caught in a bear trap!* Professor

"ON RISING, HE WAS ASTOUNDED TO FIND THAT HE WAS CAUGHT IN A BEAR TRAP!"

Schmidt believes that had not fortunately the bag of stones got into the trap at the same moment as his own person, the bone of his leg would have been crushed, so great was the force with which the trap shut. You see, the tremendously powerful jaws first struck the bag, and then, with considerably diminished violence, his leg.

"The first moment or so after my capture," says the professor, "I did not deem the affair

so very serious, believing myself strong enough to press down the spring and thus release my imprisoned limb. With all my might and main, therefore, I pressed the spring with my right foot, at the same time endeavouring to lever open the jaws by inserting my alpenstock between them; but it was in vain. Then I tried another way, but equally unsuccessfully; the spring was altogether too strong. There was apparently no getting my foot out. Next I began to consider matters as more serious. 'And yet if I cannot get out,' I said to myself comfortingly the next moment, 'why, I must try and reach the valley with the trap on my leg. The peasants will laugh heartily on seeing what a strange bear they have caught!'

"Then came my second disappointment, and it was far bitterer than the first. *The trap was fastened to a stout beech-tree by means of a strong chain;* and when I endeavoured to unhook the latter I found to my horror that it was impossible, as the two ends were held together by a padlock. With my pocket-knife and geological hammer I tried to open a link in the chain, and to break the lock—but it was in vain; all my efforts were fruitless. Soon the conviction forced itself upon me that I had no means whatever of releasing myself, and, therefore, there was nothing for it but patiently to wait till somebody should visit the trap. 'To-morrow,' said I, trying to comfort myself once more, 'a hunter or peasant will certainly come and let you out; and you certainly can bear it till then.' But, despite a hundred repetitions of this comfort, I was growing very depressed, I frankly confess. I called out as loudly as I could, but at length I became too hoarse to shout any more; and besides, who could possibly be near that lonely spot at that hour? In my wanderings through the mountains I had not seen a single soul all day long, and the nearest farm was, at the very least, several miles from my remarkable prison!

"The pains in my leg grew rapidly more and more intolerable; and there was not a single thing I could do to relieve them. I did not dare to cut off my leather legging, for fear that the jaws of the trap should penetrate still deeper into my flesh and injure the bone. Nor had I even any water wherewith to cool the suffering part, which already burned in an agonizing way. Only a few paces from me a brook ran murmuring by, but it might as well have been a mile off, for my chain was too short to allow of my getting a drop. My wine-flask, too, was well-nigh empty, and I resolved to spare the little still left in it for the next day. With food I was better supplied. Not having been hungry all day, my knapsack still contained two hard-boiled eggs, a bit of meat, and some bread. Contenting myself with an egg, some meat, and a little bread, I saved the rest for the next day.

"Meanwhile it had been growing darker and darker, till at last it was quite night. Imagine the situation for yourself. The darkness, the loneliness, the intolerable pain, and the absurd situation—a man of my position caught by the leg in a bear trap! In Bosnia the spring nights are pretty cold, the temperature often falling below freezing-point. The night on this wretched occasion promised to be cold, and despite the fact that I had put on my overcoat I began to shiver a great deal. 'I shall be frozen to death, if I sit still on this cold ground,' I said to myself. 'I must take some exercise, otherwise it is all up with me.' I thought to walk round the tree to which I was chained, but I had forgotten my injured leg. Even standing increased the pain to an unbearable degree, and so walking was utterly out of the question, as it would have involved dragging the heavy trap with my suffering leg. After standing for a while leaning against a neighbouring tree I sat down again, contenting myself with doing gymnastic exercises with my arms. Then for a change I took my long, iron-pointed alpenstock and stabbed at the trees within my reach.

"In this manner I succeeded in passing a few awful leaden hours, but I felt convinced I could not continue the gymnastic exercises all night—although they had certainly warmed me a little. At last, however, my arms grew so tired that I could hardly move them at all. Accordingly I resolved to rest for a little while. But when I wanted to resume my gymnastics I found my arms even more tired than before. Also my eyes closed, and it became clear that I should be overcome in my resistance to sleep. By the light of a match I looked at my watch and found it was a quarter to twelve. How was it possible, I thought, for me, in my exhausted state, to keep awake the six dreadful hours of the night? My leg, it is true, still pained me, yet not so intensely as at first; it was, however, just as though it had been plunged into hot water up to the knee. Was it, I wondered, getting numbed? I thought of blood-poisoning, of limbs falling off, and other gruesome things. At length, giving way to my fatigue, after wrapping my overcoat tightly round me, I lay down as comfortably as circumstances permitted. Yet I did not drop off to sleep so quickly as I had expected. My excited brain kept me awake. I thought and thought, and wondered how long my captivity would last—how it would end, and whether there were not some possibility of getting out of the horrible trap without help from anybody. Suddenly it dawned on me that *perhaps the bear for which the trap had been intended might soon come along.* The thought filled me with horror. Cold drops of perspiration stood out on my forehead. 'If the bear comes you are lost,' said I to myself. 'In this position — immovable, unarmed, and caught, literally, like a rat in a trap — how could you resist the fierce creature? It would eat you up as it would a lamb or a goat.'

"When this thought came it banished all sleep. I could not get the bear out of my head. Years before I had passed some weeks in Croatia, and had ample opportunity of learning what bears are like. How, when once they have become accustomed to eating meat, they are very dangerous and relentless enemies of man. Consequently, I knew precisely what fate awaited me if the bear found me during its nocturnal rambles.

"Some hours must have elapsed when suddenly, from a distance, and in the direction of the plain, I heard a low, unmistakable growling, which I knew must come from a bear. Then it was quiet again for a time; but soon the growling recommenced, louder and more angry than before—as if the beast were irritated. I listened with an indescribable feeling of helpless horror. All grew quiet again; then once more I heard the violent growling. Next a perfect Babel of sounds reached my ear, without, however, my being able to decide from what animal they came. 'Ah! the bear is fighting with some other animal,' said I to myself. 'But what animal?' For a while quiet again prevailed. At last, when the beast made itself heard again, its growling was much more distinct than before — as if it had approached the spot where I was. When, after a few minutes' pause, its voice was heard again, it was quite close to me. The bear at this time could not have been farther from me than the breadth of the glade before me. Distinctly I heard the twigs cracking. Evidently the forest there was very dense, and at times I even thought I heard the beast snorting. My excitement, my torture, my helplessness, were something truly awful. It could not be long before the bear, which, as is well known, has a very acute sense of smell, would find me out. A short struggle—its result certain beforehand—and I should be dead, torn to pieces. And yet what I could never have hoped for actually took place. The bear left my vicinity and took its way towards the valley. Soon its voice sounded far away, and finally all was silent again. Once more I breathed almost freely. I listened a long time, but all remained quiet, and at last I fell asleep, not to wake until it was broad day.

"The first thing I did was to try every imaginable means of getting free, whether by opening the lock, a link of the chain, or the jaws of the trap itself. But all my efforts were in vain—despite all I could do I remained a helpless prisoner. Then I examined my leg, and found it terribly inflamed and swollen almost up to the knee. It was now causing me considerably more pain even than it had the evening before. Something had to be done, otherwise I think I should have gone mad. With my clasp-knife I dug up some earth, and applied it to the inflamed part as far as possible. Finding this peculiar compress brought me some relief, I renewed it several times in the course of the day. On feeling my pulse I found I had a little fever, and probably that was the reason of a want of appetite, which made half a hard-boiled egg enough for my breakfast. My thirst, however, became very tormenting, and soon the little remnant of wine I had saved was all gone.

"Hour after hour passed without anybody coming to see after the trap. I cried for help as loudly and as long as I could, but no one came to my rescue. Knowing that the hunters usually start to look after their traps soon after daybreak, I had confidently reckoned on being freed in the course of the morning. But noon came and found me still fastened in agony to the tree. How much longer, I wondered dizzily, was I to remain in that torturing condition? When would *somebody* come up the mountain? And suppose that the trap had been altogether forgotten? Or the man who looked after it been taken ill, or otherwise prevented from coming—what then? Then indeed I should perish miserably of hunger and thirst. However small the rations I allowed myself, my provisions could not possibly be eked out for more than another day, and to drink I now had nothing whatever. Deep depression took possession of me. For a long while I sat resting my head on my hand, brooding in melancholy and despair. I thought of my aged parents—what a terrible blow it would be to those dear ones to lose their only son. Then I remembered a saying my father was fond of using: 'Don't despair!' And curiously enough, those words encouraged me. Taking heart again, I roused myself from my useless lethargy, and again made every possible effort to free myself from my hateful captivity. The result was the same as in all my innumerable previous attempts. Then I began considering whether it would not be possible to burn down the beech-tree to which the trap-chain was fastened. But soon I was forced to the conclusion that if the trunk of the tree were on fire I, who was hardly two paces from it, should inevitably be consumed also—apart from the fact that at the same time the whole forest would be set on fire. But then again, could not I cut down the tree with my clasp-knife? I had asked myself the question long before, it is true, but had concluded that such a manner of deliverance was both impossible and grotesque. The beech was a thick one, with a diameter of almost 2ft. How then could I even dream of felling it with my pocket-knife? But even presupposing the bare possibility, it was a job that would take not mere hours, but whole days. And, besides, I could not conceal from myself the possibility that the falling tree might crush me to death, so that my efforts would result only in my own speedier destruction. All these things occurred to me, and yet I had a much greater mind to try than I had had previously.

"Losing no more time, I set about my apparently absurd work. As my painful leg compelled me to sit all the time, I was forced to make the incision pretty near the ground, where the trunk was, of course, thickest. I began by cutting two rings right round the tree about a foot apart, and then stripping off the bark between them. That was comparatively easy. But when I began cutting the wood itself I found at once how hard beech is. Very soon the perspiration was running down my face and my right hand was covered with blisters; but the result of this labour was very unsatisfactory. Next I tried another way, which proved much more effectual. I put my knife—which, as I omitted to mention, had a large, strong blade—slanting against the tree, and with my hammer drove it downwards towards a cut I had made lower down, and then with little trouble I could break off large chips; for beech wood splits easily. I worked hard all the afternoon and evening, and when increasing darkness compelled me to stop, I was well satisfied with what I had accomplished. Fancy a feeling of comparative content under such circumstances —the second night darkening down. I had got on unexpectedly quickly, because the wood was diseased and soft in one place, where the cut

"I PUT MY KNIFE SLANTING AGAINST THE TREE, AND WITH MY HAMMER DROVE IT DOWNWARDS."

it. Imagine my despair! The work had been progressing remarkably well, and just when success became probable —nay, well-nigh certain—this new misfortune occurred to dash my hopes. I lost my one and only tool—the sole thing that could possibly deliver me from my amazing bondage and save my life. But now I was reckoning how long I could eke out my scanty remnant of food, and how many days after it was gone I should have to endure the awful tortures of hunger before I finally died of starvation. I remembered reading of imprisoned miners who had lived without food for a week or more.

"It was long before I had sufficiently recovered from the shock to consider that after all it might be possible to use the broken blade. The break was a favourable one, being not in the middle, but close to the handle. My first task was to get the blade out of the wood in which it was stuck—a difficult operation, as it did not project enough to enable me to catch hold of it with my fingers. After considerable exertion, however, I at last succeeded in wrenching off the chip with my alpenstock and getting out the precious blade.

"Meanwhile it had become so dark as to make it impossible to do anything more that night. Having nothing to eat, all I could do was to stretch myself on the sodden ground, and there I slept for some hours, despite the pouring rain.

"As soon as the next day began to dawn I resumed operations on the cruel beech. I found I could use the broken blade like a chisel; but separating the chip was much more difficult and slow. Nevertheless, I did not lose courage; my progress was slow, it is true, but still it was constant, notwithstanding my increasing weakness. But would my strength, I wondered, hold out until the tree fell? I worked with feverish haste—my hands trembling and my temples throbbing. I was fully convinced that, unless release came soon, exhaustion would overcome me and put an end to everything. My excitement increased so, that repeatedly I hit my left hand a smashing blow with the hammer. But, regardless of the pain, I worked on and on breathlessly.

"At last I had got so far that the tree might fall at any moment. Now my fate should soon be decided. Either I would be free or crushed to death. The rain had ceased in the early hours of the morning, and the wind had risen and blew a gale at noon; it had, however,

was already almost as deep as the large blade of my knife was long. After eating a few mouthfuls of meat, I was about to arrange my primitive bed, when it suddenly began to rain very heavily, so that in half an hour there was not a dry thread about me, despite my overcoat. Nevertheless, I was heartily glad of the rain, for I was already suffering dreadfully from thirst, which now, thank God, I could quench. I caught the water in my hat, and dug a little hole in the ground in which to store some more. I also drank as much as I wanted, and filled my flask besides.

"After a few hours the rain ceased. Although I was so cold in my wet clothes that my teeth chattered, I was so very tired that I soon fell into a sleep, which fortunately lasted all night, undisturbed by any bear.

"When I awoke the next morning it was raining again, and it hardly left off the whole day and the succeeding night. The inflammation had by this time extended farther up my leg, which I could not now bend without frightful pain. My fever, too, had increased, as I found on feeling my pulse. Nevertheless I immediately set to work at the tree once more, and continued working almost uninterruptedly till evening, when I sustained a fresh blow. Just as I was getting out a rather large chip my knife-blade broke—evidently I had overstrained

"I GAVE ONE LAST DESPAIRING CRY FOR HELP, AND THEN FAINTED."

I had to remain four days before I was able to return to Sarajevo.

"The reason why no one had come to look after the trap was as follows : The bear, whose growling had so frightened me the first night, had been caught in another trap which the peasants had put in a meadow, and which, for want of a tree near by, they had fastened to a large log of wood. Thus, though the bear was caught, it could walk about. Evidently it meant to go to its lair in the mountains, and on its way had passed very near me. On arriving at the glade it must have changed its mind, so to speak, and gone down towards the Krupar brook. There its log was caught in the thicket, and so in the morning the men found the captive beast with little trouble. Joyful at catching their enemy, they very naturally omitted looking after the other trap, and the following day they were again deterred by the torrents of rain. Besides, in the conviction that there was no second bear in the neighbourhood, they naturally were not in any hurry to visit the other trap.

"My leg was in a terrible condition ; but fortunately it had not sustained any permanent injury, and in a short time was perfectly well again.

"My knife, despite its broken blade, has a place of honour on my desk. Although the sight of it reminds me of three woful days, such as I hope never again to experience, yet I treasure the simple thing as the saviour of my life."

moderated since then. Towards one o'clock there was a sudden gust, and to my delight my beech cracked, and then slowly fell on to its neighbours. Finally, it fell to the ground with a crash like thunder.

"Unhurt—free! A seventy hours' captivity over! Not quite, however, for the trap and chain were still attached to my leg. But yet I could by some means now get into the valley, not that that was an easy undertaking—even to a man full of strength. Being unable to use my left leg I could only slide along in a sitting posture. At first I got on pretty well, but after a while the unwonted mode of motion tired me so very much that repeatedly I was forced to rest awhile through sheer inability to move. For six dreadful hours this extraordinary journey continued before I reached the village of Pazaric, which I entered with my clothes rent and my face so torn by the bushes and boughs that the blood was running down it. My hands also were bleeding and blistered. But summoning up the last remnant of my strength I gave one last despairing cry for help, and then fainted.

"On coming to again I found that some men had removed the huge trap from my leg, and that I was in a peasant woman's house. There

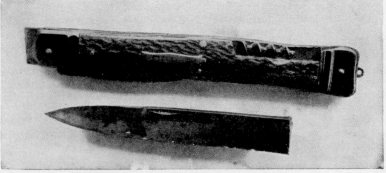

THIS IS THE PROFESSOR'S TRUSTY POCKET-KNIFE, WITH WHICH HE CUT DOWN THE TREE, AND TO WHICH HE OWES HIS LIFE. IT WAS SPECIALLY PHOTOGRAPHED FOR THIS NARRATIVE.

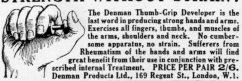

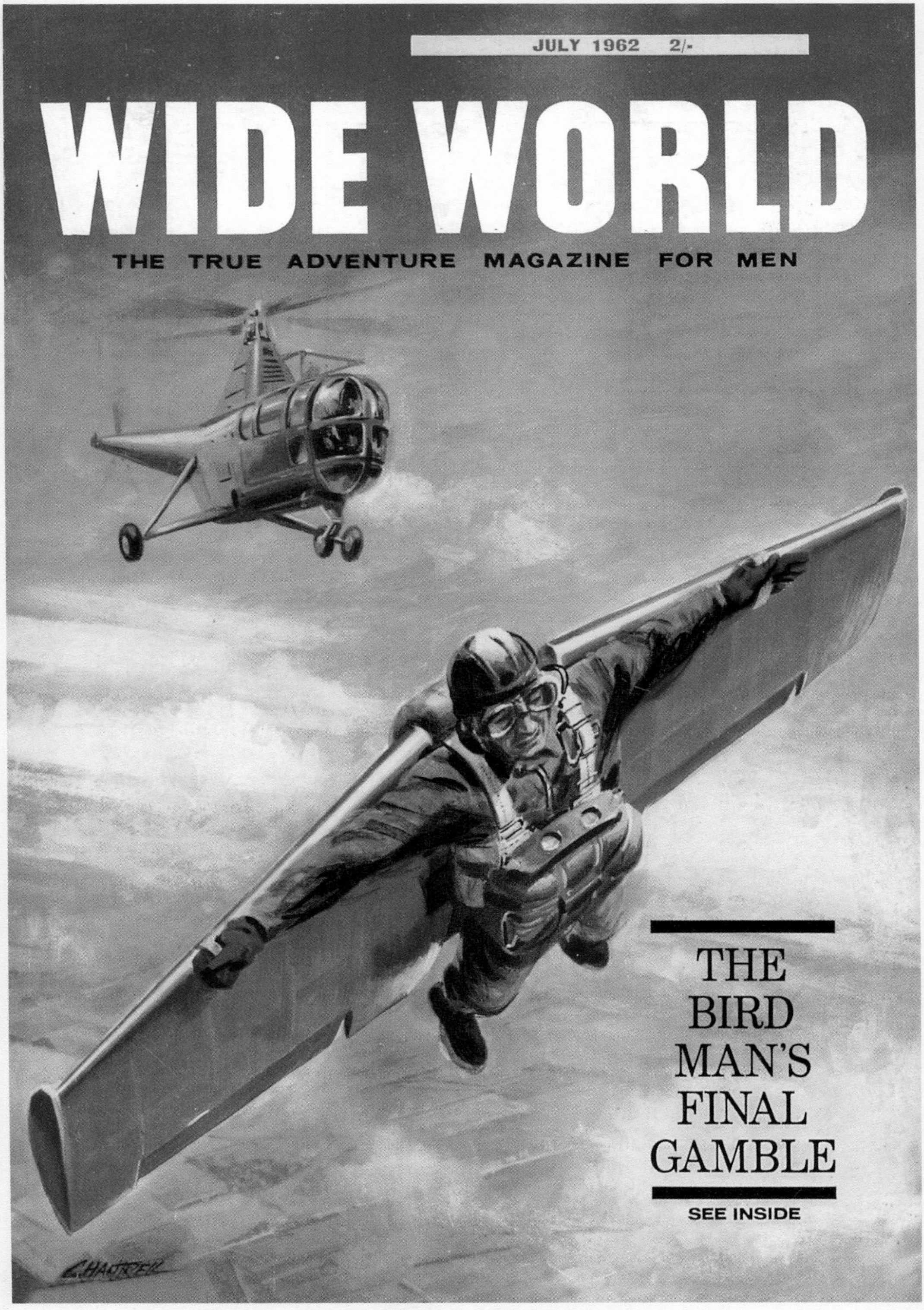

JULY 1962   2/-

WIDE WORLD

THE TRUE ADVENTURE MAGAZINE FOR MEN

**THE
BIRD
MAN'S
FINAL
GAMBLE**

SEE INSIDE

THE BIRD MAN'S FINAL GAMBLE

He had devoted his life to planning the conquest of the skies, and now he was to gamble his life to fulfil his long-cherished dream of flying just like a bird . . .

A SHIMMERING haze of heat blankets the crowd of 100,000 that has come to see the International Air Display. The sky is Mediterranean-blue, the tarmac and terminal buildings of Speke Airport, Liverpool, gleam an eye-searing Tangier-white, and the grass of the airfield is scorched yellowish-brown in patches.

A Sipa Minijet zooms low. A gasp scythes across the crowd. The sun stabs off the sleek, silver bodies of 'planes that buzz, like angry gnats, through the tepid air.

Very soon now, the great event of the pageant is scheduled to take place. Thousands of programmes rustle an overture of anticipation.

The cause of all this excitement is a slight, swarthy, 37-year-old Frenchman. His name is Léo Valentin, and ever since he was a small boy, watching the storks and buzzards soaring above the trees of the great park that surrounded his home at Epinal in the Vosges department of France, he has devoted his life to the dream of flying like a bird.

Today is to see the climax of that dream, for, billed as the Bird Man, he is to jump from an aircraft at 8,500 feet and, with the aid of a pair of wooden wings, attempt to glide for several miles before parachuting down on to the airfield.

He is the last of the twentieth-century disciples of Icarus. He is to try to realise the age-old dream of the ancient Greek, and challenge the sky. And I am to go up into the sky with him, to witness his supreme effort.

Léo Valentin was born of humble parents at Epinal in 1919. Before he was ten, fascinated by aeroplanes, he was spending most of his time wandering around the hangars of Dogneville Aerodrome, gazing enraptured at the quaint flying-machines of those days, and sometimes actually talking to the leather-suited and goggled demigods, the pilots who flew them.

Young Valentin left school at sixteen to become, first, a butcher's boy, and then an apprentice locksmith; but the urge to fly persisted, and he scraped together sufficient money to attend lectures at the Vosges Air Club in his spare time.

COVER AND
ILLUSTRATION
BY CHANTRELL

By RICHARD WHITTINGTON-EGAN

In 1938, when he was 19, he enlisted in the *Armée de l'Air,* was sent to Blida in North Africa, and soon became a corporal. Impatient, though, at the prospect of the three years' pilot's course one had to take, before starting to fly, he volunteered to train as a parachutist at the Maison Blanche centre in Algiers.

He made his first jump over Baraki on 15th October, 1938.

The following year war was declared, and the French parachutists were, for a time, transformed into mountain troops. That did not suit young Valentin at all.

When France fell, he was fighting on the Pyrenean frontier, but he managed to escape, via the underground, to North Africa. There he joined the parachute school which had been formed at Fez and, with more than 80 jumps to his credit, became, before he was twenty-one, a sergeant-instructor.

Soon, however, the monotony of camp life began to bore him. He wanted action, and so, at the end of 1942, he embarked on a troop-transport, and a few days later found himself in Liverpool.

From there he was sent to a camp near Glasgow, where the British Special Air Service was undergoing intensive training in preparation for the invasion of the German-held Continent. *(continued overleaf)*

On 9th June, 1944, Valentin parachuted into Brittany. He dropped over Morbihan and, after blowing up the railway lines between Vannes and Rennes, made his way to the St. Marcel Plateau.

During the next few months he took part in some fierce fighting and, after a brief respite back in England, was sent into the Loire pocket where, in the course of an engagement with the SS, his right arm was shattered. He was treated in the hospital at Issoudun, and convalesced on the Marne and in England.

When the war ended, Valentin was promoted to sergeant-major, and posted as an instructor to the parachute school at Lannion. A few months later the school was transferred to Pau, and there Valentin remained, until he decided to quit the *Armée de l'Air* in 1949.

It was in the Pau library that Léo Valentin first began to pore over certain old books in which was embalmed the history of man's long fight to conquer the heavens.

He read, with mounting excitement, of the pioneer parachutists—of old Fausto Veranzio, the Venetian mathematician who, in 1616, first described an apparatus resembling a parachute; of Sebastien le Normand, the father of parachuting; of Berry, the first parachutist to be launched from a 'plane, and of the American, Irvin, who, on 28th April, 1919, jumped from an aeroplane flying at 1,800 feet, and fell to 600 feet before opening his parachute, thus accomplishing the first delayed-action drop ever.

He read, and he resolved that he would have *his* place in the sky.

Work In Secret

This ambition was achieved when, on 23rd March, 1948, he jumped over Pau from a height of 22,000 feet, allowing himself to fall to 1,800 feet before opening his parachute.

That exploit put in his pocket the world record for a free drop without a respirator.

During those four years at Pau, Valentin made one other great advance. He invented a method of controlling his position during a free fall. It is still known as the Valentin Position.

Naturally, all these activities made him something of a star in the world of aviation, and when he retired from the *Armée de l'Air*, he made up his mind to turn to stunt-parachuting as a profession.

It was then that he began to consider again the whole question of flight. He wanted to fly like a bird—like those storks and buzzards he had loved to watch so long ago at Epinal. He decided that, like a bird, he must sprout wings.

Working in secret, he made himself a

THE BIRD MAN'S FINAL GAMBLE

(continued)

pair of canvas wings. He tried them out on 30th April, 1950, at Villacoublay, before a crowd of 300,000.

They were not a success, and nearly cost him his life.

Undeterred, he attempted a second flight with them, over Meaux-Esbly Airfield on 4th May. Once again they proved dangerously unsatisfactory.

It was then that Valentin realised that he must abandon canvas wings. What he really needed, he told himself, were wooden feathers.

Throughout the last six months of 1950, and the first six months of 1951, he and his friend, Monsieur Collignon, spent many, many hours in the latter's workshops on the outskirts of Paris, constructing a pair of wooden wings.

Valentin made his first test jump with them at Cormeilles-en-Vexin on 8th June, 1951. He launched himself from a platform attached to the side of a helicopter.

A terrific gust of wind closed the wings and he got into a terrible spin. He only just managed to pull out of it, and landed with the hard-won knowledge that some way must be devised to prevent the wings from closing.

His Worst Drop

A month later, his wings now provided with automatic locks, the indomitable little Frenchman was ready to try again.

This occasion—2nd July, 1951—was, for him, a rather special one. The venue for the jump was that same Dogneville Airfield where, nearly a quarter of a century before, the young Valentin had watched and envied his heroes of the sky.

He soared to 9,000 feet, in a Junkers 52, and leapt into the void. He had just time to glimpse the well-remembered landscape of his childhood, spread like a tawny map below him, and then found himself plunged into a bewildering spin.

The lock of his right wing had been damaged. The left wing was firm, locked, but the right wing hung limp and flapping at his side.

The spin intensified and the earth whirled like a vortex. The blood rushed to his head, and his vision blurred.

On the point of fainting, he just managed, by a gigantic effort of will, to pull the ripcord of his 'chute.

Trembling like a leaf, he landed on the very brink of the Moselle. It was the worst drop he had ever made.

It says much for the man's nerve that, after such an experience, Valentin could again entrust himself to the mercy of those fickle wings. As it happened, victory was just around the corner.

Three years later, on 13th May, 1954, at

Valentin, with his " bat's wings ", flying earthwards from 6,000 feet. ▶

Gisy-les-Nobles, near Pont-sur-Yonne, Léo Valentin, the Bird Man, using his wooden wings, "flew" for a distance of at least three miles over Thorigny, and landed, safe and sound, in a field of lucerne.

And so to Whitsun Monday, 21st May, 1956, at Speke, Liverpool, where he plans to experiment with a new pair of wings.

They are of bright, orange-coloured balsawood. Four-feet high, and with an overall span of nine feet, they are attached to a light metal alloy corset, and fitted with ailerons. The whole apparatus weighs 28 lb.

Before a bank holiday crowd of 100,000, the Bird Man is to fly again, and I am to fly with him.

It is 3.40 p.m. precisely. I follow the diminutive figure of the Bird Man across the tarmac, and clamber after him into the waiting Dakota.

Five minutes later, the engines are revving up, and then we begin to taxi slowly out to the runway.

"*Un moment! Un moment!*" shouts Valentin.

He has forgotten something. We stop. He leaps out and runs across the tarmac to a small shed.

A minute or so later he is back, with a box spanner. I help him into the 'plane and we move off again.

At 3.55 we roar across the field. The ground drops away and we are airborne.

We bank out over the Mersey River, describe a vast circle over Cheshire, and climb steadily and smoothly to 9,000 feet.

The earth is spread out below us, like a green patchwork quilt. It looks far away and very harmless. The late afternoon sun glints gold across great cotton-woolly patches of cumulus cloud, bunched like irregular icebergs in a blue and misty sea of sky.

It is cold in the aircraft. Icy air comes rushing in through the seven-foot gap where the port-side freight doors have been removed to facilitate the Bird Man's exit.

I glance at Valentin. He is sitting hunched like a broody bird on the back seat. The wind ruffles his hair, combed straight back

(continued overleaf)

THE BIRD MAN'S FINAL GAMBLE

(continued)

over his balding head, and it stands up like the crest of a bird.

He seems nervous and ill at ease, and crouches on the very edge of the seat, sucking his lips and looking out of the window.

I go across and speak to him. He confesses that he hates heights, and tells me that an ascent of the Eiffel Tower once made him sick.

At 4.06 we top 9,000 feet, and then drop to 8,500, the height from which the jump is to be made.

"Five minutes from now," says the pilot.

Valentin rises to his feet and struggles into his parachutes. He has two of them, in case one "candles." He fixes his main parachute to his back.

"Four minutes."

He straps the other to his chest. That is his emergency 'chute. On top of it is a wooden panel, carrying a stop-watch and an altimeter.

"Three minutes."

Tension increases in the 'plane, and I find myself noticing little things, like the bright-blue wool jumper Valentin wears under his olive-green flying-suit, the brown, lambs'-wool-lined suede boots with zip-fasteners and crêpe soles to take the shock on landing, the large gold ring on the little finger of his left hand.

"Two minutes."

Valentin puts on his goggles and crash helmet, and a pair of red rubber gloves, rough-surfaced like those used by a gardener or a wicketkeeper. With his hands, he indicates that his heart is fluttering. He crouches down in front of the wings and starts to adjust the straps.

"One minute."

Valentin is not even nearly ready.

"Non, non, non!" he exclaims.

We begin a second circuit.

"Five minutes from now," says the pilot.

The Bird Man steps into his wings. He is facing the back of the aircraft, and he gazes wistfully out of the open hatch. Squatting on his heels, he inches infinitely slowly forward to the edge of the hatch.

At 4.16 we reach the jumping point for the second time.

"Now!"

Valentin braces himself. Leans outwards.

"Non, non, non!" he almost screams. "A gauche. A gauche. La rivière à gauche."

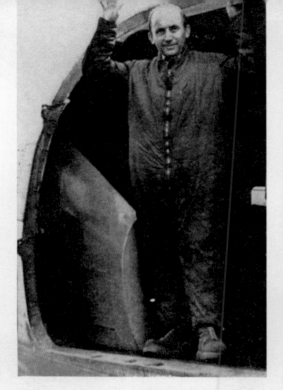

Valentin waves to the crowd before leaving on what was to prove his last flight.

He wants the River Mersey on his left.

For the third time we start that circuit. We have been in the air barely twenty minutes, but time seems somehow to have clicked into another gear.

Monotonous, and as inevitable as a dripping tap, the count-down begins again.

"Five minutes."

Once more Valentin begins to edge towards the hatch, and fights the roaring, blustering gale that plucks at his clumsy wings.

"Four minutes."

Slowly—so slowly—he advances.

"Three minutes."

His wing-tips keep catching in the ridging of the metal floor.

"Two minutes."

There can be no mistaking the strain he is undergoing. It seems to me almost as if Valentin has a premonition. I *know* he does not want to jump. Can he see death below, through a mist of cloud? He shuffles doggedly forward into the main aperture.

"One minute."

I go over to Valentin, pat him on the shoulder and say: "*Bonne chance!*"

He pulls a wry face, gives the thumbs-up signal, and replies: "*Merci, monsieur.*"

The time is 4.21.

"Now!"

What happens now, happens so quickly that it is difficult to be sure of it.

Valentin steps backwards and sideways to the brink of the exit, his closed wings held straight in front of him, his body bent, leaning backwards and half supported by the outside pressure.

He looks rapidly up, once . . . down, twice . . . and then it seems to me that a buffet of wind catches him and whips him out of the aircraft into the slipstream.

At the same time, I hear a terrific splintering noise above the roar of the engines. I lean forward, and see a tiny fragment of orange wood whisked away by the wind.

Another piece hits the fuselage, and goes spiralling, like an autumn leaf, to earth. The Bird Man has clipped his left wing on the side of the exit hatch.

A second, even less than a second later, there is another crack, and the 'plane, which has been flying so smoothly that you could have balanced a threepenny-bit on edge in it, gives a lurch.

For a moment I am afraid that our tailplane has been fatally damaged. All is well, however, but Valentin is in serious trouble.

Leaning out, I am almost caught in the slipstream. I feel myself being sucked out of the 'plane. I am out almost to the waist, when a colleague grabs my legs and manages to drag me back; but I have caught a glimpse of Valentin. He is spinning, clockwise, towards the earth like a top—rolling, spiralling, crazily pirouetting to certain death—his smashed, orange wings glistening like blood in the sunlight.

He has two chances—two parachutes.

We bank off to the left, and anxiously circle above his tumbling body, watching helplessly.

He has fallen, I should judge, about a thousand feet, when I see a little puff of white. His parachute is opening.

But no! Instead of mushrooming out, it remains cylindrical like a candle—a Roman candle—the stuck silk rippling like a flame.

Chance number one is lost.

Down . . . down . . . down he hurtles. Although he is plummeting at 120 miles an hour, the fall seems interminable. Time is eternity up here.

What about that second parachute on his chest?

Heart-in-mouth, I strain to see. He is now about 1,000 feet from the ground.

The second parachute opens, but fails to develop.

That has candled, too! It lashes around his face, and wraps itself about his body like a shroud. I see him frantically struggling to free himself . . .

The long agony is almost over now.

Our 'plane dives steeply in the wake of Valentin, to within a few-score feet of the ground.

There, below me in a green-and-yellow cornfield, spread-eagled, I see the figure of a bird—a bird with splayed and broken wings.

He lies on his face, absolutely still, the only movement a slight ruffling of the white silk, which looks, from this height, for all the world like the snowy pinions of a swan.

Léo Valentin once wrote: "You cannot continue to stretch the limits of what is possible without provoking death—and that slut is not very loving if you flout her, or pretend to ignore her."

"Death Is For Others!"

Yet more than 600 times since he first discovered what he called "that dark mistress, fear" in the sky above Baraki, he had flung himself into the spacious jaws of death.

He had seen others "make a dent in the ground"—young Raoul Sabé, his army comrade whom he had seen plunge to death in 1938, just two days before he had to make his own first drop; Clem Sohn, that other bird man; Salvator Canarrozzo, and female-parachutist Baby Monetti.

"But death is for the others, not for me," he would say. "I always get the firm conviction, before I do anything, that I am going to come out alive."

Circling above his body, we saw them cover him with his parachute—it was his shroud.

As we flew off, heading back to the airfield, I gazed up at the sky. It was blue—like a baby's eyes. How innocent it looked! Why shouldn't it? It was the earth that killed Léo Valentin, for, as he himself once wrote: "The lost parachutist knows the face of death. It is the face of the earth."

The end of the Bird Man. Valentin lies dead after the Liverpool disaster.

"THERE WAS NOTHING TO DO BUT TO CHARGE THEM."

The Grey Scourge.

SOME ROUMANIAN WOLF STORIES.

BY ROOK CARNEGIE, OF BRAILA, ROUMANIA.

Harmless and cowardly in summer, when he hunts alone and there is plenty to eat, but a deadly menace in winter, when hunger gnaws at his vitals and he joins his grey-coated fellows in concerted attacks upon hapless travellers — such is the dreaded wolf of the Carpathian forests. In this article, Mr. Carnegie, who has lived in Roumania for many years, tells some enthralling Christmas stories concerning life-and-death fights with the "grey scourge."

IN England the worried mother, in order to make her child keep quiet, threatens it with, "If you are not good I'll give you to the sweep!" In Roumania the peasant mother says, "Be quiet, or the wolf will come and take you!" And it is not only the children of Roumania who fear the wolf, for its presence is a terrible menace to old and young alike. A fearful coward in summer, when he has plenty to eat and lives alone, it is only in winter that, emboldened by strength of numbers and desperate from the gnawings of hunger, he becomes a savage and ruthless beast of prey. The trackless forests of the Carpathians teem with the grey brutes, and thence in winter they come down to the plains in search of prey, travelling hundreds of miles across the frozen wastes, attacking and devouring anything and everything that comes in their way. For this reason all live stock is kept under cover throughout the whole of the winter.

Even in the daytime the peasants move from village to village only in large, well-armed groups. Every winter the newspapers are full of accounts of encounters with wolves or deaths from their attacks. The annual quota of the latter must always run into three figures. Organized "drives" are sometimes made, but with small

success so far as the wolves are concerned, instinct apparently warning them to save themselves ere the network of beaters is drawn too close.

In times gone by they were more numerous than at present. Even in the larger towns no one stirred out alone after dark, as the marauding brutes often penetrated to the very middle of the town itself. In Tulcea, on the Lower Danube, there exists the tale of how, many years ago, some thirty people, guests at a wedding, started for home in the small hours, with gipsy music in front, to conduct each family in turn to their dwelling. *None of them arrived home!* I have been assured by several inhabitants of the town that this is absolutely true, and I fully believe it to be so. One can imagine the size of a pack that would dare to attack and kill a party of thirty people.

The following three stories I can personally vouch for, as the particulars show.

The winter of 1901 was an exceptionally severe one. So heavy was the snow that on one occasion the train service was interrupted for ten days, during which time we received no word from the outer world.

Five privates of the 6th Regiment of Militia, with its head-quarters in Galatz, obtained leave of absence for the Roumanian Christmas (our

7th of January). Their names were: Vasili Stan, Vasili Omescu, Ghitza Maorodin, Ilie Stephanescu, and Alexandru Balceanu, all belonging to the village of Pekie. On the 7th of January, their Christmas, they set out for home, a distance of from five to seven miles.

The three days' leave expired, and all those who had been on leave reported themselves with the exception of our five. They were marked as not having returned to barracks, and after a week's time were regarded as deserters, and warrants were issued for their arrest.

On the military authorities inquiring at the village, however, they were surprised to hear that the men had never arrived there. The matter was given over to the police, but though a hue and cry was raised and their description circulated throughout the country, nothing could be heard of them.

A fortnight later some peasants with sleighs went to collect firewood in the woods lying between Galatz and the village of Pekie. On the outskirts of the forest they came on a terrible sight, and reported it at once to the mayor. I was stopping for a few days with a landed proprietor in the neighbourhood, and so heard of the affair. My host had horses put in the sleigh and we drove over. Everything remained as the peasants had found it, waiting for the military authorities.

The snow inside a circle of thirty yards was beaten and trodden down, soaked a deep crimson with frozen blood. Buttons and five sword-bayonets, with blood frozen deep on the blades, one of which had a portion of the vertebræ of a wolf's backbone still on the point, lay about. There were also scabbards and belts, much gnawed, some few human and wolf bones, scraps of cloth, and—five pairs of feet! For wolves never eat the feet of their human victims, which fact I have never yet seen noted in print.

It was not much, but enough to tell us what had happened. The poor militiamen—tramping happily over the frozen snow, carrying their little presents for those at home, joining, perhaps, in one of their patriotic songs—little thought of the unseen enemy treacherously skulking along in the undergrowth on their left, watching for a favourable opportunity to make the final rush.

Then came the sudden attack, the fierce fight for dear life—fists and bayonets against those terrible sharp fangs. And at last the end, one after another being pulled down, with the final fight among the pack, those killed by the soldiers being also hungrily devoured.

Some of the peasants had reverently fixed up a holy candle or two, and a few of their relations were praying on all fours—the peasantry of the Balkans do not kneel.

It is not often that a man lives to tell the tale of escape from these four-footed fiends of winter, but here is a tale by one who fought an immense pack single-handed and saved himself by coolness and bravery.

On December 24th, 1903, Barbu Calinescu, a sergeant of the rural gendarmerie, was returning to the town of Ploesti, having been on his weekly patrol through some of the outlying villages. I will give his story as nearly as I can as he lately retold it to me.

It would be about five and getting dusk as I came along the road where it cuts into the edge of the forest of Vadeni. My horse began to get a bit restless, but I did not attach any importance to its behaviour till it began to snort and shiver. Then I heard what the animal had heard—the far-away baying of a pack of wolves. I knew what it was, though I had never heard the sound before. My charger began to get very nervous, and for this reason I commenced to trot—not that it ever struck me for a moment that they were after me. After a time the sound died down, and I supposed the brutes had gone off in some other direction. Suddenly, however, it broke out again from the forest on my left, this time very much closer. Then I heard the crackling of broken twigs, and soon the baying appeared so near that I wondered I could not see some of them.

Never thinking of danger—for he who rides always feels safe on his horse—I unslung my carbine, meaning, when I got a look at them, to give them a fright, expecting one shot would send them flying. We always carry two blank cartridges above three bulleted ones in our carbines.

I had not long to wait. A minute or two more, and I saw weird grey shapes flying along among the under-brush and between the fir trees; as they got nearer their numbers increased, and I could barely keep my terrified horse at a short canter.

Presently, as though at a preconcerted signal, they all showed themselves; I should think there were two hundred at least! Taking up my reins, I fired my two blank cartridges, but, to my consternation, the reports had no effect on the brutes! Now, for the first time, I began to realize that the matter was serious. Looking behind me, I saw some of them crossing the road, so as to hem me in on both sides.

Then I fired my three bullets at them—bang! bang! bang! I heard yelps of pain, but what damage I had done I could not see, for by this time I was galloping. Slinging my carbine strap over my head, I sat down to ride hard. The road here was straight, and I looked anxiously ahead in the hope of seeing some carts or other signs of human presence. But there was nothing to be seen! I knew now that I must make a fight for my life. I had a good hour to ride, going my best, before I could hope to reach a place of safety. There was no need to spur my steed; the poor beast was snorting and sweating with fear as he dashed along. Happily I managed to keep him in hand; had he lost his head and gone rushing away into the woods it would have been adieu to both of us!

Sergeant Barbu Calinescu, who found himself surrounded by a huge pack of hunger-maddened wolves, and only narrowly escaped with his life.
From a Photograph.

Now, for the first time, they came close to me. Eight or ten great brutes leapt out into the road and raced along, looking up at me; and to my dying day I shall never forget their cruel red eyes. The great danger, I had always heard, is when they jump at a horse's shoulders and fix on with nails and teeth, driving their victims mad with fright and pain. Against this, I knew, I must be on guard. Presently one ran forward, clear of the others, looking up

and obviously preparing for a jump. I leaned forward and gave it a revolver bullet. With a yell it sprang into the air and dropped. Some few rushed at it, but, as I said before, I was galloping just as hard as my horse could go, so I did not see if they stopped to eat it. They were now flying along all round me—regularly, steadily, making hardly a sound. This noiseless manner of rapid progression—gaunt, red-eyed brutes waiting their chance to pull me down to death—was most terrifying.

We fairly flew along. Happily the snow was neither too hard nor too soft, and gave good foothold, for had my charger stumbled we should both have been finished.

Again one made a rush; then two others. Each time I bent forward and, shooting carefully, dropped each in turn at close quarters as they approached my horse. I had only two more bullets left, and they soon went in the same way—six cartridges, six wolves.

Presently, to my amazement and joy, the pack dropped back and disappeared from sight. Had the shooting been too hot for them, and were they cowed, I wondered? I did not relax my pace at first, but, hearing nothing, I finally slowed down and allowed my panting charger to walk. At last, however, as the light was getting bad, I broke into a trot again. I was just turning a bend in the road when, with a gasp, I realized the cause of the wolves' sudden disappearance. The cunning brutes had cut off a corner and were waiting for me; the road was black with them!

I had no more bullets, but I had my sabre, and glad I was then to think that I knew how to use it. There was nothing to do but to charge them, I decided. To diverge from the road meant certain death; to keep straight on was my only hope.

"I brought the heavy hilt of my sword down on its head with all my strength."

My poor charger was panting and groaning with fear and the hard going, but there was no stopping. Using my spurs freely I dashed on, and almost before I had time to think the wolves were all round me. Sword exercise! I went through it with a vengeance during the next few minutes! It was slash, slash, slash, right and left, as wolf after wolf tried a leap at my charger's shoulders. But I was soon through them and racing along again, with the pack—thinned a little, I tell you—on each side of me.

Suddenly my horse gave a scream and a leap that nearly unseated me. A wolf had sprung on to his quarters; I turned in my saddle and, as it was too close to cut, I brought the heavy hilt of my sword down on its head with all my strength. I heard the skull crack. It dropped off – dead, I suppose—and on we flew.

My poor horse was sobbing now, and I felt every stride was an effort. It seemed cruel to spur, yet I had to for both our sakes. Soon he began to flag. Would this awful race never finish, I asked myself despairingly. Then, all in a moment, as though by an order, the pack dropped back, trotted, and turned. Was it some trick of the devils to catch me?

I kept on, but they did not follow me. Then I looked ahead and saw lights. Thank Heaven, I was nearing the outskirts of the town! In the excitement of the race I had had no time to note any landmarks. My charger dropped to a walk, panting, and with head hanging down. With trembling fingers I tried to return my blood-stained sabre to its scabbard, but, now that the excitement was over, my arm was too tired, and I could not raise the point sufficiently high.

The people in the cottages on the outskirts gazed at me in wonder. At the barrier I stopped, and the policeman outside the office came over. He told me afterwards that he thought I was drunk. I got down, but went lurching all over the place, finally staggering into the office and dropping on a chair. They got me wine, and that freshened me a little. They would hardly believe my story, but my sword and some nasty bites on my horse's shoulders and flanks told the tale. I had been about an hour over that ride; it seemed like a month. I have often been over the ground again by day—and sometimes in my dreams.

Next day four of us, with plenty of cartridges, went along the road and found remains of wolves and the marks where they had eaten their dead brothers. That same evening, not far off, a peasant and his two horses were attacked and devoured—no doubt by the same pack.

Of the many wolf stories I have heard, the following is by far the most romantic. It was told me some years ago by the mayor of the village of Borcea Verde, a village in the Carpathians. If anyone looks at a map he will see the sources of the River Tekete on the Hungarian frontier and the Chuzzitza on the Roumanian side. Between the two lies the village in question. We had been shooting all day, and, sitting down after long toiling among the mountains, the subject of wolves came up. A certain Belgian engineer, who was of the party, gave it as his opinion that no wolves would stand against a bold front. Various tales were told to disprove this, and finally our host for the night, the mayor, gave us the following.

A few years since, gentlemen, there lived in this village a girl named Katinka Gaitan. She was a great beauty, very fair and blue-eyed, like many of the Mo-Kanch (a word meaning the women of the Roumanians settled in Hungary). Her father possessed some forest land, and some dealers from Budapest came and bought up all the timber, and so he became the richest man in the village. Therefore Katinka was a great *partie*—a good catch, for she was the only child and would inherit everything. But, if pretty, she was a terrible coquette, always leading some young fellow on and then throwing him over for another. At last, however, something happened that taught her a lesson. One day two of her suitors got to words about her, and one, losing his temper, drew his knife and struck the other.

Then there was a fine row. First the gendarmes came, and then the "Procuror" (Public Prosecutor). It looked like being a murder case, but the wounded man got over his injury in time, and the other—Ilie Pantu, son of a very well-to-do man—bolted, no one knew where.

From that time Katinka seemed an altered being. There were no more flirtings, no more standing about with the other young people of an evening; nor did she join in the "Hora" and other national dances on Sunday afternoons, though she was considered one of our best dancers. She remained at home, working with her mother. The Katinka of before was not the Katinka of now, people said. So, gentlemen, three years passed away, and on the few occasions we saw Katinka she was quiet and staid, and we thought her more beautiful than ever.

Then we were all surprised one day at being invited by her parents for the following Sunday to her "logodna" (betrothal ceremony). To whom? we asked one another.

There was in the village a very quiet and staid young fellow named Radu Patricin. He was an orphan, living in his own house, which he had inherited, with only an old woman to look after him. He was a "venator," or professional hunter, trapping foxes and other animals for their skins, and shooting game, which he disposed of to the Jew traders. He lived very simply, and it was known that he saved money; but who ever thought of Radu as a husband for Katinka?

Well, we went to the "logodna," ate and drank, played cards, and danced all night, leaving at daylight, wishing prosperity and happiness to the young people. But we knew it was only a marriage of arrangement—got up by Katinka's uncle, who owed money to Radu—and that, so far at least, there was not much love.

The "logodna" was on December 1st, as I remember, like all of us here in the village do, only too well.

"Beside him, muffled up, was a figure the hunter knew only too well."

A fortnight later who should ride into the village but Ilie, the man who had, three years before, stabbed the other in the quarrel about Katinka.

He came in the gay uniform of a Hungarian hussar, mounted on a splendid grey charger, and with a "wachtmeister's" stripes on his arm.

His parents received him with open arms. All the past was forgotten, and nothing was too good for him; you see, they were "Mokani," and so actually Hungarian subjects. Ilie was the hero of the village. Every day saw him at the "caritchima," paying for wine for everybody, whilst he recounted to the open-mouthed idlers the wonders of Budapest and Kecskemet, where his regiment was stationed.

No one saw them meet, and so everybody was surprised on the following Sunday, when Katinka came walking to church between Radu and Ilie.

Then, very soon, we began to see Katinka and Ilie alone, and began to remember how, in the old days, Ilie always seemed the most favoured of the crowd of Katinka's followers. But, as Radu was out with his traps and his gun all day, he was the only one who saw nothing, and nobody cared to be the one to tell him — only everybody hoped Ilie's leave would soon be at an end.

Christmas Day, as we reckon it, came round, and then something happened. We were able to put two and two together because we found, afterwards, a trap in the snow—fixed, but not yet set up—over there on one of the mountain slopes which overlook the roadway leading towards the frontier.

Radu was setting his traps, no doubt, when, looking down on the road below him, he saw a sleigh coming along, driven at a rapid rate. The man who was driving was urging his horses to their best pace, but there were no bells on the horses. This would strike Radu at once as strange. Then he saw it was Ilie, wrapped in his soldier's cloak, and beside him, muffled up, was a figure the hunter knew all too well. In a moment he understood—it was an elopement! And as he gazed, spellbound, the sleigh went out of sight.

There was a knock at Katinka's parents' door. I happened to be there, with some certificates to do with timber sales. Radu looked in, white and trembling.

"Where's Katinka?"

"Down the village at Rosa's," was the reply.

Radu turned hurriedly away. It was only after he had been gone some time that it struck us how pale and disturbed he looked. He hurried to the house of Rosa's parents.

Katinka was not there! He rushed home, threw down his gun and traps, and unhooked a heavy revolver from the wall. Then in came his old servant. Terrified at Radu's deathly colour and trembling fingers as he loaded the revolver, she shrieked. Radu sprang over, put his hand on her mouth, and forced her backwards on to the bed, where he gagged and bound her; then out he rushed, took a horse from a neighbour's shed—unnoticed, for it was growing dusk—and rode away after the fugitive pair.

Next morning, someone looking in at the

The little wooden cross erected on the spot where Katinka and her two lovers were devoured by the wolves.
From a Sketch by the Author.

window saw the old woman tied to the bed. He raised the alarm. The door was knocked in, and the poor old lady, half dead with cold and terror, was released. Then she told, in broken words, how she came to be there.

Then we learnt that Ilie had gone and that Katinka was missing, as also were the father's sleigh and horses. We saw it all. What fearful crime had Radu committed?

There was a rush of getting out sleighs and harnessing horses and of loading guns; for it was a severe winter, and the wolves were many and fierce.

The mayor paused and gazed before him, as though looking at something afar off.

"What did you find?" asked the Belgian.

The mayor looked up from his reverie and said, very slowly:—

"We found, gentlemen, a broken sleigh, some horses' bones, a few buttons, and the blade of a sword with blood frozen on it. There were also a revolver, the handle actually gnawed away, some empty cartridges, much blood-stained snow, and three pairs of human feet."

"Radu must have caught up with the runaway pair just as a pack of wolves attacked them. Instead of killing his faithless 'mirassa' (*fiancée*) and her abductor, he joined them in a fierce fight for life against hopeless odds. What the moon saw that night when it rose must have been very terrible."

Those three pairs of feet lie buried together near where they were found. The cross, as in my sketch, was put up by the fellow-villagers, and it is the custom each Christmas for the priest of the village to go out and say a mass. A little light is always kept burning, the shepherds and others keeping it supplied with oil.

LUMBERJILLS OF JAPAN

CANADIAN lumberjacks are rightly renowned for their ability to ride spinning logs on fast-flowing rivers; lesser known, though no less experienced, are Japan's "lumberjills." Roping long piles of logs together in the upper reaches of Japan's rivers, the women send them down to the mills unaided.

When the girls want a week-end in town, they take neither bus nor lorry, but simply hitch a ride on the floating timber. Hanging

on to a rope tied to a centre log, the lumberjills speed down the narrow, rock-strewn rivers, at times resembling cowboys at a rodeo, as the logs plunge and toss but are unable to dislodge the tough riders. Sometimes, while racing at over forty miles an hour on the swift current, one of the log-rafts hits a rock in the centre of the river and bounces half-a-dozen or more feet into the air. Yet the lumberjills ride with the blow and, beyond a wetting from the spray, rarely lose their grip or balance to take an undignified plunge in the river.

The WIDE WORLD

THE TRUE ADVENTURE
MAGAZINE FOR MEN

SEPTEMBER — 1956 1/6

THE HAIRY GIANTS

SEE INSIDE

A Lady's Meteor=Hunt Above the Clouds.

That the person who went through the following exciting and well-told adventure is a lady renders the narrative doubly interesting. During November of last year it was arranged that Miss Bacon should accompany her father, the Rev. J. M. Bacon, F.R.A.S., as assistant in the balloon generously placed at his disposal by the "Times" newspaper for the observation of the expected meteoric display. All three aeronauts narrowly escaped with their lives, our authoress herself sustaining a broken arm. Her photos. will be found most interesting.

 HE great shower was generally predicted by astronomers for the early morning of Thursday, November 16th; but since we were warned that it might very possibly arrive twenty-four hours earlier, it was decided to have the balloon inflated and ready by the previous night.

For this purpose Messrs. Spencer and Sons, the well-known firm of aeronauts, in whose capable hands the necessary arrangements were left, elected in favour of a large balloon fitted with a solid or "ripping" valve, which would allow of little or no leakage of gas during the many hours the silk might have to remain filled. It is, perhaps, scarcely necessary to say that an ordinary balloon valve is provided with a spring, by which it can be opened and shut at pleasure. A solid valve, on the contrary, is hermetically sealed until the last moment, when a sharp wrench tears the whole away, leaving a large orifice which cannot afterwards be closed. Owing to this circumstance, and to the large amount of gas liberated, such a valve can only with safety be ripped open when the balloon is quite close to earth, otherwise an ugly fall is the consequence.

The scene of the ascent was the inclosure of the Newbury gas-works, where Mr. Stanley Spencer, to whose personal care we were committed, arrived with

THE REV. J. M. AND MISS G. BACON AS THEY APPEARED ON REACHING THE EARTH ONCE MORE. MR. BACON'S CLOTHES ARE TORN AND HIS CAP MISSING; WHILST OUR AUTHORESS HAS A BROKEN ARM.
From a Photo. by Rev. J. S. W. Stanwell.

his aerial craft during the Tuesday morning. The aerial ship that he brought with him was worthy of his command—a shapely monster of 56,000 cubic feet capacity. The process of filling was shortly commenced.

Tuesday night, November 14th, was luckily a clear one, and we were able to satisfy ourselves that there was not sufficient promise of the expected display to warrant our ascending. On Wednesday night dense clouds overspread the entire heavens, and we decided to make the ascent at about four o'clock in the morning, from which hour until six astronomers had predicted the height of the brilliant heavenly shower. We reached Newbury at midnight.

There was something strange and unusual about the scene of our start which rendered it not a little effective. A moist, heavy mist, through which the light of the almost full moon could scarcely penetrate, lay like a pall over all, and damped the folds of the great balloon as it towered up into the darkness, rustling gently, every now and then, to the light night breeze blowing from the eastward. Despite the hour a large crowd had gathered around, dimly revealed in the light of the gas-lamps. There were many kind friends present to wish us "bon voyage," and many eager hands were extended to help our skilled and genial aeronaut, who, in gold-laced naval cap and jacket, swinging

122

himself deftly among the ropes as he made his final adjustments, looked every inch the sailor he has such good right to consider himself. Many were the surmises as to the course we were likely to take, the general opinion being that we should travel due west, following the

FILLING MR. BACON'S BALLOON AT NEWBURY GASWORKS.
From a Photo. by Miss Gertrude Bacon.

course of the great Bath Road; and since this would bring us to the sea-coast in about sixty miles, we agreed that in the event of our losing sight of the earth above the clouds, it would scarcely be safe to remain aloft more than three hours—or four at the outside.

Our paraphernalia was soon stowed away in the car. It comprised a camera for a possible shot at the stars; a specially constructed apparatus for collecting meteoric dust that might be floating in the upper regions; note-books and pencils, a Davy lamp, rugs and great-coats, and a thick packet of sandwiches. Nothing had been omitted. Even life-belts were provided in view of possible accidents, but being at the last moment deemed unnecessary, they were left behind. Lastly we ourselves scrambled into our wicker basket, the superfluous sand-bags were lifted out, the last restraining rope released, and then swiftly and smoothly we rose into the air amid the cheers of the crowd. "Which way are we drifting?" shouted my father to the sea of upturned faces below, but the answer was drowned in the general outcry; and in another moment the noise had died completely away and perfect calm and stillness wrapped us round.

It was then half-past four. In five minutes we had reached 1,500ft., as indicated by the sensitive aneroid slung in the light of the Davy lamp overhead. The lights of the sleeping town were still beneath us; but now we discharged our first bag of ballast, and immediately found ourselves enveloped in dense cloud. The heavy folds of damp, clinging vapour hung like a smothering blanket round our already moisture-laden balloon, and two more ballast bags had immediately to be emptied over the side. Nor was this enough. At 4.50 we were 3,000ft. high, proving the mist to be 1,500ft. thick at least; and as we rose no more, another 50lb. was got rid of — an almost unprecedented loss of sand for so short a period.

But the contents of the fourth bag had scarcely been discharged when, as in a flash, the moon burst forth in matchless splendour and the stars shone down from a perfectly clear sky. And into what a fairyland had we penetrated! And what a sublime panorama was spread around! The moon was of a strange, tawny, copper hue; and round her was a large and glorious halo of brightest prismatic colours, weird and wondrous, but supremely lovely. The stars twinkled vividly overhead, and beneath lay a sea of snow-white cloud, all piled and heaped in waves and mountain billows, as of some wind-tossed ocean—but with this difference, that the outlines were all of the softest filmy vapour, glistening in the moonlight, with deep purple shadows beneath. And from this calm, still sea came no murmur of waters, but an utter silence prevailed and a perfect peace that might have belonged to Heaven itself.

For a moment we were lost in breathless admiration. Then we thought of the meteors, and realized that the stupendous shower we had learned to expect so much of was *not* in progress. Not a single shooting star would issue from the radiant, and we shortly found ourselves sinking back into the mist. Another bag was swiftly dispatched, and immediately after we saw our first meteor. But one shooting star doesn't make a shower, and we were much more concerned to note that we were still falling earthwards. It was scarcely five o'clock. We had already sacrificed five bags, and two more had to go almost immediately. It was altogether beyond Mr. Spencer's experience, as it was also against his professional instinct, to part with weight so rapidly. He could only

THIS ONE OF MISS BACON'S SNAP-SHOTS GIVES A BEAUTIFUL VIEW OF THE OCEAN OF CLOUD THAT GLISTENED BELOW THEM.

From a Photo. by Miss Gertrude Bacon.

which now hid her in a thick veil, and then, falling away again, allowed us one more peep of her darkened, misshapen face. Then from below came such a chorus of shrill, piercing cock-crows that it seemed as if the whole country-side must be one vast poultry farm; and the lowing of cattle and yelping of dogs rose up as joyful greeting to another working day.

In twenty minutes it was broad daylight, and the moon had fled for good. Again we turned to our aneroid, expecting our descent to be near at hand; but we were still riding at 3,000ft. though no more ballast had been discharged. And now for the first time a new and uncomfortable thought stole into our minds. In a short time longer the sun would have risen upon us, and his warm beams would be drying the silk and expanding the gas—in which case should we not rise instead of fall, and rise for how long?

"Would it be safe to pull the valve-rope," I asked Mr. Spencer, "supposing that in half an hour we were still at our present height?" But he answered most emphatically that it would not, and henceforth we watched the drifting cloud banks anxiously, as they stretched up clammy arms towards us, yet ever just too far away to reach us in their damp embrace.

Half an hour passed, not over happily, despite the changing beauty of the dawn; and then at length, in golden splendour, the glorious sun appeared. All eyes turned once more upon the graduated dial, and then, indeed, it is no shame to own, as we owned to each other—if not in actual words, at least in sobered faces and gloomy hints—that our hopes sank within us. We had risen almost another 500ft., and were still rising. The mists fell away below us for the last time, like baffled spirits of the night, and the tightened red and yellow silk spread its dry folds to a cloudless sky.

One thing was abundantly clear. Under no circumstances could we hope to come down to earth till noon (distant five long hours) was passed. As the day wore on we must surely rise up into the heavens, where no cloud would form to shield us; and if this had been the only consideration it would not have seriously distressed us. The difficulty lay in the awful un-

suppose it due to the enormous condensation of moisture upon the silk during the passage through the cloud, and the chilling of the gas in the colder upper regions. However, we had come to see the shower of meteors, or prove its absence, and we urged him to keep above cloud-level for at least a short while longer; and indeed, after the seventh bag we noted with satisfaction that we sank no more, but preserved a uniform height of about 3,000ft.

For an hour or so we floated thus, keeping a sharp look-out upon the meteors, of which, altogether, we caught a glimpse of some nine or ten. It was just upon the stroke of six, as tolled out from some village steeple far beneath, when we first beheld in the eastern sky the breaking flush of day. Very lovely was this rising dawn of green and copper shades, and very rapidly it overspread the heavens; while opposite in the westward the dulled moon was slowly creeping behind the eddying mists,

MR. STANLEY SPENCER, THE WELL-KNOWN AERONAUT, AND CAPTAIN OF MR. BACON'S BALLOON.

From a Photo. by G. W. Austen.

certainty of our whereabouts; our inability to see the earth or judge in any way our direction or speed; and the probability, growing every moment nearer a certainty, *that we were approaching the sea*, out over which we must surely float mile after mile, beyond the reach of aid, till with declining day our balloon settled down upon the watery waste to rise no more.

And in order to demonstrate that this danger was a very real and very near one, let it be borne in mind that we had already been aloft almost the full time that had seemed to us safe, even with but a light wind, considering the direction we believed ourselves to be taking. Already the coast must be no considerable distance ahead; and yet many long, inevitable hours were surely before us. Could there be even a reasonable hope that afternoon would find us yet within the bounds of the United Kingdom?

The one thing that afforded us some satisfaction was the conviction, based on the sounds of earth, that we were travelling extremely slowly. At one time for the space of a good half-hour we hovered over one particular farm-yard, whence the braying of a donkey, the bellow of a cow, and the specially strident and high-pitched voice of an insistent cock formed a continual concert very gratifying to our strained ears. But we were rising rapidly, at the rate of 600ft. in every quarter of an hour, so that such rural sounds were before long lost to us—though the whistle of locomotives still came up shrill and clear. The thought that we might presently rise so high as to lose sounds of earth altogether was a far from pleasant one, and served to intensify the loneliness, isolation, and danger of our position. We were now high above the cloud-floor, which lay some thousands of feet below us like a boundless frozen sea. The sun was blazing full upon us with such overpowering brilliance that we were glad to tie handkerchiefs and scarfs round the ropes of the car to form some kind of shield for our heads. My father in particular stood in need of such protection, for he had contrived to drop his cap over the side, and now was wearing a handkerchief instead, the knots hanging down in unbecoming fashion about his face. In truth, we presented a woebegone appearance; but despite the gravity of our position the ludicrousness of it all at once overcame us, and we burst into hearty laughter over a situation that contained not a little of the comic as well as the tragic element.

Indeed, the brightness and beauty of the scene, as well as its novelty and charm, would have dispelled all gloomy forebodings had this been possible. But now occurred an incident that brought us back sharply to the realities of our position. We had been making a frugal breakfast off our somewhat dry sandwiches, and had forgotten for the moment to strain our ears for the now faint echoes of earth, when suddenly there rose to us a wild, piercing note that held us breathless for an instant ere, with mutual accord, we exclaimed to each other, in consternation, "We are over the sea!" The sound was the familiar and unmistakable wail of a steamer's siren, and mingled with it the clash and clang of metal in the dockyards of a seaport town. Aye, and what was that soft and sighing murmur that rhythmically rose and fell in gentlest accompaniment, so faint, and yet fraught with such awful significance? It was the breaking of waves upon a shingly beach.

And still the sun blazed down, and still the tense silk rose into the cloudless sky; and our hopes sank low indeed. To climb the netting and pierce the balloon above the equator was out of the question. To pull the valve meant in all probability to fall like a stone. And though a chance there was that the silk might form itself into a parachute, and if we threw everything out of the car might bring us down alive, still it was but a chance, and the alternative was so fearful that we unanimously chose to wait the consequences as we were, trusting to the chance of a possible rescue by a passing ship or boat from the shore, and preferring in any case to be drowned rather than dashed to pieces in such an appalling descent to earth.

That we were over some big seaport city at this moment was amply evident. The roar of crowded streets and busy life was filling our ears with a deep, continuous hum. Was there no help for us from the thousands beneath, so ignorant of our peril above the clouds that hid us from their view? It so happened that we had with us a thick budget of Press telegram forms, ruled one side and plain the other, and these, at my suggestion, we now employed as means of communication with earth. With red and black pencil I scrawled on each a hasty message of distress. My father then folded the paper into three-cornered notes, which Mr. Spencer labelled "Important" and dispatched over the side. They ran as follows:—

"URGENT! Large balloon from Newbury overhead above clouds. *Cannot descend*. Telegraph to sea-coast (coastguards) to be ready to rescue.—(Signed) BACON and SPENCER." I thought it might be interesting to give a facsimile of one of these identical messages on which we considered our lives depended.

Work such as this helped to divert our thoughts and occupy our time. During the next two hours we wrote and threw over some

T.—No. 43.   POST OFFICE TELEGRAPHS.   Page____

(For use as second and subsequent sheets of Press Messages only.)

URGENT

Large Balloon from Newbury overhead, above clouds, cannot descend. Telegraph to Sea Coast (Coast Guards) to be ready to rescue —

Bacon & Spencer

11.15 a.m. Thursday

G & S 3122 6/98—[2895] 300m 7/96ev

REDUCED FACSIMILE OF ONE OF THE URGENT MESSAGES FOR ASSISTANCE WHICH WERE DROPPED FROM THE HELPLESS BALLOON.

we craned our necks over the basket, and beheld clearly enough that the boundless cloud-sea, though still resembling a vast expanse of snow, had now the appearance of melting under a noonday sun, and was breaking here and there into small black pits and holes through which, every now and again, fleeting glimpses could be caught of infinitely tiny roads and fields, trees and buildings, all sweeping past at a great rate, but proving conclusively that earth and not sea was yet beneath us.

Already it seemed to us that our troubles were over, and our hopes rose with a bound, only to receive a temporary check on finding that we were again rising. True we did not

three dozen of these missives. Where they went to is still a mystery. Doubtless the majority fell into the Bristol Channel, twenty miles of which we were now unknowingly traversing. Only in one case have we since heard the fate of our labours. One of the earliest, written at a time when it now appears morally certain we had scarcely reached the eastern suburbs of Bristol, was picked up next day on the top of a mountain in Glamorganshire, twenty miles only from where we eventually landed three hours after our letter was dispatched !

Shortly before twelve o'clock we found we had attained the height of 9,200ft., almost two miles high —a fact not calculated to allay our fears. A few more minutes elapsed, devoted to our literary efforts and to taking a snap-shot or two of the clouds, of ourselves, the balloon above us—anything to pass the time that dragged so wearily. Suddenly my father, who had again turned to the aneroid, announced the unexpected tidings that we had fallen nearly 2,000ft., and were still steadily sinking. This was good news in truth, nor was it all, for almost simultaneously Mr. Spencer, whose keen eyes had been searching the cloud-floor, suddenly exclaimed that he could see land. Eagerly

NEARING EARTH AGAIN—THIS VIEW AFFORDED THE AERIAL PASSENGERS HEARTY RELIEF, FOR THEY FEARED THEY WERE OVER THE SEA.
From a Photo. by Miss Gertrude Bacon.

attain to our former elevation, and shortly after fell to still lower levels; but we saw that our descent, though sure, was also going to be a very slow one. Our stout old balloon was dying hard; while it had become clear that our velocity before the wind was considerable. Should we not, we wondered, even now, reach the ocean before our wonderful voyage had ended?

And thus for two long hours more we watched —with what eagerness!—the fateful race between cooling gas and freshening breeze. Two hours of keenest suspense and alternate hopes and fears. It took three-quarters of an hour to sink 5,000ft., but another hour elapsed before a height of 3,500ft. was recorded, while through the opening cloud-pits the landscape rushed past with ever-increasing speed. At length we were level with the mist, and after another long delay the white arms of cloud had claimed us, and the sun was hidden for good. A few minutes we were lost in the bosom of the stifling cloud, and then we emerged, beneath, this time. And, oh, joy! a peaceful prospect of green fields and quiet pastures spread before us. We were falling very fast, too fast, perhaps—though not for worlds would we risk another rise by parting with a grain more ballast. Our trail-rope already swept the tops of the trees, and the grazing horses scattered in terror at the strange monster bearing down upon them. Then came in the skill of the practised aeronaut. Only a few seconds remained to him, yet in that time he had chosen his landing-place—a green paddock. He had given the sharp wrench that ripped the valve, cast over a ballast-bag to check the fall, and released the cunning catch that sends the grapnel crashing down to the ground. All beautifully done, without hurry and without delay.

And if our landing had depended on Mr. Spencer's skill alone, surely none would have been safer or easier. But there was another unsuspected power to reckon with. We were descending among the mountains of the western coast of Wales, and the breeze which had there been blowing a gale the last few days was still gusty and boisterous, as it swooped down among the hills. We pitched, indeed, on the spot chosen, but with a crash that strained every groaning twig of our wicker car and broke my right arm near the wrist, as we rolled over together, well-nigh out on the ground. And then, as with a mighty sail, the wind caught the flapping silk in a wild gust and swept us madly across the ground in a furious steeplechase, while we held on like grim death and wondered what the end might be. An ugly five-strand barbed wire fence loomed first in the way. Through this we crashed, cutting the wire like pack-thread. The basket shielded us somewhat, yet one strand passed above it and tore the garment almost entirely off my father's right leg. Then came a half-grown dead oak tree, and this also we passed through, carrying away the whole upper portion in our ropes, while the branches swept our faces. But the root at least held firm, and in this our grapnel was now secured. Presently, as we lay tossed and breathless in the car, came cheery voices and brawny arms, and the yet struggling monster was held to earth while we scrambled out at length, too devoutly thankful for our safety to pay much regard to what Mr. Spencer considers the roughest landing he has ever experienced, even as the whole voyage was the most perilous of the many hundreds he has made.

Perilous, indeed! Almost the first words addressed to us by our kindly helpers were that we had descended at Neath, in South Wales, only a mile and a half from the open sea, to which we were heading when we fell. For nine and a half hours had we been drifting above the clouds, and less than ten minutes more would have seen us out over the Atlantic, twenty miles of which we had already traversed. But nowhere in all the world could we have met with a warmer and more hospitable welcome; and in the kind hands of Mr. Jones, of Westernmoor, and his daughter our troubles were soon forgotten.

Thus ended happily a voyage fraught with deepest interest from first to last, and which we three who braved its perils together are likely to remember for the rest of our lives.

THE COLLAPSED BALLOON, SHOWING A BRANCH OF THE OAK TREE IT CARRIED AWAY IN ITS HEADLONG FLIGHT OVER THE GROUND.
From a Photo. by Miss Gertrude Bacon.

"At last I reached the stern and was sucked helplessly towards that whirling propeller."

"MY STRANGEST EXPERIENCE"

I.—RUN OVER BY A SHIP.

By HARRY C. JOHNSON.

ILLUSTRATED BY E. VERPILLEUX.

One of the first stories produced by the competition recently announced. It is a strange experience—one of the most remarkable, surely, that a man ever went through and lived to tell of.

NO, there is no mistake in the title. Strange and thrilling accidents happen every day, but I believe that the incident I experienced is unique of its kind. I shall endeavour to set forth the facts just as they occurred, adding nothing and leaving out nothing.

I was a seaman in the United States Navy at the time, attached to the U.S.S. *Annapolis*. She was not a particularly formidable vessel, and not by any means new. She carried some sail—used only for drill purposes—and was a single-screw ship with a maximum speed of about fourteen knots.

In the early part of 1915 we left San Francisco bound for Panama, in Central America. We stopped at San Diego to take on a few supplies, staying there one day. Leaving San Diego at eleven o'clock, we headed s o u t h, but I, for one, was not destined to see Panama that trip.

On occasions when the weather was favourable our sails would be set and the crew instructed in the almost-forgotten art of handling a ship under canvas. When we were about a day and a half out of San Diego, and just passing the famous Magdalena Bay, on the peninsula of Lower California, the captain gave orders to make sail. Helped by this additional power, the small cruiser pushed ahead at a great rate.

Towards evening a gasket broke loose on the jib, and I was ordered out on the jib-boom to secure it. Being a sailor and accustomed to such duties, I was quite at home upon the jib-boom, and perhaps a little inclined to be careless.

The Author, after his discharge from hospital.

The U.S.S. *Annapolis*, showing the jib-boom from which Mr. Johnson fell.

There happened to be a line leading out to the jib-boom, the end being loose on deck. Sure of my footing, and intent upon my work, I mistook this loose line for a foot-rope, and unthinkingly stepped upon it.

It all happened very quickly, and before I could grasp at anything to save myself I had fallen overboard, directly in front of the ship's bows.

The next thing I remember is striking the water on my back, with my hands and feet in the air, and my eyes glued upon the on-rushing ship. Suddenly the great curving cutwater was upon me, and, striking me on the top of the head, rolled over me and passed on.

Up to this time I had literally had no time to think, let alone attempt to save myself. Opening my eyes under water, I found myself directly beneath the ship, half on my back and half on my side, with that black hulk above me moving at express-train speed, it seemed.

My first thought, naturally, was to swim clear, which I proceeded to do with all my might and main. In spite of my efforts, however, the suction drew me back against the ship, from whose bottom I bounced again and again like a cork. As sailors say, I was being "keel-hauled"! It was then that I learned the truth of the statement I had often heard—that persons near to death review all the events of their past life. Everything that had transpired during my life was gone over by my subsconscious mind, and still I had time for conjecture and a prayer or two.

It seemed hours that I lay beneath the ship, striving desperately to clear myself from the powerful suction. All the time the swish, swish of the propeller, drawing momentarily nearer and nearer, and the thumping of the propeller-shaft, turning over and over in the shaft-alley, drummed into my ears and considerably increased my apprehensions.

And then, at last, I reached the stern and was sucked helplessly towards that whirling propeller! Thud! thud! I received two terrific blows across both legs, delivered by the swiftly-revolving blades, and my body was wrenched from head to toe. Everything grew black before my eyes, and I felt myself going down—down—down!

Hitherto I had not thought of breathing. Now the effort to hold my breath and the desire to exhale maddened me, and I tore at the water frantically in a desperate effort to reach the surface. The momentary shock had passed, and my vision cleared somewhat. The effort to keep my arms in motion was appalling, but I could hold out no longer. My bursting lungs seemed to lose all their power, and I exhaled. A million bubbles rolled over my face and eyes on their way to the surface. I did not dare to inhale, but I tore savagely at the water with my tired and aching arms, my one thought being to get fresh air. The will to live was probably all that kept me going. I held my breath through sheer will-power, but it was torture.

But there is a limit even to will-power, and presently, almost involuntarily, I inhaled deeply. Instead of the choking salt water that I dreaded, however, a rush of sweet fresh air filled my lungs. I opened my eyes tentatively, afraid that I was suffering from a delusion. My head was above the water!

After the first shock of the blow from the propeller, my wounds did not bother me; in fact, but for a dull ache I should not have been conscious of the fact that I was injured. Having breathed my fill of air, I glanced about me. Straight ahead, about a hundred yards away, floated a copper life-buoy—one of those big affairs, lit up with phosphorus, that are carried by all men-of-war. Being a good swimmer, I immediately set out for this buoy, little knowing at the time that both my legs were hanging to my body by mere shreds of skin.

Before reaching the life-buoy I felt a faintness coming over me, and when I got to it I was quite exhausted, due, of course, to the shock and the enormous amount of blood that I had lost. However, faint and nauseated as I was, I hung desperately to the life-buoy, chilled and sick, and with my strength fast ebbing.

Imagine my relief when I was picked up by one of the lifeboats which had set out from the ship shortly after I had fallen overboard. During all this time I never once lost consciousness, and it was only upon being given an anæsthetic by the ship's doctor that I fell into a happy nothingness.

The ship put back to San Diego, the nearest port, and I was transferred to a local hospital. I will not go into details regarding the suffering I endured, what with losing both legs close to the hips and all my scalp—the latter caused from the blow of the bow of the ship. In six months I was discharged from the hospital, and now, with the exception of the injuries I have described, I am just as well and happy as before.

This is the account of my adventure just as it happened, although most of the sensations I experienced cannot be put into words, and the reader will have to imagine them for himself.

I think that I have the distinction of being the only man on record who has experienced the effects of being " run over " by a ship, " keel-hauled " along her bottom, and chewed up by the propeller, and who has lived to tell of it.

BURIED·ALIVE·BY·A· DEAD·ELEPHANT

A dramatic, weird, and all but incredible story.   Read it and judge for yourself whether this phrase is exaggerated.

WHILST with my regiment in Secunderabad towards the end of the forties, I became very chummy with Walker, a lieutenant in one of the other regiments. Everybody liked him. He was a good sportsman, and had the reputation of being the very soul of honour. His regiment left *en route* for Jaulna, and shortly after it was reported that Walker had disappeared, and that there were large defalcations in the mess accounts, of which he had been secretary for some years. So high was his reputation for probity, that the mess president, his own commandant, had passed the accounts time after time without going into them.

On the march Major Randell and Walker had a quarrel about getting ordinary fresh stores, and Walker was removed from being secretary and directed to give over charge of the mess to a brother officer— which he readily and cheerfully agreed to do in a few days. Randell had removed Walker in a fit of temper, and was rather sorry the next day he had done so, and meant to reinstate him shortly. His consternation

THE AUTHOR—COLONEL F. T. POLLOK.
From a Photo.

may be imagined when, on the regiment resuming its march, the adjutant reported that Walker was missing. There were no telegraphs in India in those days, and although every search was made for Walker's whereabouts, he was never discovered; but on the mess accounts being scrutinized, a deficiency of over 4,000 Rs. was discovered, and which Major Randell had to make good. At long intervals there were rumours that Walker had escaped to Bombay in native disguise, and that he was a trooper in the Cape Mounted Rifles, and finally that he had met with his death by an elephant.

So universal a favourite was Walker, that nearly everybody but his commandant was rather glad that he had got away— especially when, some years afterwards, we heard that the sum deficient had been repaid. He was some five or six years senior to me, and was very kind to me when I was a griffin. Walker was never in want of money, and Bunseloll, the soucar, would cash a cheque for him to any amount. His friends would have found the money for him at any time. Why, therefore, should he be a

131

defaulter for a paltry 4,000 Rs., and become a dishonoured wanderer? For upwards of forty years I never heard anything more of him, and, indeed, had almost forgotten all about him.

A few years ago I was residing in a seaport town in the North of France, and during the season, accompanied by my son, a lad of ten, used to go to a village about ten miles off to fish. Occasionally I saw an invalid being wheeled about in a Bath chair, and somebody told me he was an Englishman, believed to be a retired officer, who lived in a cottage near our fishing-place—that he was a great invalid, and associated with no one. Poor fellow! I could sympathize with him, for we knew scarcely anybody, and a new acquaintance would be a godsend. I called on him, but was not admitted. I left my card, but as no notice was taken of my visit I did not repeat it. One day my son was alone and had caught a couple of fine trout, and coming across the invalid accosted him, and asked him to accept one, which he did, adding, "I presume you are the son of Colonel Pollok, who called on me some days ago? Tell him I am not equal to receiving him, but I will write to him some day."

I saw him some time afterwards, but beyond taking off my hat, no intercourse took place between us. I could not help thinking that his face appeared familiar to me, but I could not catch his name; the French villagers distorted it beyond recognition, nor could I think where I had known or seen him, and I heard nothing more till one day I got a letter from a notary requesting me to attend the funeral of Captain Walker, who had died a day or two ago at the village. "Walker! Walker!" I kept repeating. "It can't be the Walker I knew in India, who disappeared suddenly?" It was no use speculating—a day or two would remove all doubts. I attended the funeral, and asked the notary why I had been sent for. "I have a packet to deliver to you," he said, and produced a parcel, which he gave me. I lost no time in returning home and reading its contents. Its writer was indeed my old friend Walker, and this is the story he related:—

"I did not like to receive you, Pollok," he wrote, "as I did not know whether you would care to renew our old friendship. The poor have few friends, the dishonoured none—and I am both. My sad history is this: I never was in want of money, for I had an interest in a large manufactory, which my father left me, and I was entitled to several hundreds a year, an income which, however, fluctuated. The partners always cashed my drafts, which were never very heavy, and, as I intended to take furlough, as soon as it was due I drew only a portion of my income, leaving, as I believed, ample funds for home expenses.

"I was very unlucky in the Mole Alley Races, the year I disappeared, and lost over 4,000 Rs. I gave Bunseloll an order for the amount, which he paid over to me at once—he had often cashed cheques for me before, and they had always been met—but this was returned indorsed, 'Refer to drawer.' I was astounded; there ought to have been, at least, a couple of thousand pounds due to me. Bunseloll behaved very shabbily, and declared that, unless I paid him the amount, with interest, within three days, he would report me to the Commander-in-Chief. I had a Hoondie for 3,000 Rs. which I was just going to remit to Madras on account of our mess, but there was no hurry for the payment, and in a weak moment I gave it to him, together with the balance in cash, thinking I could easily replace it in three months, and as the mess accounts had only just been audited, I never doubted I should be able to remit the amount to the agents in Madras before the next inspection. I wrote home very strongly, and directed that the whole of the amount due to me then was to be remitted to Arbuthnot & Co., in Madras, and that in future all sums that were mine should also be remitted there when due.

"Two months and a half passed. I expected the letter in reply to mine at Jaulna. We were on the march when that unfortunate quarrel took place, and I was removed and directed to hand the mess accounts over to Gray. I could not obtain the money where we were, and in a day or two I should be a dishonoured man under arrest, and the result must be exposure, dismissal from the service, and most probably imprisonment. This prospect was more than I could bear. About a mile off our camp was an Arab dealer returning to Bombay with some horses. He was an old acquaintance, and we had had dealings together. I went to him and tried to induce him to advance me the money, but he said he was not a usurer. I told him I should be disgraced if I did not get it within twenty-four hours—still he would not or could not help me. Then said I, 'Will you help me to escape to Bombay?' He agreed to do so if I would pay him down 500 Rs. and hand him over my three Arab horses. It was a hard bargain, but I saw no other way of getting out of the difficulties I was in. I had some 300 Rs. of my own, and I took 300 more from the mess moneys. I dressed up as a groom, or syce. I could talk Hindustani like a native, and went off quietly at night riding one horse and leading the others—without anyone being the wiser. Within a couple of hours of my departure my steeds, from being

"I SAID, 'WILL YOU HELP ME TO ESCAPE TO BOMBAY?'"

grey, had become bay, chestnut, and black, and I their syce.

"In the hubbub attending the discovery of my absence, no one thought of visiting the Arab dealer, barely a mile away, but search was made for me far, far away. The Arab dealer remained where he was for a couple of days, and then leisurely marched by the regular stages to Bombay. I remained two months in his stables, and then he told me he had sold a couple of Arab stallions for stud purposes for the Cape, and that I could go with them if I wished. I accepted, of course, and no one suspected that Abdullah the syce was the Walker so well known throughout the Madras Presidency. After I had duly delivered over my steeds, I discarded my disguise and enlisted in the Cape Mounted Rifles.

"I remained with them for five years. I then obtained my discharge and returned to England. I found the business that my father had established so firmly in a tottering state, and that no more money had been remitted to India on my account. However, I got sufficient from my partners to repay Randell, and with the balance, some £500, I returned to the Cape. I had

made the acquaintance of Gordon Cumming, the famous hunter, and at one time it was in contemplation that we should conjointly make another trip into the interior of Africa. But Cumming changed his mind, preferring to remain at home with his exhibition, but he gave me many useful hints, and, purchasing all I required, I set up as a professional hunter. I bought two waggons and two teams of bullocks, and five good horses, went inland, and traded and hunted for ten years. I was very lucky, and by the sale of ivory, hides, horns, and curios, I made sufficient money to buy myself an annuity which would suffice to keep me in comparative affluence for the remainder of my life. But the devil tempted me to make one more trip before leaving Africa and settling in Western Australia, as I had determined to do. I was luckier than usual—had my waggons full, and I was returning when the fly appeared, and my cattle and horses died off one by one. Forming a camp near water, and leaving my waggons and men there, I, with a gun-bearer, set out to try and reach a missionary station some sixty miles off, and there get a span of cattle to remove my goods, which were worth fully a thousand pounds. We had a dreary trudge, for people do not walk as a rule in South Africa, and we subsisted on what we shot. We had completed forty out of the sixty miles, and I hoped in another twenty-four hours to be at my destination. The country was hilly, cut up with ravines, and most unexpectedly we came upon a herd of elephants. It would have been as well if I had left them alone. But I was covetous of the ivories carried by several of the bulls, and killed three and wounded a fourth. This one would not die. I had fired some dozen bullets into him, but he seemed to bear a charmed life. We lost sight of him amongst the kopjes, and in tracking him up, he suddenly charged down upon us. I escaped by throwing myself behind some creepers, but my gun-carrier stood in his path and fired both barrels of my heavy rifle into his head. Before the smoke cleared away my poor attendant was a shapeless mass of clay. I now thought only of the death of the monster, and of avenging my follower—but he led me a long chase. At last, from the top of an eminence I saw him standing near some rocks, evidently waiting for me. I took the bearings, and by walking round some outlying hillocks I hoped to creep up near enough to administer a *coup de grace*. I got to the place I wanted to all right. I was between two rocks, and close by was a deep trench, about 7ft. broad, which I could easily jump, but which would stop any living elephant.

"I was thinking of advancing, when the monster evidently got the wind of me and charged headlong. I let him come within 6ft. or 8ft., and then let him have the contents of both barrels, and sprang backwards, intending to clear the trench—but my foot slipped and I fell headlong into it, and in a moment I was in total darkness. I was a good deal shaken, and on recovering my feet I found I was in a living grave. The walls were scarped granite and the aperture above was closed by the huge body of the elephant, who filled it completely. I lit a

match to examine my position more carefully—there was a lot of *débris* at the bottom of the trench and an inner cave—raised above the outer portion about two feet. For a wonder there was also a small trickling stream which flowed along on one side, disappearing in a fissure at the extremity. I collected the decayed *débris* and formed of them several torches. To escape seemed impossible—to move that mass of flesh above would tax the strength of a team of cattle—I alone could not have moved it an inch.

"I was in the wilderness. To hope for help was futile—there were no inhabitants. I knew of no hunters living in the neighbourhood. The missionary I was about to visit was a fair sportsman and a lay brother, but he would not be likely to wander in these wilds, as he could get what game he required within a mile or two of the station. I saw no prospect before me but a slow and painful death. The heat was stifling—there was just enough air circulating to keep me alive. Still, I did not quite despair. Vultures would be attracted by the mass of flesh, and perhaps induce some wandering locals to follow them—then there were lions, who would demolish the flesh in a few days, and I should be able to scramble out of my living grave.

"I had a few biscuits in my pocket—what had become of my rifle I did not know, as it was not in the trench with me. My cartridges (for breechloaders had just been introduced) were useless. My flask contained some brandy, and if very hard up for food I could cut a steak out of the Goliath above me. I cleared out the cave, which ran underground about 8ft. I had

"MY FOOT SLIPPED AND I FELL HEADLONG."

to be careful with my matches, for I had only one box with me, and it was hard to distinguish day from night except by the weird cries of jackals, hyenas, and other wild beasts. I could hear the rush of wings, and knew that the obscene birds were collecting in their thousands, but even they with their powerful beaks could make no impression on the pachydermatous hide until decay set in. I was in a sort of stupor. I heard no lions roaring, but the snarling of hyenas was incessant, and whilst it lasted I knew it was night. My biscuits were soon exhausted —fortunately the rill of water was sweet and cool.

"I CUT OUT A PIECE OF FLESH ABOVE ME."

bereft of both my legs from the knee down. Then I had a relapse, and lay between life and death for fully three months. I can never sufficiently express my gratitude to Mr. Mason and his wife for all the kindness they showed me, and the care they took of me. When I was sufficiently well to be carried into the veranda, he told me some wandering bushmen, attracted by the chattering of the vultures, visited the spot. They heard groans, and on dragging away the skeleton of the leviathan to extract the tusks, they saw my legs hanging down from the cave. They lifted me from my living grave and carried me to the missionary station, where it was found necessary to amputate both my legs, for they had been riddled through and through by hundreds of maggots, and doubtless in a day or two mortification would have set in.

"I had been imprisoned eight days, and it was a marvel I had not died.

"It was useless my going to Australia in my crippled state. I had a widowed sister living in the North of France, and, after realizing the money by the sale of my last venture—for the missionary sent for my waggons when I was able to indicate where they were, and where they were found — but no traces of the men who had been with me were ever discovered, and whether they got back to civilization or died on the way I never knew. They had deserted the waggons. I left the Cape, purchased a further annuity, joined my sister, and have lived ever since where I am now. She died some time ago, and my life has been, indeed, dreary since."

This was the letter handed to me; portions have been omitted, having reference to purely private affairs of others. I have no doubt in my own mind that the writer was my former friend, Walker, who so mysteriously disappeared all those years ago.

"At last, pressed by hunger, with my shikar knife I cut out a piece of the flesh above me and broiled it in the embers of a fire I lit out of the *débris*, but the smoke nearly blinded and choked me, and the stench sickened me; the meat was so tough and nauseous that I could not swallow it. At last I heard lions roaring, and a report above convinced me that the body, extended with gas, had burst. Now all the quadrupeds and bipeds could devour it; but would they do so in time to save my life? I feared not, for hunger and want of fresh air were slowly, but surely, killing me. Driven to desperation by hunger, I stepped out of my cave into the trench, intending to cut out a portion of the now putrid flesh, when I felt a shower falling on me, and, lighting one of the few matches left, I discovered to my horror that not only was the floor several inches deep covered with maggots, but that they were raining down on me.

"I staggered back towards the cave, and there consciousness left me. When I regained my senses I found myself in bed attended by the missionary and his wife, and it was many days before he would relate how I came to be under his care—for, alas! I soon discovered that I was

By PETER BARNES as told to GRAHAM FISHER

HAD we been superstitious, I suppose we should have turned back while still 450 miles short of Kano, which is justly nicknamed "Gateway to the Desert."

It was there that jovial Alan Cooper, leader of our little expedition, broke the string of coloured glass beads that the natives on his coffee plantation, near Nairobi, had given him as a good luck charm before he left.

Alan had worn the beads carefully about his neck until that day when the string broke and the beads cascaded into the dust at his feet. The superstitious would say that our luck broke with them.

For me, the grim adventures that followed had all started with a newspaper advertisement. Alan Cooper, a big, bluff, strongly-built man in his late forties, had advertised for three other people to share the expenses of an 8,000-miles overland trip to England

—a car journey by way of Uganda, the Belgian Congo, French Equatorial Africa, Nigeria and the blazing sands of the Sahara.

I was eighteen at the time, and an engineering student in Nairobi, and it seemed an excellent opportunity to see my grandparents in England.

I was a little surprised when I first saw the small, 8-h.p. station wagon in which it was proposed to make this long and hazardous journey, but Alan, in his bluff way, assured me that it was just the car for the job. Some years before, he had achieved prominence as the first man ever to cross the Sahara in a baby car, and I judged that he knew what he was talking about.

I was also rather surprised to discover that both our travelling companions were to be women—Freda Taylor, a lively, attractive brunette, a schoolmistress returning to England at the end of a six-months' stay in Africa,

ILLUSTRATION BY HENRY FOX

DEATH IN THE DESERT

and Barbara Duthy, a Kenya Government zoologist, a more dominant and dogmatic personality altogether.

It was 16th April, 1955, when we set off. The first 3,000 miles—over the mountain passes of Uganda, along the narrow, winding jungle roads of the Congo, and through the stunted grasslands and semi-desert of Nigeria—were comparatively uneventful.

This stage of the journey took us the best part of three weeks, with Alan Cooper and myself sharing the driving.

The two women did the cooking and washing for the party, and we augmented our stock of canned food by trading cigarettes with the Congo pygmies for poultry and fruit.

To Freda and me, the whole business, at this stage, was just one great, gay adventure. I don't suppose any other woman has ever tackled the Sahara with seven pairs of flimsy, high-

heeled shoes as part of her desert wardrobe.

It was Freda who added a touch of youthful flamboyance to the proceedings, by painting on the rear of the station wagon :

"Kenya to England
via
Uganda, Belgian Congo, French Equatorial Africa, Nigeria, Sahara Desert, Spain and France."

Then came the incident of the broken beads.

That very day, soon after the incident, a sharp rock, churned up by one of the front wheels, pierced the sump of our station wagon. Unnoticed, the oil ran out, and we finally limped into Kano on three cylinders, only after plugging the hole and putting in fresh oil.

The station wagon, which had responded splendidly hitherto, consistently gave us trouble from then on. Three times we had the engine repaired—in the bush town of Maiduguri, in Kano itself and in the desert outpost of Agades, and each time it let us down again.

Though we were heading north from the Equator, the temperature was rising as we neared the vast, three-million square miles of the Sahara. It was up to 115 degrees Fahrenheit when we reached Kano.

There, we took on extra water, two four-gallon drums of petrol and two spare cans of oil. This extra load made it rather cramped for the four of us in the station wagon, and we adopted a system of changing seats at intervals, to ease our aching limbs.

However, there was nothing we could do to ease the strain on the vehicle, which was now so overloaded that the rear end actually banged against the ground whenever we drove over a particularly bad stretch of the route.

Our top speed was down to 15 m.p.h.—and our average nearer 12—as we drove over roads the like of which I had never seen. Razor-backed ridges, dangerous gulleys, stretches of treacherous sand and huge potholes barred our way in turn.

The last time Alan Cooper had crossed the Sahara, he had taken the west route to Oran. This time, eager to break new ground, it was decided to try the west route—the Hoggar route—to Algiers.

An execrably bad road brought us to Zinder, a back-of-beyond township of flat-roofed houses of mud and straw, entirely cut off from civilization, except for a lorry that brought in supplies.

The French authorities at Zinder warned us that we could get no more petrol until we reached Agades, 250 miles farther on. The engine of the station wagon was giving trouble again, but there were no repair facilities at

Zinder—nothing but mud huts, so we limped onwards on three cylinders.

We reached Agades safely, however, and persuaded the French commandant there to loan us a mechanic to fix the engine.

It was May 8—exactly seven days before the date on which the French authorities ban all travel across the Sahara until the scorching sun has passed its summer peak of intensity.

The commandant told us to go back and see him once the engine was fixed. We never went—unwisely, as it turned out.

The temperature was up to 120 in the shade when we left Agades to drive out into the desert—and there was no shade except for the white-painted roof of the station wagon itself. All around us, a pitiless sun beat down on grass scorched yellow, on stunted thorn bushes and a limitless vista of flat sand.

We were pitifully ill-equipped for the desert crossing. We had neither shovels nor sand-mats. How we were to wish for them, later !

We had only forty litres of water with us. The French authorities, I learned afterwards, normally insist on a minimum of 160 litres.

Ahead of us stretched 1,800 miles of pitiless desert, with an oasis situated roughly every three-hundred miles. The only road was that left by the fading tracks of vehicles which had made the crossing before us, and the only signposts were the black oil drums that the French had set up, at intervals of one kilometre, to mark the route.

It is, almost assuredly, the loneliest road in the world—and the most dangerous.

We drove only in the early morning and at evening. During the heat of the day—from eleven o'clock until three in the afternoon—it was far too hot to drive—and too hot even to move. We just lolled listlessly in our seats while the sun beat down on the roof of the station wagon, and the perspiration streamed off us in rivulets.

Our first stopping point was the oasis of In-Abangaret, 175 miles north of Agades. The oasis consisted of a well, a solitary mud-hut and a handful of skin tents inhabited by a group of wandering Tuaregs.

We filled everything that would hold liquid with water from the well, drank greedily of the camels' milk which the Tuaregs offered us, and pushed on again into the hellish heat of the desert.

Now there were no longer any tyre tracks for us to follow. A sandstorm had blotted them out as effectively as a wet duster would have rubbed chalk marks from a blackboard. There were only the black-painted oil drums, spaced at intervals of one kilometre, to guide us on our way.

At midday we camped near a small cluster of stunted trees, rigging a tarpaulin at the side of the station wagon to keep off the worst of the scorching heat of the sun.

Trouble started when we tried to go on

again. The rear wheels of the station wagon would only spin uselessly and helplessly, digging themselves ever-deeper into the soft, hot sand, until the vehicle was buried right up to the axle.

Without shovels or sand-mats, it took us three hours of digging with our bare hands to free them.

Alan brought his previous experience of desert travel into use. He carefully detoured anything that looked like a particularly bad patch of sand, or rushed it at speed, banking on our impetus to carry us through before the rear wheels bogged down again. Despite all his experience, however, we were stuck fast three more times that afternoon.

Each time, we had to get down on our hands and knees, scraping away at the sand with our fingers, sweltering in the hot sun, and tormented by ants and flies, in order to free the vehicle; then, heaving and straining, we had to push it forward on to firmer ground, before starting it again.

That day we covered only 25 miles. Our next stopping place—the oasis of In-Guezzam —was still 95 miles distant.

Anxiously, we checked our water supplies. To our dismay, there was a mere one-and-a-half gallons left—and a gallon of that was in a can which had previously held petrol. It tasted horrible.

Alan's face had lost its usually cheerful grin. He had lost his trick of wisecracking when things went wrong. The nerves of all of us were becoming tense and edgy.

Next day, things went from bad to worse. We started the station wagon—and the wheels simply burrowed into the sand as the vehicle was put into gear.

There was nothing for it but to unload all our equipment and supplies, and carry everything 150 yards or more to where the ground was firmer. Again we had to dig the station wagon out with our bare hands, manhandle it on to firm ground and load it up again.

Again and again it stuck—and again and

again we went through the struggle and torment of setting it free.

We were now in the *fêche-fêche* area—a treacherous mixture of powdery, yellow-white sand, fine black gravel and sharp rocks.

Again the station wagon stuck, and again we struggled to free it; but this time, with our hands blistered and our clothes soaked with stale perspiration, we had to give up. The sweltering heat and the first torments of thirst were beginning to tell on us.

We rigged up some blankets to give us a little extra shade, and then lay prostrate in the shade, too dead-beat even to eat.

Alan and I talked in whispers, so as not to alarm the two women.

We knew that this time we were really stuck fast. Without help and proper equipment, we would never free the station wagon.

"There's only one thing for it," I said. "I'll try walking to In-Guezzam to get help."

In-Guezzam was still 65 miles away across the burning sands of the desert. In my innocence, I failed to realise that to try to walk there was inviting almost certain death.

Alan Cooper did realise it, I think; but to stay where we were was to die, anyway. The chances of another vehicle coming along that desert trail were one in a million.

"If anyone's going to try to reach In-Guezzam," contended Alan, "it's going to be me."

"I'm younger than you are," I retorted. "My chances of making it are greater."

Freda and Barbara heard us arguing, and wanted to know what it was all about. When we told them, they both supported Alan, and said that he should go. He had the experience, they pointed out.

Alan took his share of what little water we had left—two one-pint bottles, and Freda offered him her share as well, but he wouldn't take it.

"You'll need it yourself," he said.

Barbara offered him her wide-brimmed

Peter Barnes sits in the shade of the station wagon while Alan Cooper measures out the meagre water ration to Barbara Duthy.

DEATH IN THE DESERT

(continued)

hat as protection against the sun, but he wouldn't take that, either.

With only a knotted handkerchief to protect his head against the heat, he set out across the sand on one of the most terrible walks any man ever attempted.

I looked at his footprints as he trudged away from us across the desert. They were a full two inches deep.

At dusk, while the women enjoyed the sleep of the exhausted, I tried again with the station wagon. Using a folded camp-bed as a base, I jacked up each wheel in turn, and began to scrape away the sand.

Several times the jack slipped—and I had to start all over again.

Eventually, I managed to work a camp-bed under each of the rear wheels, and then laid a carpet of mattresses and blankets on the sand in front of the vehicle.

Trembling and exhausted, I climbed into the driving seat and started the engine.

I gripped the steering wheel with blistered hands, and put the vehicle gently into gear. Gradually it eased forward on to firmer sand.

My excited shout of triumph awakened the two women. We lost no time in loading the vehicle again, and impatiently waited for dawn to come creeping across the desert.

It was now Wednesday, May 11.

At the first sign of light, we started off across the desert, following in Alan Cooper's footprints.

Seven more times the station wagon bogged down in the treacherous *fêche-fêche*, and six times we managed to wrestle it free, and set off again. On the seventh occasion, however, the growing heat of the sun forced us to give up. There was nothing we could do but wait for the sun to go down, and then we set to work again. After four back-breaking hours, we were on the move again.

The next day we got bogged down four times. We were struggling, the fourth time, to push the station wagon towards a patch of seemingly firmer sand, about a hundred yards farther on, when I thought I saw something move on the horizon.

I rubbed my eyes with my hand, and reached for the binoculars. I was trembling so much that I could hardly get them into focus.

I was terrified that the moving speck in the distance should prove only a mirage; but through the binoculars, the moving speck divided up into a car and a lorry. I let out a shout of joy.

The lorry, zig-zagging towards us, to avoid the bad spots, finally stopped at a safe distance from where our station wagon was trapped.

Barbara burst into tears as we rushed

towards it. Help had come only just in time. Our water supply was down to a mere two cupfuls.

A man climbed slowly down from the lorry. I scarcely recognized him at first, so terribly had he changed.

Then I saw that it was Alan Cooper, but not the Alan we had known. This was a living skeleton—his fat all gone, melted away by the blazing sun.

His eyes were sunken hollows in his head. His face was burned almost black, except for livid white patches here and there, where sand and dust had stuck to sweat, and shielded a portion of skin from the sun's glare. His feet were bare, and he had to clutch at the side of the lorry to keep himself from falling.

We hugged each other in frantic joy.

In disjointed sentences, Alan told of his terrible ordeal.

From five o'clock on Tuesday, when he had left us, he had walked until dusk; then, exhausted, he had rested until the moon came up. By moonlight, he started again, plodding doggedly on, following the dotted line of black-painted oil drums stretching across the desert.

He took an occasional sip of whisky, conserving what little water he had for the greater ordeal which would come with the sun.

Towards dawn, disaster overtook him. He had stumbled among some rocks, shattering one of his precious bottles of water.

On he went into the heat of the day, ticking off each oil drum he passed with pencil and paper.

Presently, as the sun climbed higher and hotter, he collapsed. For a while, he lay there on the sand, the sun beating down on him. The only shade in sight was that offered by the next oil drum. He staggered towards it, scooped away the sand and crawled inside.

It was a terrible mistake. The fierce sun, beating down on the metal drum, turned it into a raging furnace. Realising this, Alan tried to wriggle out again, but failed; then, mercifully, he lost consciousness.

When he recovered his senses, the sun had gone, and the moon had risen.

He crawled out and somehow staggered on, past ten more oil drums.

Another dawn came, and another day of unbearable heat. He forced himself to go on.

He had ticked off 70 oil drums—43 miles of desert—when he came upon footprints in the sand.

Horrified, he realised that they were his own—he had somehow walked in a circle!

He was found, face down in the sand, by the lorry driver, a French-Algerian named De Zorzi—who was escorting a Swiss-driven Volkswagen across the desert.

When Alan recovered sufficiently to explain what had happened, they set out to look for us.

The lorry driver and the rest of his party helped us to manhandle the station wagon on to firmer ground again, and then we set off in convoy across the desert.

Alan Cooper, because of his condition, travelled with us in the station wagon, so that Freda could nurse him. Barbara took his place in the lorry. The lorry driver gave us an extra gallon of water, just in case anything went wrong.

Inevitably, it did.

I was ahead of the other vehicles when Freda's sudden shout startled me.

"Hold it, Peter—we've lost them."

I stopped the station wagon on top of a slight rise. Freda was right. There was no sign of either the lorry or the Volkswagen. We found out later that the Volkswagen had broken down, and the lorry driver had stopped to help; but we did not know it at the time.

There seemed nothing for it but to drive on. Presently, we struck another patch of the treacherous *fêche-fêche*, and became bogged down again.

We waited for the others to catch up again and help us out, none of us realising that we were now off the track altogether !

We had already drunk the last of our water, when Alan became delirious. In desperation, I drained the water from the radiator and Freda gave him that.

By three o'clock in the afternoon, the last drop was gone.

Night came. Freda and I sat in the front seats, taking it in turns to flash our headlamps at five-minute intervals.

At dawn, I tried to rig an improvized shelter. I fixed one corner of the tarpaulin to the luggage rack on the roof, and another corner to the bonnet. I filled empty cans with sand, to weigh it down at the other corners.

At about half-past eight, the Volkswagen appeared suddenly on a nearby ridge, but the occupants failed to see us, and it went off in another direction.

It was Friday, May 13.

All day we lay motionless in the shelter of the tarpaulin, while the sun beat down upon us. By evening, Alan Cooper was dead.

Freda refused to believe it at first.

"He's only sleeping," she insisted, over and over again. "He's only sleeping."

But he wasn't.

I staggered out of the lean-to, only to collapse in the sand. When I recovered, I crawled painfully towards the rear wheels.

All night I worked, scraping the sand away, jacking the wheels up, and pushing the camp-beds under them. It took me eight hours, but I made it.

Freda helped me to get Alan's body into the back of the station wagon, and cover it with a blanket; then I remembered that there was no water in the radiator. I put some oil in instead.

We covered twelve miles in slow spurts, stopping the engine each time it showed signs of overheating, but at dawn on Saturday,

May 14, the engine refused to start. The battery was flat. I tried cranking by hand, but my strength had gone.

The heat of another desert day beat down on us in great waves. Overhead, the first vulture wheeled in patient anticipation.

We made a tent with the blankets, and crawled in. I bandaged Freda's mouth and eyes, and plugged her ears, to preserve the moisture content of the body. We bathed our faces in some perfume she had.

At about five o'clock, the lean-to fell down, and neither of us had the strength to rebuild it.

When night came, Freda suggested, "Try the lights again."

They came on—faintly—for a few minutes, but then went out altogether.

We prepared for the next day's ordeal. We lifted Alan's body from the station wagon, and covered it with a blanket. We opened the rear doors and draped a blanket across them, and we fixed a towel and bathrobe across the windows.

We then collected what perfume, eye lotion and skin tonic we could find, and placed them handy.

As the sun came up, we plugged our ears, and bandaged our mouths and eyes. When it became too difficult to swallow, we rinsed our mouths with perfume or eye lotion.

It was Sunday, May 15. We had had no water to drink since the Thursday.

I dabbed my face with skin tonic, and reached over to do the same for Freda. It was then that I discovered that she was dead.

I decided to get out of the station wagon and die in the open. I remember staggering out, but then the sand seemed to rise up and meet me.

Consciousness came back. I felt vibrations with my fingers in the hot sand.

Not twenty feet away from me were two desert army lorries. I thought at first that they were another mirage. I tried to cry out, but couldn't utter a sound with my tortured mouth.

Even as the lorry driver and a Tuareg ran towards me, I collapsed again into the sand.

They gave me some water—and the pains started. My weight, when they got me to hospital, was down from 145 to 98 lb.

The search party which found me had been alerted by the other lorry driver, De Zorzi. They had come up with a party of Tuaregs who spoke of lights flashing in the desert night. The Tuaregs had guided them to the lights—and to me !

It was Freda who had suggested trying the lights yet again. In doing so, she had saved my life, but not her own.

She and Alan lie buried in the Sahara, their graves marked with rough, wooden crosses, and just deep enough so that the vultures cannot disturb them. ▲▲▲

MAY 1961   1/9

WIDE WORLD

THE TRUE ADVENTURE MAGAZINE FOR MEN

MY WORLD BENEATH THE SEA

by

HANS HASS

Out of the depths came a fighting fury
to turn a quiet fishing trip into
a terrifying ordeal □□□ By FRANCIS J. HUSSEY

Even clamped in the jaws of an eel catcher the Moray is to be feared.

GREEN KILLER

SOME years ago I spent a holiday with an American friend in Bermuda. It was to be a fishing holiday, a lot of goggle, lance and spear-gun fishing. Jim Braybon had a smart little fishing boat, and we had been cruising around the islands and had made our way over to Key West for a drink, then on to the Dry Tortugas. We had headed back by easy stages to Bermuda, stopping here and there among the islands on our way. Mornings we'd take turns over the side with mask and lance. Afternoons we did hook and line fishing.

We had found a tiny cove with one of the most beautiful coral reefs we had ever seen. Not only was it a good safe anchorage for the boat but it seemed to be a good place for the amazingly varied fish of the tropical reefs.

We would take our turn in going over the side, often drop down along the bright reef and jack lance through a blue sturgeon fish, or a green wrasse, or a bright red, big-eyed squirrel fish.

One morning, near noon, we had something to eat. Then after a rest we did some hook and line fishing. The last thought in our minds was danger.

Suddenly I felt a terrific tug on my line. I started pulling away. I could not hold it. Oddly, it did not feel like any fish I knew.

I called to Jim to give me a hand. He grabbed hold of the line with me. We knew that the line would hold. Slowly but surely our combined strength was pulling whatever it was to the top. Jim leaned over the side and looked down into the clear water.

"Moray!" he yelled. "The biggest moray I ever saw. Cut the line!"

Jim took a hitch in the line to a deck cleft and ran for his knife. I looked over the side and saw the green monster flailing wildly.

"Hurry, Jim," I shouted loudly. In my excitement I must have given a heave on the line because the monster's vile, ugly head came level with the boat rail. At that moment the creature gave a tremendous eel-like surge and, lunging, came aboard. I could see that the moray was free of the hook which was loose on the bottom of the boat.

A moray looks rather similar to an eel. It is, in fact, related to the eels. There are many species of morays, but of them all the green moray is probably the largest, and certainly the most dangerous at close quarters.

It is thick like a rattlesnake. Longitudinal creases showed in its leathery hide. It is solid muscle and solid ugliness, a slimy, yellow-green thing which looks for all the world like an enormous elongated cucumber.

As I leaped out of the way the moray writhed and floundered, beating a violent warning upon the deck. Slime from its great body was greasing the boat's bottom, and its beady eyes burned first on me and then on Jim as he stood knife in hand.

Its mouth filled with needle-like teeth capable of rending any flesh with which they came in contact, kept snapping open and shut as it lunged.

I plunged over the side and came up the fore-end of the boat, got my lance gun from the deck, moved back beside Jim and let fly a shot at the snapping killer there below us. The lance twanged, pierced the skin of the big green killer and pinned him to the bottom of the boat.

At that moment, Jim made the biggest

ODDS AND ENDS

A SUIT MADE ENTIRELY OF SEAWEED.
From a Photo. by Underwood & Underwood.

The oddly-dressed gentleman in the foregoing photograph is a lunatic incarcerated in the asylum at Mendrisio, in the Canton of Tessin, Switzerland. The most dangerous of the patients at this institution are kept in cells containing no furniture whatever, only a heap of "varech," or dried seaweed, which serves as a mattress. The unfortunate man here shown passes his spare time in daubing on the walls of his apartment curious allegorical drawings; but perhaps his most remarkable feat was the weaving, from the smaller threads of the dried seaweed, of the suit he is seen wearing in our snap-shot.

GREEN KILLER *(continued)*

mistake of his life. Apparently thinking the moray was lanced through and held solidly, Jim jumped to the bottom with a fish club in his hand. He aimed a tremendous blow at the head of the green moray.

As the club swept the air straight at its target, the head of the monster shot aside and upwards. The leathery skin pinned tight by the lance ripped free. The giant green moray leaped off the boat's bottom like a striking rattler to meet Jim's low-bent head.

The cruel mouth opened and snapped. I heard the club bang harmlessly on the boat's bottom, and I heard Jim make a peculiar startled sound.

Then he was down, rolling over and over frantically, fighting. His hands were gripping, slipping and gripping wildly at the enormous slippery body. Jim was now on his back slithering helplessly in the slime of the beast.

I saw with horror that the great green moray was at his throat.

It shook its head, ripping at Jim's flesh. It let go and struck time after time, into his face, his shoulders, his neck. The boat's bottom was a welter of red blood and yellow slime.

I leaped down to help him and at the same time Jim managed to stagger upright. He had the moray wound round his arm. I was grabbing for the lance. I knew I had to act quickly because he was almost fainting with pain.

Jim was making a choking, sobbing sound, fighting the beast off, and then with a wild flailing of arms and legs and green-snake-like body both Jim and the moray went plunging over the side.

I saw him break away and beat the water frantically. I saw the creature strike once more at Jim's legs, ripping a terrible gash in his thigh. Then Jim was heaving himself over the rail again, and the giant moray had disappeared, slithering into his hole in the coral down below.

I remember thinking in a flash that my hunts down there must have been in sight of the giant moray's den. I had not known the monster had been there. A shudder went through me as I rushed to help Jim.

The rest of the story is a nightmare.

I raced the boat as fast as it would go to the nearest port. With help I got Jim to a doctor. He was in very bad shape. For nearly two weeks Jim fought to live. Everything possible was done for him. The end came late one night.

Any one who has seen the lacerations a giant green moray can inflict will realise the terrible condition Jim was in!

I have never through the years which have passed been able to erase the terrible sight from my memory. ▲▲▲

Across America by Airship.

THE STORY OF AN ILL-STARRED ENTERPRISE.

BY ARTHUR INKERSLEY, OF SAN FRANCISCO.

Now that airships are so much to the fore, this account of the meteoric career of the largest "dirigible balloon" ever constructed—larger even than Count Zeppelin's unfortunate monster—will be read with interest. The inventor had an ambitious scheme for running luxuriously-fitted aerial liners between New York and San Francisco, but his first ship got no farther than the ascension ground. The photographs accompanying the article are particularly striking.

SOME time last year there came from the windy city of Chicago to the hardly less breezy San Francisco a man named John A. Morrell, who built a small airship with a balloon of insufficient size to lift the engines and netting. The craft got loose before the crew of twelve had taken their places and rose from a hundred to two hundred feet in the air, floating away in a southerly direction down the San Francisco peninsula and coming to rest at Burlingame, in San Mateo County, twenty miles from its starting-point.

Nothing daunted by this mishap, Morrell organized the "National Airship Company," incorporated under the laws of South Dakota, established offices in a leading street of San Francisco, and put forth a glowing prospectus, in which people were invited to invest their money in a sure thing—to wit, an airship a quarter of a mile long, already under construction, and intended to make regular trips between San Francisco and New York City, carrying

passengers as comfortably as a Pullman car. The chairs in this remarkable craft were to be made of hollow aluminium tubes and to weigh only seventeen ounces; the bedsteads, of the same material, weighing twenty-seven ounces. The mattresses were to be inflated with a very light gas of a secret nature. Extravagant and fantastic though all this sounds, Morrell possessed the enthusiasm and glibness of the genuine promoter, contriving to obtain many thousands of dollars from credulous people in support of his wild project.

The National Airship Company established shops in San Francisco, and went to work upon the airship, which was named "Ariel." The construction was under the direction of George H. Loose, who has had considerable experience in building aeroplanes and airships. It was intended that Loose should be first officer of the aerial liner, but, when the time for making the first ascent came, Loose wisely threw up his job, because Morrell had disregarded his advice in the construction.

MORRELL'S MONSTER AIRSHIP BEING INFLATED, READY FOR ITS FIRST ASCENT, IN THE PRESENCE OF A VAST CROWD.
From a Photograph.

A NEAR VIEW OF PART OF THE AIRSHIP, SHOWING ONE OF THE ENGINES AND PROPELLERS — NOTICE THE FLIMSY NETTINGS AND THE
MATTRESSES INTENDED TO SUPPORT THE CREW.
From a]   *[Photograph.*

Nearly every well-known principle of airship construction was violated. The proportions were impracticable, the craft being four hundred and eighty-five feet long and having a diameter of only thirty-four feet. The gas-bag was like a huge snake, having no rigidity, either horizontally or vertically, and not being stiffened by trussing of any adequate sort. A gas-bag of such length and proportionately small diameter should have been strengthened by a vertical framework, or by trusswork of rope or wire, so as to impart rigidity; but nothing of this sort was done. The motive-power was supplied by six separate four-cylinder forty-horse-power automobile engines, hung below the balloon at intervals.

From a]   THE AIRSHIP LEAVING THE GROUND AMID THE CHEERS OF THE EXCITED ONLOOKERS.   *[Photograph.*

These concentrated weights were carried on a platform, not of planks, but of mattresses, laid down on mere canvas, supported by the netting which covered the gas-bag. Ropes placed round the gas-bag at the points where the engines were situated cut deeply into it, and no arrangements whatever were made to meet the special stresses caused by the steering of so long-drawn-out an affair. Loose's chief reasons for refusing to make the ascent were that if the envelope were filled with enough gas to render it rigid the emergency valves would open, and if these were tightened the envelope was liable to burst.

Serious as the various defects mentioned were,

strangely enough, the greatest difficulty was experienced in keeping people off the craft. One man, a well-known aeronaut named Captain Penfold, repeatedly begged Morrell to let him make the ascent, but his request was flatly refused. Yet so eager was Penfold that at the last minute he smuggled himself on to the craft and went up with it and—a few moments later —came down with it.

Some time before the attempted ascent was made the airship was conveyed from San Francisco across the Bay to Berkeley, in Alameda County, Cal. The trial trip was fixed for Saturday, May 23rd, and on that morning thousands of excited people were on hand to

THE "ARIEL" IN MID-AIR—ITS NOSE HAD A DECIDED TILT DOWNWARDS, AND THIS INCREASED UNTIL ALL EQUILIBRIUM WAS LOST.
From a Photograph.

the most fatal one was the fact that nothing had been done to prevent collapse or deformation caused by sudden expansion or contraction of the gas from changes of temperature. The balloon was one great, undivided bag, containing from four hundred thousand to five hundred thousand cubic feet of gas, but having no compartments or internal air-bags. Its lifting capacity was from eight to ten tons, so that it was much the largest airship ever built in America, even exceeding in dimensions the great "dirigible" of Count von Zeppelin.

It might be supposed that it would be pretty hard to get together a score of persons who would be willing to risk their lives in such an unpractical affair as the Morrell airship; but,

watch the ascent. The airship was released from its moorings and began to mount into the air, its nose having a decided tilt downwards. The machine had risen scarcely two or three hundred feet when the rear of the balloon had an upward inclination of as much as forty-five degrees.

Morrell shouted to his crew, consisting of engineers and valve-tenders, numbering fourteen or fifteen, to go aft, so as to depress the stern of the machine and cause it to resume its equilibrium. But the shouts and cheers of the people below drowned his voice so that he could not be heard. A moment later the gas rushed into the after-end of the bag with great force, bursting the oiled cloth of which the

"THE HORROR-STRICKEN CROWD SAW THE GREAT BALLOON COLLAPSE AND COME HEADLONG TO THE GROUND WITH ITS NINETEEN PASSENGERS." NOTICE THE VALVE - TENDER SCRAMBLING WILDLY ALONG THE NETTING ON TOP OF THE GAS-BAG ; HIS AGILITY STOOD HIM IN GOOD STEAD, FOR HE ESCAPED ALMOST UNINJURED.

From a]   *[Photograph.*

envelope was constructed, and the cheers had hardly died away before the horror-stricken crowd saw the great balloon collapse and come headlong to the ground, with its nineteen passengers, who included Morrell, eight engineers, five valve-tenders, two photographers with their assistants, and the aeronaut already mentioned.

The unfortunate men were entangled in the wreckage of flapping cloth, network, and machinery, running the danger of being struck by the propellers of the engines or of being suffocated by the great volumes of escaping gas. One valve-tender, who was on the top of the great bag, can be seen in one of the photographs climbing along the netting. His agility stood

GATHERING UP THE WRECKAGE AFTER THE COLLAPSE OF THE AIRSHIP.
From a Photograph.

him in good stead, for he escaped from the wreck almost uninjured.

It might be supposed that nearly all the men on the ill-fated craft were killed; but, remarkable to relate, not one lost his life. Morrell himself sustained severe lacerations, and had both his legs broken by one of the propellers; Penfold, the persistent, had his right ankle and left instep broken; Rogers, an assistant engineer, suffered a broken right ankle; and another engineer met with broken ribs and ankles. Others were bruised or rendered unconscious by the gas.

Morrell ascribed the disaster to the fact that he was forced by impatient stockholders in the National Airship Company to make the attempted flight before he had worked out

certain details of the vessel s construction thoroughly. It is believed by those who saw the luckless craft that it was constructed flimsily of poor materials and not inflated sufficiently. The ill-starred aeronautic adventure not only cost many broken bones, but some forty thousand dollars (more than eight thousand pounds) in money.

It would naturally be supposed that so complete and disastrous a failure, after the expenditure of so large a sum of money, would have destroyed all confidence in Morrell as a designer of airships, and would have put him out of the business of aerial navigation for all time. But it was not so; the enthusiast still asserts that he has discovered the true principle of the navigation of the air, and that the National Airship Company is ready to proceed with the construction of another craft, much larger and costlier than the first one.

The new airship is to be seven hundred and fifty feet long and forty feet in diameter, equipped with eight gasolene engines, developing nearly three hundred and fifty horse-power and operating sixteen propellers. The inside bag will be of light silk and the outside bag of heavy silk interwoven with a material known as "flexible aluminium," of which Morrell possesses the secret. The new balloon is to have more than a hundred compartments, many of which might be broken without disturbing the buoyancy or equilibrium of the vessel.

A rigid platform is to be substituted for the canvas and netting cage in which the unfortunate participants in the attempted ascent of the "Ariel" rode. The new vessel is to cost one hundred thousand dollars (more than twenty thousand pounds), and to be capable, if the inventor is to be believed, of a speed of a hundred miles an hour. The really marvellous things about the whole business are the unquenchable enthusiasm of the inventor and the unfailing credulity of those who believe in him.

APRIL 1962   2/-

WIDE WORLD

THE TRUE ADVENTURE MAGAZINE FOR MEN

DEATH WAITS ON THE ICE

————————— SEE INSIDE —————————

"STRANGE AS IT MAY SEEM, NOBODY THOUGHT OF LOOKING UNDER THE TRAIN."

Under the Train

THE STORY OF A TERRIBLE JOURNEY.

BY W. S. MEARS.

Being the unique experience which befell Mr. John Eke, a Great Northern Railway foreman. Clinging desperately to an iron rod, and with his feet braced against a brake, he travelled underneath the Manchester express from London to Grantham, a distance of over a hundred miles, at a speed of nearly seventy miles an hour. Only an iron will and extraordinary endurance saved him from a fearful death.

HERE are several trains leaving King's Cross daily for the North of England and Scotland which run for long distances at a rate of well over sixty miles an hour. A few of these trains make almost "record" daily runs of over a hundred miles from the Great Northern Railway terminus before their first stop.

The famous Manchester express, which leaves King's Cross every afternoon at 2 p.m., is one of the best known of these. It is timed to reach Grantham exactly at 4 p.m., and runs to that town without a stop. Now, Grantham is one hundred and five and a half miles from King's Cross, and so the express must on an average run close on fifty-three miles an hour for the whole journey.

As it takes some time in getting up full speed, however, and as there is now and then an occasional slowing down when signals are adverse,

or when the permanent-way is on an ascent, it is clear that in some portions of the one hundred and five and a half miles the train must be going considerably over a mile a minute in order to keep its scheduled time at the Lincolnshire town. As a matter of fact, I believe it is well known that these Great Northern Railway expresses to the North have often gone at the rate of over seventy miles an hour over a good portion of the line between King's Cross and Grantham.

Mr. John Eke is an unassuming, kindly-featured man, now about fifty-nine years of age. He has for some years held the very responsible post of a foreman at King's Cross Station. His work is to superintend the vacuum and Westinghouse automatic brakes attached to all the trains, and he must personally see that these brakes are in perfect working order before the chief expresses leave the platform daily on their great journeys. Mr. Eke is about the medium

MR. JOHN EKE, WHO TRAVELLED UNDERNEATH THE MANCHESTER
From a] EXPRESS FROM LONDON TO GRANTHAM.   [*Photo.*

height, somewhat thinly built. He does not look nearly so strong as this story will prove him to be; yet his eyes are bright and keen, and his face suggests a wonderful amount of experience and confidence.

It certainly should do, for Mr. Eke had, nearly six years ago, such an experience as fortunately falls to the lot of but few men. As a trial of nerve and endurance it is probably unique. For this slightly-built, quiet, unassuming man actually rode *under* the Manchester express, going at seventy miles an hour, from King's Cross to Grantham —and survived!

It was on Satur-

day, June 25th, 1898, that this terrible adventure occurred. Needless to say, the experience was both unsought and undesired. It arose from a pure accident, simple enough in its nature, but fraught with tremendous issues to Mr. Eke. Let me tell the story in his own words, as he has told it to me more than once.

The Manchester express, due to leave King's Cross at 2 p.m., was standing by its accustomed platform waiting for the signal to start. This platform was the one known to us as " E." My last observation as to the brakes being right is generally made by walking along the train on the side away from the platform, and on the afternoon in question I was doing this part of my duty as usual.

Whilst walking along I heard the slight hissing which betokens a small leakage in the vacuum brake, and I judged immediately that this ought to be made right in order to avoid any risk of accident. It would be a light, easy job, I supposed; and as there was, according to my reckoning, plenty of time to do it myself, I got down under the carriage to put it right. I certainly made a mistake in not calling out to the guard or driver that I was going to do this, but my mind was so intent on avoiding any risk to the train's passengers, and I expected the job to be so easily and quickly done, that I never thought about that at the time.

I fancy the work must have taken me longer than I anticipated, and in my anxiety to do it well and thoroughly I doubtless did not notice how time slipped by just then. The carriage was a composite one, and I was bending down

From a]   MR. EKE STANDING BESIDE THE ENGINE AT KING'S CROSS STATION.   [*Photo.*

on the ground beneath it when I became conscious of a little jerk and of the train moving forward slightly. Of this, however, I took hardly any notice, nor did it alarm me in the least, for when the hand-brake is taken off previous to the starting of a train a jerk and movement of that kind is a perfectly usual thing. It was to this cause I attributed the motion, and I merely went on with my work, going forward for a step or two with the moving carriage.

I moved involuntarily, so to speak, for half-a-dozen steps. Then it dawned upon me that the train was really going faster. I was in a quandary which ever way I turned, as you will understand if you know the "make" of the underbody of a carriage. Getting out at the sides below it was of course impossible ; the wheels would have caught me. Nor could I lie down and let the train pass over me, for owing to the construction of that particular carriage it would not have passed along without serious injury to me.

My resolution was quickly made. It came to me like a lightning flash. My only hope of safety consisted in lying flat on the brake itself. So I passed my leg across a transverse rod under the carriage, and placed myself lengthwise as far as I could stretch on the brake.

I am bound to admit that even at this point I had hardly grasped the fact that the train had actually started on its journey. What I have described took such a few seconds that I had no time to think about anything but what I have told you. I fancied that the express was merely moving forward a little for some purpose unknown to me there under the train, and that was why I did not shout out immediately I felt it move, or just after getting my body on the brake. My mind was full of the certainty that I should get out or be rescued from my awkward position within a minute or two, and I cannot say that I felt in any way afraid or even upset at my precarious situation.

A few more seconds, however, made a wonderful difference, both in my real danger and in my views respecting it. As I lay there I could distinctly feel the train gathering speed, and then, almost for the first time, there burst upon me with all its horror the dreadful truth

"I BECAME CONSCIOUS OF A LITTLE JERK AND OF THE TRAIN MOVING FORWARD SLIGHTLY."

that the express was fairly off on its long journey !

One hundred and five miles without stopping ! Two hours' run ; in some places going more than seventy miles an hour ! And there was I, John Eke, lying full-length on the brake, with only that and the rod to cling to ! Only physical strength, presence of mind, and terrible endurance could save me from an awful death. That was now clear to my mind.

I realized all this ere the train was away from the platform, and I called out loudly for help with all my might. I was heard by many people, for from my position I could see them running to the end of the platform and looking eagerly everywhere to see whence the cries came. But, strange as it may seem, nobody thought for a moment of looking *under* the train. They gazed at the top, at the carriages, at the wheels ; they saw the permanent-way appear all right as the train passed along. I then tried to shout

out to them that I was under the carriage, but by this time we had reached the end of the platform and were going fairly fast, so I could not make anyone hear.

Then I almost despaired, for I saw no prospect of release. Yet, stay; one hope filled my breast at something I saw. I could make out from my cramped position that an official was running along the lines and over the metals, and I felt sure somebody had noticed my absence, had guessed its cause, and was running to the signal-box to get the train stopped. Yes, I thought I should be rescued, after all.

Alas, it was a vain hope! The porter, or whatever he was, could not have known anything about my plight; for, instead of the train being slowed down, I began to feel that it was going faster every minute. For a moment I seemed to lose all hope of living longer. The prospect was so terrible, it made my blood run cold to think of.

One hundred and five and a half miles without stopping—in two hours! Picture it to yourself, and try to imagine how you would feel if you were clinging for life to a narrow rod under a train, with the jarring and roaring of the wheels about you.

I am glad to say, however, that though the first prospect of the awful fact somewhat unnerved me, I kept perfect presence of mind, and it is to that I owe my wonderful escape. There were, after all, one or two things I had to be thankful for. The first was that I knew precisely what to do; the second, that the carriage I was under was placed almost in the centre of the train; the third was that this carriage had a peculiar pipe running along below it which I could grasp, a pipe other carriages were without. So I lay close down on the brake, twisted one leg round it, and tightened the other round the rod I spoke of before, which was above the brake. Then I grasped the

pipe firmly with both hands, to hold on by. I made myself both as comfortable and as secure as I possibly could, and husbanded my strength and courage for the tremendous tussle that I knew would come before and after leaving Peterborough.

Thirteen miles from King's Cross is Potter's Bar. I was getting badly cramped as we flew past it at a great rate, gaining speed every moment. The famous Welwyn tunnel—twenty-two miles

"I LAY CLOSE DOWN ON THE BRAKE."

from London—was the next goal that loomed up in my mind. My whole body, but especially my hands and legs, felt stiff and numb by the time Welwyn was reached. I shut my eyes as often and as much as I could, for the terrible speed made the ground—so close to my face—seem to be flying away from beneath me so fast that I got dizzy. I was also nearly blinded by dust. My face began to be cut with the small stones and grit that were dashing past me with the force of big hailstones in a severe storm, and the roar of the train deafened me and numbed my senses. The blasts of air that rushed past, too, were enough to blow me clean off my insecure perch. For we were, on leaving Welwyn tunnel, beginning to attain a regular speed of nearly a mile a minute, and the displaced air goes by with a rush, and no mistake, when the train gets to that speed!

I should probably have had to give up the

struggle for life, owing to the awful cramp in my limbs, had it not been for a lucky chance.

I was beginning to feel more comfortable in my strange position—at any rate, more secure—from having lasted out so far. But would my grasp hold good, or would my muscles presently refuse to do my bidding and send me hurtling down among these flying wheels, pounding along at fearful speed? That would assuredly happen unless I could obtain a little respite from the strain. So with some risk and with much nervousness as to the result, I let go with one hand to rest it, and clung only by the other. When I found I could manage this it was like a Heaven-sent help. After that I rested my hands alternately as we flew along.

Before we got to Peterborough the speed almost attained its maximum, being close upon seventy miles an hour. I knew that we should slow down a good deal in order to go through the station, and I yelled out my hardest as we did so in the hope that somebody either near the permanent-way or on the platform would hear me and effect my rescue. By this time my face was bleeding freely from the stone-cuts, for the flying pebbles cut like a whip-lash, and I can hardly imagine what I must have looked like, caked with dirt and dust.

We went through the station, and my heart sank within me, for no one heard my cries. In spite of this disheartening fact I remembered that we had gone seventy-seven miles—more than two-thirds of the journey—and I prepared for a last great fight for my life. After succeeding so far it would be terrible to succumb now, I thought.

I did not underrate the task before me. I knew my strength was failing; I knew my limbs might refuse to hold on any longer from sheer exhaustion, however clear my mind might be and however determined I was not to give in. I knew that the speed between Peterborough and Grantham, especially as we neared the latter, would exceed anything we had done so far. But I braced my nerves, breathed a quiet prayer, and resolved to do my utmost. How I survived that last part of the run I can scarcely tell you. We travelled at more than seventy miles an hour when near Grantham, and I was nearly killed by the cutting showers of stones and cinders from the track as we literally flew along. Though each moment brought me nearer to the "first stop" and to safety, the anguish of those last ten minutes was, perhaps, the worst phase of all the long-drawn agony of those awful two hours.

Did you ever dream of falling down a deep pit, and then, just as you were expecting to be smashed to atoms at the bottom, wake to find you were in your own soft, safe, comfortable bed? Did you ever, after giving up all hope on a sinking ship, when death was awaiting you, suddenly see a sail and know it was coming to rescue you?

If you have experienced any sensations such as those you will guess how I felt as the train drew into Grantham Station and came to a stop alongside the platform there. Curious to relate, professional pride seemed to come over me the very first thing! I gazed from below the carriage at the well-known clock, and saw that its big hands pointed to exactly 4 p.m.! And you will think it strange that I felt, after all my awful experience, a sort of pride in the grand engines of the line I had worked for during so many years. One hundred and five miles in two hours—and I had ridden underneath the train all the way!

My hands were so stiff and cramped that I could hardly get them free from the pipe, and my feet clung heavily to the brake. As the man came round to test the wheels I crept stiffly out from my cramped position. He stared in utter astonishment, and no wonder, for I must have been a shocking sight. When he did find his tongue he naturally jumped to the same conclusion that I should have done had I met a stranger in similar circumstances at King's Cross.

"Halloa, old fellow!" said he—not unkindly, however—"so you've been having a ride without paying, have you? Been doing it on the cheap!"

I could not help smiling grimly at his mistake, and he became, if possible, more mystified still.

"Yes, far too cheap," I retorted, huskily, and briefly explained to him my plight. He gave a short, quiet whistle, shook my hand, and stared again.

I climbed up on the platform and made my way to the office of the chief of our department at Grantham. I told him my story. I will pass over all the fuss they made of me, of the hero-worship they gave me. I am a quiet man, and even now care little to talk about that awful June day. I will merely say that they gave me a good wash and that I had a splendid meal, which I badly needed.

Strange to say, I was little the worse for my unique experience, and I returned to King's Cross the same evening—but, as you will guess, not in the same way! I went in an ordinary carriage, and felt much more comfortable and safe.

Mr. Eke usually stops when he has got thus

"I CREPT STIFFLY OUT FROM MY CRAMPED POSITION."

interesting little episode which came later.

When he heard of Mr. Eke's extraordinary ride, the present King (then Prince of Wales) sent for him, asked him all about it, shook hands with him warmly, and offered his hearty congratulations upon Mr. Eke's nerve and his escape from such a terrible position. Mr. Eke received hundreds of kind letters and messages from all classes of people when the story of his ride became known, but nobody could possibly have been kinder or more sympathetic than was the King.

Mr. Eke still pursues his ordinary duties at King's Cross. Everybody respects him; and he is the hero of boys all over the district. You may see the spare figure of the foreman standing on the platform noting the testing of the brakes of the Scotch express, or watching carefully over the safety and comfort of the passengers by the famous Leeds dining-car trains. If you observe him closely, you may see him give a slight twitch when the 2 p.m. Manchester express—"First stop, Grantham!"—draws gracefully away from the platform to begin its long journey.

far with the marvellous story of his escape. But those who, like myself, know him well will not allow his modesty to suppress an

And then you can point out to your friends the man who rode under the Manchester express for two hours, at a speed of seventy miles an hour—and survived.

From a Photo. by]   THE MANCHESTER EXPRESS ENTERING GRANTHAM STATION.   *[J. Miller, Grantham.*

The Peril of Seaman Diver Young.

By Major Charlton Anne.

Going down as a diver to retrieve a lost torpedo belonging to the first-class battle-ship "Hood" he fouled his lines, got turned completely upside down, and remained in this fearful position in total darkness at the bottom of the sea off Crete for five hours.

OWARDS the latter end of the month of September, in the year 1896, Her Majesty's first-class battleship *Hood* was lying in Suda Bay, looking after British interests in Crete (a photograph of the great ship is reproduced herewith). The battleship had only just been re-commissioned, and had recently arrived from Malta with an entirely new crew.

is doubly severe on all newly-commissioned ships, until such time as the crew have got thoroughly knocked into shape. And, of course, strict discipline, combined with hard work, and plenty of it, is the surest way of arriving at this much-desired consummation on board a British man-of-war.

Despite the fact that the month of September is the hottest month of the year in the Mediterranean, drills and gun-practice (with

H.M.S. "HOOD" TO WHICH SEAMAN GUNNER AND DIVER JOHN YOUNG BELONGED.
From a Photo. by Symonds, Portsmouth.

Whilst in Suda Bay the officers of the *Hood* amused themselves by organizing shooting expeditions to the neighbouring marshes, where duck and snipe abound. There was also a certain amount of exercise to be got in the shape of walking and riding — under somewhat stringent rules, however. For at that period the island was in an unsettled condition.

Officers' bathing parties also took advantage of the many small coves lying around the Akrotiri peninsula, which was destined shortly to become famous as the principal stronghold of the Christian insurgents in Crete. The ordinary seamen, however, were on no account whatever allowed to land. They had to put up with the usual service routine and strict discipline, which, as in the case of the *Hood*,

greater or lesser quick-firers) were the order throughout each day of the *Hood's* sojourn in Suda Bay. And when the sea was smooth enough there would be torpedo practice with those small torpedoes which are usually in vogue on these occasions. These are only about 12ft. long, so the sailors affectionately call them "babies."

Now, a torpedo is a thing with apparently as capricious a temper as that of a spoiled child at times. And so it happened that one of these infants, when fired from the *Hood* one morning, instead of pursuing an even and horizontal course in the direction of the target which it was intended to hit, suddenly took a turn, and tossing its tail upwards in derision in the face of the whole ship's company, ran down vertically at full speed. The result was that its other end, or "nose" as it is called, became embedded some 6ft. or 7ft. in the stiff clay which lines the bottom of Suda Bay. It was afterwards found that one small split pin had come out of a rod, causing the torpedo to run vertically instead of horizontally.

At that time the *Hood* was anchored in about thirteen fathoms of water. A merciful Providence has apparently decreed (doubtless with a view to economizing much time, bad temper, and scarlet language on the part of ships' officers) that an escaped torpedo shall always let those above know its whereabouts by the bubbles which the compressed air, which works the mechanism inside it, discharges to the surface. Thus, a lost torpedo will sometimes continue to give off bubbles for days after it has disappeared.

In this instance the truant was quickly located through its boiling up like a veritable geyser in miniature, some fifty yards from the ship. Even a "baby" torpedo is too costly a thing to be lost without the utmost being done for its recovery, so preparations were at once made on board the *Hood* to do so in this case.

The ship's divers, of whom there were three, were immediately warned to get ready. The launch was manned and lowered alongside, furnished with all the apparatus necessary for diving operations. She carried one of Siebe and Gorman's patent three-cylinder air-pumps. These pumps are capable of supplying ample air to two divers simultaneously, at the depth of twelve fathoms. Beyond that depth, it is safe only to allow the pump to supply air to one diver at a time. In this instance, the lost torpedo being about thirteen fathoms down, it was not thought advisable

SEAMAN GUNNER AND DIVER JOHN YOUNG, THE HERO OF THE TERRIBLE ADVENTURE RELATED HEREIN.
From a Photo. by Arthur Burgess, Folkestone.

LIEUTENANT (NOW COMMANDER) E. CHARLTON WHO HAD CHARGE OF THE DIVING OPERATIONS.
From a Photo. by G. West & Son, Southsea.

to send down more than one diver at a time during the subsequent operations.

In the course of the afternoon which followed, two divers had descended and found the torpedo. They had attached three-and-a-half-inch grass ropes to it, but these had broken at every attempt to drag the torpedo out of the mud in which it was so firmly embedded. At 5.45 p.m. it fell to the lot of No. 148,127, Seaman Gunner and Diver John Young (whose portrait, specially taken for this article, is here reproduced), to descend and make a final attempt for that day.

On this occasion the torpedo was (it was hoped) to be raised by attaching a five-inch hemp hawser to it.

It was rapidly growing dusk. The sea was smooth, with an occasional ripple on its surface, raised by the soft evening breeze. The temperature on the surface was about 85deg. Fahrenheit, and that of the waters underneath from 7deg. to 10deg. lower. A few yards beneath the surface it was practically dark, and it is necessary to bear in mind all these conditions and circumstances, they being essential to a right appreciation of the narrative. Diver Young had donned a brand-new dress for the occasion. Before the helmet was screwed home he assured his assistants that he would "have the blessed thing up in half a mo'." Only Seaman Gunner and Diver John Young did *not* say "blessed." He went over the side, his weights were put on over his shoulders, the cranks of the pumps began to revolve, and with the signal "All right," given by two pats on the top of his helmet, John Young gently sank beneath the waves, easing himself down his shot-rope as he went, as seen in the first diagram reproduced.

NO. 1.—5.45 P.M.
Sea moderate. Depth, 78ft. Diver Young descending.

spot by the officer who was in charge of the diving operations; this was Lieutenant (now Commander) E. Charlton, of the *Hood* (his portrait is reproduced on the previous page). The admirable diagrams help us to realize the different stages of the diver's fearful position. These diagrams were originally drawn on the spot whilst the diver was below. It would appear that in Suda Bay there must have been a submarine current, probably only very slight, but nevertheless sufficiently strong when Young descended to turn him gradually, but completely, round, so that ere he touched the bottom he had unknowingly already got foul. Diagram No. 2 shows the position at this moment.

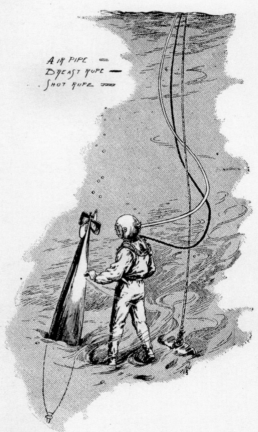

NO. 2.—5.50 P.M.
Diver sees torpedo and signals for hawser. He has unconsciously taken a turn round his shot rope and is already foul.

It may be here mentioned that the shot-rope is an inch line, to which a half-hundredweight "sinker" is attached. This is always the first thing to be lowered from a diver's boat, and is a guide to the diver himself both in descending and ascending. Besides the shot-line—to which he is *not* attached—the diver is also connected with the boat by a breast-line which is fastened to his shoulders, and, of course, there is likewise the air-pipe, which is screwed into the side of his helmet, and then connected with the air cylinders above.

A pressure gauge on the pump indicates through a dial the exact depth at which the diver below is working. It must be borne in mind that the adventures of John Young after he became submerged could only be subsequently guessed after unravelling the incredible tangle of his various ropes and the air-tube after his rescue. But a careful note of the time of all his signals from below, and of every effort made above towards his aid, was kept on the

Utterly unaware of this, and finding the torpedo immediately, Young gave the signal— a pull on his life-line—which had already been agreed upon, and which meant that he was ready for the 5in. hawser to be lowered to him.

This being done, and catching hold of the end of the hawser, he groped his way to the torpedo, wading through the heavy bottom mud, which was nearly up to his knees. Making the hawser fast to the tail of the torpedo he must have moved completely round the submerged weapon from left to right, thus making another foul. (See Diagram 3.)

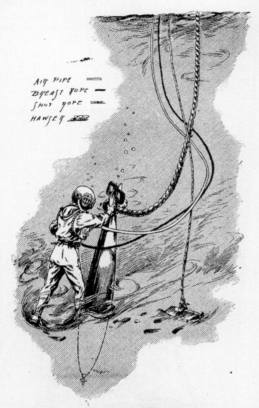

NO. 3.—6 P.M.

Making fast. The diver here walks completely round the torpedo.

The hawser being made fast, Young now started to ascend up the shot-rope, quite unaware that he had made a hitch round both it and the torpedo with both his air-pipe and breast-line. The muddle so far can be realized by a glance at Diagram 4.

But to return to the surface. It was now 6.30 p.m. The wind, which had been hitherto blowing gently from the westward, suddenly increased and, with the sunset, veered round to the north.

The huge battle-ship swinging to it threatened to carry away both the launch and the whole diving apparatus. This would, of course, have meant instant death to the diver below. Happily,

such a terrible catastrophe was averted by a kedge anchor and line being promptly laid out from the off-quarter of the *Hood*. The next diagram (No. 5) explains this situation.

By this time Young must have come to the conclusion that he was fouled, for he had ascended a short distance and then found he could not move. Therefore, like a wise man, he went down again and tried to find out where the trouble was; but owing to its being pitch dark where he was, it is not to be wondered at that he failed to do so.

Almost despairing of being able to free himself, and dreading to resort to the last resource (that of cutting himself clear with his knife), lest he should get foul again whilst going up, the unfortunate man gave four pulls on his air-pipe. This is the most urgent signal that a diver can send to his friends above. It means, "Pull me up at once by my life-line." (See Diagram 6.)

At first the operators hesitated to act on this,

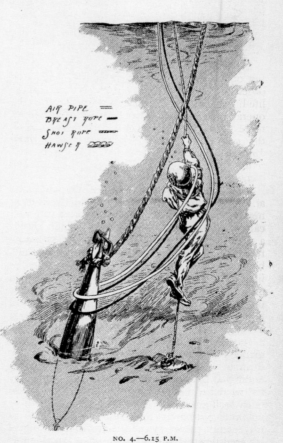

NO. 4.—6.15 P.M.

Diver tries to ascend on shot-rope, having got a hitch round it and also round the torpedo with air-pipe and breast-line.

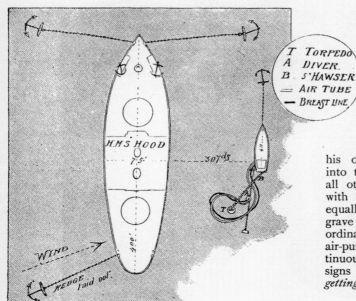

T TORPEDO
A DIVER.
B 5" HAWSER
═ AIR TUBE
— BREAST LINE

WIND

KEDGE laid out.

HMS HOOD
75'

30 yds

NO. 5.—6.30 P.M.
The wind shifts, and the battle-ship threatens to swing over the fouled diver. A kedge anchor averts this.

but on the urgent repetition of the signal, the order was given on the launch to haul in the life-line. But on commencing to do this the operators found it was impossible to bring up more than a fathom of the line. Worse still, the only result of this operation was to *turn Young completely upside down!* The very first pull on the line—entangled as it was round the torpedo—must have done this.

Now, once a diver loses his perpendicul and gets horizontal, the air gets into the legs o. his dress—up they go, and then nothing that he can do will ever bring them down again. He is a mere helpless wind-bag, quite incapable of reversing himself. This is precisely what must have happened to Young. The loop of his life-line round the torpedo pulled him on to his chest; the hapless man's legs immediately went up, buoyed with air, and so he remained, bumping about on his head in total darkness, 78ft. at the bottom of the sea. The accompanying diagram (No. 7) shows at a glance the effect of trying to haul up poor Seaman Diver Young, who was now hopelessly entangled. Of course, those above could not tell what had happened, although they may have fairly well guessed. Unable to bring the diver up, and getting no more signals from him, a fifty candle-power electric submarine lamp was lowered down to him at 7.30 p.m. To this was attached a slate and pencil, so that the helpless

man could write on the slate and inform those above precisely what his dilemma was. (See Plate 8.)

After his rescue Young said he remembered seeing the light, but he never had any recollection of the slate. All this time he was floating at the bottom of the sea, heels uppermost, the monotony being varied by his occasionally thumping his head into the mud. During the next hour all other expedients to communicate with him were tried, but all proved equally fruitless. And now another grave danger entered upon the extraordinary scene. The cylinders of the air-pump, which had been working continuously for some eight hours, showed signs of over-work, and *were rapidly getting red-hot.* In this case they would

AIR PIPE ═
BREAST ROPE —
SHOT ROPE —
HAWSER ▨▨

NO. 6.—6.55 P.M.
Descending again, Diver Young concludes he is foul. It is now pitch dark. He signals " Pull up at once.'

AIR PIPE ═══
BREAST ROPE ▬
SHOT ROPE ═══
HAWSER ▬▬

NO. 7.—7 P.M.
The result of hauling up the fouled diver. People above
do not know. Diver now helpless and upside down.
Dress leaks and water accumulates in helmet.

At 9 p.m. all lines attached to Young, which had previously been kept taut, as well as the hawser which he had fastened to the torpedo, and the shot-line — all were simultaneously eased. The result of this was that the unfortunate man gradually ascended — though of course he was still head downward. At 9.45 p.m. the second diver from the *Dolphin* descended, and by the aid of the electric light he found Young bobbing about in a perfectly helpless condition. He shook the luckless diver by the hand, and tried in other ways to attract his attention. Getting no response to his efforts, he came up and reported Young quite dead. The next diagram (No. 9) depicts for us this remarkable greeting. The unfortunate man was now actually sighted from the launch, legs up and head down, about 24ft. below the surface of the translucent water. There

have to be stopped altogether. However, luckily there was a plentiful supply of ice on board the *Hood*, and by packing this continually round the pump it was kept cool enough to work.

While these operations were going on, Her Majesty's sloop *Dolphin* hove in sight, and joined her huge consort in Suda Bay. A signal was at once made to her from the flag-ship to send immediately a boat, with diver and apparatus. The *Dolphin's* boat brought at once a couple of divers and a one-man pump. One of the divers went down as quickly as possible in search of Young, but he was a new hand at the work, and speedily returned to the surface, having failed to see anyone or anything !

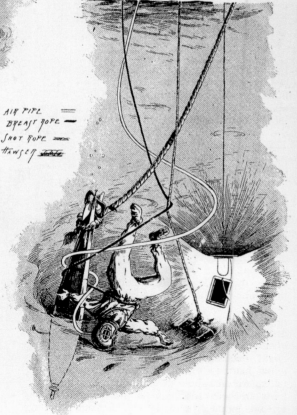

AIR PIPE ═══
BREAST ROPE ▬
SHOT ROPE ═══
HAWSER ▬▬

NO. 8.—7.30 P.M.
A 50 candle-power submarine lamp is lowered ; also a slate for messages.
Diver floats, but often bumps his head against the bottom.

164

remained only one thing to be done—namely, to pull up the torpedo by main force by means of the hawser attached to it. It was a desperate and last resource.

In a letter written home the next day, Lieutenant Charlton—who has already been referred to—said, "I had to decide and take the risk of the hawser being round the diver,

When all was in readiness the signal was given, "Full steam ahead." This was done twice, each time in a different direction, but without any apparent result. The torpedo firmly wedged in the clay would not budge! Then again once more—this time spurt at right angles to previous pulls and at full speed. Again eighty brawny arms in the launch heaved

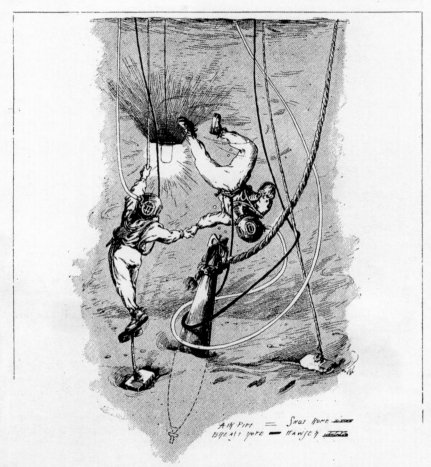

AIR PIPE === SHOT ROPE ━━━
BREAST ROPE ━━━ HAWSER ▪▪▪▪▪

NO. 9.—9.45 P.M.
Another Diver from H.M.S. *Dolphin* goes down. On coming up he reports
John Young dead hours ago.

when we put the launch and steam pinnace on her. Had the diver got the strain he must have been torn to pieces." The launch was now manned by a picked boat's crew of forty men, who laid hold of the hawser. The launch was in her turn taken in tow by the ship's steam pinnace, the latter's furnace burning for all it was worth, and her boilers carrying the fullest head of steam possible. (See Diagram No. 10.)

and hauled with a will; the steam pinnace panted and puffed, her screw beating the calm waters into a milky foam. Both boats were at a standstill, quivering with the immense strain put upon them from stern to bow.

Then, suddenly, and without any apparent warning, the torpedo, having given way at last, the helpless diver came shooting out of the water feet foremost, with an impetus that almost landed him into the arms of the crew of the launch. The lost torpedo came alongside almost at the same moment.

The shot-line was found twisted round Young's right arm, and the limb was apparently broken. The face-plate was quickly removed from the poor fellow's helmet, which was found three-quarters full of water. The new

supposed dead man opened, and a very sepulchral voice murmured, in feeble protest: "Don't cut the blankety dress; it's a new 'un!" An immense cheer—such a one as only British tars can give—rent the air from the boats, and was quickly taken up on board the war-ship. The whole vicinity was filled with

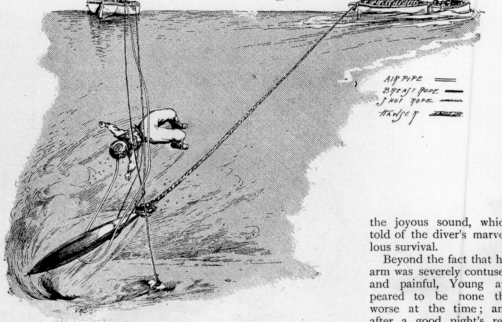

AIR PIPE
BREAST ROPE
SHOT ROPE
HAWSER

NO. 10.—10.25 P.M.
The last desperate course : Main force.   Full steam ahead and forty men pulling.
Diver and torpedo come up with a run.

the joyous sound, which told of the diver's marvellous survival.

Beyond the fact that his arm was severely contused and painful, Young appeared to be none the worse at the time; and after a good night's rest he was going about his duties as usual next day. When we consider that he

dress had evidently leaked slightly, and all the while that Young had been bumping about on his head the sea had been slowly oozing through and accumulating in his helmet. *It had reached his eyebrows* when he shot violently to the surface. Another quarter of an hour and his mouth and nostrils would have been covered.

The shot-rope was cut away. Every soul in the boat thought that the man had been dead some hours. They were beginning to cut away the sleeve of the indiarubber dress, so as to free his arm, when suddenly, and to the utter amazement of all present, the eyes of the

was under the water, 78ft. deep, for over five hours in total darkness, most of the time upside down and hopelessly entangled with two ropes and the torpedo, we can safely say that his experience was unique, and in all the records of diving his escape may be taken as the most wonderful known.

Young evidently kept his head with great coolness from first to last, especially when he found he was foul. But it is surmised that for some time before his rescue he was probably almost unconscious, since he said, when asked about it, "that the time had passed very quickly!"

APRIL 1963   2/-

WIDE WORLD

THE TRUE ADVENTURE MAGAZINE FOR MEN

THE TORMENT OF TITOV

The truth about the human terrors of space flight.

LONG JOURNEY

Why did three
well-equipped explorers
just lie down and
die in a frozen
wilderness? Today
science provides
a solution to a
sixty-year-old mystery
of the Arctic.

TO NOWHERE

By WILBUR CROSS, with THORLEIF HELLBOM

THE summer of 1930 was hot. In the mid-western United States farmers were battling to save parched crops; on the Continent people with money were flocking northward to the Scandinavian countries, only to find that the beaches there were baking in the sun. Even in Russia, the big subject of conversation was the heat.

Farther still to the north, between Spitsbergen and Franz Josef Land, the tubby and smelly little Norwegian fishing vessel, *Bratvaag*, cruised easily through waters that even the oldest and most experienced hands had never seen before because they were usually locked solidly in ice. Unlike their countrymen back home, the members of the crew had only good things to say about the weather, for it meant that they could heave in close to shore off Great Island, Victoria Island and White Island and surprise large herds of walrus.

No one, however, was more complimentary about the weather than Dr. Gunnar Horn, a geologist, who had booked passage aboard the *Bratvaag* with two other scientists from the

Andrée, Fraenkel and Strindberg made their final checks of the balloon and its basket. Minutes later they took off across the bleak Arctic Ocean bound for the Pole, trailing their ballasting lines, to vanish and become a legend.

The three explorers set up camp on the last fatal march.

LONG JOURNEY TO NOWHERE

Spitsbergen Bureau of Norway in order to study whatever land masses they could reach while the ship engaged in her regular hunt for walrus, seals and whales. In the early evening of August 5, 1930, Dr. Horn became greatly excited when the little sealer nosed in to an anchorage off White Island. Taking meteorological observations, he discovered that the island was way off the location shown clearly on the charts.

Important though this discovery was, it was not to compare with the significance of a find the next day, August 6.

That morning, as Horn poked among the rocks, gathering geological specimens that had lain for decades under the snow and ice, he heard shouts from two of the crew members, Olaf Salén and Carl Tusvik, who were looking for water.

"What's the matter?" Horn called.

"We've found something," replied Tusvik, motioning from an outcropping.

It was a rusty tin can. This was odd because, to Horn's knowledge, no white man had visited the island for many years. He began poking around in the rocky crevices and in a large, melting snowbank. Under the snow, his geologist's pick struck something solid, but definitely not stone. Scooping away the snow, the three men uncovered an object that made them gasp: the prow of a small boat. On it was distinctly lettered, "ANDREE'S POLAR EXPEDITION, 1897."

"Andrée!" Was it possible that here was a clue to the greatest Arctic mystery of all time: the disappearance of Salomon August Andrée and two companions, who had

vanished 33 years earlier while trying to reach the North Pole in a balloon?

In feverish haste, working against the threat that bad weather might force the *Bratvaag* to leave her exposed anchorage, Horn and his colleagues dug furiously through other snowbanks. The more they found, the deeper the mystery grew, a mystery that was not to be solved until the 1950's.

That day in 1930, the time and place of Andrée's death was confirmed beyond any doubt. But the puzzle which no Arctic expert could solve was this: *Why had three strong, experienced men, with plenty of food, shelter, clothing, weapons and other equipment died, after battling elements and severe hardships of the most rigorous sort to reach what should have been safety and security?*

Salomon August Andrée, a wiry, intense Swede whose system was constantly supercharged with energy, was only 22 when he tasted his first absorbing experience with balloons while working at the Philadelphia World's Fair. From that day on, he began to devote himself to the study of aeronautics. He was an individualist who could pursue one line of thought as tenaciously as a tightrope artist performing on the high wire. Veteran balloonists were astonished that a man so young and inexperienced could take to the air, in varying weather conditions, and never once exhibit any signs of fright.

His first craft was the *Svea,* which he had persuaded the publisher of *Aftonbladet,* an evening newspaper in Stockholm, to buy for him, "to promote public welfare and science." From that moment on, ballooning was his

mistress, his religion, his entire life. In *Svea*, he made many significant weather observations, studied the speed and movement of sound, and took some remarkable aerial photographs. His greatest accomplishments in the early 1890's were several daring, and unprecedented, f l i g h t s across the Baltic Sea. Then, in 1895, Andrée startled his associates by announcing :

"It is possible—and feasible—for a balloon to fly to the North Pole !"

Even the sceptics listened as Andrée passionately explained just why and how a balloon could forever outmode the plodding, laborious method of packing across the ice on foot or with dogs and sledges.

"The w i n d s are steady," he pointed out. "From Spitsbergen, you can almost count on a northerly wind of two weeks' duration. It will carry a balloon across the roof of the world, and beyond to Alaska."

"But," came the objection, "how can a balloon stay aloft that long?"

Andrée had the answer to this question, too. "In the summertime, conditions would be ideal. Constant daylight would keep the temperature variation within a few degrees. Therefore, the gas would neither expand much nor contract. The result would be a minimum amount of leakage and no need to valve off

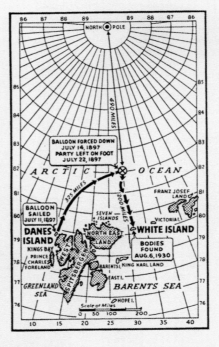

precious gas because of expansion. By attaching a sail to the bag, a balloonist could increase the speed so that the distance would be covered well within the 15- to 20-day period of buoyancy his craft could have."

On May 31, 1896, after more than a year of preparation, the *First Andrée Polar Expedition* left Stockholm on a tidal wave of patriotic fervour. Andrée hit headlines all around the world as he left for D a n e s Island, Spitsbergen. Then, for six weeks, the world—and especially S w e d e n — waited expectantly while the expedition remained weathered in at the advance base.

The right wind and weather never came. On August 17, Andrée dejectedly gave up. The balloon was deflated and the expedition crept back to Stockholm in a state of abject depression. Almost overnight, the man who had been labelled a national hero because of his previous, daring flights became an object of criticism and ridicule. He was called a "fraud" by some journalists, a "publicity seeker" by others. Even the most sympathetic newspapers conceded that his chances of ballooning to the North Pole were as limp as the deflated bag.

All autumn and winter Andrée brooded. Then, in the spring of 1897, buoyed by new

LONG JOURNEY TO NOWHERE

hope and financially backed by the noted Alfred Nobel, inventor of dynamite and donor of the Nobel prizes, Andrée decided on a second attempt. This time, the Swedish Government assigned a gunboat, the *Svensksund,* to accompany the expedition to Danes Island, with an expert crew to repair the balloon hangar, dig the gas apparatus out of the snow and help with launching.

"We *cannot* fail," said Andrée again and again with an almost pathological insistence, indicating that this time he would get his balloon, *The Eagle,* airborne at all costs.

Accompanying Andrée on the flight would be Knut Fraenkel and Nils Strindberg. Fraenkel was a civil engineer, with considerable Arctic experience. At 27, he was a mountaineer, gymnast and railroad builder— a man in the tradition of the old Vikings. Though he had crashed twice while ballooning, he regarded the experience as "rare sport." Strindberg, 24, was more of an intellectual, with a background as a university professor. He was strikingly handsome, a fact that brought the expedition a multitude of female well-wishers. A photographer, he had designed a special reflex camera, in a sealed case, to take pictures as the balloon soared over the polar ice. Some of the pictures accompanying this story were taken with the camera.

By mid-June, 1897, Andrée was back at Danes Island with *The Eagle,* whose bag was 97 feet high and 68 feet in diameter, made from 600 pieces of pongee silk. Maker Henri Lachambre had personally tested all the pieces before stitching and cementing them together. Andrée, in his thorough, meticulous way, had even arranged for two engineers from the Nordenfelt Company to follow each step in the manufacture and make regular tests. The upper two-thirds of the bag was three-ply, both for strength and reduction of leakage; and the lower third was two-ply. The finished bag was carefully varnished inside and out so that, though weighing a ton and a half because of this extra process, it was supposedly impervious.

More than 380 hempen cords formed a netting over the bag. On the underside, they were woven together to form a dozen ropes, which then passed through a bearing ring shaped from American elm and were secured to the basket. The basket was made of wicker and wood, and designed as a double-decker. On top, in an area about six feet in diameter, was the observation platform, similar to that on most balloons. Below was a compartment which had a mattress and sleeping bag of reindeer skins and was tight and solid enough in construction to serve as a dark room. Andrée's idea was to develop photographs along the way, and send prints back by carrier

pigeon and by cylinder dropped into the sea. In this way, a valuable record of the Arctic would get back to civilization, even if the expedition did not.

Around the walls of both decks were small compartments with the wide variety of equipment the three men had gathered: photographic supplies, food, extra clothing, navigational instruments, maps, books, utensils and other items. Guns and ammunition were fitted into a space in the floor of the lower compartment.

The expedition had enough food for an estimated three and a half months. Included were special lemon lozenges to prevent scurvy, a concoction made of 55 pounds of chocolate and pulverized pemmican shaped into solid cakes, and two bottles of port presented to them by the King of Sweden.

There were also 36 homing pigeons, in wicker cages, which had been trained in the Arctic and were supposedly capable of taking messages back to Spitsbergen from any faraway point along the route. Andrée, something of an inventor, had devised a sledge that would come apart to form two, a collapsible canvas boat and other unique items of equipment. He had also devised a clever system of "automatic ballasting" that did not necessitate valving or throwing sandbags over the side. This consisted of a harness with three heavy coconut fibre ropes, each a little over 1,000 feet long. The ropes, waxed at the lower ends, were supposed to drag easily across the surface of water and ice, their combined weight being enough to pull the balloon down about 10 feet for each 20 feet of length the aeronauts hauled into the basket. In the standard trailing position, the ropes would hold *The Eagle* at about 600 to 700 feet as she rode.

Despite Andrée's foresight and attention to detail, the balloon had one dangerous flaw: she leaked. While in the shed being readied for flight, it was found that she lost about 35 cubic metres of gas per day. Andrée tried to stop the leakage by varnishing the seams, but without much luck. The advice of everyone, including the balloon maker himself, was that the expedition should be postponed and the bag rebuilt.

"I do not have the courage to postpone the flight again," Andrée replied, remembering the ignominy of the year before. He was strongly supported by both Strindberg and Fraenkel, even though it had been demonstrated that *The Eagle* was losing a lift capacity of 99 pounds every 24 hours.

On July 11, 1897, at 2.30 in the afternoon, the flight order was given.

"Strindberg! Fraenkel!" The three men climbed into the basket, reaching out to give last handshakes to the men on the ground.

"Cut!" shouted Andrée. A sailor took his knife to the anchor rope.

"Oh, hell!" the man muttered as the blade nicked his finger.

Andrée leaned over the basket at the exclamation. "Hell—that is where we are going," he retorted as the balloon leapt skyward.

The Eagle wobbled erratically as the wind caught the sail, and headed northward. Passing over the shore, one of the three long trailing ropes caught on a rock. Snagged, the balloon dipped dangerously, so low that the bottom of the basket touched the water. Andrée and his companions struggled to maintain their balance. Then the balloon righted itself again, as the trailing line yanked free, losing a whole section of the end, and the bag began to rise. For almost an hour *The Eagle* could be seen against the grey north sky, growing smaller and smaller.

Then it vanished and was never sighted again.

In August of 1930, the news of the curious discovery by the men of the Norwegian sealer *Bratvaag* was slow in reaching the outside world. The skipper wanted to complete one of the most profitable fishing cruises he had ever enjoyed. So word of the find was shouted across to one Capt. Gustav Jensen, whose ship, the *Terningen,* was sighted a few days later. When Jensen reached port, his statements touched off a large journalistic bomb. Newspapers of all nations frantically began hiring small steamers to go to look for the *Bratvaag,* to get the first story. Radio appeals were made (the *Bratvaag* had a receiver, but no transmitter), pleading with the skipper to meet at a designated mid-ocean rendezvous and give the sender an "exclusive" for which his editors would pay a huge price.

When two weeks went by with no contact, reporters began hinting that Captain Jensen of the *Terningen* had concocted the whole story for publicity, or that the relics discovered had nothing to do with the Andrée expedition.

Finally, on September 3rd, the *New York Times* headlined the true significance of the story:

"BODIES OF AIRMEN LOST 33 YEARS FOUND NEAR WHERE BALLOON FELL IN ARCTIC."

During the next few days, the story was patched together. There was no doubt that the relics on White Island were from the Andrée Expedition: the canvas boat, a sledge, some food, a rusty rifle, clothing, a cooking stove and a camera, still loaded with film.

Two skeletons had also been found, still dressed in furs. One was Andrée's, leaning against a supporting ledge of rock; the other was that of Strindberg. The bones of Fraenkel were not found until a few weeks later, when

The remains
of the last
camp on
White Island.

further searches were made at White Island.

Most important of all, there was a diary.

Now the entire world waited to see whether the writing was still legible, after 33 years under the snow; and, if so, whether the pages contained a complete record of the struggle. Andrée, even in his dying hours, had fortunately practised the same meticulous care that had been characteristic of his life. He had padded the diary in straw, then sealed it as tightly as possible in oilcloth. Even as he died, the book was clutched to his chest, inside the protective clothing he wore. Its recordings were as nearly complete as anyone could have wished.

All Sweden rejoiced that the greatest of all Arctic mysteries would be solved: how had the three men met death? But the mystery was not solved. If anything it was intensified. There was no reason at all why the explorers should have perished when and where they did, no more reason than had they been on a camping trip in the Kjölen Mountains of northern Sweden.

On July 11, 1897, three hours after the start of the flight, the three explorers were in high spirits. The barometer was rising, the wind steady, though with a slight drift to the east. Andrée was not worried about the drift. With proper handling of sail and trailing lines, *The Eagle* could be steered at an angle as much as 30 degrees to the right or left of the true wind direction.

Andrée decided, with his usual restlessness, that it was time to send some messages to the outer world. Consequently, he wrote four notes and tied them to four of his carrier pigeons. Later, he placed another message in a metal cylinder and dropped it over the side. It read:

"Buoy No. 4. The first one dropped. July 11, 10 p.m. G.M.T. So far our trip has gone well. We continue at a height of about 250 metres, with a course at first north 10 degrees east, true, but later north, 45 degrees east, true. Four carrier pigeons were dispatched at 5.40 p.m. Greenwich time. They flew westward. We are now over ice, which is much broken in all directions. Glorious weather. Excellent spirits, Andrée, Strindberg, Fraenkel. Above clouds since 7.45, G.M.T."

A second buoy, dropped less than an hour later, showed that *The Eagle* had risen to about 1,800 feet and was at about 82 degrees of latitude and 25 degrees longitude east. The balloon's speed was remarkable.

Hour after hour passed, with a monotony that quickly replaced the initial exhilaration of the start. There was nothing to do but eat and sleep. Below, the Arctic wastes had a

hypnotic sameness, one ice floe after another, sometimes jammed together by wind and currents, at other times broken up, with patches of dark water showing through. The three men wrote their observations and made notations about the temperature, the wind, the weather. But, with continual daylight and almost no change in weather conditions, there was little to record.

On the third day out, Andrée wrote another note and attached it to several carrier pigeons:

"From Andrée's Polar Expedition to *Aftonbladet*, Stockholm. July 13, 12.30 noon. Lat. 82 degrees, 2'. Long. 15 degrees 5' east. Good passage each 10 degrees south. All well on board. This is the third pigeon post. Andrée."

This was the only carrier pigeon message ever received.

That day, the men began to hear a disturbing sound: the crackling of ice, forming a thin veneer over the fabric and breaking off in small sheets. Slowly the weight increased, pushing the balloon lower—so low that finally the bottom of the basket touched the ice hummocks for the first time. Like a ball, the balloon bounced up to 500 feet, then slowly settled again.

The afternoon of the third day was the beginning of the "Hell" that Andrée had prophesied in his caustic final remark as the flight started. Hour after hour, *The Eagle* continued its exhausting cycle: rising, falling, dragging the gondola for long stretches over the choppy ice, then rising again as the men jettisoned ballast.

From later evidence, from correspondence with the explorer Fridtjof Nansen and from remarks he had made, Andrée had known for many weeks that the flight would be a failure. Perhaps he had pictured at least reaching the Pole and being able to send out one glorious message by pigeon and buoy before vanishing forever. But he had never anticipated trouble so soon.

It was ironic that the balloon carried a preposterous collection of entirely useless objects, many of which the three men clung to when all hope of flight had ended and they were forced to march across the ice. These included quantities of Russian and U.S. money in silver and gold, a white dress tie, an expensive porcelain bowl, the heavy silver base for a German vase, a white shirt in its original wrappings, a large collection of heavy towels, old newspapers, packets of personal letters and two tickets to the Stockholm Exposition of 1897.

On July 14, *The Eagle* unaccountably rose for a few hours, perhaps because of a tempera-

A cup and a
spirit stove
lead to the
discovery of one
of the bodies.

ture change. But by afternoon, luck ran out. The constant jolting had loosened an escape valve and hydrogen could distinctly be heard hissing out above the heads of the three men. *The Eagle's* life blood was draining away, and nothing could be done about it.

By 7 p.m. that day, after a long, punishing drag over the sharp ice hummocks that threatened to rip the gondola to shreds and matchwood, Andrée gave the order which all three knew was inevitable: "Get ready to open the ripvalves."

By 7.30 they were down for good, untangling the ropes on an ice floe, trying to furl the sail so it would not catch the wind, and despairingly watching the great bag grow limper and limper as it settled down into a great, dark blob of fabric.

There was one small blessing: for the first time in four days, the men slept soundly, securely wrapped in sleeping bags and canvas.

For the next seven days, the men camped at the scene of the landing, sorting out their equipment, readying the sledge, and putting together the collapsible canvas boat. There was one great decision to make: which direction to march in? The men used the time in trying to determine the drift of the ice. The obvious course would have been to head south, and slightly to the west, toward North-east Land off Spitsbergen and the Seven Islands, where there were known to be caches of food and supplies. Instead, for a reason that will never be known, they headed almost due east, towards the barren, and little-known, Franz Josef Land.

Perhaps, since the wind had carried *The Eagle* much farther eastward than estimated, Andrée was convinced that the moving ice would also carry them east. On July 22, 11 days after the glorious start from Danes Island, Andrée, Strindberg and Fraenkel began their laborious march across the ice pack.

The difficulties were overpowering. The men kept slipping into pools of melting ice; the sledge runners caught on hummocks; breaks in the ice made it necessary to go hundreds of yards out of their way to avoid open water; the constant glare of 24 hours of daylight made their eyes bloodshot and blackened their skin wherever it was exposed. To make matters worse, the general drift of the ice was now seen to be westward, taking them farther and farther from their objective each day.

"We will have to change the direction of march," said Andrée finally, not giving in to the elements until August 4. They had already abandoned a few things each day, and a bulky 220 pounds of baggage on July 27. "We will make for the Seven Islands."

On taking observations in his diary, he noted that they were then at Latitude 82:7 North and Longitude 22:43 East. During almost two weeks of plodding, therefore, they had progressed about 60 miles from the point of landing.

With feet cut and frost-bitten, and arms bruised from many slips and falls on the ice, the men found it a relief to arrive at open water somewhere off North-east Land. They stowed their gear in the canvas boat and set out with paddles and oars. Then the whims of the elements caught them again. Suddenly the current changed from westward to south-easterly. Again they saw their objective, the Seven Islands, fade away. From September 12 to 17 they drifted, partly on open water, but

LONG JOURNEY TO NOWHERE

mostly encamped on floes. The days were beginning to shorten. The nights became pitch dark and brought bitter cold and dangerous squalls.

On September 17, they sighted the first land in 68 days—White Island. Working toward it frantically, on foot and by boat, they paused long enough to make two important kills: a seal on September 18, a bear (Andrée's diary refers to bears as "the wandering meat shops of the Arctic") on September 20. They also took time for as weird a celebration as has ever been recorded in polar history. The details were found in the remains of Strindberg's diary. This was a feast of "seal steak, seal liver, seal brains, seal kidneys, butter, and Swedish bread, *gateaux aux raisins,* with raspberry sauce, and port wine for dessert." The wine was the gift of King Oscar II, vintage 1836. With it, they drank a toast to the king, unfurled a small Swedish flag carried for the occasion (or any other that might arise), and made the Arctic wastes echo with their National Anthem, sung at the top of their voices.

A day later, the triumph of approaching land was shattered when the ice beneath them suddenly started to break up. Part of their supplies were thrown into the water. A small hut-like shelter they had erected against the night's cold was torn apart. But somehow they all escaped alive, managed to salvage a good part of their equipment (Andrée had insisted on having sinkable items lashed, whenever possible to floatable ones), and eventually reached land. Drenched, exhausted and frozen, the three men began the last phase of their historic ordeal.

They actually reached White Island with enough food, shelter and equipment to survive from that first week in October, when they set foot ashore, through the winter. They had already conquered the worst hardships—weathering out some 11 weeks on the dangerous, shifting ice. It only remained now to hold out until the winter ice became firm and they could sledge across some 50 miles to North-east Land, where they would find natives and shelter.

For a week, the three men had been suffering stomach cramps, diarrhoea and other intestinal upsets. They were badly weakened, constantly in pain, and often too exhausted to cook the rich polar bear meat they had saved from their recent kill. They had, however, a small primus stove, in such good condition and with enough fuel remaining that it was actually used when found 33 years later.

There was, however, one small factor, not considered in 1897—and not even suspected in 1930—which was to cause tragedy.

Andrée's diary does give a clue to one

death, that of Nils Strindberg, who was the first to go. Shortly after the three men had pushed and tugged the sledge and the canvas boat across the rocky shores of the island, he was seized by what the other two men decided was a heart attack. He died within a few hours. The last entry in Strindberg's diary, on October 6, was "Resignation."

Andrée and Fraenkel lived about two weeks longer. The condition of the camp, with no real shelter constructed and with equipment strewn around, indicated that the two men were too weak to work. It was contrary to Andrée's nature that he should have left valuable instruments and ammunition in the canvas boat, where they were found by the *Bratvaag* sailors in 1930: or that he would not have used loose rock to construct a wall for protection against the wind and the cold.

And so the record fades away, rather than ends. For the last few entries in Andrée's diary are indecipherable, and the last recognizable date is October 17th. Knut Fraenkel died in his sleeping bag, and Salomon August Andrée died propped against a rock. The Great Adventure had ended.

After the discovery of the three skeletons in 1930, there were several theories as to how they died. The immediate belief was that they had frozen to death. None had very heavy clothing, since Andrée had not foreseen (or else had decided to ignore) the possibility of having to winter in. Yet there was one great flaw in this theory. The records of meteorologists in Spitsbergen showed that in the autumn of 1897, the temperature could not have fallen much below 15° by the time the men died, hardly bitter enough cold to have killed off three Swedes, used to harsh climates. The sleeping bag was in good condition, and they had bear skins for extra protection.

A second but not very common theory was that they had committed suicide, knowing that their position was hopeless. Yet no expended ammunition was found near any of the bodies; there was no clue pointing to suicide, nor was there any real motive.

The third and gradually accepted theory was that the three men (or at least Andrée and Fraenkel) had suffocated to death. The small tent which they carried was of rubberized silk. The sides and ends were sealed to a floor of the same material, so that the only open part was the entrance. And even this could be snapped tight. The primus stove could have consumed much of the oxygen in the tiny space. Yet it hardly seems possible that Andrée would not have taken this into account, or at least noticed it in time to open the tent.

Into the mystery, in late 1930, stepped one Ernst Adam Tryde, late physician and scientist from Denmark. As a boy, Tryde had been fascinated by polar expeditions. He knew all there was to know about Andrée,

LONG JOURNEY TO NOWHERE

and studied the theories about his death; he read the diaries; he inspected the relics brought back from White Island. As a medical man, he was curious about the symptoms which Andrée had so painstakingly described: eyes burning, noses running, diarrhoea and stomach cramps, the everlasting sense of exhaustion . . . .

"The symptoms sound like those of a bad cold," said Tryde, "but it is well known that this ailment does not exist above the Polar Circle."

Tryde was a busy man. He could spend little time seeking a solution to the mystery during the 30's. Then came the war years, and Salomon August Andrée was pushed into the background. But in 1947, Ernst Adam Tryde read a medical report that made him pause and think. A mysterious epidemic had broken out among the Eskimos at Disco Bay on western Greenland. Most doctors had determined that it was paratyphoid. A Danish medical expedition was sent to the scene with lab equipment.

There, the doctors diagnosed the outbreak as trichinosis, caused by a walrus the Eskimos had eaten. After that, the bio-bacteriological laboratory at Copenhagen started to examine skins from many polar animals at the zoological museum. For a long time, results were negative.

Then, in late 1948, a doctor discovered the first trichina capsules, in a polar bear which had been shot in eastern Greenland in 1908. Continuing examinations showed that about 30 per cent of all polar bears in the area were infected with trichinosis.

Tryde began to devote all of his spare time to a private study of his own. He unearthed a carefully-kept secret: that a group of German soldiers at an outpost on Franz Josef Land had to be evacuated because of trichinosis from eating improperly-cooked bear meat.

Excitedly, Tryde received permission to examine the Andrée diaries. The pieces began to fit together. On about July 19th, or 20th, the three explorers ate their first bear meat.

"July 27. Fraenkel complains of fatigue. July 30. He is snowblind." Those were indications, said Tryde; extreme fatigue and an eye inflammation that would have made him susceptible to snow-blindness . . . .

"August 3. We . . . suffered severely from heat in the tent. We have decided to eat outside today . . . It is so warm that we proceed without coats . . ." The first signs of fever, said Tryde.

On August 8th, Andrée, thinking himself a victim of snow-blindness, described having to pinch his eyes together in order to see properly. The inflammation was common to the disease. Andrée also made an entry that day, "Our noses are running all the time. A permanent catarrh." Another symptom.

Other clues fell right in line: diarrhoea, joint and muscle pains, stomach cramps. By now the three men were taking morphine and opium to combat the excruciating pain.

Circumstantial evidence, but the last conclusive proof was still missing. In November, 1949, Tryde took the train southward from Stockholm to Gränna, Andrée's birthplace, where a museum had been built, with most of the relics from the expedition. For two days and nights, he worked with little sleep in the unheated museum searching for evidence. He did not find what he wanted. More than a month later, however, he was more successful. On January 6, 1950, he told a reporter from the Stockholm newspaper, *Dagens Nyheter,* "On the bottom of the boat, I have found a small packing case where there were lots of skin-tufts from a polar bear. I had picked them up carefully, piece by piece, and then I found three small fragments from Andrée's sleeping bag, mended with bear-skin taken from the front paws. I have also found a polar bear cranium, vertebrae, a knee-joint and some ribs. I have scraped off 14 tiny pieces of dried meat and I am taking these pieces back to Denmark to get them examined."

Dr. Tryde returned to Copenhagen with his tiny samples, which altogether amounted to not more than three grams, and submitted them to the bacteriological laboratory of the Veterinary School. It was almost three months before the tests were finished. Then, on April 20, 1950, Tryde received an official report. In the samples, 12 trichina capsules had been found and positively identified.

It proved beyond a doubt, when coupled with the detailed symptoms reported by Andrée in his diaries, that the three explorers had been beaten, not by cold or Arctic winds, but by a minute, unseen worm whose existence was not even known by the three men who perished because of it.

Had the men known enough to avoid bear meat, or to cook it thoroughly, they might have survived to march the 50 miles across the ice that separated them from North-east Land and safety.

The final chapter still remained to be written. In 1961, a Swedish journalist, studying the documentary proof that Dr. Tryde had assembled just before his death a few years ago, stumbled across the most ironic of all the many strange ironies that had plagued the explorers. The doctor, quoting an entry in the expedition's diaries for September 20, 1897, had underlined the words of Salomon August Andrée, written 64 years ago in his careful, scientific hand:

"The bear is the best friend of the explorer."   ▲▲▲

Travellers' Tales

Make-it-yourself Frogmen

At 100 feet . . . I began to panic. Fatigue was making my limbs heavy. I dropped the axe, the weight of which was braking my ascent. With the reduced pressure the valve let a little fresh air through, but suddenly my head began to swim. I could see the rope bending and dancing through the haze. Perhaps Alan was clinging there. If only I could see him. But no, I was all alone. My body was letting me down. I had every reason to be afraid. Was I going to faint? Whatever I did, I must not let go of the mouthpiece. I must clench my teeth on the rubber. My hand clutched the chromium-plated branch-tube. Up, up. Just a few more thrusts with my flippers.

Everything was shifting, swaying, tilting, and everywhere were bubbles, in clusters, in swaying columns, all air that had come from my body. I was suffocating. I had a great lump in my throat. It was pretty certain now that I was going to faint before I could get back to the surface and the light. If I had had a weighted belt I would have undone it. But I didn't have a belt at all. The sea would take hold of me and take me slowly down again.

That is a description of the less enjoyable side of skin diving and is quoted from a book, "The Marvellous Kingdom," by Pierre Labat (Odhams, 15s.).

Home-made diving apparatus. From "The Marvellous Kingdom," reviewed above.

A Training School for Cowboys.

By Scudamore Jarvis.

At Shepperton-on-Thames there is a unique educational establishment whose purpose it is to convert youths intended for a Colonial career into more or less expert cowboys and stockmen, with a varied list of accomplishments such as are likely to be required in the wilds. The striking photographs which accompany the article give one a vivid idea of the thoroughness of the training at the "Cowboys' College."

Standing on a horse's back at the gallop.
From a Photo. by Halftones, Ltd.

NOW that the Colonies have been brought so near the mother country through increased facilities offered by modern transport, and that competition for employment in all walks of life has overcrowded every profession and trade, it has become a recognized thing for a large percentage of the boys of British middle-class families to proceed to Australia, Canada, or one of our other dependencies in search of a living.

The desire for a life in the open, with the sky for a roof, lies dormant in every Britisher, and each year sees some thousands of the youth of England sailing away, with hope beating high in their hearts, to carve for themselves a living, if not a fortune, in lands beyond the seas.

That so many return within a year or so, disappointed, and resolved that life on a sheep-run or ranch is not all their fancy depicted it, is due almost solely to the fact that the altered conditions of life are such that a youngster is appalled at his own ignorance, and, unable to withstand the good-natured chaff of his new comrades, decides to return to England, where at least some of his good qualities were recognized.

A certain number also find the hardships of

their new calling unbearable, and, although a few months would have shown them that it is possible to become acclimatized to anything in time, they take ship for home to help overcrowd the employment market, and incidentally spread reports in no way calculated to popularize the Colonies.

The need, therefore, of some institution where the would-be Colonist

West, has long been felt, and this want is now supplied by the " Imperial School of Colonial Instruction," run by Captain Morgan and Mr. ffrench at Shepperton-on-Thames. Here, within a few miles of London, in sight of one of the loveliest reaches of the Thames, embryo stockmen and cowboys, in moleskins and " shaps," live the life which is to be theirs in the future, as if the busy whirl of the

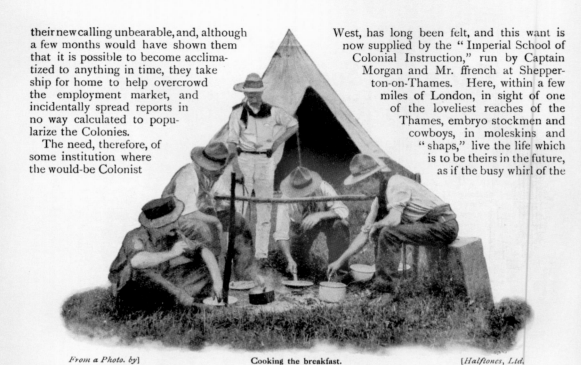

From a Photo. by] **Cooking the breakfast.** [*Halftones, Ltd.*

might learn the rudiments of what is required in the bush or on the prairie, without going to the expense of visiting either the Antipodes or the

Metropolis were some thousands of miles distant. Pupils are taken at the school for a course of six months, or any less period if desired, and learn during that short time the ins and outs of a wonderful variety of subjects, from elementary carpentering and cooking to the more fascinating art of roping cattle and using the stock-whip. The idea is to give the youth a rough knowledge of everything that forms part of the daily curriculum of the cowboy or stockman, and to do this thoroughly the instructors see that life in the bush or prairie is imitated to the minutest detail.

The pupils live in bunk-houses during the winter and tents through the summer months, and their day's work starts before the ordinary city dweller's hot water has been placed

From a Photo. by] **Cold shoeing.** [*Halftones, Ltd.*

From a Photo. by]   Teaching a horse to stand fire.   [Halftones, Ltd.

outside his door. The food is cooked by the pupils themselves in a Dutch oven and over the open fire, and they are not even spared the drudgery of washing up and bed-making.

Riding, of course, is one of the most necessary accomplishments of the Colonial, and great attention is paid to this feature ; but the budding stockman must also learn how to look after his horse—to saddle him, groom him, and even shoe him. Among other things that the young Colonial learns may be mentioned packing packsaddles, repairing saddlery and leather work, making fences, gardening, branding cattle, rifle, revolver, and gun shooting, boxing, ju-jitsu, etc. It will thus be seen that the pupil, after six months' training, is a man of much knowledge and an individual to be treated with respect.

Tying a man up from a distance of thirty feet by throwing a succession of half-hitches over him.

From a Photo. by Halftones, Ltd.

181

Some of the feats which the embryo cowboys are taught to perform.
From Photos. by Halftones, Ltd.

The WIDE·WORLD

THE MAGAZINE FOR MEN

FEBRUARY 1948 1/3

First published 2004 by Macmillan
an imprint of Pan Macmillan Ltd
Pan Macmillan, 20 New Wharf Road, London N1 9RR
Basingstoke and Oxford
Associated companies throughout the world
www.panmacmillan.com

ISBN 1 4050 4931 6

A CIP catalogue record for this book is available from
the British Library.

Printed and bound in Great Britain by
The Bath Press

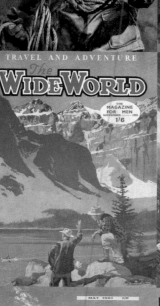